GUARDIANSHIP AND DEMOCRACY IN IRAN AND TURKEY

GUARDIANSHIP AND DEMOCRACY IN IRAN AND TURKEY

Tutelary Consolidation,
Popular Contestation

Karabekir Akkoyunlu

EDINBURGH
University Press

Edinburgh University Press is one of the leading university presses in the UK. We publish academic books and journals in our selected subject areas across the humanities and social sciences, combining cutting-edge scholarship with high editorial and production values to produce academic works of lasting importance. For more information visit our website: edinburghuniversitypress.com

Edinburgh University Press Ltd
13 Infirmary Street
Edinburgh EH1 1LT

Typeset in 11/15 EB Garamond by
IDSUK (DataConnection) Ltd, and
printed and bound in Great Britain

A CIP record for this book is available from the British Library

ISBN 978 1 3995 0610 6 (hardback)
ISBN 978 1 3995 0612 0 (webready PDF)
ISBN 978 1 3995 0613 7 (epub)

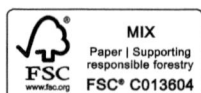

FSC
www.fsc.org

MIX
Paper | Supporting
responsible forestry
FSC® C013604

CONTENTS

ACRONYMS

ADD	Atatürkist Thought Association
AİHM	European Court of Human Rights
AKP	Justice and Development Party
ANAP	Motherland Party
AP	Justice Party
CHP	Republican People's Party
CUP	Committee of Union and Progress
ÇYD	Association in Support of Contemporary Living
DP	Democrat Party
DSP	Democratic Left Party
EC	Expediency Council
ECHR	European Court of Human Rights
FP	Virtue Party
GC	Guardian Council
GNA	Grand National Assembly
HDP	Peoples' Democratic Party
IRGC	Islamic Revolutionary Guard Corps
IRI	Islamic Republic of Iran
IRP	Islamic Republican Party
JCPOA	Joint Comprehensive Plan of Action
JRM	Society of the Militant Clergy

Kargozaran	Executives of the Construction of Iran Party
MEK	People's Mojahedin of Iran
MHP	Nationalist Action Party
MRM	Association of Combatant Clerics
MÜSİAD	Independent Industrialists and Businessmen Association
NSC	National Security Council
NSPD	National Security Policy Document
OYAK	Armed Forces Pension Fund
PKK	Kurdistan Workers' Party
RP	Welfare Party
RTÜK	Higher Council of Radio and Television
SCC	Special Court of the Clergy
SCF	Free Republican Party
SCFR	Strategic Council for Foreign Relations
SNSC	Supreme National Security Council
SSC	State Security Courts
TCF	Progressive Republican Party
TSK	Turkish Armed Forces
TUSKON	Turkish Confederation of Businessmen and Industrialists
TÜSİAD	Turkish Industry and Business Association
YAŞ	Supreme Military Council
YÖK	Council of Higher Education
YPG	Kurdish People's Protection Units

PREFACE

This book is the product of a long and winding journey. I first began thinking and writing about regime guardianship in Iran and Turkey in late 2009. I had just started my PhD studies at the London School of Economics. In Turkey, the power struggle between the 'Kemalist establishment' (i.e. the secular nationalist military and senior bureaucracy) and the AKP government had taken a critical turn following the launch of the Ergenekon court case. The investigation and the trial divided observers and scholars of Turkey, as well as the wider public, on whether they represented a watershed moment in the country's struggle for democracy and fight against 'the deep state' or a judicial coup and power grab by the ruling Islamists and their allies, a divide that would only deepen in the following years. That was the same year when Iran's own century-long struggle for democracy, and the more recent fight between the supporters and opponents of reform, had reached a bloody turning point. I first visited Iran in the summer of 2009 and was struck by the palpable atmosphere of anxiety, frustration and paranoia that seemed to have pervaded its urban middle class in the immediate aftermath of the bloody crackdown of mass protests against election manipulation and the suppression of the Green Movement by the guardians of the Islamic Republic.

I was also struck by the prominence of the themes of tutelage (*vesayet* in Turkish and *velayat* in Persian), the deep state, democracy and reform in the public discourses and debates, as well as private conversations, in both countries. Few seemed to have noticed this similarity and even fewer made an effort to make sense of it in a scholarly fashion. As I discovered, there was limited contact between scholars of modern Turkey and modern Iran, both within these countries and in English-speaking academia. In the field of comparative politics, the political systems of Turkey and the Islamic Republic were considered simply too different or inimical to merit serious comparison. I thought that the secular versus Islamic or the Sunni versus Shi'a binaries were not only overly simplistic, but that they also concealed an underlying similarity, namely the ideas and institutions of guardianship, around which much of politics in Iran and Turkey revolved at the time. Furthermore, I saw in the emerging literature on hybrid regimes a conceptual framework to ground the comparison, and in turn an opportunity to contribute to that growing literature.

An immediate obstacle I faced as I set out for research was access to resources. Few researchers, myself included, worked with both Turkish and Persian-language sources. To this end, I took Persian courses at SOAS and spent part of 2010 studying the language at the University of Isfahan. I returned to Iran periodically afterwards for research and travel. Although my Persian never reached the level of my English or native Turkish, I was surprised by how quickly I became proficient in it, both in conversation and in reading newspapers and following the news, thanks in large part to the shared cultural and linguistic heritage between Turkish and Persian.

History seems to have accelerated in the 2010s, when transformative events that shook the world and the region also shaped my personal and intellectual trajectory. The 'Arab Spring' uprisings and their bloody aftermath, and in particular the Gezi movement of 2013, which I was actively and enthusiastically engaged in, were the genesis of this personal transformation. After finishing my PhD in 2014, like many young academics and activists involved in Turkey's democratic struggles, I committed myself almost exclusively to making sense of, resisting and contending with the country's deep dive into conflict, violence and authoritarianism. This was a time when, to paraphrase novelist Ahmet Hamdi Tanpınar, Turkey truly did not allow its children to be occupied with anything other than itself. My academic production during my post-doctoral fellowship in Modern Turkey Studies at the University of Graz reflected this focus and urgency. I postponed turning the dissertation into a book and gradually drifted away from Iran academically, although never losing sight of it personally or politically.

I picked up the book project again only in late 2018. By then I was married, living in Brazil, and had just started a two-year visiting fellowship at the Institute of International Relations, University of São Paulo, still doing research on democratisation, autocratisation and tutelage, with a growing focus on Latin America, particularly Brazil. The revision of the text took place in fits and starts – periods of productivity punctured by other professional commitments and major life events, namely the birth of our daughter Yasmin, the Covid-19 pandemic and the decision to move back to the United Kingdom in 2021. Every time I returned to the manuscript, I saw it in a different and more critical light against the backdrop of fast-paced global and personal transformation, which led to moments of self-doubt and hesitation. I could not have overcome these without the patience of my editors at Edinburgh University Press and their confidence in this project, the encouragement and guidance of many a close friend and colleague and the unwavering support of my partner, Izabela, and parents, Pınar and Ali Cevat, all of whom I owe an enormous debt of gratitude.

The present monograph contains traces of every step taken on this winding path since 2009. It also draws from my more recent publications, from conversations with colleagues and students, and from the courses I taught in Graz, São Paulo and London on the history of modern Turkey, the politics of the Middle East, international development, comparative politics and social science research. I believe that the final product, albeit far from perfect, is a balanced synthesis of these different insights and experiences. As I write this in my office at SOAS, fourteen years after sitting in my first Persian class in the same institution, there is still a dearth of comparative research on the politics of modern Iran and Turkey, and as far as I am aware, no comprehensive study of their tutelary politics. Let us hope, then, that this book serves as a beginning and inspiration for further conversation and deeper research on the subject.

London, November 2023

For Yasmin and Izabela

INTRODUCTION

In order to discover the rules of society best suited to nations, a superior intelligence beholding all the passions of men without experiencing any of them would be needed.

– Jean Jacques Rousseau

Civilisations as yet have only been created and directed by a small intellectual aristocracy, never by crowds. Crowds are only powerful for destruction.

– Gustave Le Bon

A party is the vanguard of a class, and its duty is to lead the masses and not merely to reflect the average political level of the masses.

– V. I. Lenin

Distrustful of the masses, guardianship, or rule by self-appointed philosopher kings, challenges the basic democratic assumption that ordinary people are capable of defining and defending their own interests. From Plato's treatment of politics as a 'royal art or science' to the epistemic paternalism inherent in the Confucian philosophy of government, from Gustave Le Bon's virtuous, rational and skilful aristocrat to Lenin's 'vanguard party' shepherding the proletariat, the idea that society as a whole is better off when guided by an elite group of administrators with superior knowledge, values and skills has been a potent vision throughout history. Robert Dahl considered guardianship not only 'a fundamentally different *kind* of regime', rather than a mere modification of democracy, but also democracy's 'perennial enemy' and its 'most formidable rival'.[1]

This book offers a comparative study of the foundations, consolidation and contestation of guardianship in two countries where tutelary bodies and democratic institutions and processes have co-existed in a hybrid arrangement: The Islamic Republic of Iran (IRI), featuring a presidential system, republican institutions and competitive – albeit tightly controlled – elections under the guardianship of a supreme clerical authority, and the Republic of Turkey, where until recently parliamentary democracy and electoral competition were constrained by military tutelage. It traces the political and ideological trajectory of the two republics, starting with their imperial legacies and engagement with modernity, through their foundational experiences and subsequent institutional evolution, leading up to the power struggles between tutelary actors and popular challengers in the twenty-first century, and asks the following questions: What is similar – and what is different – about the way guardianship has been conceptualised, established, legitimised, consolidated and contested in these two republics with seemingly inimical founding ideologies? How and why did guardianship unravel in Turkey, but survive in the Islamic Republic in the course of the 2010s? And what does a comparative study of guardianship and democracy in Iran and Turkey tell us about political systems that combine tutelage with competitive elections and popular representation?

Historically speaking, socio-political change within Turkey and Iran has had reverberations beyond the two countries' boundaries. The causes and the consequences of the contemporaneous power struggles taking place between the self-appointed custodians of the Kemalist and Khomeinist republics and their popular (and populist) challengers since the turn of the millennium should be of concern to wider audiences and geographies. Yet the literature analysing the domestic politics of the two countries from a comparative perspective is surprisingly thin. In the absence of a well-developed body of comparative scholarship, the mainstream discourse on these countries has been largely shaped by caricaturised portrayals often conjured outside of academia.

Ever since the Iranian Revolution of 1979, the popular tendency has been to view Turkey and Iran through the framework of their geopolitical and ideological differences: Turkey, a pro-western secular democracy, albeit a flawed one, and Iran, an anti-western theocratic dictatorship. Although this simplistic depiction started changing with the rise of the Justice and Development Party (*Adalet ve Kalkınma Partisi*, AKP) in Turkey in the 2000s, the underlying dichotomous approach survived, with references to Ottoman versus Persian imperial rivalry, or Sunni versus Shi'a Islam gradually supplanting the secularism versus Islamism binary. Occasionally, political elites and the media in both countries made use of caricaturised portrayals to criticise, even demonise, the other side's ruling elites as 'godless imitators of the West' or 'rabid religious fanatics', although these were typically meant for domestic consumption and did not constitute the basis of the two countries' relationship.[2]

Nevertheless, the scholarship dealing with the two countries often took these portrayals on board without sufficient scrutiny. At least until the late 2000s, when Ankara and Tehran started improving their bilateral ties, this was the subtext to the dominant international relations (IR) approach to the two countries, and a large part of the English-language scholarship dealing with their politics has been IR-based.[3] This black-and-white approach arguably led scholars of politics and IR and to overlook the two regimes' shared tutelary architecture and its impact on their domestic and foreign politics. Of the handful of comparative works on modern Turkey and Iran available in the English language, only two – Shambayati's comparison of the Turkish and Iranian judiciaries, and a single chapter in Tezcür's book on Muslim reformers – are fully devoted to the institutions of regime guardianship in the two republics.[4] I started this research with the purpose of addressing and filling this gap.

Historians have offered more nuanced accounts of the two countries' entangled pasts, drawing on similarities and interlinkages as well as differences and rivalries.[5] These range from discussions over the 'Turco-Persian tradition', emanating from centuries of intermingling between Turkic and Iranian peoples and cultures,[6] to analyses of the two countries' simultaneous engagements with modernity, including Ottoman and Iranian constitutional movements, modernisation attempts under Westernising strongmen, Mustafa Kemal Atatürk and Reza Shah Pahlavi, or the developmentalist states of the 1960s and the 1970s.[7] Yet the need for historical distance and contemporaneity have generally kept historians away from sinking their teeth into more recent episodes or engaging in asymmetrical comparisons between non-contemporaries, as this book does between Turkey under Atatürk and Iran under Khomeini.

Meanwhile, scholars of comparative politics have often struggled with categorising the political systems of Turkey and, in particular, Iran, treating them as exceptions or anomalies to existing regime typologies. In the *Third Wave*, Samuel Huntington placed Iran 'elsewhere'.[8] Juan Linz admitted in his *Totalitarian and Authoritarian Regimes* that it was 'difficult to fit the Iranian regime into the existing typology'.[9] Houchang Chehabi suggested that 'the comparativist has literally no previously developed tools for analysing [Iran's] political system'.[10] Similarly, Larry Diamond categorised Turkey in 2002 as an 'ambiguous regime', lying somewhere between competitive authoritarianism and electoral democracy.[11] Since the mid-2010s, the country has served as a 'theory-busting case' of democratic backsliding,[12] variably described as having transitioned from tutelary or semi-democracy to delegative democracy, illiberal democracy, competitive authoritarianism, electoral authoritarianism, weak authoritarianism, cartel state, neo-fascism and Bonapartism.[13]

One exception is provided by Leah Gilbert and Payam Mohseni, who, in their reconceptualisation and classification of hybrid regimes between 1990 and 2009, categorised both Turkey and Iran as 'tutelary hybrid regimes'.[14] The authors further qualified Iran as an 'illiberal tutelary hybrid regime' – illiberal, due to the poor enforcement of civil liberties – while suggesting that Turkey had transitioned from being an illiberal to 'liberal tutelary hybrid regime' after 2003, thanks to its EU-backed liberal democratic reform initiatives. Despite being rather clunky sounding, for the purposes of the book's comparative framework, I follow Gilbert and Mohseni in treating Turkey between 1960 and 2011 and Iran after 1989 as 'tutelary hybrid regimes', as this conceptualisation puts both the tutelary and hybrid institutional architecture of the two republics at the centre of the analysis.

Comparing the foundations, consolidation and contestation of guardianship in Turkey and Iran does not only help us move beyond such caricaturised dichotomies towards an appreciation of the political and institutional dynamics that the two republics, which emerged under very different historical and ideological circumstances, had in common; it also allows for a more nuanced discussion of what separated them. In Iran, for instance, guardianship has been designed and constitutionalised as an explicit and permanent fixture on politics, whereas in Turkey, it developed in an ad hoc manner and was justified as a temporary necessity. The Iranian system under the Islamic Republic ultimately subordinated popular rule to divine rule, while the Turkish Republic at least paid lip service to the supremacy of popular sovereignty. The international geo-political conditions for the emergence and survival of guardianship in Iran and Turkey have also been markedly different. Such differences are key to explaining the divergent outcomes for guardianship in the two republics during the twenty-first century.

Finally, the comparison has relevance beyond the cases of Iran and Turkey, the Middle East or hybrid regimes. With far-right populists in established democracies employing a similar rhetoric to that of their counterparts in tutelary hybrid regimes, insights from this study can contribute to efforts to make sense of the global phenomena of democratic erosion and autocratisation. From 'the People versus the Establishment' dichotomy that is increasingly at the core of power struggles in liberal democracies, to allegations of shadowy deep states meddling in the affairs of elected governments, it is difficult to distinguish the discourse of right-wing anti-establishment figures like Donald Trump in the US, Matteo Salvini and Giorgia Meloni in Italy, or Jair Bolsonaro in Brazil, from Iran's Mahmoud Ahmadinejad and Turkey's Recep Tayyip Erdoğan. Even the term 'deep state', which has become popular in US and UK politics since the late 2010s, seems to have made its way into the Anglo-American political discourse from Turkey.[15]

As this book demonstrates, tutelage in its various forms can pose a veritable obstacle to democratisation. But 'the fight against tutelage' can also be an opportunistic banner to conceal and justify attacks on democratic institutions and state capture in the name of 'the People'. Distinguishing the myth of a deep state from the socio-political reality, and democratic challenges to guardianship from attacks on democratic checks and balances – not after the fact, but as these happen – has never been more urgent or important.[16] The case studies in this book, particularly the Turkish experience of disassembling undemocratic tutelage only to end up with a more autocratic arrangement, serve as a cautionary tale of getting this distinction wrong.

On Guardianship and Democracy

In socio-legal usage, guardianship, or tutelage (used interchangeably in this book), refers to the position of being responsible for the care of individuals who are unable to manage their own affairs. This definition comes with two implicit assumptions. First, guardianship implies exerting limitations on the autonomy of a person in exchange for their protection and supervision, but not total control over them or their absolute submission. Secondly, unless the person under guardianship is permanently incapacitated or disabled, the role is meant to be transitional: a legal guardian protects and supervises a minor until they reach adulthood, a tutor provides tuition until the student reaches a desired level of education and maturity. The political meaning of the term follows from this legal definition and carries its core assumptions.

In a political context, guardianship refers to the limitations imposed upon the independence, autonomy or sovereignty of a people, nation, ethnic group or other entity in exchange for a degree of protection or guidance.[17] Political guardianship comes in different forms and ideologies. It can be found in sub-national, national and international levels of government, based on a conservative or progressive vision of social change, and built upon varying sources of legitimacy and levels of consent. Yet whatever the form or ideology, guardianship everywhere embodies the inherent paternalism of the adult–minor/tutor–tutee relationship. It is the adult/tutor that upholds 'the truth', knows the logic and the direction of change to attain that truth, and judges when or whether it has been attained.

By nature and definition, conservative guardianship, such as traditional monarchy and aristocracy, views social change as mostly undesirable or threatening, and aims to protect and preserve the traditions, morals and power relations in society from its corrosive effects. Progressive guardianship, in contrast, is based on the assumption that society can and should change for the better, and it is the duty of the guardians to oversee this progress. Unlike the conservative kind, which sees the masses as permanently unfit to govern, progressive guardianship is meant to be a temporary fixture on society, ideally disappearing once the people reach the desired level of maturity. The typical example is Lenin's concept of the 'vanguard party', which is composed of class-conscious cadres that lead the proletariat to revolution and is meant to disappear once socialism is achieved. Whether the mandate system of the League of Nations, the single-party or military-led developmentalist governments of post-colonial nation-states, or supranational aid, finance and development agencies, tutelary arrangements emanating from the modernisation paradigm of the twentieth century also fall into this category.

In practice, however, there may be little difference between conservative and progressive guardianship. Modernising monarchs and their bureaucrats also want to transform state and society, but their plans are unlikely to ever involve the eventual disappearance of the monarchy. Socio-political reform is intended to reformulate and strengthen state–society relations and ensure the survival of the system of guardianship, although top-down change can yield unintended outcomes, as the experience of nineteenth century reforms in the Ottoman Empire, the fate of the Pahlavi dynasty in Iran or the consequences of *glasnost* for the Soviet Union demonstrate. By the same token, progressive systems of guardianship may outstay their welcome because the desired social transformation has not been achieved or was simply too utopian in the first place. A tutelary arrangement initially intended as temporary and transformative can turn into a permanent mechanism of power preservation.[18] The paternalism inherent to tutelage can be the very cause of 'stunted development', which is in turn used to justify continued tutelage. Still, as the Turkish and Iranian cases in this book demonstrate, whether tutelage was originally designed and propagated as temporary (Kemalist) or permanent (Khomeinist) can have long-term implications on the system's self-justification, perceived legitimacy and survival.

The legitimacy and survival of guardianship also depend on the type and degree of consent it generates. Guardianship can involve a good deal of coercion, in particular during its founding and consolidation. But no system of guardianship, however coercive, can be preserved without generating a degree of consent from those in whose name it governs. As with any political system, the most successful systems of guardianship are those that enjoy the highest level of consent and rely on the least amount of coercion possible. A fine example was the European Union in its heyday of seemingly limitless expansion in the 2000s, when democratically elected national governments raced to limit their own sovereignty and come under the tutelage of a liberal supranational order.[19] Although consent provides legitimacy to guardianship, it does not rule out its paternalistic logic, not least because, as scholars both ancient and modern remind us, ruling elites can devise sophisticated ways of manufacturing consent among the populace.[20] Popular consent can show the degree to which the values, ideas and interests upheld by the guardians have been internalised and accepted as the norm (i.e., have become hegemonic).[21]

Rather than a coercive apparatus aimed at ensuring total submission, which may neither be feasible nor desirable, guardianship, then, is the institutional mechanism through which a dominant group attempts to establish and maintain socio-political hegemony. The greater the need for physical coercion, the more tenuous the guardians' position tends to be in society.

The vision of government as an exclusively elite preoccupation and the infantilisation of large segments of an adult population stand as anathema to the democratic ideal of a people managing their own affairs, directly or through their elected representatives. Yet virtually all modern political systems feature a combination of these two inimical philosophies. Modern representative democracies feature an in-built tension between the promise of popular sovereignty and the reality of elite domination of political institutions, which occasionally gives rise to populist reactions.[22] Post-World War II liberal democracies, having emerged out of a gradual process of elite accommodation of popular demands and challenges in Western Europe and North America, boast a range of institutions that are designed to safeguard the established order and keep unwanted intruders away from the levers of power.

As noted earlier, non-democratic tutelage should be distinguished from institutions of horizontal accountability, such as 'constitutional courts, accounting offices, ombudsmen or human rights commissions', which are vital to the functioning of modern democracies.[23] But the line separating the two may not always be crystal clear, especially when they are blurred by the populist discourse of the people versus the establishment. An independent judiciary, for instance, is an integral part of a democratic system based on the rule of law and separation of powers. But when courts become too powerful and judges engage in political engineering, the judiciary can stifle democracy.[24] In both Iran and Turkey, judiciaries acted as bulwarks for Khomeinist and Kemalist guardianship. In Turkey, elected Islamists succeeded in breaking the 'Kemalist juristocracy', only to make the courts subservient to an increasingly authoritarian executive, showing that majoritarian populism can pose just as big a threat (if not a bigger one) to democracy as its antidote, tutelary elitism.

Politics in Tutelary Hybrid Regimes

In the interest of a workable, and therefore inevitably simplified definition, I propose that tutelary hybrid regimes are political regimes that stand upon twin pillars of legitimacy: a democratic pillar based on popular sovereignty manifested through periodic elections, and a guardianship pillar that might claim legitimacy from traditional, divine, legalistic, charismatic or revolutionary sources of authority. What sets these regimes apart from full-blown autocracies is the existence of institutions and processes of procedural democracy, namely competitive elections and representative legislative and executive branches. What sets them apart from consolidated democracies is the existence of unelected and unaccountable tutelary actors, or regime guardians, who draw and enforce formal and informal boundaries of politics without taking part in the democratic process themselves.

Guardians in tutelary hybrid regimes are powerful actors that 'exercise broad oversight of the government and its policy decisions while claiming to represent vaguely formulated fundamental and enduring interests of the nation-state.'[25] These can be praetorian militaries (Chile after Pinochet, Myanmar after 2011, Pakistan, Thailand, Turkey until the 2010s), clerical bodies (IRI), monarchies (Thailand and much of pre-1914 Europe) as well as intergovernmental organisations (the interwar mandate system in the Middle East, post-Dayton Bosnia and Herzegovina, Kosovo). In these hybrid regimes, guardians do not enjoy absolute authority, but tend to hold 'constitutionally defined final decision-making power in crucial policy areas that normally would fall under democratic control', such as foreign policy or national security.[26] These are also called 'reserved domains'.[27] In addition to formal institutions, guardians may also use informal channels, such as political parties, media and business organisations, civil society groups as well as semi-official or clandestine agencies – to shape public opinion and influence political decisions.

On the other hand, despite being constrained by the guardians, democratic institutions in tutelary hybrid regimes are not mere façades. Electoral politics features real competition and produces meaningful outcomes, which can serve as a counterweight to tutelary power. As such, the boundary between the tutelary and democratic pillars tends to be continually negotiated and in flux. Unless one of the two pillars is dismantled (through reform, revolution or coup) or retained in a purely symbolic capacity (as in many constitutional monarchies, or dictatorships with democratic façades), these fluctuations reflect shifting balances of power between tutelary and electoral politics and not a transition to a different regime type.

It is important to emphasise at this point that this dual institutional architecture does not on its own capture the complexity of politics in tutelary hybrid regimes, as the two pillars rarely correspond to two monolithic groups of opposing actors, guardians on one side and democrats on the other. In fact, one of the central arguments of this book is that it would be misleading to think about electoral politics under tutelage purely as an elite versus popular, or authoritarian versus democratic, power struggle. As both the Iranian and Turkish cases demonstrate, social classes, political factions, ideological affiliations and interest-based networks and alliances often cut across the two pillars. In particular, intra-elite cooperation and competition play a key role in shaping the processes of consolidation and contestation of tutelage. Indeed, it only makes sense to talk about 'the guardians' while keeping in mind this elite factionalism, as well as the shared networks, interests and worldviews beyond the tutelary–electoral divide.

Politics in tutelary hybrid regimes, in other words, does not take place exclusively along the guardianship versus democracy cleavage. Elected politicians, for one or more of the reasons mentioned above, may see in the preservation of the hybrid regime architecture clear benefits for themselves. They may internalise and uphold the existence of tutelary red lines, and refrain from questioning the legitimacy of tutelary actors (such as in the case of Thailand's deeply revered monarchy), therefore presenting no threat to the status quo. Meanwhile, the guardians may also view the popular legitimacy that the existence of a democratic pillar lends to the political system as a whole as necessary for the regime's (and by extension, for their own) survival. Electoral politics, as we will see in both the Iranian and Turkish cases, can be used by the guardians to deflate societal tensions and manage expectations. In short, both the guardians and participants in electoral politics may see the maintenance of the regime's hybrid architecture as in their best interest – or, at least, challenging this status quo as being too costly and dangerous. Based on a shared understanding that neither pillar should overcome the other, and that factional or partisan divisions should not openly exploit the guardianship versus democracy cleavage, actors can reach a modus vivendi, rendering tutelary hybrid regimes more stable and flexible than their contradictory nature would lead us to assume.[28]

Nevertheless, power struggles can still erupt along the guardianship versus democracy cleavage, whether: (a) out of intra-elite competition (such as when an elite faction that dominates the tutelary pillar then goes on to emasculate the democratic pillar, or when a faction that is driven out of the tutelary state apparatus turns to popular politics to reform or re-enter that apparatus), (b) due to the emergence of popular movements and actors outside the regime elite that openly challenge the guardians and their privileges or (c) a combination of both (i.e., when an elite faction forms an alliance with popular outsiders against a rival elite faction). In these scenarios, the 'foundational tension' of these regimes – the tension between elite and popular rule – comes to surface, triggering institutional clashes that can destabilise and even result in the collapse of one of the two pillars. This is the basic story of the regime crises that both Iran and Turkey experienced during the first decade of the twenty-first century.

Iran and Turkey as Tutelary Hybrid Regimes

Despite the differences in their formative experiences, geopolitical orientations and institutional architecture, the Republic of Turkey, founded on the secular nationalist ethos of Mustafa Kemal Atatürk and the Islamic Republic of Iran, built upon Ayatollah Khomeini's *velayat-e faqih* (guardianship of the Islamic jurisprudent) thesis, shared one basic feature: powerful tutelary actors watching over democratic institutions and defining the rules and boundaries of electoral competition. *Velayat* and *vesayet,* two terms with Arabic origins that mean guardianship, have been at the centre of the Iranian and Turkish political discourses, respectively, for decades. The military in Turkey and the Shi'a clergy in Iran sought to legitimise their tutelary roles on the basis of their historical prominence as institutions negotiating power with the Ottoman sultans and Iranian shahs, their heroic roles in the foundational episodes of the two republics (the Turkish War of Liberation of 1919–22 and the Iranian Revolution of 1978–9), as well as their claim to inherit the charismatic legacies of Atatürk and Khomeini.

Upholding the ideological legacy of the founding fathers is the self-assigned and proclaimed duty of the guardians in both republics. But the interpretation of these legacies has varied considerably depending on the changing worldview and interests of different elite factions in changing times. Already containing internal contradictions during the leaders' lifetime as a result of years of pragmatic decision making, Kemalism and Khomeinism have come to embody different meanings and priorities for different actors at different historical moments. This ideological fluidity is immediately observable in Iran, where factional divisions amongst the Khomeinist elite have become a core characteristic of politics in the IRI. These divisions do not only reflect divergent interpretations of Islamic jurisprudence by the historically decentralised Shi'a clergy, but also the different prioritisation of the 1979 revolution's meaning and key promises by the traditionalist, modernist, reformist and neo-conservative factions, as well as the class interests that each group represents.

Divisions among Turkey's ruling elites have also played a key role in the consolidation and the subsequent contestation of tutelage in that country. The nationalist leadership of the Liberation War was split in the immediate aftermath of victory in 1922 over personal rivalries and disagreements over the nature and intensity of Mustafa Kemal's reforms. Although Kemalist one-party rule was secured by 1925, a new factional division emerged within the ruling Republican People's Party (*Cumhuriyet Halk Partisi*, CHP) that pitted statist officers and bureaucrats against the urban bourgeoisie and rural landlords. While the first group had the upper hand for much of the single-party period, the latter group dominated the first decade of multiparty politics in Turkey under the Democrat Party (*Demokrat Parti*, DP) government in the 1950s. Yet even as the statists consolidated their grip over the state apparatus with the 1960 military coup, ideological splits and generational shifts within the Turkish Armed Forces (*Türk Silahlı Kuvvetleri*, TSK) continued to shape Turkey's political trajectory. For instance, the religious–nationalist agenda promoted by the 1971 and 1980 coup-makers, known as the 'Turkish–Islamic synthesis', stood in stark contrast with the secularism enforced by both the 1960 junta and the perpetrators of the post-modern coup of 1997. Nevertheless, all of these interventions were carried out in the name of safeguarding 'Atatürk's principles and revolution'.

In both the Turkish and Iranian cases, early intra-elite rivalries and splits created institutional path dependence. As those elite factions that were sidelined from the regime's core decision-making apparatus turned to popular politics, they focused on mobilising the electorate by claiming to represent the people's true demands and interests. This won them widespread backing from societal groups with a wide range of grievances towards the state. Although their leaders came from within the state elite and had no particular interest in overturning the regime, their insider–outsider status and electoral popularity posed a threat to their elite rivals. This threat perception, in turn, prompted these latter factions to channel their energies to further entrench themselves within the state apparatus, maintaining a grip over tutelary institutions and strengthening them against popular challengers, effectively turning the intra-elite rivalry into tutelary–popular competition. It was the successive election defeats of the CHP in the 1950s, together with the DP's increasingly majoritarian politics, that prompted statist officers to carry out the 1960 coup and establish new institutions of tutelage. Likewise, the sweeping reformist victories in the 1997 presidential and 2000 Majles elections in Iran propelled the decidedly unpopular traditionalist faction to focus on dominating the judiciary, the Guardian Council and the security establishment and to use them aggressively against the elected government.

A long-term consequence of tutelary entrenchment in both Turkey and Iran has been the gradual yet constant expansion of the guardians' political authority and constitutional jurisdiction at the expense of democratic politics. In Turkey, each 'self-correcting coup' saw the constitution amended or rewritten, the electoral space tightened and veto institutions established, as the guardians set out to reverse the unforeseen consequences of the previous generations' ill-conceived socio-political engineering projects. In the IRI, the legalisation of the Leader's powers with the 1989 Constitution, the 1991 expansion of the Guardian Council's supervisory and vetting authorities, and the 2008 Majles decision exempting the Leader from any theoretical parliamentary oversight are examples of the expansion of the guardians' formal authorities. Parallel to this was also an informal process, whereby Supreme Leader Ali Khamenei strengthened his grip over the state apparatus through his personal representatives, control over the *bonyads* (semi-public economic foundations) and the growing politico-economic clout of the Islamic Revolutionary Guard Corps (IRGC). In both cases, the predominant tendency of those who held unaccountable power has been to maximise it – not to relinquish or share it with others.

Yet despite this tendency, even at the peak of their institutional power, the guardians in both countries remained reluctant to rule without electoral legitimation. If one of the lessons of the Khatami presidency (1997–2005) for Iran's traditionalist guardians was to tighten the tutelary controls over the republican institutions and search for a presidential candidate who would be loyal to the Leader, the other was the need for the traditionalists to be able to compete in popular politics. It was this pragmatic concern that led Ayatollah Mesbah Yazdi, an influential ultra-conservative cleric and a firm believer in absolute guardianship without any need for popular legitimation, to support Mahmoud Ahmadinejad as a conservative populist antidote to the liberal-minded reformists. Likewise, survival instincts in response to the popular legitimacy crisis that engulfed the Islamic Republic after the 2009 election eventually led Khamenei and the traditionalists to accept a new factional modus vivendi with the modernist and reformist leaderships and attempt to restore the regime's republican pillar with the 2013 presidential election.

In Turkey, the decision to return power to civilian governments after every coup d'état demonstrated the guardians' reluctance to govern directly. Even as senior generals dictated ultimatums to prime ministers behind the scenes through the powerful National Security Council (NSC), the Turkish Armed Forces carefully upheld an image of a professional body, disinterested in politics and interfering reluctantly in civilian affairs only to preserve the republic's core principles, thereby placing the burden of public opinion on the shoulders of elected officials. While the guardians in both Iran and Turkey viewed the electoral process as inherently risky and sought to mitigate its unpredictable outcomes, they also knew that rendering the democratic process meaningless or cancelling elections altogether carried greater risks for regime stability and survival.

In other words, just as in consolidated democracies, competitive elections were the sine qua non of the Turkish and Iranian tutelary hybrid regimes. In Turkey, a high level of public confidence in the integrity of elections and belief in the validity of outcomes provided legitimacy to the political system, including to the military's guardianship role. In numerous crises, elections were used to resolve deadlocks and deflate socio-political tensions. From 1950 onwards, the Kemalist guardians recognised the outcome of every election, even when these threatened the institutional status quo. The operational logic of guardianship in Turkey was to define and enforce the rules and boundaries of electoral politics through veto actors – not through electoral manipulation and vote rigging.

The inherent risks for the guardians of allowing the electoral process to run its course became apparent as the popular AKP governments used successive referenda and election victories to deconstruct the military–bureaucratic tutelage in the 2000s. This process provoked and exposed bitter divisions among the tutelary elite over how to respond to the existential threat facing the Kemalist establishment. Erdoğan invoked the 'nation's will' obtained through the ballot box as a licence to overcome undemocratic tutelage. But under the guise of fighting tutelage, he also targeted democratic checks and balances, and gradually established his own personalistic rule at the expense of rule of law and civil liberties. Ironically, electoral integrity started deteriorating in Turkey not under military rule but under civilian governments that turned increasingly authoritarian in the post-tutelary setting, and demonstrated a growing reluctance to share or relinquish power through the ballot box.

Compared with Turkey, the democratic space has been more tightly restricted in the IRI, where the powerful Guardian Council limits participation in elections by keeping out candidates that are deemed a threat to the tutelary establishment. Despite this rigid filtering mechanism, elections in the Islamic Republic have also served a crucial function. The belief (or at least the hope) that election outcomes would have tangible policy implications repeatedly drove Iranians to the ballot box in large numbers, frequently rebuffing the preferences of the regime's top guardians and providing much needed popular legitimation for the Islamic Republic. In turn, the regime elite used elections to manage popular participation in politics, socialise younger generations into the IRI system and to negotiate factional rivalries.

Underpinning this process was a tacit social contract, whereby the Iranian public by and large came to accept the restrictions imposed upon electoral competition, and expected in return a reasonably fair and lawful campaign process and vote count. That agreement gradually came undone as factional rivalries intensified and the traditionalists perceived in the reform movement an existential threat to the IRI system. Perceptions of manipulation of the vote started with the Majles elections in 2000 and grew with each election, culminating in the mass uprising that followed claims of systematic fraud in the 2009 presidential election. Khamenei and the traditionalists suppressed this uprising by force and secured their grip over the state apparatus at the expense of the regime's popular legitimacy. Even though the factional modus vivendi of 2013 surrounding the election of Hassan Rouhani was aimed at bringing the IRI back from the precipice, the experience of 2009 dealt a long-term blow to the regime's republican pillar. By 2017, much of the hope that the system could be reformed from within appeared to have been lost. When the ballot box no longer offered a remedy to the society's grievances, the streets became the outlet for the people's frustrated energy.

In short, the fight over electoral politics and institutions has been an integral part of the power struggles between the guardians and their popular challengers in the two tutelary hybrid regimes in the twenty-first century. How did these power struggles unfold and why did they yield such divergent outcomes? The answer this book puts forward through tracing the long-term institutional evolution of the two polities involves a combination of structure and agency-related factors, including the legal/constitutional remit and justifications of guardianship in both countries, the degree to which guardianship has been integrated into the Western-led international order and global economy, as well as the fateful decisions by key tutelary and elected actors in critical junctures.

Organisation of the Book

The book consists of four parts, each divided into two chapters. The first part – Foundations – explores the historical and ideological roots of the Iranian and Turkish tutelary hybrid regimes. Dankwart Rustow once said 'the study of democratic transitions will take the political scientist deeper into history than he has been willing to go. Man did not become a political animal in 1960 or in 1945, as much of our recent literature pretends to suppose'. In this spirit, Chapter 1 delves into the two countries' long imperial histories to explore the emergence, institutionalisation and evolution of the idea of state and legitimate authority as the two polities grappled with the challenges of modernity. In particular, I discuss the persistent vision of an antagonistic duality between state and society in Iran versus the influential nationalist myth of a hierarchical unison between the state and the nation in Turkey. Chapter 2 focuses on the foundational experiences of the two republics – the Anatolian resistance movement of 1919–22 and the Iranian revolution of 1979 – and compares and contrasts the pragmatic politics and ideological legacies of their charismatic leaders, Atatürk and Khomeini, which underpin the systems of guardianship in both republics.

The second part of the book – Consolidation – is about the institutional entrenchment of Khomeinist and Kemalist tutelage in both countries.

Chapter 3 discusses the establishment of institutional duality in the IRI that is embodied in the regime's Islamic and Republican pillars, its evolution following the death of Khomeini in 1989, the role of elections in this hybrid arrangement and the role of factional politics in the institutionalisation of a leader versus president rivalry. Chapter 4 analyses the consolidation of military tutelage in Turkey in a more gradual and ad hoc fashion than in Iran in the context of the Cold War and parallel to the development of multiparty democracy, through periodic 'self-correcting coups'.

Part Three – Contestation – is about political competition in the two tutelary hybrid regimes. Chapters 5 and 6 focus on the power struggles between the guardians and elected contenders in Iran and Turkey, respectively, at the turn of the millennium. These power struggles brought to surface the foundational tension of the two regimes between popular and elite rule, and culminated in the end of hybridity in both republics by the late 2000s. The fourth part – The Outcome – discusses what follows the suspension of hybridity: Chapter 7 explains how the erosion of the IRI's democratic legitimacy after 2009 brought the entire system to the brink of collapse in an atmosphere of geopolitical and socio-economic tension and compelled rival factions to put aside their differences to establish a new modus vivendi to revive the republican pillar and ensure regime survival. Chapter 8 discusses the use and abuse of tutelage as a populist strategy in the undoing of Kemalist guardianship and the establishment of Erdoğan's 'New Turkey', as well as the changes and continuities between these supposedly old and new Turkeys.

I conclude with reflections on the two puzzles that the comparative study of the two cases leaves us with. The first is how and why the guardians came out on top in their respective power struggles against popular contenders in Iran in the 2000s, while they were defeated in Turkey. The second puzzle concerns the remarkable persistence of patriarchal authority in both polities despite their divergent trajectories, and what this means for the study of political transitions and democratisation in general.

Notes

1. Dahl, *Democracy and its Critics*, p. 52.
2. See Akkoyunlu, 'Turkey's Iranian Conundrum: A Delicate Balancing Act', in Kadıoğlu et al., *Another Empire?*

3. See for example, Özbudun, 'Khomeinism – A Danger for Turkey?'; Rubenstein and Smolansky, *Regional Power Rivalries in New Eurasia*; Barkey, *Reluctant Neighbour*; Olson, *Turkey – Iran Relations 1979–2004*.

4. Shambayati, 'A Tale of Two Mayors'; Tezcür, *Muslim Reformers in Iran and Turkey*.

5. For an overview of the comparative literature on Turkey and Iran up to 2014, see Hazır, 'Comparing Turkey and Iran in Political Science and Historical Sociology'.

6. 'Turkish and Iranian Political Theories and Traditions in Kutadgu Bilig,' in İnalcık, *The Middle East and the Balkans under the Ottoman Empire*; Lewis, 'Iran in History'; Canfield, *Turko-Persia in Historical Perspective*.

7. Sohrabi, *Revolution and Constitutionalism in the Ottoman Empire and Iran*; Issawi, 'Egypt, Iran and Turkey 1800–1970' in Bairoch and Levy-Leboyer, *Economic Development since the Industrial Revolution*; Perry, 'Language Reform in Turkey and Iran'; Atabaki, and Zürcher, *Men of Order*; Atabaki, *The State and the Subaltern*; Kamali, *Multiple Modernities, Civil Society and Islam*.

8. Huntington, *The Third Wave*, p. 141.

9. Linz, *Totalitarian and Authoritarian Regimes*, p. 36.

10. Chehabi, 'The Political Regime of the Islamic Republic of Iran in Comparative Perspective'.

11. Diamond, 'Thinking About Hybrid Regimes'.

12. Sarfati, 'How Turkey's slide to authoritarianism defies modernization theory'.

13. Taş, 'Turkey – from tutelary to delegative democracy'; Esen and Gümüşçü, 'Rising competitive authoritarianism in Turkey'; Akkoyunlu and Öktem, 'Existential insecurity and the making of a weak authoritarian regime in Turkey'; Yılmaz and Turner, 'Turkey's deepening authoritarianism and the fall of electoral democracy; Bozarslan, 'Rejecting democracy'; Tugal, 'Turkey coup aftermath'.

14. Gilbert and Mohseni, 'Beyond authoritarianism'.

15. Gingeras, 'How the Deep State came to America'; Ellidge, 'Don't fall for Boris Johnson's "deep state" conspiracy theory'.

16. Though they can overlap to some extent (in that, tutelary regimes can have their deep state), tutelage and deep state remain separate concepts. Tutelage refers to a formal and visible institutional arrangement, whereas the deep state implies an opaque power structure entrenched within the state apparatus, wielding influence behind the scenes, hindering accountability and undermining democratic process. Because of its clandestine, extra-legal nature, telling the true scale and structure of the deep state can be difficult, allowing for myth to mix with fact and for a conspiratorial discourse to flourish around the notion.

17. Di Cosmo, 'From alliance to tutelage', p. 190.

18. Of military praetorianism, Huntington wrote: 'As society changes, so does the role of the military. In the world of oligarchy, the soldier is a radical; in the middle-class world he is a participant and arbiter; as the mass society looms on the horizon he becomes the conservative guardian of the existing order' (*Political Order in Changing Societies*, p. 21).

19. Closa and Palestini, 'Tutelage and regime survival in regional organizations' democracy protection'.

20. Long before Chomsky and Herman published *Manufacturing Consent: The Political Economy of the Mass Media*, Plato considered how the people could be won over by the guardians. In the *Republic*, the guardians are *aristos*, selected from among the populace for their skills, intelligence and moral virtue, and rigorously trained for the task of governing. In this meritocratic utopia, the *demos* give the *aristos* their implicit or explicit consent to govern. But since the people are not fully aware of their interests, they may resist the stewardship of a professional ruling class. Plato suggested that the guardians then produce a 'noble lie' (also interpreted as 'magnificent myth' or a founding religion) to win over the society's consent, an advice that political leaders everywhere have taken to heart. See Ferrari, *Plato: The Republic*.

21. Nowell-Smith, *Selections from the Prison Notebooks of Antonio Gramsci*; Lull, *Media, Communication, Culture*.

22. Canovan, 'Trust the people!'.

23. Wigell, 'Mapping hybrid regimes', p. 239.

24. A number of established democracies have long featured heated debates about whether their high courts help sustain or undermine democracy. Dahl, for instance, referred to the US Supreme Court as a 'quasi-guardianship' institution. Also see Guarneri and Pederzoli, *From Democracy to Juristocracy?*, and Hirschl, *Towards Juristocracy*.

25. Valenzuela, 'Democratic Consolidation in Post-Transitional Settings' in Mainwaring, et al., *Issues in Democratic Consolidation*, p. 67.

26. Wigell, 'Mapping hybrid regimes', p. 238.

27. Mainwaring et al., *Issues in Democratic Consolidation*.

28. Stability, it is worth adding, does not imply politics stops and institutions remain static. It means that change happens incrementally and without a rupture, through processes such as 'layering', 'drift' or 'conversion'. See Streeck and Thelen, *Beyond Continuity*.

Part I

FOUNDATIONS

1

OF POWER AND LEGITIMACY: THE IDEA OF STATE IN IRAN AND TURKEY

We expect the fulfilment of whatever we desire initially from the government, and if not, then from God Almighty. There should be no doubt that a government is neither the father nor the teacher, neither the guardian nor the nanny of its people.

– Namık Kemal, Young Ottoman intellectual and reformer, 18 June 1872

The Iranian clergy should learn from the Sunnis who publicly remember their king at the end of each prayer and pray for him. Of our clergy the less said the better.

– Mohammad Reza Pahlavi

Most accounts of contemporary Iranian and Turkish politics and international relations start with the region's encounters with Western modernity and imperialism in the nineteenth century and the subsequent development of modern nation-state institutions and identities in the twentieth century. This approach treats these polities' long pre- and early modern histories as a distant past that is, while intriguing as a source of nationalist mythology, nonetheless irrelevant to how institutions were formed and politics is conducted in these countries. The implicit assumption is that the genesis of global politics as we know it is the European exportation of the modern state to the rest of the world, which knew no such concept previously. As others have pointed out, that is a flawed assumption.[1] In both Iran and Turkey, images, ideas and symbols of statehood, sovereignty and legitimacy that predate encounters with Western modernity continue to cast a shadow in contemporary politics. Guardians in both countries have routinely drawn from these deep-rooted reservoirs of power projection and legitimation to justify their claim to ownership of the state and paternalistic relationship with society.

With this in mind, this chapter presents a (necessarily non-exhaustive) *longue durée* account of the emergence and evolution of persistent ideas of statehood and legitimate authority in Iran and Turkey. I argue that despite references to a shared Turco-Persian culture, institutional self-images and perceptions of political authority have developed in their distinct historical contexts in the two polities. In particular, I contrast what Katouzian refers to as the 'dialectic of state and society' in Iran with the idea of a hierarchical unison between the state and society in Turkey and look at the political impact and implications of these images in the two tutelary hybrid regimes.

Despite – and perhaps also as a result of – a history of frequent foreign invasions and occupations, Iran has come to embody a supra-political meaning, associated not with any political authority in the first place, but rather with a cultural, linguistic and geographic space. The perception of political authority as foreign and fleeting has found embodiment in the pre-Islamic, Shi'a and modern revolutionary concepts of resistance to externally imposed tyranny and has reinforced the persistent image of an antagonistic dualism between state and society, invoked by the numerous popular movements against governments viewed as illegitimate. In contrast, it is the political authority that appeared constant under 600 years of Ottoman rule, and survived, albeit in new ideological garments, in what became Turkey in the twentieth century while everything from borders to languages, demographic make-up to socio-economic infrastructure went under violent transformation as the Ottoman Empire entered its catastrophic demise from the late nineteenth century onwards. As a result, 'the state' (*devlet*) emerged as both the main architect and a central pillar of modern Turkish national identity.

I should underline that the intention here is not to explain state–society relations through a simplified lens that treats the state as a monolithic entity existing separately from society.[2] Migdal wrote that the state has a paradoxical quality that must be thought of 'at once (1) as the powerful image of a clearly bounded, unified organization [. . .] and (2) as the practices of a heap of loosely connected parts or fragments'.[3] The idea in this chapter is to focus on (1) without losing sight of (2). In other words, while recognising that state and society are mutually constitutive and entangled through class dynamics, interest groups and networks, I am interested in the simple yet powerful popular imaginations of what the state is, where these imaginations originate from, how they have evolved, and the non-imaginary effects they have on institutional legitimation and political decision-making in modern Iran and Turkey.

On 'Iran' and 'Turkey': What is in a Name?

Beyond the modern construct of a nation-state, Iran refers to both a geographic and, more importantly, cultural concept that has been in continuous use for millennia. Despite periodic ethno-nationalist efforts to place it among the 'civilised' white/European races by asserting the nation's Aryan roots, we cannot define Iran as the exclusive domain of any single tribe or ethnic group.[4] Nor does Iran singularly refer to a political regime or dynasty. Iranian history is awash with dynasties that have come and gone, of indigenous as well as foreign origins, some fleeting, others more enduring in impact and legacy. Iran is not exclusively defined by the Achaemenid, Sassanid or Safavid empires, the Qajar or Pahlavi dynasties or the Islamic Republic for that matter, even though all of these political entities are part of the history of Iran.

In this sense, Iran is analogous to China for being, first and foremost, the centre of a 'shared imaginary geography' based on a 'common understanding of the relationship between language and power'.[5] Both have been subjected to foreign conquest and rule at various moments in their history. Yet on each occasion, a degree of assimilation of the conquering peoples, through partial or full adoption of the language, political institutions and administrative practices, has allowed for the idea of Iran and China to survive, adapt to and even flourish under 'foreign' domination. Today it is commonplace to count the Turkic Seljuk, Mongol Ilkhanid and Azeri Safavid states as Persianate dynasties, just as it is to list the Manchu Qing or the Mongol Yuan dynasties as Sinicised dynasties.[6]

This does not imply the existence of a single Iranian identity that has remained unchanged since the dawn of history. Although the notion of an unchanging Iranian national identity has been propagated by westernised intellectuals as part of the modern nation-building process, as well as by rulers aiming at self-legitimisation, the vast number of dynasties, regimes and ideologies that have dominated Iran alone is a testament to the existence of diverse and often clashing identities.[7] The idea of Iran propagated by the Pahlavis is clearly at odds with the one envisioned by Khomeini. We should, however, distinguish between social history and nationalist propaganda. Regardless of its fluid or even mythical nature, the enduring reference to a concept of Iran at the centre of a 'Persianate cosmopolis' allows us to speak of a continuity defined by 'an aesthetic and literary sensibility [and] an integrated understanding of moral and social order'.[8] In this respect, Iran stands apart from other nation-states in its neighbourhood that are more easily categorised as modern constructs.[9] As Anthony Smith argued in his critique of the modernist view of nationalism, Iran embodies a certain 'participants' primordialism': the persistent notion of a homeland, names, symbols and memories, however fluid or selective, at a collective level despite conquest and colonisation.[10]

Turkey shares few of these characteristics. In contrast to Iran, Turkey as a political or geographic term does not evoke a similar sense of historical continuity. For centuries, it was exclusively in Europe that the Ottoman Empire was referred to as Turkey, and the subjects of the sultan as Turks, often regardless of their ethnicity or religion.[11] Prior to the emergence of Turkish nationalism at the turn of the twentieth century, Turkey meant little, if anything, to the inhabitants of the geographic area that the Turkish Republic comprises today.[12] In fact, a corresponding term did not exist in most languages spoken within the Ottoman borders, including in Turkish.[13] This was a rather inaccurate way of conceptualising the Ottoman Empire, as there was little that was exclusively Turkish or Turkic about the vast realm. The Ottoman Empire was a multi-ethnic, multi-religious and multi-lingual empire that in no clear way constituted a land of Turks or even a 'Turkish empire'.[14]

For centuries, the official name of the Ottoman Empire as it was known to its subjects was *Devlet-i Âliye-yi Osmâniyye*, the Sublime Ottoman State, or simply the Sublime State (in contrast the Qajar state was called *Dowlat-e Aliyye-ye Irân*, emphasising its Iranian identity). In the sense that the state was at the centre of the definition of both the political and the geographic entity, the Ottoman Empire was closest to the polity it had supplanted: The Byzantine Empire. But whereas in Byzantium, dynasties replaced one another while the state lived on, 'in the Ottoman case the dynasty *was* the state throughout its 622-year career'.[15] The Ottoman dynasty meant the state, while the state – as it evolved into the complex administrative machinery overseeing the affairs of a domain spanning three continents – became analogous with the empire.

Official republican historiography sought to construct a purely Turkish identity by claiming an unbroken link between early Turkic tribal confederations of Central Asia and modern Turkey. This view conceives of the nation not as a people with a purportedly timeless attachment to a homeland, but as a people on the move, whose nationhood is derived primarily from its construction of successive political entities (i.e., statehood). A representation of this idea of nationhood-via-statehood is found in the official seal of the President of the Turkish Republic. First adopted in 1925, it features a pointed sun at the centre, representing the Turkish Republic, surrounded by 16 stars, each symbolising a historic Turkic state. One of the intended effects of this effort was to diminish the role played by the Ottoman dynasty – portrayed by the early Kemalists as an initially pure and heroic, but ultimately corrupted and decayed establishment – in the evolution of key institutions that also constituted the central pillars of the new republic: the military and the bureaucracy. But while numerous pre-Ottoman Turkic administrative and military traditions have survived into the Ottoman and republican periods, it would be impossible to get an accurate picture of the idea of the state and perceptions of legitimate authority in modern Turkey without taking into account their construction and evolution within the Ottoman context.

The state, both as an abstract idea and in terms of the physical apparatus used to forge the nation-state, is at the heart of modern Turkey's national identity. *Devlet* remained one of the few persistent associations in the lives of ordinary Muslims, particularly in the cities and towns of Ottoman Anatolia, as the familiar world around them – from socio-economic composition to the alphabet – changed radically and violently in the early twentieth century. And as far as anyone could remember, *devlet* had always been there, even if in a distance, in one form or another. Indeed, the Ottoman state's resilience was a remarkable feat that has been surpassed by few others in history, and none in the history of Iran. As many as twelve different dynasties ruled Iran in part or in whole during the reign of the Ottoman dynasty. Yet despite the frequent turnover of political authority, Iran did not experience such a profoundly traumatising demographic transformation as the Ottoman Empire did during its catastrophic demise, when entire communities arrived as refugees, while the old ones were decimated by war and famine, or uprooted, expulsed and annihilated in state-led ethnic cleansing.[16] 'Present-day Iranians live more or less within the same borders as their great-grandparents,' notes Abrahamian.[17] This is not the case for many citizens of modern Turkey, or the grandchildren of Christian communities of the Ottoman Empire.

To sum up, if Iranian national identity derives its key references from geographic space, language and culture, rather than government institutions, Turkish national identity is very much built around the idea of the state. Turkish nationalism sanctifies the state and conceives it as inseparable from, yet also exalted above, the nation.[18] Ottoman reformers in the nineteenth century, military commanders in the twentieth century and President Erdoğan in the twenty-first century have all have all invoked 'ensuring the state's perpetuity' (*devletin bekası*) as their most urgent and sacred duty.[19] Unsurprisingly, this has also been used to justify tutelage, the 'deep state' and systematic violations of democracy and rule of law in Turkey. In popular discourses, the state is likened – sometimes affectionately, sometimes mockingly – to a father (*devlet baba*) who loves his children, beats them up for their own good and is often absent from their lives. Such a patriarchal predilection is not absent in modern Iran, though it tends to be less directed towards the abstract idea of the state than to individual leaders and is counteracted by the entrenched suspicion of political authority as fleeting and foreign and therefore against 'the people'.

From *Farr* to Shi'ism: Divine Sanction in Iran

The right to rule is one of the most enduring and controversial themes running through the history of Iran. References to divine grace or sanction (*farr-e izadi*, henceforth *farr*) are traced to the early Median populations and feature prominently in Achaemenid and Sassanid-era inscriptions and symbolisms.[20] *Farr* indicates the qualities a ruler must possess in order to obtain God's grace, without which his rule would be illegitimate. In Zoroastrian imagery, the possession of *farr* was marked by a mystical aura, or halo, around the sovereign's head, a symbolism later adopted by Abrahamic religions to denote sainthood.[21]

Divinely obtained legitimacy constitutes the basis of Weber's concept of patriarchal patrimonialism.[22] In patriarchal patrimonial systems, kings are not bound by an earthly contract; they are 'above society and not just at the head of it'.[23] Yet unlike the European concept of the divine right of kings, which Weber's ideal type is based on, the concept of *farr* in Iran has embodied distinctly secular and practical provisions concerning the conduct and legitimacy of rulers, akin to the Confucian idea of the Mandate of Heaven. According to these provisions, *farr* could not be inherited or obtained by brute force. It was invested according to one's personal worth, judged not only by success as a military commander but also by commitment to Mazdaism, the highly moralistic precepts of which emphasised personal choice and responsibility.[24]

According to the Zoroastrian book of *Zadspram*, a ruler's legitimacy depended on three qualities: his attachment to the faith, his efforts to fight his personal evils (namely pride, conceit and falsehood) and fulfilling of his duty towards the people, understood as delivering justice, charity and good fortune.[25] Another Zoroastrian scripture, *Zamyad Yasht*, explains that 'the Glory that cannot be forcibly seized' is bestowed upon those who endeavour to improve the world of Ahura Mazda through 'good thought, good word and good deed'.[26] Ferdowsi's eleventh century epic *Shahnameh*, which has over 450 references to *farr,* recounts the legend of the Turanian king Afrasiab, who tries three times to seize the kingly glory by force and fails each time due to his tyrannical and deceitful nature.[27]

Divine grace was also conditional and non-permanent: a king could lose his *farr* if he became unjust or unable to maintain peace and security within his realm. In such a case, *farr* would be bestowed upon someone else, the figure of a divinely ordained saviour. Crucially, the new recipient of *farr* did not need to belong to the ruling dynasty (as it could not simply be inherited) or have any noble credentials at all, which meant the top job within the realm was theoretically open to all mortals. In theory, this was a rather meritocratic way to ensure just rule.[28] In practice, however, the fluctuating nature of divine sanction and its dependence on the personality and achievements of the ruler made dynastic continuity an elusive ambition. Similar to the Confucian Mandate of Heaven, the idea that a ruler could lose his legitimacy meant that revolt against an illegitimate ruler was not only considered justified, but also a duty. In Katouzian's view, this impermanent, conditional and ultimately subjective conceptualisation of legitimate authority, which could be observed in Iran's pre-modern and modern history, has led to frequent crises of succession and rebellions against authority that chronically destabilised Iran, rendering it a 'short-term society' (*jame-ye kutah moddat*).[29]

Another point that needs emphasis is the availability of divine sanction to all social classes. According to the ninth century Zoroastrian text *Denkard*, legitimate authority was originally bestowed in its entirety on one ruler, King Yima (Jamshid in *Shahnameh*) who ruled all of humanity for 300 years, until he became proud and conceited. Upon his eventual fall from God's grace, it was divided into three parts reflecting the three classes of people: the warriors (including kings and princes), the priests and 'the producers of material wealth' – or the bulk of Iran's working population.[30] This division reflected the role of both the clerical establishment and the common people (understood interchangeably as the masses, the workers or merchants and traders, i.e., *bazaaris*) in the legitimation of authority in Iran.

Here, the universalistic dualism between good and evil enshrined in Mazdaism – one of the earliest faiths to move beyond cult and totemism to address moral issues, with great influence on Abrahamic religions – plays a governing role.[31] Mazdaism places currency on the individual's responsibility to shape his or her own destiny by committing to 'the truth' and refraining from evil. Thus, the goal of every individual should be to attain perfection that is symbolised by the possession of *farr*. This notion opens space for any individual to strive for greatness and prepares the ground for a vast literature on heroism, leadership and martyrdom. One of the most cherished heroes of *Shahnameh* is the blacksmith Kaveh, who leads a mass revolution and helps the rightful king-to-be Fereydun on his mission to dethrone the despotic ruler Zahhak. Their legend embodies some of the themes that feature prominently in modern Iranian political discourse: the loss of legitimacy, the rightful struggle against injustice and resistance to foreign rule (the tyranny of Zahhak, a Babylonian king, has been understood as a metaphor for Arab oppression in Ferdowsi's epic).

Kaveh and Fereydun remain popular symbols in modern Iran, frequently invoked in reference to contemporary political struggles. Indeed, the historical importance of Ferdowsi's *Shahnameh* is based not only on its role in preserving Persian language at a time of Arabic domination, but also in bridging Islamic Iran with its pre-Islamic past in the construction of a proto-national Iranian identity. Like a number of other pre-Islamic traditions, such as Nowruz and Mihragan, the idea of justice-based divine sanction survived the Arab and Mongol conquests, adopted Islamic references (both Sufi mysticism and Shi'a) and found its way into modern political symbolism. The myth of Imam Hossein's marriage to Shahrbanu, the daughter of the last Sassanid emperor Yazdegerd III, although highly dubious as a historical fact, nonetheless facilitated a psychological reconciliation between Islam and Iran's pre-Islamic past.[32] 'Shi'ism,' wrote Behnam, 'essentially mitigated Arab encroachment in the minds of the vanquished'.[33] With its emphasis on the perfection and divine legitimacy of the Imamate, and the ideas of justice and struggle against tyranny characterised by the tragic martyrdom of Hossein bin Ali in Karbala, Shi'ism eventually came to represent both a distinct Islamic identity for Iran, and an Iranian mark on Islam. The term *farr-e izadi* itself remained in continuous use as post-Islamic dynasties of Iran, from the Ghaznavids to the Qajars, laid claim to divine sanction.

The universal availability of *farr* granted 'the people' a remarkable voice in Iran. It also legitimised two conflicting forces at the same time: divinely ordained patriarchal authority and popular resistance to unjust rule. This dichotomy resonates in modern Iran. Reza Shah Pahlavi, for instance, was widely seen as Iran's long-awaited saviour when he emerged out of virtual obscurity to impose order on a chaotic country and resist foreign encroachment (epitomised by his refusal to ratify the 1919 treaty that would expand oil concessions to Britain). That he was also an iron-fisted dictator did not seem to put his legitimacy into question, at least until the latter half of his reign.[34] His successor, Mohammad Reza Shah, was very much aware of the traditional symbolism of divine grace. At the same time as he projected an image of himself as a visionary reformer and a patriotic leader, he claimed that he was 'an agent of the will of God'.[35] He was more successful, however, in convincing his immediate entourage and Western supporters than his own subjects, many of whom saw the monarch as a 'foreign imposition'.[36] They found a new Fereydun in the charismatic leadership of the exiled Ayatollah Khomeini and new Kavehs in the supporters of the revolution. Khomeini himself did not only lead the Iranian revolution as a divinely sanctioned struggle against tyranny and injustice, but also established the Islamic Republic with *velayat-e faqih* at its centre very much on this premise.[37]

Justice lies at the heart of the Iranian concept of legitimacy, but what exactly constitutes a just ruler remains ambiguous and subjective in practice. On balance, much depends on the ruler's personal success – or rather, the perception of success – as a military commander and skilful administrator. Darius, Khosrow I and Abbas I were such figures, and they personify the idea of the just ruler. The verdict is less clear on Reza Shah, who lost much of his popularity due not only to his increasingly autocratic rule but also his failure to prevent the Anglo-Soviet invasion of Iran in 1941, which culminated in his dethronement. Success, to a notable extent, depends on conditions and circumstances beyond one's immediate control, such as the availability of resources and the presence of powerful external rivals, internal power struggles and political intrigues. Does failure, then, automatically imply illegitimacy, and conversely, does the legitimacy of a rebellion rest largely on its popularity and success?

The answer may not be a straightforward 'yes' as some scholars, including Katouzian, suggest.[38] Another modern Iranian leader, Prime Minister Mohammad Mosaddeq, was overthrown for nationalising the Anglo-Iranian Oil Company and ended his days in relative obscurity under house arrest. Yet even when the details of the US and British-backed coup that toppled him in 1953 were unknown to the public, and the Shah's regime portrayed the old man as an obstinate fanatic, Mosaddeq remained popular among Iranians, many of whom saw him as a legitimate champion of Iran's national interests, a secular martyr of sorts. What seems clear instead, and therefore worthy of repeated emphasis, is the central role that popular perceptions of justice play in ascribing or denying legitimacy to rulers, as well as to rebellions and revolutions, in Iran.

From *Beylik* to Empire: The Ottoman Idea of Statehood

In contrast to Iran, the popular featured less prominently in the Ottoman concept of legitimacy. The dynasty did assert a divine aura of sanctity to emphasise the justness of its claim over a vast territory and its diverse populations, the leadership of Islam and patronage of the Orthodox Church. Nonetheless, the Ottoman production of legitimacy bore 'a distinctly elitist character. At least in its written texts it did not address the general public and was meant to serve philosophical and one might even say aesthetic demands'.[39] This is not to suggest that the Ottoman state existed in a vacuum, cut off from society. On the contrary, part of the explanation for the empire's impressive longevity rests on its ability to devise an effective administrative system that could accommodate diversity, local customs and decentralised government, at least until it was forced to adapt to European modernity from the eighteenth century onwards. Even so, the pyramid-shaped structure of the Ottoman state, with the monarch sitting alone at the top, reflects a hierarchical conception of authority and of the state–society relationship.

In theory, Ottoman sovereigns were less constrained than their Iranian counterparts to negotiate their personal legitimacy with the Muslim clergy (*ulama*) or their subjects. What explains this difference? We may find an answer in the geopolitics of the fourteenth and fifteenth century Anatolia, where the Ottoman polity emerged and replaced the Byzantine Empire. The early Ottoman state was among two dozen tribal principalities (*beylik*) that gained independence after the demise of the Seljuk Sultanate of Rûm in the thirteenth century. The political structure of the Ottoman *beylik* displayed quasi-feudal characteristics. Reflective of the traditions of Turkmen tribal confederations, Ottoman rulers until Mehmed II, the conqueror of Constantinople, were *primus inter pares* in a frontier state at the border of Islamic and Christian realms. Warlords who led the expansion into the Christian Balkans held significant sway over the early Ottoman sultans. These early aristocrats, in turn, were dependent on their overlord (*bey*) who, with their access to the Anatolian hinterland, provided them with a market for 'frontier booty' and a steady flow of holy warriors.[40]

This quasi-feudal arrangement gave way to a centralised structure from the mid-fourteenth century onwards as Ottoman rulers increasingly relied on non-Muslim converts, recruited from the newly conquered European lands and trained to serve in the state's elite military and bureaucratic posts. The introduction of the *devshirme* (convert) system and the creation of a highly disciplined central military apparatus (the janissary corps) took place at the expense of the peripheral warlords, whose status and power gradually waned. The new system gave the Ottomans a distinct military advantage over their decentralised adversaries on both frontiers: the Muslim principalities of Anatolia and the tribal confederations of Iran to the East, and the feudal Balkan princedoms to the West. A comparable central military structure, with the *gholam* (slave) army at its core, was only established in Iran during the reign of Shah Abbas I in the early seventeenth century.

The great leap from sultanate to empire and the reformulation of the Ottoman concept of statehood occurred as a consequence of this military superiority, which culminated in the conquest of Constantinople in 1453. The inclusion of *the* city to the Islamic realm, an ambitious dream first articulated by Prophet Mohammad, not only contributed enormously to the prestige of the Ottoman sultans, and hence to their legitimacy in the eyes of their subjects, as well as the Muslim *umma* beyond it, it also served as a critical stepping stone in the transformation of the Ottoman state from a regional sultanate to a cosmopolitan empire with a claim to universal sovereignty. In the process, the Ottoman state adopted several key institutional features of the empire it had supplanted. One example is the assumption of the title '*Kayser-i Rûm*', or Caesar of the Romans, by Sultan Mehmed II. In the words of Kunt, Mehmed 'regarded himself as a sultan in the Islamic tradition and a great khan in the Inner Asian mould as well as a "kaiser" of the Romans or the Rumi, Byzantine and Turkish'.[41] 'Mehmed II', wrote Zarakol, 'tilted the empire away from the frontier practices towards an even more imperial conception of universal sovereignty, by drawing from as many wells of legitimation as were available'.[42]

Exactly how much the Ottomans borrowed from Byzantium was a polemical debate during the first half of the twentieth century, an authoritative account of which can be found in Cemal Kafadar's *Between Two Worlds*. That debate saw European Orientalists argue that 'uncivilised Turks' owed much of their state tradition to Greeks, and Turkish nationalists retorted, in a bid to assert modern Turkey's right to nationhood, that the Ottoman idea of statehood had its roots in Turkic-Mongol and Persian traditions.[43] Beyond the polemic, it is safe to suggest that Turkic, Mongol (Timurid), Persian and Byzantine traditions all played a role in shaping the Ottoman state architecture. In the sense that the overwhelming authority of the central government became the most obvious characteristic of the empire, with the ruler standing at the pinnacle of legitimate secular authority and religious establishment remaining a department of the state, the post-1453 Ottoman Empire closely resembled Byzantium.[44]

The sultans' expansive legal remit was codified in a series of imperial laws and investitures (*kanun* and *berat*) promulgated between the late fifteenth and the late sixteenth centuries. Starting with the reforms of Mehmed II, these laws and investitures institutionalised the authority of the central government, formalised the organisation of religious communities into autonomous socio-political clusters (*millets*) and regulated provincial administration, finances and land tenure within the empire. In an attempt to assert the state's claim to the absolute ownership of all arable land, and to raise funds for the janissary corps, Mehmed II confiscated land that was controlled by provincial aristocrats and Sufi orders and fraternities.[45] His legal code (*kanunname*) of 1475 sought to bring independent religious endowments (*vakıf*) and artisans' guilds (*ahi*), which had formed the basis of civil society in Anatolia since the Seljuk era, under the supervision of the central government, albeit with limited success.[46]

The imperial laws and decrees issued during the reign of Mehmed II defined the basic institutions of the Ottoman state, which were elaborated and refined under his successors, Bayezid II, Selim I and Süleyman I, and survived more or less intact into the nineteenth century. With the sultan at the top, the central administrative mechanism represented the 'eternal state' (*devlet-i ebed müddet*) responsible for preserving the 'world order' (*nizam-ı alem*), a concept further supported by the implementation of Sunni legal-ism in the late sixteenth century. The administrative formula for preserving the world order was known as the 'circle of equity' (*da'ire-i adliye*), which conceptualised a reciprocal relationship between the state and its subjects, whereby the state would provide order, welfare and a reliable justice system, in return for the routine collection of taxes, manpower for its troops and respect for its symbols.[47]

The practical reality of Ottoman rule, of course, was more complex than this straightforward philosophical conceptualisation would suggest. Despite its extensive legal and political remit, the central government possessed neither the intention nor the capacity to exercise direct control over the vast domain, and opted to delegate authority. The Ottoman legal system allowed a con-siderable degree of autonomy to relatively organised segments of the popula-tion, ranging from 'tribes, villages, residents of the same urban quarters, and artisanal groups (*esnaf* or *ta'ife*) in the marketplace to religious communities (*ta'ife* or *cemaat jama'a*) and provinces at large, in handling their affairs and internal differences according to their own custom' as long as public peace and order were retained.[48] Societal actors were not merely passive recipients of state policy. Outside the capital, entrenched local elites played a key role as intermediaries between the government and the people, often working with, as well as against, state representatives.[49]

The maintenance of this complex web of interdependencies in a vast realm necessitated a strong and effective bureaucratic apparatus. Over time, the empire's administration passed into the hands of viziers, and later, westernised bureaucrats and military officers. Bound by tradition and the state's bureaucratic rituals, the personal charisma of Ottoman sultans was gradually attributed to an abstract notion of the state, which was seen as the provider of order, a process Karen Barkey refers to as the bureaucratisation of patrimonial authority.[50] Unlike their illustrious ancestors, many of the latter-day Ottoman sultans became little more than figureheads, withdrawn from the affairs of the state.[51] As the fate of eleven sultans would illustrate, they could be deposed, murdered and replaced with a more favoured candidate – always from the same family – in the interest of the state.

State versus Clergy: Institutionalisation of Religious Orthodoxy in Iran and Turkey

The institutionalisation of Sunni legalism in the Ottoman Empire and Twelver (*Ithna Ashari*) Shi'ism in Safavid Iran as state doctrine further defined the legal remit of Ottoman and Iranian rulers. This process took place in the context of the geopolitical rivalry between the two states during the sixteenth century as both sides tried to establish their moral and political authority over Eastern Anatolia. At the same time, they faced the need to move away from millenarianism and formulate an institutional rationale to accommodate the transformation towards urban-based, bureaucratic empire.[52] However, these contemporaneous processes yielded markedly different long-term results for the two polities in terms of state organisation vis-à-vis the relationship between temporal and religious authority.

In the Ottoman case, the gradual move away from heterodox Turco-Islamic (Sufi) traditions into canonical Sunni Islam, hastened by the conquests of the Levant and Egypt and the power struggle with Safavid Iran, gave further theoretical legitimacy to the sultan and consolidated his position vis-à-vis the clergy. Conversely in Iran, the gradual marginalisation of the millenarian Sufism adhered to by the early Turkmen followers of the Safavid Shah Ismail, and the rise of an autonomous Shi'a clerical establishment starting under Tahmasp and consolidating under Abbas I, eventually constituted a counterweight to the authority of the ruler and placed the absolutism and legitimacy claimed by secular governments on tenuous ground.

The Sunni interpretation of the principle of *maslahat,* translated as public interest or expedience, granted legitimacy to de facto rulers as long as they protected and served the Islamic community, even if they seized power by force. Borne out of pragmatism and survival instincts, this principle reinforced the Ottoman concept of eternal state upholding the world order.[53] The acceptance of the dynasty's authority as legitimate by the Sunni *ulama* allowed Ottoman rulers to promulgate secular laws and justify them in the name of religiously provisioned order. It was in keeping with the public's interest that the Ottoman clergy sanctioned Mehmed II's *kanunname*, which included the legalisation of fratricide in order to prevent a succession crisis. Süleyman I was known to his subjects as 'Kanunî', or lawmaker, on the basis of his legal reforms. The modernising and secularising reform edicts of 1839 and 1856 were likewise justified by religious edicts (*fatwa*) even though they were widely unpopular among the empire's Muslims. In 1826, Sultan Mahmud II dismissed his *şeyhülislam*, the highest-ranking religious official in the empire, who refused to issue an edict supporting the abolition of the janissary corps, and replaced him with a more compliant public official.[54]

In contrast to the Sunni interpretation of *maslahat,* Shi'a jurists maintained that only a divinely sanctioned Imam could make and promulgate laws.[55] In the absence of the Mahdi, the saviour, the task of interpreting the divine law to reach a legal decision (*ijtihad*) was vested in the *mojtahed*, or qualified scholars of Islam, instead of the temporal ruler. The gradual institutionalisation of Twelver Shi'ism as the state religion of Iran under the Safavids also brought with it an institutional double-headedness that involved a trade-off between protection provided by the political establishment in exchange for religious endorsement from the autonomous clergy. This double-headed arrangement remained a basic tenet of administrative organisation in Iran until the Islamic Republic.[56] This is not to suggest that the Shi'a clergy was actively involved in government affairs from the beginning. In fact, a strong quietist tradition that decreed political inactivity until the return of the Mahdi remained dominant among the *ulama* until the faith became politicised and the clergy mobilised in the late nineteenth century.[57] Coupled with a growing practical predilection towards stability, the *ulama* often struck a compliant chord vis-à-vis the political authority, especially when the ruler was strong and popular. But from the late nineteenth century onwards, the *mojtahed*, in reaction to perceived injustice, did not refrain from using their legal influence to challenge the legitimacy of secular governments to defend traditional social structures, or to maintain their own class interests.

To be sure, neither the Ottoman nor the Iranian religious establishments were homogeneous entities. Behrooz Moazami provides a detailed account of how the Shi'a clerical establishment started transforming from a decentralised entity without a distinct institutional identity into an organised structure with an official hierarchy and powerful political networks only in the late nineteenth century, in the context of Iran's centralisation and modernisation.[58] Meanwhile, not all religious clerics in the Ottoman Empire were on government payroll. *Medreses* (religious schools) produced many scholars who did not work for the sultan, although these scholars also benefited from the numerous state endowments that sustained the *medreses* and *zawiyas* (monasteries), mosques and libraries across the empire. There were periods, such as in the late seventeenth and early eighteenth centuries, when the *ulama*, alongside the *janissaries*, wielded considerable influence on government affairs, checking the power of the sultans.[59]

Finally, as noted above, there were also deeply entrenched Sufi orders and fraternities that pre-dated the Ottoman state and enjoyed considerable autonomy despite being nominally bound to the sultan. They provided an alternative social network, source of spirituality, and in those parts of the empire where the sultan's authority was weak, a source of protection and stability. The relationship between these Sufi orders and the Ottoman state was complex and dynamic, shifting between interdependence and rivalry. The same should be said for Iran, where Sufi millenarian practices never died out, certainly not in socio-cultural spheres. Although institutionally sidelined, Sufi mysticism had a lasting influence on Shi'ism. Khomeini's esoteric worldview and idea of *velayat* (guardianship) were shaped by the gnostic strand in Sufism.[60]

These being said, both in terms of jurisprudential basis and administrative structure, it is safe to argue that the Shi'a *ulama* enjoyed a greater deal of independence from the political authority in Iran compared with the Sunni clergy in the Ottoman Empire. While the Ottoman government closely monitored the private funding of the office of the *şeyhülislam* and local religious judges (*qadi*), in Iran the *ulama* enjoyed extensive financial freedoms. Funded directly by public endowments, they were able to operate a wide network of religious schools and foundations that commanded significant socio-political influence under limited government interference. The fact that Najaf and Karbala, the traditional centres of Shi'a scholarship in modern day Iraq, had come under Ottoman rule in the sixteenth century also limited Iranian monarchs' control over the clergy, granting popular religious figures a valuable refuge in times of dispute with the authorities. Grand Ayatollah Mirza Hassan Shirazi triggered the Tobacco Protests of 1891 from Samarra in Iraq. It was during his sixteen-year exile in Najaf that Ayatollah Khomeini devised a radical political agenda for Shi'ism and led the mounting opposition against Mohammad Reza Shah.[61]

The dichotomy of a subservient *ulama* in the Turkish case and an autonomous one in Iran becomes especially visible in the course of the twentieth century. Besides abolishing the caliphate, the Kemalist rulers of the young Turkish Republic replaced the office of the *şeyhülislam* with the Presidency of Religious Affairs (*Diyanet*), a state department, demoted in official hierarchy, serving the interests of the secular military-bureaucratic guardians. Meanwhile, the relationship between the state and religious orders turned increasingly antagonistic in the process of Ottoman modernisation, centralisation and secularisation, ultimately culminating in the banning of religious orders by Mustafa Kemal in 1925. Islam, however, always remained a powerful societal force that wielded influence on modern Turkish politics, especially from the 1980s onwards.

In contrast, the 1907 supplements to the Iranian Constitution, establishing a committee of *mojtahed* to oversee the Islamic legality of legislation proposed by the parliament, were a manifestation of the *ulama*'s growing involvement in state affairs. Although never fully implemented, the Supplementary Fundamental Laws served as a precursor to Khomeini's *velayet-e faqih* theory and the Guardian Council in the Islamic Republic.[62] The Pahlavi shahs despised the institutional double-headedness of Iranian politics and yearned for a system where the government controlled the religious establishment. Mohammad Reza Shah expressed this resentment and yearning in the following words: 'The Iranian clergy should learn from the Sunnis who publicly remember their king at the end of each prayer and pray for him. Of our clergy the less said the better'.[63]

Change and Continuity in the Age of Revolutions

The nineteenth and the early twentieth centuries were defined by turbulent and often traumatising change impacting both the Ottoman and Iranian states and societies. Long convinced that they occupied the centre of the world, the Ottoman and the Iranian ruling elites slowly came to the realisation that they now inhabited the margins of a new world order, shaped by the economic and territorial ambitions of European imperialism. In the context of this geopolitical and psychological marginalisation, nostalgia for bygone glory days and the sense of urgency to fix a broken order created fertile ground for new and radical ideas to emerge. During this period, ideas that successfully fused elements of modern European thought with traditional concepts of authority and legitimacy had profound political and intellectual impact on both polities.

Two common external factors contributed to this sense of marginalisation: the Ottomans by the eighteenth century and the Qajars by the nineteenth century had become engulfed in lengthy, costly and mostly unsuccessful defensive wars against powerful imperial rivals, particularly Russia. At the same time, both were being integrated into the emerging global economy. Flung unprotected into capitalist competition with industrialising Western powers and their manufactured goods, the predominantly agrarian Ottoman and Iranian economies experienced profound shifts in production patterns and trade volumes, resulting in rising inflation, excessive taxation, mounting foreign debt and the institutionalisation of a culture of corruption.[64] As their political and economic fortunes declined, the Ottoman and Qajar states assumed an increasingly arbitrary character with state officials being seen as 'plunderers of their own society'.[65]

Encounters with European modernity and systematic reactions to it occurred earlier in the Ottoman Empire than in Iran, partly due to the former's territorial presence in and around Europe and the existence within its boundaries of large non-Muslim communities that had direct access to Western goods and ideas. From the eighteenth century onwards, with growing financial problems and military defeats, the central government's ability to administer its vast territories started to deteriorate. With land turning into a source of revenue rather than military retinue, a tax-farming scheme was introduced, leading to the rise of a new class of local notables (*ayans*) who collected taxes on behalf of the imperial government and served as an intermediary between the sultan and his subjects in the provinces. Increasing tax burden without a corresponding rise in productivity led to popular unrest among agricultural workers, who overwhelmingly formed the backbone of the Ottoman economy. In the nineteenth century, rebellions proliferated among the non-Muslim *millets*, who were now armed with the revolutionary idea of nationalism, as well as the empire's increasingly disgruntled Muslim subjects.

In response, throughout the nineteenth century the Ottoman state underwent an ambitious project of modernisation and reform, whose principal aim was to restore the authority and the legitimacy of the state and its image as the provider of peace and order throughout the realm. This process featured two simultaneous power struggles with lasting impacts on modern Turkey's institutional character: one between the state and the provinces, and the other within the state, between the sultan and an increasingly influential class of westernised bureaucrats and military officers.

Sultan Mahmud II (r. 1808–39) and his grandson Abdulhamid II (r. 1876–1909) were both ambitious modernisers and ardent believers in the absolute authority of the sultan. Both rose to power at a time when their personal security, the institutional authority of the sultan and the territorial sovereignty of their empire were being threatened by a host of domestic and foreign challenges. Mahmud II owed the throne to a powerful *ayan*, the governor of Ruscuk province, Alemdar Mustafa Pasha, who marched into the Ottoman capital to suppress a janissary rebellion that had killed the young sultan's reformist predecessor, Selim III. In exchange for this support, Mahmud agreed to sign a pact of alliance (*Sened-i Ittifak*) in which the state guaranteed land ownership and hereditary rights to the *ayan*s.[66] In his early years on the throne, Mahmud had to contend with rebellious janissaries as well as ambitious provincial governors.[67] One governor in particular, Mohammad Ali of Egypt, threatened the empire with full scale invasion, which was only averted after a desperate plea by the Ottoman government for Russian help.

Like his grandfather, Sultan Abdulhamid II rose to power on the shoulders of the powerful bureaucrats of the *Tanzimat* (Reform) era of 1836–76, who had previously deposed both his uncle and his brother and forced the young monarch to promulgate the empire's first constitution. The empire that Abdulhamid inherited was losing territory and facing disintegration as a result of financial bankruptcy, military defeat (most heavily inflicted by the forces of Tsar Alexander II in the war of 1877–8) and nationalist uprisings across its Christian communities. Labelled by the Russian tsar as 'the sick man of Europe', the Ottoman state's loss of sovereignty, and the dismemberment of its territories, was eagerly anticipated both by the Great Powers and smaller nationalist aspirants.

Both Mahmud II and Abdulhamid II were convinced that the only way to ensure their personal safety, the authority of their office and the integrity of their domain was by building a thoroughly modern central state apparatus in the European model that would monopolise decision-making.[68] Consequently, they invested heavily in creating a modern military, bureaucracy and education system, as well as improved transportation and communication infrastructure linking the provinces to the capital. In 1826, having consolidated his position, Mahmud II abolished the janissary corps and replaced it with a European-style conscript army. He also nullified the agreement with the *ayans* and executed headstrong provincial notables, like Ali Pasha of Tepelena. The authority of the central government over the provinces was further asserted in the *Tanzimat* era with the Land Code of 1858 and the Provincial Administration Law of 1864.

Abdulhamid II suspended the constitution and the parliament within a year of his reign. His rejection of the *Tanzimat*-era attempt to forge a civic Ottoman identity on the basis of equal rights for all religious communities, and embrace of pan-Islamism instead, won him the label of 'Oriental despot' in the twentieth century European and Turkish historiographies.[69] But despite the change in the political rhetoric, and the growing paranoia that led him to establish a repressive police state against which the Constitutional Revolution of 1908 took place, Abdulhamid's ambitious modernisation initiatives were very much a continuation of both the policies of the Westernising *Tanzimat* pashas, and his centralising grandfather, Mahmud II. These included the opening of the University of Istanbul in 1900 and 51 new secondary schools, mostly in the provinces, between 1882 and 1884, the connection of Istanbul with Vienna and Baghdad by railroad and the expansion of modern military academies across the empire.[70]

Ironically, the greatest opposition to the sultans' authority – as well as the ultimate demise of the dynasty – came from among these new classes of westernised bureaucrats and officers trained in Hamidian schools and serving in Mahmud's modern military. These bureaucrats and officers differed with the sultans on how to reform the legal and the administrative system, but not on the importance of re-establishing the state's authority and capacity to maintain order. Both the *Tanzimat* bureaucrats of the nineteenth century and the Young Turk officers who led the Constitutional Revolution of 1908 saw themselves foremost as servants of the state.

Crucially, when these bureaucrats and officers seized the reins of power, the patriarchal tendency they displayed was not fundamentally different from that of the two sultans. Namık Kemal, a leading Young Ottoman intellectual and advocate of constitutional monarchy, quoted in the beginning of this chapter, described the Ottoman government under the *Tanzimat* pashas as 'the system of many sultans'. The Young Turk officers that rose to prominence with the Constitutional Revolution of 1908 were initially in coalition with the empire's cosmopolitan urban intelligentsia and fledgling socialist movements under the slogan 'liberty, equality and justice' (*hürriyet, müsavaat, adalet*).[71] But the group's militaristic nationalism, shaped by the brutal experience of fighting militias in the Macedonian mountains and the existential trauma of the First Balkan War, culminated in the coup d'état of 1913 by the Committee of Union and Progress (*İttihat ve Terakki Fırkası*, CUP).[72] Embodying the hybrid results of Ottoman modernisation, Unionist Young Turks combined the radical militancy of French Jacobins, the conservative militarism of Prussian officers and the Ottoman tradition of guardianship that considered government 'the prerogative of a properly trained elite'.[73] The military-bureaucratic cadres that that led the Anatolian resistance movement and established the Turkish Republic carried this hybrid outcome into the twentieth century.

In his review of the changes in the Ottoman judicial system in the eighteenth and nineteenth centuries, Akarlı demonstrates that as the Ottomans grappled with the challenges of decline, the interactive judicial processes 'that helped connect the formulations of common good or public interest to the "public" to which it applied' became gradually marginalised and forgotten:

> Administrative decisions began to define public interest, which became increasingly hard to distinguish from the interests of the state as defined by the people in charge of it. Thus, the concept of *maslahat* lost its connection to a set of basic rights and conditions that made civic life possible. Rather, it became associated with *raison d'état*.[74]

Ottoman/Turkish modernisers, in other words, were armed with the self-legitimising philosophy of patriarchal authority that envisioned an all-powerful state at the centre of the world as the provider of peace and order. But while their predecessors were primarily interested in maintaining a functioning order, and thus content with interfering minimally in the public's affairs as long as taxes were collected, order maintained and symbols of the state respected, the modernising successors were in pursuit of establishing a new order in a changing world. This entailed turning the idea of the all-powerful state into reality. It was in this process, aided by technological change, that the state apparatus became a mechanism of social intervention, coercion and transformation in the hands of officers, bureaucrats and monarchs with clashing ideologies but a shared acceptance of the state's central place in upholding the world order.

Unlike their Ottoman neighbours, the Qajar rulers of Iran, who only came to power in the late eighteenth century after a century of internal strife, lacked the resources and the infrastructure to carry out a similarly ambitious reform project. The Qajar state was highly decentralised and the central government had little control beyond the new capital, Tehran. The Qajar shahs relied on local notables such as tribal leaders, merchants and senior clerics to administer the provinces.[75] Even at the centre, the state had 'few government institutions worthy of the name', including less than a dozen underfunded ministries of limited practical authority, some of which had been controlled by the same families since the early Safavid era.[76] Despite assuming *farr*-invoking titles such as King of Kings (*Shahanshah*) and Shadow of God (*Zillallah*), the Qajar shahs hardly fulfilled Wittfogel's definition of Oriental despotism as 'a political arrangement in which the state is stronger than society'. In the twentieth century, Mohammad Reza Shah commanded a much more formidable central state apparatus and adopted similarly grandiose titles including *Shahanshah* and *Aryamehr* (Light of the Aryans). Yet in both instances, the rulers' actual authority was checked by powerful and persistent societal forces.

With a feeble central state apparatus and a poorly armed and trained army consisting in large part of tribal contingents, Iran under the Qajars could provide scant resistance to the imperial ambitions of Russia and Britain. During the nineteenth and early twentieth centuries, Russia, motivated by territorial expansion, and Britain, by securing trade routes to India (and later by access to oil), played an increasingly ruthless game of domination over Iran, culminat-ing in the 1907 Anglo-Russian agreement that partitioned the country into zones of influence.[77] Humiliating defeats by Russia in 1813 and 1828 on the one hand, and the example of the Ottoman *Tanzimat* on the other, prompted Qajar shahs to attempt administrative and military reform in the 1830s and then in the 1870s under Naser al-Din Shah, who established the Russian-trained Cossack Brigade, Iran's first organised military in the modern sense.[78]

On the whole, however, these reforms remained intermittent and superfi-cial, largely due to the government's inability to raise the necessary funds. As a result, Qajar rulers came to rely on granting lucrative concessions to foreigners as a means of income, a policy widely despised for its impact on the local econ-omy and for increasing Western political and cultural influence. The impres-sion that whatever revenue the state managed to accumulate was squandered by corrupt officials and on lavish royal trips to Europe added to the growing popular resentment against the state. Thus, by the late nineteenth century, the Qajar state appeared to possess all the characteristics of a temporal government that had lost its legitimacy: self-interested, corrupt and inept, it had failed to provide for the people's well-being and security and defend the realm against foreign intervention. Rebelling against its authority could be justified.

The *ulama*'s prominent role in the Iranian Constitutional Revolution of 1905–6 has been widely noted. We should also remember that for the greater part of the struggle, the *ulama* acted in a coalition with a diverse range of soci-etal actors, including disgruntled notables, *bazaar* merchants, westernised intel-lectuals, as well as social democrats, socialists and radicals, mostly inspired and organised by contemporaneous movements in Russian-controlled Armenia and Azerbaijan. Afary argues that by emphasising the *ulama–bazaari* alliance as a guideline for the struggle against the Pahlavi regime, the ideologues of the 1960s and 70s effectively ignored the key role played by the socialists and radicals during the Constitutional Revolution.[79] Instead, both Afary and Keddie point to the importance of the 'radical-religious' alliance, and particularly the radicals' conscious decision to reach out to the 'progressive' members of the *ulama*, as the decisive factor behind the initial success of the movement.[80] Such an alliance, of course, was possible to the extent that the radicals and the *ulama* shared the same goals and principles, namely the struggle against foreign imperialist influence and unjust, arbitrary rule – central themes of both the revolutionary left and Shi'ism.

The radical-religious alliance, a marriage of convenience from the outset, collapsed soon after the immediate goals of the struggle had been reached. The split became manifest in dramatic fashion when a key clerical supporter of the Constitutional movement, Sheikh Fazlollah Nuri, switched to the royalist side and issued a *fatwa* condemning the constitutionalists as atheists and 'secret Bahai's'. In reaction to his support of Mohammad Ali Shah's 1908 coup against the parliament, Nuri was branded a traitor and executed by the constitutionalist forces that reclaimed Tehran the following year. Following the 1979 revolution, the IRI government rehabilitated Nuri as a martyr who had given his life in defence of the faith; a testament to the enduring rupture not only between the *ulama* and the secular left, but also within the *ulama* itself, as well as the emphasis of the 'Islamic' over the 'Republic' in post-1979 Iran.[81]

Sohrabi explains the failure of constitutionalism in Iran with the lack of a comprehensive state-driven modernisation project preceding it. As a result, unlike in the Ottoman Empire, the demand for constitutionalism was formulated largely outside the institutional framework of the state.[82] Likewise, Abrahamian attributes both the success of the Constitutional Revolution and the eventual collapse of the parliamentary system it put in place to the lack of a viable central state. Reza Shah Pahlavi, the former officer in the Cossack Brigade who carried out a coup d'état in 1921 to put an end to the constitutional era, must have reached a similar conclusion. As the man who set out to westernise and modernise Iran from above, Reza Shah is often compared with his contemporary, Mustafa Kemal Atatürk.[83] It is true that the Iranian ruler found inspiration in the Turkish leader's reforms, with the notable exception of his republicanism. But Atatürk had inherited a well-organised central state apparatus with a functioning bureaucracy and a standing army, the product of a century of modernisation, which was able to negotiate or impose its will with relative efficacy on an exhausted and traumatised population, whose traditional social fabric had been torn apart in the course of a decade of war and ethnic cleansing.[84] In contrast, Reza Shah took over a weak central state that had to contend with powerful and well-entrenched societal forces.

In fact, as the absolutist architects of the modern Iranian state, the historical role and the ironic fate of the Pahlavi monarchs have more in common with the modernising Ottoman sultans of the nineteenth century, Mahmud II and

Abdulhamid II, than with Atatürk. Like the Ottoman sultans, the Pahlavi shahs were firm believers in the divinely ordained traditional authority of the monarchy over state and society. And like the Ottoman sultans, both men assumed power in precarious political circumstances, which convinced them of the need to build a powerful central state apparatus that would protect the crown from societal challenges and foreign encroachment. Reza Shah's primary concern and main accomplishment was to establish this absent authority by building railways, nationalising and expanding the telegraph and postal systems, modernising the military and enforcing conscription, crushing tribal dissent and imposing a rigid central tax-collection system. His efforts to impose the state's authority on the *ulama* turned out to be less successful and fleeting.

During the reign of his son, Mohammad Reza Shah, the central state apparatus evolved into a behemoth standing firmly on the triple pillars of bureaucracy, military and court patronage, funded principally by oil rent.[85] Yet, crucially, like the Qajar state, the Pahlavi dynasty also failed to build and stand upon a sound social base. Launched in 1963, the Shah's White Revolution was an ambitious social engineering project aimed at weakening provincial landlords, the *bazaar* merchants and the *ulama* through a mixture of land redistribution programmes, secularising reforms and a series of nationalisation/privatisation and industrialisation initiatives.[86] But it ended up benefiting a small circle of already privileged Iranians, while creating a large number of independent farmers with too little land and no particular sympathy for the monarchy, and a new urban underclass made up of landless labourers, providing popular ammunition for the brewing uprising.

Although the Pahlavi state did gain significant powers and greater autonomy as a result of the White Revolution in the 1960s and the windfall oil income in the 70s, this happened at the expense of its social base.[87] Growing state repression further alienated the intelligentsia and brought it into coalition with other disgruntled societal forces. In the end, the Shah was left with a powerful hierarchical state apparatus that fatefully lacked public support. The dynasty's eventual fall came in another revolution that echoed 1905–6 in terms of its root causes and shifting alliances, highlighting the continued importance of popular legitimacy alongside material strength for regime survival in Iran.

Notes

1. Hobson, *The Eastern Origins of Western Civilisation*; Zarakol, *Before the West*.

2. Based on a (rather reductionist) reading of Şerif Mardin's centre-periphery thesis, the view that in Turkey a strong (secular) state existed in dialectical opposition to a (religious) society held sway over critical scholarship on Turkey since the 1990s and became influential in politics in the 2000s. As others have pointed out, this view was problematic not only for ignoring the complex interdependencies between state and society, but, as I discuss further in Chapters 6 and 8, for also overlooking the deep attachment to an idea of patriarchal state among many of those in the so-called periphery (Mardin, 'Center-Periphery Relations'; Heper, 'Center and Periphery in the Ottoman Empire'). For critical evaluations of this thesis and its various interpretations: Bakiner, 'A key to Turkish politics?'; Lord, *Religious Politics in Turkey*; Turam, *Secular State and Religious Society*.

3. Migdal, *State in Society*, p. 22.

4. See Zia-Ebrahimi, *The Emergence of Iranian Nationalism*.

5. Hemmat, 'Completing the Persianate Turn'.

6. This was of course not a one-way exchange. As Mitchell wrote, '[t]he conquests of Chingiz Khan and Timur, along with the resulting suzerain states in eastern Anatolia, Iran, and Central Asia, had fused Chingizid and Chaghata'i elements into the Persian bureaucratic culture as well as its use of terminology, seals, and symbols. [. . .] Anatolian and western Iranian bureaucratic practices experienced further changes under the Turkmen dynasties of the Karakoyunlu and Akkoyunlu'. Mitchell, *The Practice of Politics in Safavid Iran*, p. 199.

7. See Vaziri, *Iran as Imagined Nation*; Tavakoli-Targhi, *Refashioning Iran*; Zia-Ebrahimi, *The Emergence of Iranian Nationalism*. For examples of Western attempts to legitimise the Pahlavi dynasty by emphasising its place in the continuous tradition of Iranian kingship, see Bayne, *Persian Kingship in Transition*; Lenczowski, *Iran Under the Pahlavis*.

8. Eaton, 'The Persian Cosmopolis (900–1900) and the Sanskrit Cosmopolis (400–1400)', in Abbas and Ashraf, *The Persianate World*, pp. 63–83.

9. Gellner, *Thought and Change*, p. 169.

10. Smith, *Nations and Nationalism in a Global Era*, pp. 34–5.

11. In many Latin American countries, descendants of immigrants from the Ottoman Empire are still called 'Turcos' despite the vast majority of them being neither Turks nor Muslims.

12. The oldest written record of 'Türkiye' in Turkish is in Namik Kemal's 'The Problems of Ottoman Modernisation' published in 1867 when the Young Ottoman

intellectual was in exile in Paris. Nişanyan Sözlük, 'Türkiye', https://www.nisanyansozluk.com/kelime/t%C3%BCrkiye.

13. Kushner, 'Self Perception and Identity in Contemporary Turkey'.

14. Kunt and Woodhead, *Suleyman the Magnificent and His Age*, p. 4.

15. Ibid. p. 4.

16. This point stands even when we take into account the devastating human consequences of events like the Persian famine of 1917–19, during which several million people perished in Iran, a neutral country in World War I.

17. Abrahamian, *A History of Modern Iran*, p. 1.

18. And as Öktem has noted, all of Turkey's ruling ideologies have been nationalist. Öktem, 'Ruling Ideologies in Modern Turkey', in Tezcür, *The Oxford Handbook of Turkish Politics*.

19. Bora, *Cereyanlar*, p. 32; Mango, 'Reviewed Work: The First Ottoman Constitutional Period'; 'The Armed Forces is The Guarantor of the Perpetuity of the State and the Nation: Chief of Staff General Özel', *Anadolu Agency*, 1 September 2014, https://www.aa.com.tr/tr/turkiye/silahli-kuvvetler-milletin-ve-devletin-bekasinin-teminatidir/126101.

20. Root, *The King and Kingship in Achaemenid Art*.

21. Filippani-Ronconi, 'The Tradition of Sacred Kingship in Iran' in Lenczowski, *Iran Under the Pahlavis*, p. 52.

22. See 'Patriarchalism and Patrimonialism' in Weber, *Economy and Society*, pp. 1006–70.

23. Katouzian, *State and Society in Iran*, p. 8.

24. For a discussion of the enduring relevance of *farr* in legitimation of authority in Iran see Katouzian, 'Legitimacy and Succession in Iranian History'.

25. This formulation appears to stem from a practical need to 'propagate a unifying and quasi-universal concept of just authority over a vast empire'. The concept of a divinely sanctioned, just and benevolent king was the most easily translatable attribute for the empire's diverse constituencies. Soudavar, *The Aura of Kings*, pp. 89–92.

26. For an English translation see: http://www.avesta.org/ka/yt19sbe.htm.

27. 'The Role of Farr in Firdowsi's Shahname' in Bashiri, *Firdowsi's Shahname*.

28. Soudavar, *The Aura of Kings*, p. 122.

29. Katouzian, *State and Society in Iran*, p. 6.

30. For *Denkard* see http://www.avesta.org/denkard/dk3s.html

31. Axworthy, *Iran*, p. 11.

32. Momen, *An Introduction to Shi'i Islam*.

33. Behnam, *Cultural Foundations of Iranian Politics*, p. 54.

34. Katouzian, *State and Society in Iran*, pp. 14–15; Abrahamian, *A History of Modern Iran*, pp. 63–97.

35. 'I will frankly confess that I was convinced that God had ordained me to do certain things for the service of my nation, things that perhaps could not be done by anyone else. In whatever I have done and whatever I do in the future, I consider myself as an agent of the will of God'. Pahlavi, *The White Revolution of Iran*, p. 16.

36. See 'Chapter 2: The Foreign Shah and the Failure of the Pahlavi Nationalism' in Rad, *The State of Resistance*.

37. See Ghamari-Tabrizi, 'The Divine, the People, and the Faqih: On Khomeini's Theory of Sovereignty' in Adib-Moghaddam, *A Critical Introduction to Khomeini*, pp. 211–39.

38. 'Arbitrary Rule: A Theory of State, Politics and Society in Iran' in Katouzian, *State and Society in Iran*, pp. 1–25.

39. Karateke and Reinkowski, *Legitimizing the Order*, p. 7.

40. *Ghaza*, or the expansion of the Islamic realm through conquest, was a politically expedient and economically lucrative enterprise accommodating religious diversity from the very beginning. According to Cemal Kafadar, 'the culture of Anatolian Muslim frontier society allowed the coexistence of religious syncretism and militancy, adventurism and idealism'. Some of the warlords that led the expansion were not even Muslims. Mihail, for example, was a renegade Byzantine governor. Kafadar, *Between Two Worlds*, p. 89; Kunt and Woodhead, *Suleyman the Magnificent and His Age*, pp. 12–19.

41. Kunt and Woodhead, *Suleyman the Magnificent and His Age*, p. 21.

42. Zarakol, *Before the West*, p. 140.

43. For the main academic debate see Gibbons, *The Foundation of the Ottoman Empire*; Wittek, *The Rise of the Ottoman Empire*; and Köprülü, 'Bizans Müesseselerinin Osmanlı Müesseselerine Te'siri Hakkında Bazı Mülahazalar'.

44. Mango, *Byzantium*; Whittow, *The Making of Orthodox Byzantium*, p. 299.

45. For most of its history, the state was 'the only legitimate power to organise land and labor in the Ottoman Empire'. The state leased the land as freehold either directly to peasants, to cavalrymen (*sipahi*) on a non-hereditary basis (*timar*) in exchange for tax returns and support during the sultan's military campaigns, or to religious endowments *(vakıf)*. For a discussion on the origins and the outcomes of Mehmed II's land reforms, see Özel, 'Limits of the Almighty'.

46. Karpat, *Osmanlı'dan Günümüze Elitler ve Din*, pp. 47–8.

47. The origins of this administrative formula long predate the Ottomans. In his *Muqaddimah*, Ibn Khaldun refers to it three times, first in the context of an advice given to the Sassanian ruler Bahram ibn Bahram by Zoroastrian priests, second as a statement attributed to Sassanian king Anushirvan (Khosrow I) and third in reference to Aristotle's *Book on Politics*. Ibn Khaldun, *The Muqaddimah*, pp. 40–1. Also see Darling, *A History of Social Justice and Political Power in the Middle East*.

48. Akarlı, 'Maslaha from "Common Good" to "Raison d'Etat" in the Experience of Istanbul Artisans, 1730–1840', in Durukan et al., *Hoca, 'Allame, Puits de Science*.

49. See, for example, Hourani, 'Ottoman Reforms and the Politics of Notables', in Polk et al., *Beginnings of Modernization in the Middle East*, pp. 41–68; Hathaway, *The Politics of Households in Ottoman Egypt*; Meeker, *A Nation of Empire*.

50. Barkey, 'The Ottoman Empire (1299–1923): The Bureaucratization of Patrimonial Authority', in Crooks and Parsons, *Empires and Bureaucracy in World History*, pp, 102–26.

51. Notable exceptions include the reigns of Murad IV, Mahmud II and Abdulhamid II.

52. See Dressler, 'Inventing Orthodoxy' in Karateke and Reinkowski, *Legitimizing the Order*, pp. 19–58.

53. In the absence of a clear guideline for succession, and in a bid to legitimise the authority of the Abbasid rulers as well as the Umayyads before them, who assumed the caliphate through political strife, eleventh century theologians al-Ghazali and al-Mawali emphasised stability over anarchy. This did not immediately grant absolute power to temporal rulers, who still had to negotiate their authority with the ulama, local notables or provincial warlords. It was the Mongol invasions of the thirteenth century that would transmit new norms of absolute and universal sovereignty in West Asia. See Zarakol, *Before the West*.

54. The position of the *şeyhülislam* was elevated considerably during the rule of Süleyman I, and some *şeyhülislams* had decisive influence on the development of Ottoman and Islamic legal traditions. Yet even then, the *şeyhülislam* remained a servant of the sultan and could not interfere directly in government affairs, unless consulted (Karateke and Reinkowski, *Legitimizing the Order*, p. 27).

55. Shi'a imams were direct descendants of Mohammad and Ali and considered, both as private men and as rulers, to be infallible, a criterion notably absent for legitimate rule in the Sunni tradition.

56. A lucid expression of this institutional double-headedness, and of Iranian socio-political cosmology, is the *Naqsh-e Jahan* ('image of the world') Square in

Isfahan. Built during the reign of Shah Abbas I, each side of the square features a prominent building representing the key pillars of the early modern Iranian polity: the bazaar, symbolising the world of commerce, and the Imam mosque, the religiously expressed public space, face each other on the far ends. On the eastern side is the Ali Qapu Palace, the seat of the temporal ruler. Located across from it is the equally imposing Sheikh Lotfollah Mosque, the private office of the most senior Shi'a cleric and the symbol of religious authority in the realm.

57. Keddie, *Religion and Politics in Iran*; Moojan, *An Introduction to Shi'i Islam*.
58. Moazami, *State, Religion, and Revolution in Iran*.
59. Tezcan, *The Second Ottoman Empire*.
60. Melvin-Koushki, 'Early Modern Islamicate Empire: New Forms of Religiopolitical Legitimacy', in Salvatore et al., p. 365.
61. Keddie and Richard, *Modern Iran*, pp. 170–214.
62. Afary, 'Social Democracy and the Iranian Constitutional Revolution of 1906–11', pp. 36 – 37; Katouzian, *State and Society in Iran*, p. 43.
63. Quoted in Moin, *Khomeini*, p. 84.
64. Issawi, *Economic History of Iran 1800–1914*; Pamuk, *A Monetary History of the Ottoman Empire*; Akarlı, 'The Tangled Ends of an Empire'.
65. Katouzian, *State and Society in Iran*, p. 175.
66. Reflecting the aforementioned bureaucratisation of patrimonial authority, the wording of the *Sened* confirmed that this was an agreement between the notables and 'the state' – not the sultan.
67. Yaycıoğlu, 'Janissaries, Engineers and Preachers'.
68. Deringil, *The Well-Protected Domains*.
69. This view has been persuasively challenged by scholars who argue that Abdulhamid's pan-Islamism was a highly pragmatic reading of the geopolitics of the time, rather than the product of a personal or ideological dislike of the West. See for example, Akarlı, *The Long Peace* and 'The Tangled Ends of an Empire'.
70. The state-controlled curricula of these schools utilised 'European pedagogical techniques to teach modern sciences while at the same time inculcating students with the principles of Islamic morality, Ottoman identity, and loyalty to the sultan'. Cleveland, *A History of the Modern Middle East*, p. 121.
71. Zürcher, 'The Young Turk revolution'.
72. See Barkey, *Bandits and Bureaucrats*.
73. Akarlı, *The Tangled Ends of an Empire*, p. 356.
74. Akarlı, 'Maslaha from "Common Good" to "Raison d'Etat"', pp. 77–8.
75. Abrahamian, *A History of Modern Iran*, p. 9.

76. Sheikholislami, *The Structure of Central Authority in Qajar Iran*, p. 191; Ashraf and Banuazizi, 'Classes in the Qajar Period'.
77. The modern roots of Iranian suspicion of foreign manipulation can be found in the nineteenth century. For a wonderful satirical depiction of this persistent suspicion, see Iraj Pezeshkzad's classic novel *My Uncle Napoleon*.
78. Mirza Hossein Khan Sipah Salar, a diplomat and later Naser-al Din Shah's chief minister spent twelve years in Istanbul observing the *Tanzimat* reforms.
79. Afary, 'Social Democracy and the Iranian Constitutional Revolution', pp. 21–5.
80. Ibid. pp. 32–3; 'The origins of the Religious-Radical Alliance in Iran' in Keddie, *Iran: Religion, Politics and Society*, pp. 53–65.
81. Molavi, *The Soul of Iran*, p. 193.
82. 'Reform and Patrimonialism in Comparative Perspective', in Sohrabi, *Revolution and Constitutionalism in the Ottoman Empire and Iran*, pp. 287–334.
83. See for example Cronin, *The Army and The Creation of the Pahlavi State in Iran*, pp. 1–17; Atabaki and Zürcher, *Men of Order*.
84. Not surprisingly, the greatest resistance came from those parts of the country where the social fabric had remained largely intact and thus the local actors had the most to lose from the Kemalist nation-building project, in particular the Kurdish tribes of Eastern Anatolia who had enjoyed de facto autonomy under Ottoman rule.
85. Farazmand, *The State, Bureaucracy, and Revolution in Modern Iran*.
86. See Pahlavi, *Mission for My Country*, for the Shah's personal account on the needs for and aims of the White Revolution.
87. Conceived as an 'attempt by the Shah and his supporters to provide a legitimating myth for the Pahlavi monarchy by reconciling the contradictions implicit in these various ideologies [nationalism, modernism and tradition] in the person of the monarch . . . the *White Revolution* not only undermined the structural foundations of the Pahlavi monarchy, but also crucially contributed to its ideological destabilization'. Ansari, 'The Myth of the White Revolution', p. 2.

2

ATATÜRK AND KHOMEINI: POLITICAL AND IDEOLOGICAL LEGACIES OF CHARISMATIC FOUNDERS

We need to hold the nation by the hand and finish the revolution we have started.
– Mustafa Kemal Atatürk

With respect to duty and position, there is indeed no difference between the guardian of a nation and the guardian of a minor.

– Ayatollah Khomeini

Mustafa Kemal Atatürk and Ayatollah Ruhollah Khomeini are products of different times, places and conditions. In political and ideological terms, they are easily described as the antithesis of each other. A westernised military officer, Atatürk represented the increasingly potent conviction among the Ottoman and Iranian elites at the turn of the twentieth century that the only path to sovereignty was to become a modern, secular nation-state through complete socio-political transformation that included shedding backward elements of tradition and religion and adopting Western cultural tenets. His ambitious modernisation project inspired many of his contemporaries, including Reza Shah in Iran, whose dynasty was eventually overthrown by Khomeini.

Ayatollah Khomeini characterised the ideological backlash to Kemalist-style Westernisation from above. Khomeini rejected Westernisation as a cultural and developmental model as forcefully as Atatürk embraced it. He saw in the West the root causes of all the maladies that Muslims suffered from. Instead, he proposed an 'authentic modernity' that entailed an even more ambitious top-down transformation of the state and society within an Islamic framework. Khomeini made no secret of his abhorrence of the secular order put in place by Atatürk, whom he considered a pharaonic tyrant and 'the destroyer of Islam'.[1] Atatürk, of course, did not live to see Khomeini's rise as a revolutionary leader in Iran. But Volkan and Itzkowitz are probably justified in suggesting in their psychobiography of the Turkish leader that in the Shi'a cleric Atatürk would find 'a Muslim fundamentalist of the sort that would have thrown him into a blind range'.[2] For the Kemalists in Turkey, Khomeini's Islamic Revolution next door came to symbolise a nightmarish warning of the fate that could befall their secular republic if the 'religious reactionaries' had their way.

Perhaps because of their glaring differences, the similarities between the two men in the fundamental roles they played in the emergence of Turkey and Iran as tutelary hybrid regimes are often overlooked. Both men were charismatic leaders of broad-based popular movements that replaced millennia-old monarchical rule in Turkey and Iran with republican governments. They were also pragmatic political strategists, who after leading their movements into victory, ruthlessly consolidated power and went on to implement radical socio-political engineering projects from above. These tumultuous processes of forging and dissolving coalitions in turn determined the political divisions within and against the new regimes, shaping the threat perception of the Kemalist and Khomeinist elites and prompting them to establish systems of guardianship to safeguard their political and ideological hegemony.

Finally, Atatürk and Khomeini were mirror images of one another in the way they viewed the world from a dichotomous perspective based on essentialist cultural divisions. They were both motivated by a desire to cure that deep-running feeling of inferiority and injustice among the Muslims of the Ottoman and Iranian empires vis-à-vis the West and put an end to the foreign imperialist humiliation. While the ingredients of their bitter medicines were markedly opposite, their tactics were not: both projects involved an attempt to create a 'new people' and a 'new society' through mass re-education led by a new class of guardians. In short, combining both popular and elitist features in their charismatic authority, both men fit the bill of revolutionary leaders.

It is this combination that lies at the foundations of Turkish and Iranian republics and their hybrid institutional architecture. Mixing the populism of revolutionary action with the elitism of guardianship that assumes exclusive possession of 'the truth', the two men laid the groundwork for what were to eventually transform into tutelary hybrid regimes after their deaths. While they ruled as undisputed leaders and enjoyed a supra-political position during their lifetime, their passing brought new challenges to surface that created elite factions and defined the parameters of the political and institutional power struggles in Turkey and Iran in the decades that followed.

Charismatic Leaders of Popular Movements

Critically engaging with the legacies of Atatürk and Khomeini has been a sensitive endeavour in both Turkey and Iran. Official historiographies have portrayed the founding fathers as 'makers of history' who were 'unaffected by the world around [them] and who singlehandedly wrought a miracle' by creating modern Turkey and Iran: philosopher-kings 'who strove to lay down laws *de omni scibili*' in the spirit of Rousseau's legislator.[3] While they undoubtedly played the most important roles in the processes that led to the emergence of the Turkish and Iranian republics, the two men were also very much products of their time, and their worldviews were shaped by the intellectual, social and political conditions around them.

Mustafa Kemal and Ayatollah Khomeini both reached their political maturity during the periods of authoritarian modernisation and centralisation in the Ottoman Empire and Pahlavi Iran. They were members of those key institutions – the Ottoman military and the Shi'a clergy – that had transitioned into distinct political classes and come to play prominent roles in negotiating power with the sultans and the shahs since the nineteenth century. Finally, within these institutions the two men belonged to activist strands that, often in opposition to the more cautious and conservative mainstream, openly confronted the ruling monarchs and sought a more central role in decision making. Even though the two men clearly possessed leadership skills and charisma that few of their contemporaries could match, their charismatic authority was built upon the accumulated socio-political power and prestige of the institutions they hailed from.

Weber describes charismatic leadership as an innately revolutionary type of authority, which, in contrast to the bureaucratic and patriarchal authorities, 'knows no abstract laws and regulations and no formal adjudication'.

Charismatic authority 'always results from unusual, especially political or economic situations, or from extraordinary psychic, particularly religious states, or from both together. It arises from collective excitement produced by extraordinary events and from surrender to heroism of any kind'.[4] Charismatic authority, in other words, implies a leader–follower relationship, in which the latter views the former as endowed with superhuman faculties and surrenders to the leader's will. Such devotion tends to be particularly resolute among a tight-knit group of disciples around the leader, also referred to as 'coterie charisma'.[5]

Indeed, both men emerged as leaders amidst extraordinary circumstances and a sense 'collective excitement'. Khomeini rose to prominence as a gifted orator and an unapologetic critic of the government of Muhammad Reza Pahlavi in the 1960s. He gradually established himself as a major oppositional voice in exile as the Shah's White Revolution exacerbated social tensions, and together with his repressive and arbitrary rule sustained by oil rent, alienated the Pahlavi state from large sections of Iranian society. It was also during this time that Khomeini developed a coterie of devoted loyalists, the core of which was constituted by his clerical disciples.

In the Turkish case, the occupation and the planned partitioning of the Ottoman Empire after its defeat in World War I posed an existential threat to the empire's Muslims, many of whom still identified with the Ottoman order. Mobilised by former CUP officers, provincial notables and a nascent Muslim bourgeoisie, Muslim communities across Thrace and Anatolia rejected the treaty's terms and started forming armed resistance groups known as Defence of Rights Associations (*Müdafaa-i Hukuk Cemiyetleri*). United under the leadership of Mustafa Kemal, who had proven himself as a skilful military tactician during the Battle of Gallipoli (1915–16), and his fellow nationalist officers, these associations provided the popular basis and legitimacy of the Grand National Assembly (*Büyük Millet Meclisi*, GNA) founded in Ankara in April 1920 in opposition to the occupying powers and the British-controlled Ottoman government in Istanbul.[6]

Both republics were thus borne out of elite-led popular movements that united their future aristos and demos under a common and immediate purpose.[7] That said, the circumstances and the goals of the two movements were markedly different: the Iranian revolution of 1979 was the outcome of a mass uprising against the Iranian government by a domestic coalition of socio-political interest groups disenfranchised by the Pahlavi regime and the centrifugal forces of top-down modernisation, industrialisation and urbanisation in a rentier economy. It was a modern urban revolution, in which subordinate groups openly aimed to overthrow the monarchy and seize control of the state apparatus,[8] a manifestation of the 'dialectic of state and society' in a similar vein as the Constitutional Revolution of 1905–6.

The Anatolian resistance movement of 1919–22, in contrast, was an armed resistance organised and led by the Ottoman state elite against foreign military occupation. Unlike the Iranian revolution, it took place in a pre-industrial empire and mobilised a war-weary, largely rural and illiterate population in the name of saving and protecting the state and its traditional symbols – namely, the sultanate, the caliphate and the homeland (*vatan*) – from foreign invasion and occupation. At least on its surface and in its official narratives, it symbolised the existential bond that united state and society.[9] Ultimately, through this movement, and Mustafa Kemal's leadership of it, the state – and its modern westernised elite – managed to preserve itself in a new skin.

Making and Breaking Coalitions

The first major success of the leaderships of both movements was bringing together disparate interest groups and popular movements under a central command and around a common cause. It is at this stage that Ayatollah Khomeini and Mustafa Kemal emerged as pragmatic tacticians and shrewd political strategists. In striving to build and maintain broad-based coalitions, both leaders propagated straight-forward and positive goals that were acceptable to all participating actors. These did not include, certainly not explicitly, the radical socio-political reform projects that they would embark upon following victory. Hence, the periods before and after victory stand in stark contrast with each other: if the popular movements were in essence participatory, relatively egalitarian and inclusive on the basis of shared interests, the post-victory years were defined by vicious power struggles and schisms caused by clashing interests and visions, resulting in a more exclusive and homogeneous political space, dominated by the charismatic leaders and their loyalists. It was in this process of making and tearing apart coalitions that the new guardian elites, 'the people' and 'the enemies' of the Khomeinist and Kemalist regimes took their shape.

Khomeini first publicised his theory of *velayat-e faqih* (guardianship of the Islamic jurisprudent) in a series of lectures in 1971 while in exile in Najaf. During these lectures, which were later complied under the title of *Hokumat-e Islami* (Islamic Government), he declared Islam to be incompatible with monarchy and argued that 'in order to attain the unity and freedom of the Muslim peoples, we must overthrow the oppressive governments installed by the imperialists and bring into existence an Islamic government of justice that will be in the service of the people'.[10] Only under the guidance of the wisest and the most learned Islamic scholars (*fuqaha*) could such a just government be established and maintained.

Although *Hokumat-e Islami* would serve as the blueprint of the system of guardianship that Khomeini established after 1979, his early formulation of the concept, particularly the precise institutional character and sociopolitical role of guardianship, was vague and theoretical. In the years leading up to the overthrow of the Pahlavi regime, Khomeini and his disciples carefully downplayed the divisive doctrinal issues surrounding *velayat-e faqih* and instead emphasised the anti-monarchical, anti-imperialist, revolutionary and justice-seeking aspects of Islamic governance.[11] Ultimately, it was his unflinching opposition both to Pahlavi authoritarianism and its Western sponsors that had transformed the aging cleric into an icon of resistance for many Iranians – not the relatively obscure theory he put forth a decade previously, which he was criticised heavily for by the leading clerical authorities of the time.[12]

During the 1970s, Khomeini generally confined his statements regarding the Islamic character of the political system he envisioned to the 'need for the clergy to play a supervisory role' to government. In the last stage of his exile in Paris in 1978, he started speaking about an Islamic republic (*jomhoori-ye Islami*) rather than Islamic government. This was in part an effort to appeal to the various opposition groups that were 'against the Shah and [. . .] not content with just reforming the monarchy' and also to paint a favourable picture of his movement in the Western public opinion.[13] In the popular revolutionary slogan of 'independence, freedom, Islamic republic' (*esteqlal, azadi, jomhoori-ye Islami*), the idea of Islamic government was paired with the demand for a republican system that had its roots in the Constitutional Revolution of 1905–6. Even at this late stage, however, Khomeini's descriptions of what an

Islamic republic would look like remained ambiguous. In an interview with *Le Monde*, dated 13 November 1978, he said:

> By 'republic' it is meant the same types of republicanism as they are at work in other countries. However, this republic is based on a constitution which is Islamic. The reason we call it the Islamic Republic is that all conditions for the candidates as well as rules, are based on Islam [. . .] The regime will be a republic just like anywhere else.

While in Paris, Khomeini and his entourage often stressed that the future government of Iran would respect the rights of minorities, the rights of women and basic principles of democracy. 'Islamic Republic will be founded on the freedom of expression and combat against all kinds of censorship', Khomeini said.[14] He argued that 'an Islamic Republic is a democratic state in the true sense of the word [. . .] the Islamic state will respond with logic to all arguments put forward'.[15] There were also references to 'progressive Islam' where it would even be possible for a woman to become president.

During this period, Khomeini was surrounded by liberal or left-leaning Islamist activists and intellectuals, such as Ebrahim Yazdi, Abol Hassan Bani Sadr and Sadeq Qotbzadeh, who served as the link between the secular and religious wings of the revolutionary movement, as well as between the movement and the outside world. Sorbonne-educated Bani Sadr also advocated an Islamic republic, but one which opposed clerical involvement in politics and guaranteed the individual rights of citizens.[16] MIT-educated Yazdi, who maintained the movement's relationship with Iranian student activists abroad, and Qotbzadeh, Khomeini's spokesperson while in France, had set up the international branch of the Freedom Movement of Iran, a revolutionary Islamist pro-democracy movement, founded, among others, by Ayatollah Mahmoud Taleqani and former Mosaddeqist Mehdi Bazargan.

During this time, Khomeini met with representatives of secular leftist Iranian groups, who attended 'his evening consultations, and came away with the feeling that there would be room for them, too, in the Iran he was fighting for'.[17] A unity of purpose brought militant groups with wide-ranging agenda like the People's Mojahedin of Iran (*Mojahedin-e Khalq-e Iran*, MEK), which espoused a Marxist interpretation of Shi'ism, the communist People's

Feda'iyan Organisation and the right-wing Anti-Bahai Hojjatieh Society under the leadership of Ayatollah Khomeini. His rainbow coalition, which included members of the Shi'a clergy, the *bazaar* merchants, students, teachers, workers, peasants, women, liberal and leftist intellectuals, radical and moderate Islamists, communists and constitutionalists, was held together by two basic objectives: the removal of the Pahlavi regime and the establishment of a just and independent political system. While the first objective was uncontroversial to all and the most urgent, the second would prove fatally divisive.

Mustafa Kemal, too, offered a seemingly straightforward set of objectives to the disparate groups that united under his command in the Anatolian resistance movement: the liberation of the homeland from foreign occupation, the restoration of the (Ottoman) state's sovereignty and the (Muslim) nation's independence. The territorial boundaries of 'the homeland' were determined on the basis of a 'National Pact' (*Misak-ı Milli*) adopted by the last Ottoman parliament and endorsed in the formative congresses of the resistance movement in the Anatolian towns of Erzurum and Sivas in 1919 and 1920. With the exception of the Ottoman provinces of Mosul and Kirkuk, the town of Batumi and parts of Western Thrace, the territories claimed by the Pact correspond to the present-day borders of the Turkish Republic. The pre- and post-victory notions of state and nation, on the other hand, exhibited striking contrasts. If Khomeini was ambiguous about his post-revolutionary plans for Iran, Mustafa Kemal was almost completely silent. Until military victory was achieved and his authority firmly established, he did not publicise any plan to abolish the monarchy and the caliphate, establish a republic and impose radical Westernising and secularising reforms.[18]

The Anatolian resistance movement was a religiously defined project, whose leaders professed no overt desire for regime change until after its initial objectives were achieved. During the coalition-building stage, Mustafa Kemal frequently referred to the 'liberation of the sacred office of the caliphate' as one of the main goals of the resistance.[19] In his memoires, General Kazım Karabekir, a key leader and organiser of the movement, who was later targeted by the Kemalists as a reactionary, expressed his disapproval of the heavily religious symbolism used in the opening ceremony of the GNA in Ankara on 23 April 1920.[20] Mustafa Kemal's own speeches during this early period frequently emphasised and glorified Islam as a bond that united people. Likewise, his early references to the nation (*millet*) corresponded to an ethnically and culturally diverse religious community in the original meaning of the term in the Ottoman administrative lexicon, and not to the modern Western idea of a homogeneous society built upon a reconstructed history, culture and language. In a speech to the GNA on 1 May 1920, Mustafa Kemal recognised this unity in diversity:

> The people who constitute this great Assembly of ours are not only Turks, not only Circassians, not only Kurds, not only Laz, but the community of Muslims that comprises them all. [. . .] Thus, the nation that we endeavour to preserve and defend naturally does not consist of a single component. It consists of diverse components of Islam. They are compatriots who have mutual respect for each other, and [. . .] will always respect each other's ethnic, social and geographic rights.[21]

The movement's leaders stressed this historic Islamic unity particularly in their effort to win the support of Kurdish notables. The victorious powers had given the Kurds the vague prospect of a separate homeland, and for this purpose a Kurdish delegation had participated in the Paris Peace Conference of 1919. In his correspondences with Kurdish tribal leaders, Mustafa Kemal emphasised the brotherly and religious bond between Turks and Kurds, as well as the long-standing service of the Kurds to the Ottoman state.[22] In a telegraph to the notables of Malatya province, who had agreed to support the resistance, he wrote:

> It is without a doubt that as long as we have religious and noble grandees like you, the Turk and the Kurd will continue to live as inseparable brothers and as one unshakable body will form an iron fortification around the caliphate against our internal and external enemies.[23]

Finally, this language was imbued with anti-imperialist and anti-capitalist rhetoric, even though the movement's leaders did not profess a class-conscious ideology. Nonetheless on the eve of the Bolshevik revolution in Russia, and with anti-imperialist movements gaining momentum in Asia, the defiant slogans of revolutionary socialism held certain appeal for the inheritors of a crumbling empire now resisting the great imperial powers of the West. The revolution in

Russia had been a welcome development for the Ottomans during World War I, as Lenin denounced the tsarist government's territorial claims and withdrew Russia from the war. For the Anatolian movement, it also presented a practical opportunity. Days after the inauguration of the GNA, Mustafa Kemal wrote to Lenin for financial and military assistance as part of a 'joint struggle against imperialism'.[24] In an effort to appease the Bolsheviks, who were sceptical of Mustafa Kemal's revolutionary credentials, the Turkish leader allowed a group of leftist Ottoman intellectuals to establish an official Communist Party in Anatolia.[25]

A declaration adopted in November 1920, while a GNA delegation prepared to visit Moscow, summarised the anti-imperialist, religious and pro-state goals of the resistance movement with the following words:

> The Turkish Grand National Assembly has been established with a pledge to safeguard life and independence within national borders and rescue the offices of the caliphate and the sultanate. Consequently it is firm in its belief that it will succeed in liberating the people of Turkey, whose life and independence it considers its sole and sacred purpose, from the tyranny and oppression of imperialism and capitalism, and make it the master of its own will and sovereignty.[26]

Based on these objectives, Mustafa Kemal assumed the leadership of a popular Muslim resistance movement that brought together westernised Ottoman bureaucrats and former Unionist officers, the nascent Muslim bourgeoisie and urban intelligentsia with royalist, liberal, nationalist or leftist political dispositions, with provincial notables and tribal leaders of various ethnic and geographic backgrounds, in defence of the fatherland, the state and the religion against Western imperialism.

As with many elite-led popular movements, the coalitions led by the two leaders fractured soon after fulfilling their immediate goals. Part pre-meditated design and part spontaneous reaction to the ensuing period of political chaos, uncertainty and openness, Ayatollah Khomeini and Mustafa Kemal emerged as ruthless consolidators of power and pressed on with implementing their radical socio-political agendas. In Iran, the purges of the Pahlavi-era elite started immediately after the fall of the dynasty and continued in a violent manner for several years. Next, Khomeini turned against secular, nationalist and leftist groups and liberal Islamists that had supported the revolution but objected to the post-revolutionary political domination of the clergy.

Khomeini set out to establish a constitution and system that would serve as the mechanism to transform Iranian society into the ideal Islamic community. In 1980, he announced the beginning of a 'cultural revolution' aimed at cleansing the society of un-Islamic elements such as secularism, Westernism, imperialism, capitalism and communism. Growing impatient with the secular opposition to this single-minded pursuit of his revolutionary vision, he branded his critics 'xenomaniacs, people infatuated with the West, empty people with no content', questioning their loyalty to the revolution and ability to grasp its urgent needs and the truth embodied in Islam.[27] Shortly before ordering the closure of twenty-two opposition newspapers, Khomeini stated:

> If we had been truly revolutionary, we would never have allowed them [the opposition parties] to be established. We should have established one party, the party of the oppressed [. . .] I will warn these corrupt groups all over the country that if they do not stop we will deal with them differently [. . .] It is the duty of the revolutionary court to ban all these newspapers and magazines which do not reflect the path of the nation and to arrest their writers and put them on trial.[28]

The fate of the liberal Islamist intellectuals who surrounded the leader during his final months in exile illustrates the brutal course that the revolution took in its early phase. Within a few years all the men who served in influential positions in the immediate aftermath of the revolution were ousted, marginalised or executed: Bazargan, Taleqani, Bani Sadr and Yazdi were members of the Revolutionary Council (*Shura-ye Enghelab*) that Khomeini set up shortly before returning to Iran (which also included leading revolutionary clerics like Hashemi Rafsanjani, Ali Khamenei, Ayatollahs Beheshti and Motahhari). Bazargan became the prime minister of the provisional government, and Yazdi served as his deputy and minister of foreign affairs. Both men resigned in November 1979 in protest over the provisional government's inability to control the arbitrary justice dished out against the regime's opponents by the Islamic Revolutionary Guard Corps and Khomeinist vigilante groups and the creation of a *ulama*-dominated Assembly of Experts instead of a pluralistic and non-clerical constituent assembly to draft the constitution. The first elected president of the Islamic Republic of Iran, Bani Sadr clashed with Khomeini over the role of the clergy in government and the radicalisation of the revolution. Having been labelled a liberal and an imperialist lackey both by the left and the Khomeinists, he was impeached and fled the country in June 1981. Finally, in 1982, Qotbzadeh was accused of plotting to assassinate Khomeini and was executed.

The split between the Khomeinists and the leftist groups (both secular and Islamic) that the leader branded as 'hypocrites' (*monafeqin*) was more violent. Between 1979 and 1981, tensions between the MEK and the Khomeinists transformed from street battles into a bloody struggle for the reins of the regime. Khomeini blamed the MEK for collaborating with foreign intelligence agencies. Following a bomb attack at the headquarters of the ruling Islamic Republican Party (*Hezb-e Jomhoori-ye Islami,* IRP) in June 1981 that killed more than seventy high-ranking officials, the regime resorted to mass execution of opponents. 'In six short weeks', wrote Abrahamian, 'the Islamic Republic shot over one thousand prisoners. The victims included not only members of the MEK but also royalists, Bahais, Jews, Kurds, Baluchis, Arabs, Qashqayis, Turkomans, National Frontists, Maoists, anti-Stalinist Marxists, and even apolitical teenage girls who happened to be in the wrong street at the wrong time'.[29] The *Tudeh* Party, which continued to back Khomeini until 1983, was accused of spying for the Soviet Union and was destroyed practically overnight when its leadership opposed Khomeini's decision to continue the war with Iraq.[30] *Tudeh*'s fate was shared by the members of the People's Feda'iyan, which too supported Khomeini until 1983.

The period of power consolidation also saw the forced marginalisation of right-wing and religious interest groups, such as the Hojjatieh Society, which was disbanded in 1983, as well as powerful clerics who were critical of the institutionalisation of *velayat-e faqih* and the politicisation of the clergy. Chief among these dissident clerics was Grand Ayatollah Mohammad Kazem Shariatmadari of Tabriz. Throughout 1979, Shariatmadari's mainly Azeri supporters clashed with Khomeinist factions. By early 1980, his supporters were suppressed, the political party he was associated with (the Muslim People's Republican Party) accused of being infiltrated by 'anti-Islamic foreign agents' and disbanded, and Shariatmadari himself was put under house arrest. In 1982, the aged cleric was accused of conspiring with Qotbzadeh to assassinate the Leader, and in an unprecedented move that shook the clerical establishment to its core, Khomeini had this pre-eminent Shi'a scholar defrocked. His message to the clergy was that the revolution was more important than tradition.

Finally, the Leader was no more lenient towards his closest disciples who dared to publicly criticise the policies of the Islamic Republic. The most notable case is that of Grand Ayatollah Hossein Ali Montazeri, a firm believer in *velayat-e faqih* and a dedicated student of Khomeini since the early 1960s, whom the charismatic Leader would refer to as 'the fruit of my life's labour'.[31] Montazeri was Khomeini's designated successor until he was dismissed in 1989 for speaking out against the course of the revolution in the midst of a final round of mass executions following the end of the Iraq war.[32] Condemning the executions, Montazeri argued that the Islamic government had taken a path in the wrong direction and betrayed the revolution's core values and principles.[33] In a message commemorating the tenth anniversary of the Islamic revolution, he called for greater political openness, foreign trade and popular participation in government. 'The people of the world', he said, 'thought our only task here in Iran was to kill'.[34] Overnight, he was demoted from his position as the Leader's heir-designate, had his clerical title and portraits across the country removed and was forced into political obscurity in house arrest in Qom.

Opposition to the new regime also included armed insurrections by ethnic minorities demanding greater rights and autonomy in Khuzestan, Baluchistan and, most importantly, Kurdistan, where thousands were killed in clashes and executions carried out by the revolutionary government between 1979 and 1980.[35] In tightening their grip over politics and society and crushing various forms of dissent, the Khomeinists made use of two basic tools of coercion: the gun and the gavel. Armed militia groups and organisations loyal to the Leader went on to form the backbone of the regime's security establishment. These included the Islamic revolutionary committees (*Komiteh*), the *Hezbollahi* vigilantes and the Revolutionary Guards. Secondly, the Revolutionary Courts (*Dadgahha-ye Enqelab*) oversaw the incarceration and execution of thousands of perceived 'enemies of Islam and the revolution'.

Six decades earlier in Turkey, the authority of the Kemalist regime too had been established by means of coercion, through the military and the Independence Tribunals (*İstiklal Mahkemeleri*). As the unifying rhetoric Mustafa

Kemal and the nationalist leadership used during the resistance movement gave way to a project of systematic socio-political and cultural transformation, opposition to this unfolding agenda, and its top-down imposition, intensified. As in the Iranian case, dissent came in many different forms and directions. Among those who were purged, marginalised or suppressed by the Kemalists were Ottoman loyalists, liberals, socialists, Unionist officers, conservative Muslims, Kurdish nationalists and fellow leaders of the resistance movement who fell out with Mustafa Kemal for personal, political or ideological reasons.

Initially set up to maintain order and discipline and prevent desertions from the army during the resistance movement, the Independence Tribunals were equipped with extraordinary legal powers. They gradually became a vehicle to suppress opposition and consolidate power in the hands of the Kemalists. Socialists were the first to be discarded: three months after being founded on the orders of Mustafa Kemal, the Turkish Communist Party was shut down in January 1921. Socialist deputies in the GNA and several members of the Communist Party were tried and found guilty of treason, and leftist newspapers were closed down. Seventeen leading independent Turkish communists were rounded up and thrown off a fishing boat to drown in the Black Sea.[36]

Mustafa Kemal personally vetted all candidates standing for the second GNA elections in April 1923, barring standing deputies that were deemed Islamist, Kurdish nationalist, communist or simply too independent. This included an entire opposition bloc, known as the Second Group, which had resisted the concentration of power in the hands of one man and his increasingly tight-knit entourage.[37] As a result, the diverse socio-economic, political and professional backgrounds reflecting the combined will of the Anatolian resistance movement in the First Assembly gave way to the much more homogeneous Second Assembly. Dominated by loyal followers of the Leader, and organised under a new ruling party, the Republican People's Party (*Cumhuriyet Halk Partisi*, CHP), it was this Second Assembly that declared Turkey a republic and Mustafa Kemal its first president, abolished the caliphate and implemented strict social reforms such as the banning of Islamic sects and orders and the imposition of Western-style dress code.

When the reforms sparked protests and uprisings, the military and the Independence Tribunals were dispatched 'to all four corners of the land [. . .] to suppress the "reactionaries" by means of terror'.[38] One such revolt against

the central government in 1925 by the Sunni Kurdish tribes of Eastern Anatolia, led by Sheikh Said, gave the Kemalists the pretext to declare nationwide
emergency laws to decisively quash all types of opposition to what had now
become 'the Kemalist revolution'. Tens of local and national newspapers were
ordered closed, having been branded by Recep Peker, a senior government official and sympathiser of European fascism, as 'poisonous dens of snakes'.[39] Also
outlawed was the only opposition party at the GNA at the time, the Progressive Republican Party (*Terakkiperver Cumhuriyet Fırkası*, TCF) established
by prominent leaders of the resistance movement, Rauf Orbay, Kazım Karabekir, Refet Bele and Ali Fuat Cebesoy. Mustafa Kemal described the TCF in
his 'Great Speech' (*Nutuk*) as 'the product of most treacherous minds'. 'This
party', he said, 'has harboured and supported murderers and reactionaries;
assisted the plans of foreign enemies who wish to destroy the Turkish state, the
young Turkish Republic'.[40]

In fact, the TCF leaders' predicament may be comparable to that of Bani
Sadr, Shariatmadari or even Montazeri in Iran: their opposition was chiefly
against what they saw as the monopolisation of power in the hands of a single
man and his narrow entourage, and the radical nature of the reforms. This
won them the popular backing of a wide range of socio-political groups, both
within and outside the new regime.[41] According to Zürcher, the TCF 'was not
an organisation of outside opposition to the policies of the nationalists':

> The party had a real political programme and ideological stance, but it was
> not, as has been said so often, a reactionary or religious one. Its programme
> was a moderately liberal one with a distinct Western European flavour [. . .]
> less centralising, authoritarian, nationalist and radical [than the CHP].[42]

A final round of purges took place after a plot to assassinate Mustafa
Kemal in Izmir was foiled in June 1926. The ensuing trial was used as an
opportunity to deal with political rivals, including former leaders of the disbanded TCF and prominent Unionist officers, who had supported Mustafa
Kemal during the resistance movement. While the TCF leaders, who still
commanded prestige and loyalty within the military, were acquitted (albeit
marginalised from public life), the Unionists were executed. 'Sadly', wrote
Atay in his memoir, 'the regime held on to power on the gallows of Izmir

and Ankara. This definitive elimination discouraged all types of opposition and reaction. It allowed Mustafa Kemal to complete the revolution he had started'.[43]

Within four years of establishing the Turkish and Iranian republics, Mustafa Kemal by 1927 and Ayatollah Khomeini by 1983 had effectively dealt with the major domestic challenges to their charismatic authority and established themselves atop the state apparatus inherited from their monarchical predecessors. During this power struggle, both men relied on a small but fiercely loyal coterie, whose members subscribed and contributed to the leaders' visions and occupied the top administrative posts in the young republics. The Kemalist and Khomeinist projects were overseen by these core teams of dedicated operatives, many of whom owed their political careers to the leader. They were aided by the leaders' unmatched charisma, prestige and supra-political position, their growing monopoly over the security establishment and the judiciary. A permanent state of exception, justified by persistent domestic and foreign threats to the young republics (and in the case of Iran, the war with Iraq), led the revolutionary elites to securitise the political sphere, frame open criticism of their policies in the dichotomous language of revolution and counter-revolution, patriotism and treason, and justify the criminalisation of dissent.

The process of making and breaking coalitions created layers of entrenched rivalries and challenges to the new regimes. Resistance to the Kemalist and Khomeinist projects – particularly from those groups that had participated in the popular movements and felt betrayed in its aftermath – continued in various forms and intensity beyond the lifetime of the charismatic leaders. At different periods over the ensuing decades, the Kemalist elites viewed Kurdish nationalists, political Islamists, socialists and liberals as threats to the secular nationalist character of the republic. Socialists and liberals (secular as well as religious) who remained outside the Khomeinist ruling elite, ethnic and religious minorities, nationalists of different backgrounds, as well as the Iranian diaspora in the West have been perceived with suspicion by the IRI leadership. The systems of guardianship that the Kemalists and Khomeinists established to protect the revolution were, therefore, not only products of a pre-determined ideological blueprint, but also the natural outcome of these foundational power struggles and worldviews that were shaped and entrenched in the process.

Kemalism and Khomeinism: Ideological Blueprints of Tutelary Hybrid Regimes

The ideological blueprints that the founding fathers laid out in the new republics embodied many ambiguities, inconsistencies and internal contradictions, some intentional, others probably unavoidable. These allowed Kemalism and Khomeinism to be interpreted selectively by their successors and laid the groundwork for the intra-elite rivalries that were decisive in the eventual consolidation of tutelary institutions. I discuss these divisions briefly at the end of this chapter and in more detail in Chapters 3 and 4. It is beyond this book's scope to evaluate Mustafa Kemal and Khomeini, and their worldviews, in all their complexity. The aim in this part is underline the key areas that Kemalism and Khomeinism converged and diverged on, which shaped the kind of tutelary hybrid regimes that emerged in Turkey and Iran. Essentially, both men were preoccupied with securing independence against Western imperial encroachment by re-engineering society on the basis of a strictly Manichean worldview. The state, as in any revolutionary polity, became the central mechanism to carry out these social engineering projects, with maintaining state power gradually turning into an end rather than a means. Where they diverged most notably was in their views of the international order, the scope of their revolution, and, fatefully, the (im)permanence of guardianship.

National Sovereignty

The loss of political sovereignty and the sense of marginalisation and humiliation weighed heavily on both Mustafa Kemal's and Khomeini's thinking and the movements they led. The popular slogans of 'Independence or Death' (*Ya istiklal ya ölüm*) and 'Independence, Freedom, Islamic Republic' (*Esteqlal, azadi, jomhooriye Islami*) captured these sentiments. 'If a state', argued Mustafa Kemal, 'cannot practice its right to try foreigners in its own courts, if a nation is prohibited from taxing foreigners the same way it taxes its own people, if a state is prohibited from taking measures against internal elements that corrode its very being, can we believe such a state is independent and sovereign?'[44] In the same vein, Ayatollah Khomeini protested the extension of legal immunity to Americans in Iran in 1964, calling it 'a shattering blow to the foundations of our national independence'.[45] In a famous speech that helped transform him into a champion of Iran's national rights, Khomeini said:

If some American servant, some American cook, assassinates your *marja* in the middle of the bazaar, or runs over him, the Iranian police do not have the right to apprehend him! Iranian courts do not have the right to judge him! [. . .] The government has sold our independence, reduced us to the level of a colony, and made the Muslim nation of Iran appear more backward than the savages in the eyes of the world.[46]

The two leaders' popular reputation, which went well beyond the territorial boundaries of Turkey and Iran, as the men who stood up to Western imperialism to finally end the historic injustice being done to Turkish and Iranian Muslims provided immense charismatic authority to Mustafa Kemal and Khomeini.[47] This authority was not only used to consolidate the Kemalist and Khomeinist regimes, but also to justify the institutionalisation of a system of guardianship in the long run. 'Whereas Khomeini', writes Abrahamian, 'used holy texts to support the clergy's right to rule, the Islamic Republic claims the same right on the grounds that the clergy have valiantly saved the country from imperialism, feudalism, and despotism. This is legitimacy based not so much on divine right as on the secular function of preserving national independence'.[48] The same goes for Mustafa Kemal and the Turkish military, which is credited for saving the state and the nation from imperialism, foreign occupation, and, subsequently and more controversially, the backwardness of tradition.

Achieving and maintaining sovereignty necessitated not only confronting foreign powers but also defeating their domestic collaborators. In *Hokumat-e Islami*, Khomeini claimed that 'foreigners through their propaganda and their agents' inside Iran aim to 'alienate the people from Islam [. . .] in the path of their materialistic ambitions'. He frequently pointed at the monarchists, communists, non-Muslims (Jews in particular), Zionists and the Baha'is for acting as the agents of foreign imperialists, thus making official the popular distrust of social and religious minority groups. Like their Unionist predecessors, the republican elite in Turkey viewed non-Muslim communities, with their dubious loyalty to the state, own nationalist aspirations and strong ties to Europe, as inassimilable into the new Turkish nation.[49] Achieving national sovereignty necessitated creating a national (i.e. Muslim) bourgeoisie, which would serve as the socio-economic backbone of the new nation-state. Already underway since the Unionist era, the Turkification project was pursued through mass deportations and ethnic cleansing (of Ottoman Christians during World War I), legalised population exchanges (with Greece in 1923), discriminatory taxing (the Wealth Tax of 1942) and state-sponsored communal violence (such as the Istanbul pogroms of 6–7 September 1955). These policies further marginalised the already diminished and impoverished non-Muslim communities throughout the republican era.

Cultural Transformation and Guardianship

Once cleansed from the 'corrosive' and unassimilable internal elements, the Kemalist and Khomeinist regimes set out to educate and transform the people culturally based on the 'objective truths' they claimed to possess, guided either by scientific positivism (Kemalism) or neo-Platonic Shi'a mysticism (Khomeinism). The aim was to create a new (secular or Islamic) nation based on the image and vision of the two leaders. Despite attempting to achieve their goal through markedly different routes, both campaigns were based on dualistic worldviews that divided the universe into civilisation and barbarism, and a paternalistic view of society that claimed to know what is best for the people.

In his intellectual biography of Atatürk, Hanioğlu identifies four ideological strands popular among the French and German educated Ottoman officers at the turn of the twentieth century, which also shaped Mustafa Kemal's worldview: scientism, combining the nineteenth century German popular materialism, positivism and Darwinism; elitism based on Gustave Le Bon's theories of mass psychology;[50] a physical anthropology-based idea of nationalism; and republicanism inspired by Rousseau and the experience of the French Third Republic. For Mustafa Kemal a clear and absolute line divided those nations that were placed above the level of contemporary civilisation and those below it. He set the primary task of the guardians of the young republic as 'elevating the national culture to the level of contemporary civilisation'. He argued in a 1923 interview:

> There are many countries, but a single civilisation. A nation has to participate in this only civilisation in order to progress. Turks have followed but one destination over the centuries. We have always walked from the East towards the West. We want to modernise our country. Our whole effort is to establish a

modern, and therefore, Western government in Turkey. What nation desires to enter civilisation but does not turn towards the West?[51]

'Entering civilisation' was a political as well as a cultural struggle. A people could not be civilised unless they possessed a national consciousness and embraced modernity. To this end, guided by the Kemalist dictum 'Happy is he who calls himself a Turk', the guardians of the young republic set out to mould the ethnically and culturally diverse Muslim communities of the new republic into a homogeneous Turkish national identity. Cultural Westernisation was a social and political endeavour. Thus, besides adopting a secular civil code styled after the Swiss and a penal code based on Mussolini's Italy, the young regime also enforced a strict Western dress code. Mustafa Kemal said of traditional and religious attires: 'Would a civilised person wear these strange clothes and become the laughing stock of the world?'[52]

The Western Gregorian calendar was adopted in the place of the Islamic *hijri* calendar. Art, literature and music also had to be westernised, with traditional forms being expelled from the public sphere. The state radio, for example, was only allowed to play Western music during the first decade of the republic. According to Atay, who was a member of the leader's closest entourage, Mustafa Kemal 'loved classical Turkish music, but believed in Western music'.[53] Of most profound and lasting impact, the Latin script replaced the Arabic script. 'With the alphabet revolution we are totally breaking away from the Eastern-Islamic culture', wrote Yaşar Nabi, an early republican-era linguist, in his book *The Only Way: Atatürk's Way*:

> In order to truly establish our national culture inside the Western civilisation, and move from being an *umma* to being a nation, we had to get rid of the influence of the Arab's religious philosophy [. . .] Now as easy as it is for new generations to connect with the West in, say, sciences or fine arts, it has become that much harder for them to understand and digest the East.[54]

Having adopted the teleological worldview of European Enlightenment, Kemalist intellectuals and ideologues dabbled in a world of Manichean dualisms: West versus East, civilisation versus barbarism, modernity versus tradition, science versus religion, progress versus backwardness, light versus darkness. They also took pains to establish that the Turks, in fact, belonged to the civilised camp. In a reconstructed national history that depicted the late Ottoman rule as corrupt and bankrupt and harked back at an imagined past of greatness and purity, ancient Turks were credited for inventing culture and writing. Atatürk himself conjured up (and later abandoned) a pseudo-theory claiming that Turks were the founders of language.[55] 'The East is not aware of the direction where it is going and whence it is coming', wrote Peyami Safa, a prominent early republican-era journalist and novelist:

> Neither science nor criticism therefore exists in the East. So, one cannot speak of an intellectual life or even of intelligence [. . .] East is religious but not a philosopher. When compelled to describe objects, its mental ability stops. The metaphysics of India and the Far East are a play of words and have no value whatsoever. East always affirms things that cannot be proved. Its effect on nature is witchcraft.[56]

Safa then went on to explain how the Turks essentially possessed a 'European mind'. This was a deliberate effort to restore pride and inspire confidence, albeit through imagination and falsification, in a people who had experienced defeat and humiliation for centuries, and to gain acceptance in the eyes of the 'civilised world'. A *Time* magazine editorial from 1927 praised 'the Young Turks of today' for 'trying harder and with more success than any other backward people to catch up with the march of civilization'.[57]

For Khomeini and his supporters, this was a self-colonialising mindset, which nativist scholars Ali Shariati and Jalal al-e Ahmed labelled 'Westoxification' and deplored for perpetuating the very feeling of inferiority and humiliation that it sought to cure in the first place. When Khomeini rejected the Kemalist and Pahlavi arguments that attaining national sovereignty entailed Westernisation, he was equally preoccupied with restoring the people's pride and having them respected in Western eyes. 'As long as you do not put aside these imitations', he argued, 'you cannot be a human being and independent. If you want to be independent and have them recognise you as a nation, you must desist from imitating the West'.[58]

The Khomeinist rebuttals of earlier secular Westernisation projects reveal a similarly dichotomous worldview. Ayatollah Motahhari, one of the chief ideologues of the revolution and Khomeini's disciple, argued not only that philosophy had been in decline in the West since the sixth century AD, but that even at its height in ancient Greece, Western thought owed 'the origin of its principal achievements to the East'.[59] For Khomeini, the West's interpretation of human rights was bigoted, its democracy flawed and materialistic, its freedoms delusory. When adopted by Muslims, it led to a 'colonialistic freedom', which created slavery. The Iranian Leader spoke of 'deserting the West and finding the East', of leaving darkness to find light and of choosing the divine path (*rah-e khoda*) over the path of tyranny (*rah-e taghut*)[60].

At the centre of Khomeini's philosophical and political universe was the neo-Platonic idea of creating the 'perfect man' (*ensan-e kamel*) and the belief that with proper Islamic education human beings could be taken out of their primitive conditions and achieve 'awareness' (*erfan*, or gnosis). As noted earlier, Khomeini was deeply affected by the gnostic strand in Shi'ism and Sufi mysticism, which clashed with the conformism and pragmatism of the orthodox Shi'a clergy. He was particularly influenced by medieval Sufi mystic Ibn al-Arabi's metaphysical and cosmological doctrine of the perfect man and the idea of the evolution of human spirit put forth by seventeenth century Persian philosopher Mulla Sadra.[61]

Hence, like the Kemalists, the Khomeinists embarked on a project to enlighten the masses and create that ideal citizen from above: a common goal of modern revolutions. A Sharia-based legal system replaced the European-inspired civil code put in place by Reza Shah and strengthened during the White Revolution. A dress code conforming to Islamic morality was enforced. Western-style arts, literature and music – and those who practiced them – were removed from public purview, if not banned outright. As part of Khomeini's Cultural Revolution, universities were closed down for three years from 1980, during which period 'Westoxicated' and 'imperialist-minded' academics and students (including supporters of left-wing groups who had backed the revolution) were purged, and secular curricula were rewritten according to an Islamic framework.[62]

The Islamic revolution had stirred excitement among European post-modernists, with Foucault famously celebrating the triumph of 'political spirituality' against 'a *modernization* that is itself an *archaism*'.[63] For his part, Khomeini insisted that his project was not against modernity, but rather against the Western understanding of it. Its declared aim was to create an authentic Islamic alternative to Western modernity. 'We are not rejecting modern science', Khomeini declared, 'nor are we saying that science exists in two varieties, one Islamic and the other non-Islamic'.[64] He often derided as old-fashioned (*kohaniperest*) and reactionary (*ertejai*) those clerics who disapproved the use of modern technology in the creation of an authentic Islamic modernity. Khomeini emphasised this point in his last will and testament:

> The claim that Islam is against modern [technical] innovations is the same claim made by the deposed Mohammad Reza Pahlavi that these people [Islamic revolutionaries] want to travel with four-legged animals, and this is nothing but an idiotic accusation. For, if by manifestations of civilisation it is meant technical innovations, new products, new inventions, and advanced industrial techniques which aid in the progress of mankind, then never has Islam, or any other monotheistic religion, opposed their adoption. On the contrary, Islam and the Holy Quran emphasise science and industry.[65]

Finally, the Khomeinist project went beyond merely re-organising public life and, in pursuit of 'total revolution', ventured deeper into the private sphere of the citizenry than its secularising predecessors had either dared or possessed the means to do. The Islamic guardians dictated how the people were expected to behave and socialise, what they were allowed to eat and drink, in the private as well as the public sphere.

A key feature of these re-education campaigns was the role of the republican elites as guardians and teachers to the masses. The military in Turkey and the clergy in Iran, aided by cadres of revolutionary youth high in ideological fervour, were expected to both guide the masses along the leader's path and act as a role model to society. 'The Turkish people love their military,' Atatürk declared, 'and consider it the protector of their own ideals'.[66] He described the armed forces as 'not only the guardian of the fatherland and the regime, but also [. . .] an education and teaching hearth in the widest and truest sense'.[67] The central and most controversial aspect of Khomeini's ideology in terms of Shi'a legal tradition was in the way it politicised the clergy's guardianship role (*velayat*), which was hitherto limited to the protection of minors and the needy. 'With respect to duty and position', wrote Khomeini in *Hokumat-e Islami*, 'there is indeed no difference between the guardian of a nation and the guardian of a minor'.[68] Khomeini thus defined the correct function of the religious leaders and scholars as 'to guide the people in all matters'.[69]

With his immense charisma, Ayatollah Khomeini became the guide of all guides, the ultimate guardian of the revolution, a position that became institutionalised in the 1979 Constitution under the personal office of *vali-ye faqih*, or the guardian jurist. In introducing his modernising reforms to the new Turkish Republic – wearing for the first time the Western hat in public, teaching pupils the Latin alphabet or organising ballroom dancing – Atatürk too was guiding his people along the revolutionary road by example; one of his enduring epithets being *Başöğretmen*, or 'Head Teacher'. 'We need to hold the nation by the hand', the Turkish leader said, 'and finish the revolution we have started'.[70] Thus the paternalistic relationship inherent in the leader–follower bond was engrained in the institutional character of the Turkish and Iranian republics. The charismatic leaders assumed the role of benevolent patriarchs – not unlike their Ottoman and Pahlavi predecessors – presumed to be adored by the masses.

The key difference between the Kemalist and Khomeinist visions of guardianship, as concerns the future of legitimacy of the two tutelary hybrid regimes, was in their permanence. Atatürk did not envision guardianship to be a permanent fixture on Turkey's socio-political life. His self-appointed mission was, in the spirit of Rousseau's legislator, to act as the agent of transformation of a largely rural, pre-industrial, traditional society into a modern nation-state.[71] Once the desired level of development had been achieved and the people were educated enough, there would be no more need for tutelage. However imprecise and subjective it was, the fact that tutelage had a theoretical endpoint meant that as they became more entrenched, the Kemalist guardians faced growing pushback for outstaying their welcome, prompting them to constantly look for fresh sources of justification.

In contrast, Khomeini did not designate a point in time when society would reach a level of maturity that would render *velayat-e faqih* obsolete, as, for example, the socialist vanguard party was expected to disappear once communism arrived. Although perfection and wisdom were in theory available to all those who received proper and rigorous teaching of Islamic jurisprudence and morals, Khomeini did not expect all humans to reach this exalted state, nor did he think this was necessary. Until the return of the Mahdi, it was the responsibility of the *mojtahed* to protect and guide the Islamic community in the right direction. Because of this permanence, *velayat-e faqih* was, in the last instance, a conservative type of tutelage. Unlike in Kemalist Turkey, guardianship in the Islamic Republic, deriving its legitimacy from the divine as well as the revolution, was designed and constitutionally enshrined as a final product alongside republican institutions. This solid formal base rendered open opposition to tutelage much more difficult and dangerous.

State and Religion

Like in all revolutionary polities, the state played a crucial role in the realisation of the Kemalist and Khomeinist projects. Both Atatürk and Khomeini saw the existence of a powerful and capable central state apparatus, controlled by the charismatic leader and his loyal followers, as crucial for the creation of their ideal citizens and the preservation of their worldviews as hegemonic ideologies. If initially perceived as a means to a higher end, maintaining control of the state soon became the end itself, as the Turkish and Islamic Republican elites became engulfed in factional rivalries, faced persistent social resistance and grew increasingly disillusioned with their own ability to create the utopian society that they had envisioned.

As noted in the previous chapter, Mustafa Kemal's secularisation programme did not alter the basic structure of the state's relationship with religion. Far from a separation, Kemalist secularism represented a further tightening of the state's control of religion; the dramatic acceleration of a process that had started under Ottoman modernisation. Nor did the reforms make the state equidistant to all religions. The newly established *Diyanet* continued to promote the teachings of the Hanafi school of Sunni Islam. In subsequent decades, while the prescribed role of religion in public life changed according to the worldview of those in power, the essence of the state's patriarchal control of religion remained the same. Pushed out of the public sphere until the late 1940s, Islam gained greater prominence and visibility under the *Demokrat Parti* (DP) governments in the 1950s, again after the military coup of 1980, and finally, under the AKP after 2002.

It was Ayatollah Khomeini who carried out a real and profound revolution in the way the state–religion relationship was organised in Iran. Khomeini long argued, based on historical precedent and an unorthodox reading of the holy texts, that the Shi'a clergy not only could engage in political activities, but that it was obliged to do so. 'Islam', he declared, 'is a political religion'.[72] He claimed that the 'separation of religion from politics' was imperialist propaganda subscribed to only by the irreligious: 'No one can doubt that the Imam designated the *fuqaha* to exercise the functions of both government and judgeship'.[73] By uniting the clergy and the secular offices of the government within the framework of an Islamic Republic, the Iranian leader effectively put an end to the institutional double-headedness that had been a hallmark of Iranian politics for centuries.

Not only did Khomeini unite state and religion, but ultimately he subordinated the latter to the former. For Khomeini, urgent matters of government in an Islamic state had to come before the daily necessities of religion. In *Hokumat-e Islami*, he derided the quietist clergy and their followers for not taking a stance against the Shah and Western imperialism. 'Pray as much as you like', he said, 'it is your oil they are after – why should they worry about your prayers?'[74] In 1988, Khomeini took a leaf out of the Sunni rulebook of pragmatic politics when he decreed that an Islamic government could suspend any law, including religious laws, on the grounds of *maslahat* (public interest).[75] In an open letter to Khamenei, he wrote that 'the government of Islam is among the primary ordinances of Islam, and has precedence over all secondary ordinances, even over prayer, fasting, and pilgrimage'. In radical defiance of Islamic tradition, he argued that government could suspend any religious act or disregard any previous injunction of sharia law if these contradicted the interests of the Islamic government, thereby giving unprecedented powers to the ruling guardians.

For his part, Atatürk was pushing the limits of *maslahat* when his government justified secular reforms as in the interest of the public *and* Islam. He sought clerical backing to legitimise abolishing the caliphate. His followers and admirers, in and outside Turkey, even referred to the Turkish leader as 'the great reformer of Islam'.[76] Yet even some of those who were directly targeted by these reforms, such as the Sufi cleric Said Nursi, refrained from challenging the state's authority on the basis of their own consideration of *maslahat*.[77] It was Khomeini, not Mustafa Kemal, who decreed that the government could destroy a mosque in order to build a highway.[78] In their patrimonial approach to state–society relations, the Kemalists and the Khomeinists shared more than either side would be comfortable to admit.

Mission, Scope and View of the Global Order

One theme that was central to Ayatollah Khomeini's revolutionary rhetoric and became official discourse in the Islamic Republic was the antagonistic relationship between the oppressors (*mostakbaran*) and the oppressed (*mostazafan*) in society and international relations. In contrast, this distinction was almost entirely absent in the Kemalist world of dualisms. Here lies another crucial difference between the two hegemonic ideologies. Khomeini's understanding of revolution was total: it had to start in the individual's mind and spread beyond national borders, across the globe, and in particular, the Muslim world. It was revisionist in its mission and global in scope. 'We must strive to export our revolution throughout the world', the Iranian leader said in 1980, 'and must abandon all ideas of not doing so, for not only does Islam refuse to recognise any difference between Muslim countries, it is the champion of all oppressed people'.[79]

The conflict between the oppressors and the oppressed became a prominent theme in Khomeini's pronouncements once popular ideologues like Ali Shariati and Marxist Islamist groups like the MEK established the intellectual link between contemporary anti-imperialist struggles and the historical Shi'a theme of resistance to tyranny.[80] Increasingly during the 1970s, Khomeini described society as made up of a wealthy, powerful, corrupt and degenerated capitalist upper class (*tabaqeh-e bala*) and an oppressed, disenfranchised and impoverished labouring lower class (*tabaqeh-e payin*). Likewise, the international order was dominated by imperialist superpowers, the United States and the Soviet Union, which exploited the resources and corrupted the societies of Muslim countries. This view was embodied in the Islamic Republic's foreign policy mantra 'neither East nor West' (*na sharq na gharb*) in the 1980s, when the regime expressed solidarity with and lent support to third world liberation movements across the world.

The Kemalist revolution, in contrast, was neither revisionist nor global in its mission and scope. The Kemalists did not aim to upset the prevailing class structure in Turkey, save for abolishing the monarchy and eradicating the non-Muslim bourgeoisie, both of which were achieved before the declaration of the republic. Kemalist populism (*halkçılık*), which was among the six principles of Kemalism as it was codified by the CHP in the 1930s,

reflected a corporativist view of society, in which there was no class antag-
onism but instead harmonious cooperation of different social strata in
the unified body of the nation, whose head and soul were represented by
Atatürk.[81] Similarly, beyond its successful assertion for sovereign nation-
statehood, the Kemalists did not seek to challenge the existing international
status quo. Kemalism, after all, was a local reproduction of the Western
paradigm of modernisation that dominated the early twentieth century. It
did not threaten to upend the international system built upon this paradigm, but rather sought a higher place for Turkey in its pecking order.[82]
Except for one successful claim over the province of Alexandretta, which
was ceded to Turkey in 1939 by French-controlled Syria, minor border
skirmishes with Pahlavi Iran and a failed claim over the British-controlled
Mosul and Kirkuk, the new republic did not seek an expansionist foreign
policy. Mustafa Kemal had no desire to lead a revolution without borders.
Unlike the anti-hegemonic neutrality of the Islamic Republic of Iran in
the 1980s, Turkey's conformist neutrality, embodied in the slogan 'peace
at home, peace in the world' (*yurtta sulh, cihanda sulh*) was decisively non-
confrontational. As early as in 1921, Mustafa Kemal called on to the GNA
to abandon irredentist ambitions:

> Gentlemen, we drew the animosity, the grudge, the hatred of the entire world
> upon this country and this nation because of the grand and chimerical things
> we said we would do but didn't. [. . .] Instead of provoking our enemies by
> chasing notions that we will not and cannot realise, let us return to our natural
> and legitimate boundaries. Let us know our limits. For, gentlemen, we are a
> nation who wants life and independence. And only for this should we sacrifice
> our lives.[83]

Kemalist Turkey's hegemonic conformism and Khomeinist Iran's anti-
hegemonic revisionism were evident in the ways the two regimes sought recognition in the international arena. The Ankara government legitimised its
sovereignty through international organisations and treaties. The legal basis of
its political, economic and territorial sovereignty was enshrined in the Treaty of
Lausanne in 1923. In nationalising the economy, it chose to purchase foreign-
owned enterprises and infrastructure, such as railroads, factories and postal

services, rather than expropriating them without compensation, as was the case with most foreign-owned commercial interests in Iran after 1979. Even the population exchange with Greece in 1923 was carried out upon an internationally recognised bilateral agreement based on the Lausanne Convention. In contrast, the process of establishing the Islamic Republic's sovereign status took place in an environment of insecurity and hostility, characterised by the hostage crisis at the US Embassy in Tehran and the war with Iraq. During this period Tehran adopted a confrontational posture in international platforms, with Khomeini frequently slamming intergovernmental organisations and human rights groups as propaganda tools of superpowers.

Rhetoric did not always reflect actual practice: despite efforts to distinguish Western imperialism from Western civilisation, the Turkish political elite still harboured deep-rooted suspicions of foreign machinations, which surfaced during the Mosul crisis with Britain in 1926.[84] The regime readily dropped its peace-loving pretension whenever it faced resistance to its civilising mission at home, such as in the brutal campaign to crush the Alevi Kurdish uprising in Dersim in 1937–8.[85] Kurdish rebellions continued to challenge the Turkish state's authority and nationalist ideology for decades to come. Iran, on the other hand, did not always back its discourse of resistance with concrete action. Despite its resolutely anti-Israeli stance, for example, Tehran did not provide any meaningful support to rejectionist Palestinian factions until after it was left out of the US-sponsored peace talks in the early 1990s. It even continued to purchase arms from the Jewish state during the war with Iraq.[86] The 'imposed war' itself was a defensive campaign against Iraqi belligerence, at least until Khomeini rejected Saddam Hussein's offer of truce in 1982. Khomeini's eventual acceptance of ceasefire in 1988, which he described as 'drinking from the poisonous chalice' spelled an effective end to the Islamic Republic's policy of exporting the revolution.[87]

Nonetheless rhetoric – and politics – did exacerbate, or help ease, existing geopolitical tensions. By the late 1980s, Iran had found itself largely isolated in the region, with Syria, Libya and South Yemen being its only allies. Efforts by successive Iranian politicians in the post-Khomeini era to steer Iranian foreign policy towards a more pragmatic and reconciliatory line have been met with stern institutional, ideological and political resistance both at home and abroad. In contrast, the Kemalist policy of non-confrontation allowed the young republic to build stable relations with nearly all of its neighbours in the interwar era and maintain neutrality during World War II. Meanwhile, its conformist approach to the international order and general Western-orientation facilitated future Turkish governments justifying participation in imperial supra-governmental institutions like NATO or seeking member-ship of the European Union, even at the expense of compromising on the country's much cherished national sovereignty.

Immortal Leader: Succession and Institutionalisation of Charisma

While alive, Atatürk and Khomeini's unmatched charisma elevated them above the scrutiny of the regime elite, the state institutions and the general public. Although both men preferred to stay outside the tedium of daily poli-tics, delegating most duties to their trusted lieutenants, as the ultimate author-ity in all matters, they were frequently asked to weigh in on political debates and arbitrate disputes between various emerging political factions. As a result, they were often forced to make decisions on an *ad hoc* basis, balancing between opposing factions, finding practical solutions to impasses and, in the process, constantly reshaping ideology to justify the pragmatic steps taken to respond to everyday issues. The leaders, in other words, were overseeing the routinisa-tion and institutionalisation of their charisma, as extraordinary times gradu-ally gave way to the demands of everyday governance.[88]

Atay wrote that Atatürk was fond of 'ventilating the parliament' occa-sionally, meaning he would replace prime ministers and favour rival fac-tions interchangeably.[89] Two political factions emerged within the ruling CHP in the late 1920s and 30s: statist officers and bureaucrats headed by İsmet İnönü favoured a central role for the state in social and economic life, while the liberal free entrepreneurs preferred more limited and indi-rect state intervention. Led by Celal Bayar, a banker by profession, the latter group was supported by the landlords and the nascent urban bour-geoisie. Atatürk mediated between the two groups, appointing statist İnönü as prime minister in place of a liberal predecessor at the height of the Kurdish revolt of Sheikh Said in 1925, then replacing him with Celal Bayar in 1937. Khomeini also found himself having to manage the increasingly bitter clashes between the Islamic left, whose representatives advocated a statist economic policy, land reform and an anti-imperialist foreign policy, and the right (conservative) faction, which represented the *ulama-bazaar* alliance that favoured free trade, private property rights, limited state intervention in economic life and the imposition of strict religiosity in social life.[90]

Idolised while alive, the charismatic leaders were immortalised in death. Decades after their passing, their piercing gaze continue to watch over the Turkish and Iranian people through portraits hung on the walls of government buildings, classrooms, private offices and grocery stores. Their faces appear on postage stamps, paper bills and the first page of every schoolbook. The largest boulevards, biggest stadiums and most prominent airports have been named after them. Every town centre and schoolyard in Turkey has a bust of Atatürk. The murals of Khomeini adorn the façades of prominent buildings in Iranian cities. Their maxims about virtually every subject, including some that are falsely attributed to them, have been inscribed on public monuments for the inspiration of all. Their mausoleums remain places of pilgrimage for their dedicated followers.

Through immortalising the leaders, the Kemalist and Khomeinist ruling elites aimed to inherit their founders' charisma and legitimacy. While the transition of power from the leaders to their successors was carried out in a relatively smooth fashion – thereby proving wrong predictions of the regimes' demise once the leaders were dead – attempts by the successors to fill in the charismatic leaders' shoes proved more difficult and ultimately less successful. Loyal companions of Atatürk and Khomeini since the early days of the popular struggles, İsmet İnönü and Ali Khamenei had a keen instinct for power politics and considerable influence over the political machinery of the two regimes. Yet neither possessed the popularity and the charisma of the founding fathers. Nor did they boast similarly illustrious military or religious credentials, making them vulnerable to challenges from senior officers or clerics. Finally, unlike Atatürk and Khomeini, they were considered human and fallible, and therefore open to criticism.

The death of the charismatic leaders further exacerbated underlying factional rivalries within both regimes, with political groups competing to dominate key political institutions, while claiming to be the true representatives of the leaders' legacies. Although declared timeless and unchangeable, different factions interpreted what these legacies meant according to their own evolving worldview, emphasising and cherry-picking certain words and deeds and downplaying others. As a result, a different Mustafa Kemal and Khomeini have come to exist for every faction in the colourful political spectrum that emerged in Turkey and Iran after the leaders' deaths.

Some on the left remember Mustafa Kemal in his military attire as the anti-imperialist revolutionary, the ally of Lenin, who fought Western imperialists in the name of the emancipation of subjugated eastern peoples. For others, he is Atatürk, the tuxedo-wearing, waltz-dancing westerniser, who saved Turkey from the yoke of religion and oriental backwardness. For yet others, he is the gifted statesman in the true Ottoman-Turkish tradition, who successfully championed Turkey's territorial integrity, security and sovereignty. Political Islamists also call him Atatürk or just Kemal, in an intentionally crude expression of disdain for the man whom they regard as the destroyer of faith. But when they are pressed to show respect for the nation's saviour, they usually refer to him as *gazi,* or holy warrior – the honorific title the GNA bestowed upon Mustafa Kemal to embellish his religious legitimacy during the resistance movement.

In Iran, competing factions utilise Khomeinism to advocate their own interpretation of the revolution's meaning and promise. For Khamenei and the traditional right faction (also known as the principalists, or *osulgara*), Khomeinism stood for the preservation of the *velayat-e faqih* system. For Rafsanjani and the modernist right (a.k.a. the pragmatists) it meant economic development; for Khatami and the reformists, rule of law and the strengthening of the republican pillar; and for Ahmadinejad and the neo-conservatives (also known as the neo-principalists or neo-fundamentalists) social justice. During the mass demonstrations that followed the presidential election of 2009, many protestors who chanted 'Death to the dictator, death to Khamenei' were also carrying portraits of Khomeini. The security forces targeting them were determined to protect Khomeini's legacy from foreign imperialists and their Westoxicated agents at home.

Notes

1. Khomeini said in a 1986 speech, 'In the Islamic world, the ulama were led to believe that they had to obey the tyrants, oppressors, and the holders of naked power. Certain lackeys preferred to obey Atatürk, who destroyed the rule of Islam, instead of obeying the orders of the prophet. [. . .] Today, the ulama

[in Turkey] who are the puppets of the pharaonic forces, teach the people the orders of God and the prophet, but at the same time call on them to obey Atatürk. [. . .] How can one argue that this is consistent with the notion of [Islamic rulers] whom God ordered us to obey?' Quoted in Özbudun, 'Khomeinism – A Danger for Turkey?', pp. 244–5.

2. Volkan and Itzkowitz, *The Immortal Atatürk*, p. 324.
3. Hanioğlu, *Atatürk: An Intellectual Biography*, pp. 3–6.
4. Weber, *Economy and Society*, pp. 1115–21.
5. Eatwell, 'The Concept and Theory of Charismatic Leadership'; Willner, *The Spellbinders*; McDonnell, 'Populist Leaders and Charisma'.
6. Zürcher, *The Unionist Factor*.
7. I refer to these movements as the 'Anatolian resistance movement of 1919–22' and the 'Iranian revolution of 1979' or the '1979 revolution' because the commonly used terms 'Kemalist/Turkish nationalist movement' and 'the Islamic revolution' are more reflective of the post-victory ideologies and political arrangements of the two republics, than the popular movements' articulated goals at the time of mobilisation. When I do refer to the Kemalist revolution or the Islamic revolution, it is in the context of post-victory politics of the two republics.
8. Skocpol, 'Rentier State and Shi'a Islam in the Iranian Revolution'.
9. In *When the War Came Home: The Ottomans' Great War and the Devastation of an Empire*, historian Yiğit Akın details the brutal intensification of state–society relations in the course of continuous warfare and mass mobilisation between 1912 and 1922, with the state demanding and extracting, often by force, enormous sacrifices from the population. One reaction to this intensification was the vast number of desertions from the army both during World War I and in the subsequent resistance movement.
10. Khomeini, *Hokumat-e Islami*.
11. This point remains contested. Abrahamian notes, 'some of [Khomeini's] lay allies later complained that this avoidance had been part of a devious clerical scheme to dupe the public. Khomeini's disciples countered that it was the liberals and leftists who had conspired to suppress the book *Velayat-e Faqih*'. Abrahamian, *Khomeinism*, p. 30.
12. Grand Ayatollah Kho'i, the leading Shi'a *marja-e taqlid* ('object of emulation'; the highest position of leadership in the Shi'a *ulama*) of his time, was among numerous senior critics of Khomeini's thesis.
13. Shakibi, *Khatami and Gorbachev*, p. 90.
14. Interview, *Reuters*, 26 October 1978.

15. Moin, *Khomeini*, p. 219.

16. Bani Sadr, *The Fundamental Principles and Precepts of Islamic Government.*

17. Benard and Khalilzad, *The Government of God*, p. 39.

18. Once firmly in power and giving his personal account of the events to the GNA, which later became the official history of the Turkish Republic, Mustafa Kemal justified this silence as a 'pragmatic necessity' to 'prepare the feeling and the spirit of the nation and to try to reach our aim by degrees. [. . .] If I had spoken too much about future prospects, our realistic endeavours would have [. . .] caused the alienation of those who were fearful of possible changes, which might be contrary to their tradition, their way of thinking and their psychology'. See Atatürk, *The Great Speech.*

19. Atay, *Çankaya*, p. 245, 321.

20. 'Never in our history has an assembly been inaugurated with such a deeply fanatical religious ceremony'. Karabekir, *İstiklal Harbimiz*, p. 735.

21. Arsan, *Atatürk'ün Söylev ve Demeçleri*, vol I, pp. 74–5.

22. Atatürk Araştırma Merkezi, *Atatürk'ün Tamim, Telgraf ve Beyannameleri*, pp. 105, 149.

23. Quoted in Akyol, *Ama Hangi Atatürk.*

24. Dmytryshyn, *The Soviet Union and the Middle East.*

25. Tunçay, *Türkiye'de Sol Akımlar.*

26. Minutes of the Turkish Grand National Assembly, Year 1, Meeting 99, 18 November 1920, p. 414, http://global.tbmm.gov.tr/index.php/EN/yd/icerik/43.

27. From the speech marking the anniversary of the 15 Khordad uprising, 5 June 1979. Khomeini, *Islam and Revolution*, p. 270

28. Speech, 17 August 1979. Quoted in Rajaee, *Islamic Values and Worldview*, p. 100.

29. Abrahamian, *Khomeinism*, p. 131.

30. Moin, *Khomeini*, p. 255.

31. Akhavi, 'The Thought and Role of Ayatollah Hossein'ali Montazeri in the Politics of Post-1979 Iran'.

32. The split between Montazeri and other prominent Khomeinists, particularly Hashemi Rafsanjani, dates back to the Iran-Contra Affair of 1986 (Keddie and Richard, *Modern Iran*, p. 260). For the 1987–8 mass executions see Amnesty International, *Iran: Violations of Human Rights: 1987–90*, 1 December 1990.

33. In an August 1988 letter to Khomeini, Montazeri wrote, 'These mass executions [. . .] violate the fundamental principles of Islam, of the Holy Prophet, and of our Imam Ali'. In Abrahamian, *Tortured Confessions*, p. 209.

34. *Tehran Times,* 11 February 1989.
35. Cabi, 'The Roots and the Consequences of the 1979 Iranian Revolution'.
36. Tunçay, *Türkiye'de Sol Akımlar,* pp. 252–3.
37. Demirel, *Birinci Meclis'te Muhalefet*; Koçak, *Birinci Meclis.*
38. Tunçay, *Türkiye Cumhuriyeti'nde Tek Parti Yönetiminin Kurulması,* p. 77
39. Topuz, *Türk Basın Tarihi.*
40. The 'Great Speech' was delivered at the Grand National Assembly between 15–20 October 1927 and consists of Mustafa Kemal's own version of the events from the end of World War I to the Anatolian movement and the early years of the Turkish Republic. It became the basis of the official republican historiography and part of the national education curricula.
41. According to Zürcher, 'we do not have definitive analysis of the popular support of the TCF, which has been variously described as Unionists, religious reactionaries, supporters of the Second Group, democrats, conservatives, cosmopolitans, the press and sectors of the armed forces'. Zürcher, *Political Opposition in the Early Turkish Republic,* p. 113.
42. Ibid., p. 114.
43. Atay, *Çankaya,* p. 470.
44. Speech delivered at the Izmir Economic Congress, 17 February 1923. Quoted in Akalın, *Atatürk Dönemi Maliye Politikaları,* p. 26.
45. Open letter to Prime Minister Hoveyda, Najaf, 16 April 1967, in Khomeini, *Islam and Revolution,* p. 189.
46. Speech delivered in Qom, 27 October 1964. Ibid., pp. 181–2.
47. The armed resistance led by Mustafa Kemal in Anatolia had a transnational appeal across a wide geography stretching from the Balkans to Egypt and to British India as a successful anti-imperialist model for Muslims living under colonial rule. See Clayer et al., *Kemalism.*
48. Abrahamian, *Khomeinism,* p. 92.
49. From Atay's memoir: 'The Greeks were being uprooted and thrown out; and with them the entire economy of Izmir and Western Anatolia. [. . .] From small craftsmanship to trade and lucrative agriculture, the entire national economy was in the hands of the Christians' (*Çankaya,* p. 383). 'During the First World War, the Armenian tragedy took place. How sad that if it wasn't for this tragedy, the [nationalist] movement would not have succeeded. [. . .] Outside the walls of Istanbul, all of Turkey became a land of pure Muslim Turkishness', p. 520.
50. Le Bon, *The Crowd.*
51. Arsan, *Atatürk'ün Söylev ve Demeçleri,* vol III, p. 91.

52. Ibid, vol II, p. 226.

53. Atay, *Çankaya*, p. 476.

54. Nabi, *Tek Yol*, p. 16.

55. Aytürk, 'Turkish Linguists against the West'; Danforth, *The Remaking of Republican Turkey*.

56. Safa, *Reflections on the Turkish Revolution*, p. 88.

57. Time, 'TURKEY: Youth Going West', 21 February 1927.

58. Message to Faiziyeh School, 8 September 1979. Khomeini, *Islam and Revolution*, p. 29.

59. Quoted in Dabashi, *Theology of Discontent*, p. 151

60. Khomeini, *Islam and Revolution*, pp. 274–6.

61. Khomeini, *Hokumat-e Islami*, p. 163; Khomeini, *Islam and Revolution*, p. 330; Moin, *Khomeini*, p. 274–6.

62. Speech delivered in Tehran, 26 April 1980. Moin, *Khomeini*, pp. 295–6.

63. 'I then felt that I had understood that recent events did not signify a shrinking back in the face of modernization by extremely retrograde elements, but the rejection, by a whole culture and a whole people, of a *modernization* that is itself an *archaism*' (italics in original). *Corriera della Sera*, 1 October 1978. See Afary and Anderson, *Foucault and the Iranian Revolution*.

64. Moin, *Khomeini*, p. 296.

65. Quoted in Ansari, *Iran, Islam and Democracy*, p. 66.

66. Kocatürk, *Atatürk'ün Fikir ve Düşünceleri*, p. 335.

67. Arsan, *Atatürk'ün Söylev ve Demeçleri*, vol II, p. 331.

68. See 'The Necessity for Islamic Government' in Khomeini, *Hokumat-e Islami*.

69. Khomeini, *Islam and Revolution*, p. 341.

70. Kocatürk, *Atatürk'ün Fikir ve Düşünceleri*, p. 97.

71. In this, he was not fundamentally different from the leaders of other national-developmentalist states of his era. See Esen, 'Nation-Building, Party-Strength, and Regime Consolidation'.

72. Khomeini, *Islam and Revolution*, p. 22.

73. Khomeini, *Hokumat-e Islami*.

74. Ibid.

75. 'The government of Islam is a primary rule having precedence over secondary rulings such as praying, fasting and performing the hajj. To preserve Islam the government can suspend any or all secondary rulings'. *Kayhan-e Hava'e*, 19 January 1988, quoted in Abrahamian, *A History of Modern Iran*, p. 163.

76. Atay, *Çankaya*, p. 503. Also see Clayer et al., *Kemalism*, pp. 15–18.

77. Kara, *Şeyhefendinin Rüyasındaki Türkiye.*
78. Tamadonfar, 'Islam, Law, and Political Control in Contemporary Iran'.
79. New Year's message, 21 March 1980. Khomeini, *Islam and Revolution*, p. 286.
80. It was Shariati who in the 1960s translated Fanon's *The Wretched of the Earth* into Persian as *Mostazafan-e Zamin.*
81. Yaşar Yücel (1988) 'Atatürk İlkeleri', pp. 810–24. For Latin American contemporaries see Grigera, 'Populism in Latin America'. For a comparative analysis: Esen, 'Nation-Building, Party-Strength, and Regime Consolidation'.
82. Akkoyunlu, Karabekir. 'One Hundred Years of Kemalisms'.
83. Address to the GNA, 1 December 1921. Arsan, *Atatürk'ün Söylev ve Demeçleri*, vol I, p. 216.
84. See Coşar, 'The Mosul Question and the Turkish Republic'.
85. Türkyılmaz, 'Maternal Colonialism and Turkish Woman's Burden in Dersim'.
86. Parsi, *Treacherous Alliance*, pp. 106–9.
87. Hinnebusch and Ehteshami, *The Foreign Policies of Middle East States*, pp. 283–95.
88. Weber, *Economy and Society*, p. 1121.
89. Atay, *Çankaya*, p. 533.
90. See Babak Rahimi, 'Contentious Legacies of the Ayatollah', in Adib-Moghaddam, *A Critical Introduction to Khomeini*, pp. 291–306.

Part II

CONSOLIDATION

3

INSTITUTIONAL DUALITY IN THE ISLAMIC REPUBLIC OF IRAN

We believe in democracy. We believe in freedom, too. But we do not believe in liberal democracy. [. . .] We do not want to use that name for the immaculate, wholesome, righteous and pure concept that we have in mind. We say Islamic democracy, or the Islamic Republic.

– Ayatollah Khamenei[1]

Velayat-e faqih provides for a religious autocracy, or at best a clerical aristocracy.
– Mohsen Kadivar[2]

Observers of post-revolutionary Iran's political system often express a sense of bafflement by the uniqueness and complexity of its institutional architecture. Lafer and Stein describe it as a 'system with myriad overlapping centres of power', while Buchta points at the 'multitude of often loosely connected and fiercely competitive centers, both formal and informal'.[3] Chehabi admits 'the comparativist has literally no previously developed tools for analysing [Iran's] political system'.[4] In the words of Adib-Moghaddam, 'the innovative, if egregious, fusion of republicanism and (Shi'i) Islam that underpins the Islamic Republic of Iran until today is without precedence'.[5] Institutional duality is the basic character of the IRI political system on which this complex power structure has been built. This duality is represented in the name 'Islamic Republic', which reflects the foundational tension over the 1979 revolution's meaning and purpose: the pursuit of a utopian Islamic order under the guidance of religious experts, embodied in Ayatollah Khomeini's *velayat-e faqih* idea versus the pursuit of a constitutional republic based on popular will and electoral representation.

The duality is also embodied in the Constitution of the IRI, which is ambiguous as to where sovereignty ultimately lies.[6] Article 2 defines the Islamic Republican system as based on the belief in 'the One God, his exclusive sovereignty and the right to legislate, and the necessity of submission to His commands', while Article 6 stipulates that 'the affairs of the country must be administered on the basis of public opinion expressed by the means of elections'. Article 56 combines these two sources and describes popular sovereignty as a product of divine sovereignty, rendering the former subordinate to the latter:

> Absolute sovereignty over the world and man belongs to God, and it is He who has made man master of his own social destiny. No one can deprive man of this divine right, nor subordinate it to the vested interests of a particular individual or group.

The IRI tutelary hybrid regime juxtaposes Islamic revolutionary institutions with republican institutions. For every major institution associated with the regime's republican pillar, there is a parallel institution of guardianship that represents divine sovereignty and defines the limits of popular sovereignty. At the executive level, duality is represented by the offices of the elected president and *vali-ye faqih* (also known as *Rahbar-e Moazam-e Enqelab*, or the Great Leader of the Revolution, henceforth the Leader). In the legislature, it is the Majles (Parliament) against the Guardian Council (*Shora-ye Negahban-e Qanun-e Assasi*, GC). At the judicial level, the Special Court of the Clergy (*Dadgah-e Vizheh-ye Rouhaniyat*, SCC) functions independently from the civilian courts. In the security sector, the Islamic Revolutionary Guards Corps (*Sepah-e Pasdaran-e Enqelab-e Islami*, IRGC or *Pasdaran*) constitutes a parallel armed force alongside the regular military (*Artesh*).

Ayatollah Khamenei refers to this double-headed structure as 'religious democracy' (*mardomsalari dini*), the essence of which 'requires that the political system of a society should be managed through divine guidance and the will of the people. In Islam, the people are only one pillar of legitimacy, not the only pillar'.[7] In the words of Ahmad Jannati, a conservative cleric and the head of the Guardian Council since 1992, even if the clerical guardians of the regime were in a minority in society, they still had a duty to protect the Islamic order.[8]

Cutting across these two pillars are the fluid and semi-formal political factions, which are products of the ambiguities and the contradictions within Khomeini's professed worldview and his pragmatic policies, as well as rival interpretations of the revolution's goals among the Islamic revolutionary elite. Political alliances are forged and dissolved, strategies are designed and crucial decisions are made mostly at this factional level. However, it is the formal institutional structure of the IRI, which favours the guardianship institutions over the republican pillar, that determines the playing field on which factional rivalries play out and policy battles are fought.

Factional Politics in the IRI

Despite constant official emphasis on the regime's popular legitimacy, government has been by and large an elite occupation in the Islamic Republic of Iran. More than four decades after the revolution, the core leadership cadres in the IRI still consisted of an exclusive group of aging individuals, most of them clerics, who were united in their shared experiences of opposition to the Pahlavi regime and the war with Iraq, as well as a declared loyalty to the leadership and teachings of Ayatollah Khomeini. But in their interpretations of the revolution's goals and the charismatic leader's legacy, these people were sharply divided. As noted in the previous chapter, some of these divisions resulted from the ambiguities and contradictions in Khomeini's words and deeds during his ten years in charge of a modern state apparatus much more complex than the simple planning body he had envisioned in *Hokumat-e Islami*. According to Mehdi Moslem, a scholar of IRI factionalism:

> Although Khomeini's concept of the Islamic government emphasised the Islamicity of the post-revolutionary regime, he did not provide specific guidelines about what this Islamicity meant in terms of governing principles of particular policies in different spheres of government. Moreover, by repeatedly oscillating and changing his views on major issues during the ten years of his leadership, Khomeini offered differing and at times conflicting readings on what constituted a 'true' Islamic republic.[9]

These contradictions were theoretical as well as practical in nature. With regards to religious scholarship, the charismatic leader attempted to accommodate and use interchangeably two opposing interpretations of Islamic jurisprudence: traditional versus dynamic (*fiqh-e sonnati* vs. *fiqh-e pooya*).[10] Although Khomeini defended traditional jurisprudence, he also called for religious scholars to maintain a flexible attitude in interpreting Islamic law.[11] Indeed, his revolutionary programme and frequent resort to *ijtihad* (independent reasoning) and *maslahat* during his final years were exercises in dynamic jurisprudence. Factional divisions in Iran reflect Khomeini's oscillations in policy and jurisprudence as well as the conflicting goals of the Iranian revolution. Typically, the conservative clerics that dominate the Society of the Militant Clergy (*Jame'e-ye Rouhaniyat-e Mobarez*, JRM), the umbrella organisation founded in 1977 in opposition to the Pahlavi regime, have supported traditional jurisprudence, while the Association of Combatant Clerics (*Majma'-e Rowhani-yun-e Mobarez*, MRM), composed of leftists that split from the JRM in 1988, advocate dynamic jurisprudence.

The early political factions in the IRI should not be understood as mass-based political parties. At least until the rise of the reform movement in the late 1990s, these were informal coalitions that lacked explicitly stated programmes and hierarchical organisational structures and relied extensively on the personal charisma and intra-elite networks of the leading figures.[12] Frequent clashes between the conservative and the Islamic left factions dominated politics during the 1980s and eventually led Ayatollah Khomeini to abolish the official party of the regime, the Islamic Republican Party, in 1987. However, the decision to disband the Islamic Republican Party further emphasised the role of the factions as the basic vehicle of political activity in the IRI.

A consequence of the absence of institutionalised party mechanisms was the relatively weak organisational link between the regime elite and the socio-political constituencies they sought to represent.[13] In the 1980s and early 1990s, mass participation in politics took place mainly around the mosques and religious organisations. During the 1990s, the ideologues of the reform movement, which emerged from the marginalised Islamic left who had shed their uncompromising anti-imperialism and economic statism, realised the need (and the opportunity) for the institutionalisation of a formal party mechanism that would resist the traditionalist right's emasculation of the republican pillar by strengthening civil society (*jame'e-ye madani*) and energising a fast growing young generation, who were not necessarily drawn to the mosque and lacked political representation.[14]

Organised mass mobilisation brought the reformists victories in presidential, parliamentary and municipal elections at the turn of the twenty-first century. This also led other factions to put greater emphasis on mass participation as well. Ultimately, however, the reformist leadership did not succeed in institutionalising party politics within the movement, let alone in the IRI. The charisma and personality of leading factional figures and interpersonal relations between them, including kinship and marriage ties, continued to be a defining feature of politics in the IRI.[15]

Institutions of Islamic Guardianship in the IRI

The Office of the Supreme Leader

Velayat-e faqih constitutes the backbone of the guardianship structure of the IRI. The existence of a clerical leadership office at the apex of the political establishment was enshrined in Article 5 of the 1979 Constitution, which called for a just and pious *faqih* (expert of Islamic law) 'who is fully aware of the circumstances of his age; courageous, resourceful, and possessed of administrative ability' to assume the responsibilities of the Hidden Imam, until the latter's reappearance. The criteria for the selection of the 'Guardian Jurist', or the 'Leader', changed considerably following Khomeini's death. The 1979 Constitution originally stipulated that the top guardian had to be a *marja* (holding the title of grand ayatollah) as well as a revolutionary leader recognised and supported by the majority of the people. This was, in reality, a role tailored for Khomeini. Until 1988, the only candidate to fulfil the necessary requirements was considered to be Ayatollah Montazeri, Khomeini's disciple and designated successor. Montazeri's public falling out with Khomeini and his subsequent marginalisation necessitated a revision in the selection criteria to avoid a succession crisis.

The constitutional referendum in July 1989 saw Articles 5 and 109 amended and removed the requirement for the Leader to be a *marja*, thus opening the way for the rise of Khamenei, then a mid-ranking cleric, to the post. The changes emphasised political acumen over piety and popularity over scholarship. Although a pragmatic move to ensure the smooth transition of power, the new arrangement undermined the undisputed political and religious standing of *vali-ye faqih*.[16] In an attempt to make up for this loss of authority, the 1989 changes articulated the powers of the Leader for the first time and also significantly expanded them. While Khomeini's powers were unwritten and based on his tremendous charisma, Khamenei's authority had to be constitutionally protected. Article 110 outlined these powers as determining the general policies of the Islamic Republic, assuming the supreme command of the armed forces, approving the outcome of elections, dismissing the president, appointing and dismissing the head of the judiciary, the clerical members of the Guardian Council, the head of the radio and television network and the senior commanders of the security sector.

The constitutional changes confirmed the dominant position of the Leader within the IRI political structure, moving it further away from a supra-political advisory body, as it was initially conceived, towards an instrument of direct rule, or *velayat-e motlaq-e faqih* (absolute guardianship of the jurisprudent). In fact, the move towards absolute guardianship had already started with Khomeini's 1988 *fatwa,* which gave precedence to decrees issued by the Leader over those of other *marjas*.[17] After Khomeini's death, allies of Khamenei within the traditionalist faction and the security establishment emerged as the foremost supporters of *velayat-e motlaq-e faqih*. In 1994, even though he lacked the necessary scholarly credentials, Khamenei was promoted to the rank of ayatollah.

Despite the legalisation and expansion of his powers, the new Leader was aware that his practical authority was far from absolute and highly dependent on the support of guardianship institutions. Thus, immediately upon his assent, Khamenei set out to consolidate his position through a series of tactical moves and by building a network of loyalists inside both pillars of the regime.[18] Not satisfied with his constitutional prerogatives, he worked to enhance his oversight of politics, economy and the security sector through his expanding army of representatives, control over Friday prayer leaders and the Supreme Court of the Clergy, as well as his patronage over the powerful *bonyads* (foundations).

Dubbed the 'clerical commissars', the Leader's personal representatives (*nemayandegan-e rahbar*) are strategically placed in every important state institution, including government ministries run by elected officials, and serve as the Leader's eyes and hands in these institutions.[19] Within the military, the representatives have a dedicated office, known as the Ideological and Political Bureau. In universities, they supervise curricula and monitor student activities to ensure their adherence to the moral, religious and ideological guidelines prescribed by the Office of the Leader (*Daftar-e Maqam-e Moazam-e Rahbari*). While this office consisted of several dozen confidants under Khomeini, under Khamenei it became a vast bureaucratic body with thousands of representatives.

The appointment of Friday prayer leaders is another tool at the Leader's disposal. Friday sermons serve as political propaganda platforms where prayer leaders expound the virtues of the *velayat-e faqih* system and garner support for government policies. Although the Majles provides the budget for Friday prayers, it has no effective control over the contents of sermons. The Leader appoints prayer leaders for every city, and these leaders often wield greater authority than local governors or mayors.[20] Khamenei himself serves as the main prayer leader for Tehran and uses this forum to publicise his position on foreign and domestic issues or to arbitrate inter-factional disputes. However, Khamenei had difficulties monopolising this institution. While they were still alive, leading clerical figures from the revolutionary era, such as Hashemi Rafsanjani and Abdul-Karim Mousavi Ardebili, also served as prayer leaders in the capital, and within this strategic role, they were able to assert their positions in moments of internal division.

The Leader uses the Supreme Court of the Clergy to deal with clerical dissent. The SCC functions as a parallel court alongside the judiciary. Founded in the early days of the revolution in an effort to unite the clerical establishment under Khomeini, it remains an extra-constitutional institution with no civilian oversight or accountability. Although its formal function was to investigate acts of criminality by the clergy, Khamenei expanded the SCC's legal and political remit in the 1990s. Running an independent budget and its own security and prison system, and functioning behind closed doors, the court has been a key mechanism to suppress clerical opposition to the Leader.[21]

Finally, the Leader's long arm extends to the politico-economic sphere through his control of the powerful foundations, known as *bonyads*. Rooted in the tradition of clerically run religious charities, the *bonyads* have become the symbol of the politicisation of Islam and the integration of the religious establishment into the state. As the Shi'a clergy moved from being the guardians of the socially dispossessed to become the guardians of the nation, their charities also underwent a parallel transformation.[22] Over time, these religious foundations evolved into an extensive patronage network designed to ensure the loyalty of the economic elite as well as the working class by acting as privileged business conglomerates on the one hand and as mass charities on the other. Having taken over the confiscated assets of Pahlavi-era industrialists, enjoying tax-exempt status and receiving state subsidies and foreign exchange at favourable rates, the *bonyads* operate as diversified holding companies, employ hundreds of thousands of people and manage hundreds of subsidiaries in every strategic sector of the economy.[23] Answerable only to the Leader, who appoints their heads, and subject to no meaningful parliamentary oversight, the *bonyads* function as alternative power centres to governmental institutions, participating in domestic policy-making by influencing and at times directly confronting elected officials.

As he became disillusioned with the transformation of *velayat-e faqih* under Khamenei, Ayatollah Montazeri warned that the absolute guardianship of the jurisprudent would degenerate into clerical despotism.[24] Indeed, the systematic extension of the Leader's formal and informal authorities under Khamenei has been the single biggest challenge facing the integrity of the hybrid regime's republican institutions. At the same time, this expansion has turned the issue of succession into the regime's most vital long-term question, spurring a constant behind the scenes chess game for institutional positioning amongst the regime's factional elites.

The Guardian Council and the Expediency Council

The upper house of the legislative branch, the Guardian Council serves primarily as a check on the elected lower house, the Majles. Of its twelve members, six are clerics appointed directly by the Leader, while the non-clerical members are appointed by the Majles upon the recommendation of the head of the judiciary, who is also appointed by the Leader. With its influence over policy-making and elections, the GC is the 'first line of defence' of the tutelary establishment against the republican institutions in the IRI.[25] According to Article 72 of the 1989 Constitution, the Guardian Council reviews legislature for its conformity to the principles and commandments (*usul* and *ahkam*) of religion and the constitution. It also supervises 'the elections of the Assembly of Experts for Leadership, the President of the Republic, the Islamic Consultative Assembly, and the direct recourse to popular opinion and referenda' (Article 99). Articles 4 and 98 provide further constitutional powers and legitimacy to the GC: Article 4 calls for all laws and regulations to be based on 'Islamic criteria', and designates 'the *fuqaha* of the Guardian Council' as 'judges in this matter'. Article 98 stipulates, 'The authority of the interpretation of the Constitution is vested with the Guardian Council, which is to be done with the consent of three-fourths of its members'.

The GC's supervisory role over the republican pillar was expanded under both Khomeini and, especially, Khamenei. Under Khomeini, the criteria for running for office in the IRI were tightened so as to require an active religious and political commitment to *velayat-e faqih*, rather than just a lack of expressed opposition to it. Under Khamenei, in 1991, the GC's supervisory role over the elections was redefined in a manner that gave this body the power to vet and qualify all candidates running for election to the Majles, the presidency and the Assembly of Experts. The 1991 revision was a crucial blow to the independence of electoral institutions. The ability to control and manipulate elections and block legislation gave the conservatives, who dominated the GC after Khomeini's death, a clear advantage in dealing with more popular factions that controlled the presidency or the Majles. Between 1980 and 1988, for example, the GC vetoed more than a third of the bills proposed by the lower house. It disqualified more than a third and nearly half of the candidates running for Majles elections in 1992 and 1996 respectively, mostly from the Islamist left faction.[26] In 2000, only 8% of the candidates were barred from running for election, leading to a resounding victory for Khatami's reform movement. In contrast in 2004, more than half of the reformist candidates were banned and the traditionalists regained control of the Majles. Finally, the GC has also routinely disqualified hundreds of applicants aspiring to run for presidency, allowing no more than a handful of individuals who represent the tolerated political factions within the IRI establishment.

Frequent clashes between the GC and the Majles during the 1980s led Ayatollah Khomeini to establish a third legislative organ in 1988: the Expediency Discernment Council of the Order (*Majma'-e Tashkhis-e Maslahat-e Nezam*, or Expediency Council, EC). A manifestation of the institutionalisation of the *maslahat* principle, the Expediency Council was tasked with settling disputes between the lower and upper chambers. Its authority was formally recognised with the 1989 amendments to the constitution. Article 110/1 defined it as an advisory body for the Leader in determining 'the general policies of the Islamic Republic'. Article 112 tasked the Leader with appointing the permanent and temporary members of the EC.

Khamenei added a further 27 members out of loyalists to the Council, which was initially composed of 13 members and included the president, head of the judiciary, the speaker of the parliament and the clerical members of the GC. In an attempt to stem the reformist surge within the republican institutions, Khamenei departed from the previous practice of appointing sitting presidents as chairman of the EC and re-appointed former president Rafsanjani in 1998, instead of Khatami.

The Assembly of Experts

The Assembly of Experts (*Majles-e Khobregan*) embodies elements of both the Islamic and the republican pillar of the IRI tutelary hybrid regime. It was established in 1982 to uphold the popular legitimacy of *velayat-e faqih* and to prevent it from evolving into personal dictatorship. The Assembly has been tasked with monitoring the activities of the Leader, dismissing him should he be deemed incapable of fulfilling his constitutional duties, acting in his place during the period of transition and appointing a new leader upon the death or dismissal of the previous one (Articles 107 and 111). It was this body that had designated Ayatollah Montazeri as Khomeini's successor in 1983, and then following his downfall, replaced him with Khamenei in 1989.

The Assembly is the sole body that functions as a democratic check on the guardians, at least on paper. Its 86 members, who have to be qualified *fuqaha*, are elected for an eight-year term through popular vote. However, since the GC filters out those clerics who may pose a threat to the Leader, the Assembly's actual impact on politics has been negligible. To date, it has not publicly challenged the Leader or questioned his authority. Nonetheless, the Assembly remains a critical institution for the future course of the IRI, as it is this body that will determine Khamenei's successor. For this reason, it has long been regarded as a prized institution by the leading factions, which have competed to establish and maintain their influence over it.

The Islamic Revolutionary Guards Corps and the Basij

The Islamic Revolutionary Guards Corps was established as a popular militia shortly after the initial triumph of the Iranian revolution in 1979 in an effort to watch over the distrusted elements of the shah's military, defend Khomeini's nascent regime against counter-revolution and suppress opposition to the charismatic leader. It evolved over time to become one of the most powerful institutions of the IRI regime, playing an increasingly assertive role in the economy and politics of the country. Ayatollah Montazeri described the IRGC as 'the popular organ [. . .] which would protect [the revolution] and its purity and act as the powerful arm of the Islamic revolution and the protector of the oppressed the world over'. Khomeini declared in 1987 that 'the Guards were born of the revolution, grew with the revolution and will stay with it'.[27] Article 150 of the Constitution formally recognises the IRGC's role 'of guarding the Revolution and its achievements'.

The IRGC's foray into the politico-economic realm occurred in three phases. First, the loosely organised militia became a key component of the security sector during the war with Iraq. Their sacrifice in the 'sacred defence' against Iraq – through mobilising the masses in paramilitary units known as the *Basij* that served as human shields against Saddam Hussein's well-equipped army – provided the IRGC with institutional legitimacy and guardianship status. The 'sacred defence' provided the Islamic revolution with its ultimate heroes. The narrative of an army of selfless believers who, in line with the Shi'a tradition of martyrdom, willingly gave their lives to defend the faith, the country and the revolution against the mechanical onslaught of a foreign invader backed by Western imperialism readily found its place at the heart of the Islamic Republic's founding mythology.[28]

After the war, the political leadership encouraged the Guards to assume a leading role in reconstruction efforts. During this period, *Khatam al-Anbiya*, the engineering arm of the IRGC, grew into one of Iran's largest contractors in industrial and development projects, with subsidiaries in construction, mining, transport, manufacturing and energy sectors, receiving preferential treatment from the government.[29] At the same time, the *Basij* militia transformed from being a wartime mobilisation unit into a major socio-economic entity with extensive ties to the *bazaar* and presence in the construction, banking, real estate and telecommunication sectors. Providing employment and social

benefits to its members and their families, the *Basij* came to command an
extensive popular base concentrated mainly in the rural provinces and urban
working-class neighbourhoods.[30] Finally, from the late 1990s onwards, the
IRGC started playing a growing role in Iran's factional politics. Not only did
former guardsmen, such as Mohsen Rezaei, Ali Larijani and Mahmoud Ahmadinejad, emerge as prominent political figures, but the institution itself became
a direct contributor to the ideological clashes between rival factions, despite
claims of neutrality. Ahmadinejad's election as the mayor of Tehran in 2003
and the president of the IRI in 2005 confirmed the Guards' entry into their
third – political – phase.

Despite the constitutional reference to the 'brotherly cooperation and harmony' between the IRGC and the regular military (*Artesh*), their relationship
has been mired with tension. This is due to the IRGC's ambiguously defined
duty of 'guarding the revolution and its achievements' and its emergence as a
parallel military force engaged in domestic and foreign operations. Although
smaller in size and more limited in function than those of the regular military,
the IRGC possesses its own naval and air forces. Its elite unit, the *Qods Force*,
specialises in covert overseas operations. The Guards' responsibilities also clash
with those of the civilian ministries. Their intelligence arm functions independently from the Ministry of Intelligence and Security and operates its own
prisons. The law enforcement duties carried out by the *Basij*, especially in dealing with protests and demonstrations, overlap with those of the police force,
which is controlled by the Ministry of the Interior.

With these intentional overlaps and rivalries, the IRGC effectively acts as a
check on the elected government and the *Artesh*, which the guardians consider
ideologically less fervent and therefore less reliable. Furthermore, this complex
architecture becomes simpler at the very top. As the commander-in-chief, the
Leader appoints senior commanders of both the *Artesh* and the IRGC and
has the final word in the Supreme National Security Council (*Shora-ye Ali-ye
Amniat-e Melli*, SNSC), composed of the highest-ranking civilian, clerical and
military officials. Unlike the Majles, which has no oversight capability over the
IRGC, the Leader monitors and controls the entire security sector through his
representatives.

Despite this institutional supremacy, the extent of the Leader's actual
authority over the IRGC has fluctuated based on the changing balance of

powers in factional politics of the IRI. However, it is not true that the IRGC has become the most powerful tutelary actor, a praetorian guard that has gradually supplanted the clerical establishment.[31] Rather, both the Leader and the IRGC have come to rely on each other for political and institutional support.[32] It is important to emphasise that the IRGC is not a monolithic institution representing a single political agenda. Socio-economic fault lines and factional divisions have influenced the Guards as well.[33] While the IRGC will most likely play a key role in steering post-Khamenei Iran, as long as the Leader is alive and personally selects the Guards' senior cadre, the IRGC's independence should not be overstated.

Republican Institutions of the IRI

The Presidency

Elected every four years by popular vote among candidates approved by the Guardian Council, the president is the head of the government, the pinnacle of the republican pillar and the second highest office of the Islamic Republic, after the Leader. According to Article 113 of the constitution, the president is responsible 'for implementing the Constitution and acting as the head of the executive, except in matters directly concerned with the Leadership'. The president's powers include appointing and dismissing ministers, controlling the Planning and Budget Organisation (*Sazman-e Barname va Budje*), appointing the head of the Central Bank, and chairing the Supreme National Security Council. On the other hand, the president has limited authority over defence, security and foreign policy issues, which fall within the Leader's reserved domains.

Under Khomeini, the executive office of the republican pillar was split between the president and the prime minister. Despite being directly elected, the presidency, held by Khamenei after Bani Sadr's impeachment until 1989, was a ceremonial office. The main executive office was the prime ministry, held by Mir Hossein Mousavi during the same period. The charismatic leader personally mediated the frequent clashes between the two men, who represented the interests of the conservative and Islamic left factions. Following the death of Khomeini and the constitutional referendum of 1989, the office of the prime minister was abolished and the powers of the two posts were combined in a popularly elected executive presidency.

Despite systematic encroachment by the guardians, Iranian presidents since 1989 have been more than mere figureheads. As political figures with various degrees of popularity and electoral legitimacy, the presidents of the post-Khomeini era have wielded considerable influence over the political and economic trajectory of the IRI. Each presidency from Rafsanjani to Rouhani also came to represent the popular expression of discontent with the regime's failure to deliver on the revolution's numerous promises. As I discuss further below, the nature of the relationship between the head of the Islamic guardianship pillar and the head of the republican pillar has by and large determined the institutional stability of post-Khomeini IRI. Prolonged periods of discord between the two men jeopardised this stability and threatened the regime's hybrid structure.

The Majles

The Islamic Consultative Assembly, or the Majles, is the lower house of the legislature and the main institution that embodies the popular will of the electorate to the extent this is permitted by the guardians. It also symbolises the pursuit of democratic and constitutional government in Iran that dates back to the Constitutional Revolution of 1905–6. The Majles drafts legislation (Article 71), approves international treaties, protocols, contracts and agreements (Article 77), authorises imposition of emergency laws (Article 79), approves domestic and foreign loans (Article 80) and has the power to question the president and ministers and remove them from office. Its 290 members (increased from 272 in 2000) are elected every four years.

In the words of Ayatollah Khomeini, the Majles is 'the sole centre which all must obey. It is the starting point for everything that happens in the state. Submission to the Majles means submission to Islam and stands above all other institutions'.[34] Although it never really enjoyed such superior status within the IRI's hybrid architecture, during his lifetime Khomeini often used his authority in support of the Majles, then controlled by the Islamic left faction, against the conservative dominated GC. In 1981, in the midst of a row between the two bodies over land reform, Khomeini designated the Majles as the competent institution to decide on issues of necessity (*zarurat*), whereby it could ignore the objections of the GC.[35] But given the ambiguous and contested meaning of the religiously-rooted concept of *zarurat*, this intervention led to further clashes between the two bodies. In 1984, Khomeini ordered that if a bill had two-thirds majority, the Majles could override the GC's veto in the interest of expediency (*maslahat*). Until 1988, this decree empowered the Majles considerably vis-à-vis the GC. However, the arrangement was overshadowed by another decree by Khomeini, who, in his continuous effort to stem factional and institutional disagreements, established the Expediency Council in 1988.

Following Khomeini's death, conservatives who controlled the guardianship institutions set out to constrain the authority of the Islamic leftist dominated Majles. The 1989 amendments, which expanded the Leader's powers and formally institutionalised the EC, were followed by the 1991 revision to the GC's supervisory role over elections. Yet despite these limitations, the Majles elections in the IRI – like the presidential ones – often included an element of unpredictability and competition, and fielded genuine choice, albeit within tolerated and pre-determined limits. They have also featured lively debates where rival interpretations of Khomeini's legacy and visions for the future of the regime and the country clashed in public.

In other words, despite taking place in the long shadow of the guardianship institutions, elections have been a crucial legitimising force for the IRI hybrid regime. For years, they were the preferred method for 'managing popular participation, socializing the newer generations into the Islamic Republic, and regulating, and ultimately, negotiating intra-elite competition'.[36] The guardians regularly presented voter turnout in the Majles and presidential elections as evidence of continued popular support for the Islamic Republic. And until the 2009 presidential elections, they sought to strike a delicate balance between accommodating the will of the electorate without jeopardising their positions of power and institutional supremacy or compromising the dominant ideological strand within the tutelary establishment. When that balance became impossible to maintain, or the popular challenge appeared existential, the guardians opted to restrict and manipulate the electoral process.

Institutionalisation of the Leader–President Rivalry: The Rafsanjani Presidency

The post-1989 institutional arrangement of the IRI was an outcome of the ongoing factional power struggles of the preceding decade. Following Khomeini's death, Khamenei and Rafsanjani collaborated to marginalise the Islamic left, whom the conservatives had labelled 'seditionists' (*fetnehgar*).[37] The two men pushed through the constitutional referendum of 1989 and oversaw the expansion of the GC's vetting and veto powers in 1991. Rafsanjani orchestrated Khamenei's selection as Leader, and Khamenei supported Rafsanjani's virtually uncontested bid for presidency. As a result, the two allies secured the conservative domination of both pillars of the hybrid regime and started governing as a 'duumvirate'.[38]

Yet the reforms also had unintended long-term implications for the regime's institutional power dynamics. In particular, the creation of a popularly elected single-faction executive presidency at the head of the republican pillar that could potentially act as a popular counterbalance to the Leader and the guardianship pillar engrained the regime's foundational tension at the top of the state hierarchy. As long as the two office holders worked in harmony, as was briefly the case after 1989, the system would be stable. Yet if they fell apart, the resultant power struggle between 'the representative of God' and 'the representative of the People' could prove highly destabilising. Indeed, in an atmosphere of hyper-personalised factional competition, instability fuelled by Leader–President rivalry proved to be the rule rather than the exception. Starting their relationship cordially and with expressions of mutual respect, the first four presidents of the post-Khomeini era had fallen out of favour by their second terms and had their positions undermined by the Leader and the traditionalist guardians.[39]

Little separated Khamenei and Rafsanjani politically or ideologically at the outset of the latter's presidency. Both men were part of the core circle of the revolutionary elite. They were political pragmatists and proponents of dynamic *fiqh*.[40] By the late 1980s, they also appeared largely in agreement about the direction that the IRI had to take. This involved urgent economic reconstruction and a degree of foreign policy normalisation following a decade of revolution and war, which brought about severe economic disruption, societal trauma and geopolitical isolation.[41] Khomeini's approval of Rafsanjani's five-year economic plan shortly before his death in March 1989, allowing Iran to seek foreign loans, served as a blessing for a policy of gradual economic and geopolitical opening. Finally, neither man was in favour of accompanying the planned economic and foreign policy shifts with a political reform programme at home. Relaxations on social restrictions, such as the easing of censorship in the press and the arts, during the Rafsanjani presidency were piecemeal and driven by individual ministers, most notably Mohammad Khatami, the Minister of Culture and Islamic Guidance in the first cabinet, rather than part of a systematic government policy. Political reform had yet to enter the lexicon of the IRI elites in the early 1990s.

In short, the Rafsanjani presidency in no way represented a popular threat to the Leader or diversion from the *velayat-e faqih* system. Still, the Leader–President alliance soon started to shatter. By Rafsanjani's second term, it had turned into a full-blown power struggle. The underlying cause for the split was the increasingly clashing personal ambitions of the two men: Rafsanjani wanted to be the patrimonial chief executive of political and economic affairs in the IRI and Khamenei was determined not to remain in the president's shadow. This personal rivalry was also fuelled by (and in turn fuelled) a growing division within the conservative faction into modernist and traditionalist wings over the nature and consequences of Rafsanjani's economic policies.

Dubbed the 'government of construction' (*dowlat-e sazandegi*), the Rafsanjani administration set out to restructure Iran's traditional *bazaar*-based economy into an industrialised one with modern retail and banking systems. During his first term, the president reopened the Tehran stock exchange and promoted foreign trade through establishing five free-trade zones and an export bank, as a result of which Iran's trade volume soon surpassed the highest pre-revolutionary level.[42] His government also encouraged private-sector participation in the economy by initiating a process of privatisations. Rafsanjani emphasised 'expertise, technical skills and administrative abilities of the Ministers' over their 'Islamic virtues and revolutionary zeal'.[43] He was supported in this pursuit by the emerging group of technocrats and new industrialists, made up of former IRGC officers and prominent *bazaar* merchants with personal links to the president, who were given incentives to make the leap to industrial production and benefited directly from Rafsanjani's privatisation schemes. This increasingly wealthy and privileged 'mercantile bourgeoisie' formed the modernist (also known as the 'pragmatist') wing of the conservative faction.[44]

The rise of the modernists and their socio-economic worldview triggered a counter-reaction. Members of the Islamic left attacked Rafsanjani for recreating the comprador bourgeoisie of the Pahlavi era; the so-called 'thousand families' who became wealthy at the expense of the people. For the bulk of the conservative *bazaar* merchants, who were outside of this new circle, Rafsanjani's policies meant a diversion of funds from their economic activities and a long-term threat to their interests.[45] The conservative clergy started to argue that legitimising the pursuit of material wealth was threatening the moral fabric of society and exposing it dangerously to the Western-promoted ideas of liberalism and individualism. The conservative *bazaaris* and the clerics were joined by lay intellectuals and war veterans, who had returned from the frontline not so much with dreams of economic self-enrichment, but an uncompromising view of social morality and justice.

In June 1991, in an open letter to the Leader published in the leading conservative daily *Kayhan*, thirty-five university professors warned of a 'Western cultural invasion' (*tahajom-e farhangi-ye gharb*).[46] Rejecting the popular concepts of the post-Cold War neo-liberal era, such as 'the new world order' and 'the global village', the academics criticised the programmes pursued by the government for advocating 'disloyalty to tradition, family and social values', encouraging a materialistic and human-centrist view of the world and mocking revolutionary ideals. The letter also claimed that, having failed to defeat the revolution by military force, the West had resorted to exporting cultural degeneration to corrupt it from within.

This argument resonated with Khamenei, who despite initially supporting Rafsanjani's economic programme, saw both a real threat in the globalisation discourse and an opportunity to strengthen his own position by courting the reaction to the president's policies.[47] The Leader lacked a sound popular base, and the emergence of a traditionalist coalition of *bazaaris*, clerics and members of the security establishment seemed to provide him with one. As Rafsanjani became tied to the economic interests of the IRI's upper and middle classes, Khamenei refashioned himself as the guardian of its traditional structures and revolutionary values. In return, the traditionalists became the foremost supporters of the Leader and *velayat-e motlaq-e faqih*. Identifying and fighting the West's cultural invasion henceforth constituted the focus of the Leader's pronouncements, which were compiled by the Ministry of Culture and Islamic Guidance in a single volume, titled *Culture and Cultural Invasion*.[48] From the mid-1990s onwards, resisting moral degeneration associated with the Western culture, globalisation and liberal democracy became one of the main political causes and talking points of the traditionalists.

The emerging battle line between the traditionalists and the modernists became visible following the Fourth Majles election in 1992, from which the traditionalists emerged as the dominant faction. Shortly afterwards, Rafsanjani was forced to drop his reform-minded ministers, namely the Minister of Culture and Islamic Guidance Mohammad Khatami, the Minister of Interior Abdollah Nuri and the Minister of Higher Education and Culture Mostafa Moin. Having resigned shortly before the Majles election, Khatami was temporarily replaced by Ali Larijani and then, after the election, by Mostafa Mir Salim, both traditionalists with close ties to the Leader. As the new culture minister, Mir Salim quickly set out to roll back the relaxations on press censorship and artistic expression granted under Khatami.[49] Shortly after being appointed by the traditionalist-dominated Majles as its new speaker, Ali Akbar Nateq Nuri set the tone of the new legislative term by associating Rafsanjani's platform with liberalism, which he defined as a menace that had to be eradicated, arguing that 'the building of a few roads and bridges and the completion of some development projects is not the same as upholding the values of the revolution'.[50] Faced with a traditionalist-dominated Majles, Rafsanjani's economic agenda was effectively derailed for much of his second term.

Adding to Rafsanjani's setbacks was the frustration of dealing with an unsympathetic counterpart in the White House that refused to reciprocate the Iranian president's politically risky overtures to initiate a gradual improvement of bilateral ties. In 1995, the Clinton administration did not only block a major oil contract that Iran had awarded to the US firm Conoco, but it also passed the Iran Libya Sanctions Act, the most extensive economic sanctions on the Islamic Republic to that date.[51] Washington's hostile approach towards Iran shook the tenuous political ground on which Rafsanjani had to pursue his politics of normalisation at home. It also emboldened the traditionalists' view of the US as an ill-intentioned and untrustworthy counterpart, rendering future advances for rapprochement even riskier.[52]

It might seem unsurprising in hindsight that Khamenei prevailed over Rafsanjani in this first round of their decades-long rivalry. Arjomand wrote that 'it was difficult for Khamenei not to win' given the institutional arrangement following the constitutional amendments of 1989, which heavily favoured the Leader's office over the presidency.[53] Yet Khamenei's emergence as the most powerful figure of the IRI was not a foregone conclusion from the outset. At the beginning of the post-Khomeini era, many observers had expected Rafsanjani to overshadow the new Leader with his political skills, seemingly endless energy and extensive personal ties within the regime's intricate web of elite groups and factions. Stepping down as Iran's last prime minister, Mir Hossein Mousavi had warned of 'despotism and dictatorship' under conservative domination and expressed specific concern about the new president, who would wield 'powers far greater than the present prime minister and president combined'.[54] Ultimately, what Khamanei lacked in charisma, popularity or scholarly credentials, he made up for in political ambition.

The Rafsanjani presidency also demonstrated the revolutionary elite's belated recognition of the changing nature of popular politics in post-Khomeini Iran. Rafsanjani's role in strengthening both the office of the Leader and the GC vis-à-vis the republican pillar was part of his continued pre-occupation with elite-based factional rivalries, but it ended up undermining his own position as president and that of his allies in the Majles. Unlike Khamenei, whose mandate did not require periodic electoral reaffirmation, the president needed popular support and could only disregard public opinion at his own risk. With elections becoming a central mechanism for redistributing power among factions, Rafsanjani had to make promises to cater to the popular demand for economic welfare and prosperity.

However, Rafsanjani's economic policies and non-transparent privatisation schemes primarily benefited a small and privileged minority of society. Soaring food prices and inflation triggered protests in Mashhad and Shiraz in 1992 and in Qazvin and Islamshahr in 1995. The low turnout in the 1993 presidential election and the sharp decline in Rafsanjani's votes were indicators of both a general dissatisfaction with a lack of genuine choice and the government's limited popular appeal.[55] As the gap between the rich and the poor widened, Rafsanjani became a symbol of institutionalised corruption in the IRI and the face of its self-serving clerical elite, an image that still haunted him and contributed to his defeat to Ahmadinejad in the 2005 presidential election.

Having been systematically ousted from the regime's key decision-making mechanisms, the modernists, like members of the Islamic left before them, were forced to shift their focus towards building an organised party mechanism and mobilising the electorate. The decision by Rafsanjani's senior political allies to establish the Executives of the Construction of Iran Party (*Hezb-e Kargozaran-e Sazandegi-ye Iran*, henceforth *Kargozaran*) in 1996 was an overdue recognition of the necessity to strengthen the republican pillar in order to counter the traditionalists' growing control over the guardianship pillar. When his supporters' last-ditch attempt to amend the constitution to allow Rafsanjani a third term in office failed, Rafsanjani and the *Kargozaran* threw their support behind Khatami's campaign for the 1997 presidential election.[56]

While the Islamic leftist-turned-reformists focused on popular politics, the primary concern of the traditionalists remained strengthening their grip over the regime's tutelary institutions. As a result, the factional power struggles under the popular government of reformist Khatami, as well as under the populist government of neo-conservative Ahmadinejad, also took place along the guardianship versus democracy cleavage and pitted the regime's two pillars against one another. The resultant regime crises proved to be particularly destabilising and existentially threatening to the Islamic Republic.

Notes

1. Imam Khamenei's Opinion on Elections and Religious Democracy, https://english.khamenei.ir/Opinions/iranelections.
2. Kadivar, 'God and His Guardians', p. 67.
3. Buchta, *Who Rules Iran?*, p. xi.
4. Chehabi, 'The Political Regime of the Islamic Republic of Iran in Comparative Perspective', p. 48.
5. Adib-Moghaddam, *A Critical Introduction to Khomeini*, p. 5.
6. Shirazi, *The Constitution of Iran*. An English version of the IRI constitution is available at: http://www.iranchamber.com/government/laws/constitution.php.
7. 'The Supreme Leader's View of Democracy and Religious Democracy' – official website of the Supreme Leader of the IRI, 20 March 2011, http://english.khamenei.ir//index.php?option=com_content&task=view&id=1435&Itemid=12. We should note the deliberate use of the Persian word *mardomsalari* ('rule by the people') instead of the more commonly used *demokrasi*, which is a subtle yet revealing effort to promote an authentic notion of democracy, instead of one borrowed from the West.
8. 'Debir-e Shoraye Negahban: Hatti agher dar egheliyat bashim boyad nezam ra hafz konim', *BBC Persian*, 24 December 2013.
9. Moslem, *Factional Politics in Post-Khomeini Iran*, p. 4.

10. Proponents of traditional *fiqh* hold that primary sources of Islam – the Quran and the sunnah (the prophet's teachings) – are sufficient to govern an Islamic society and that religious judges should avoid resorting to secondary sources (*ahkam-e sanaviyeh*) as much as possible in everyday governance. In contrast, supporters of dynamic *fiqh* argue that although primary sources constitute the necessary base for Islamic government, changing times and the needs of modern society necessitate greater dependence on secondary sources, namely *ijma* (consensus), *qiyas* (analogy) and *ijtihad* (independent reasoning).

11. 'I believe in the traditional jurisprudence [. . .] and do not consider its violation to be permissible. This is the only correct way of *ijtihad*. But it does not mean that there is no room for further development in the Islamic Jurisprudence. In *ijtihad*, time and place occupy a fundamental position'. Khomeini, *Pithy Aphorisms*, p. 189.

12. Moslem, *Factional Politics in Post-Khomeini Iran*, p. 91.

13. Khosrokhavar, 'Toward an Anthropology of Democratization in Iran'; Brownlee, *Authoritarianism in an Age of Democratization*, pp. 157–80.

14. Razavi, 'The Road to Party Politics in Iran'.

15. A vivid example is the case of Mohsen Rafiqdoost, who once served as the head of the powerful *Mostazafan* foundation. Rafiqdoost was Khomeini's driver and was also related by marriage to Rafsanjani. Mousavi and his longtime rival, Khamenei, are distant cousins. The tradition has continued with the new generation of political elites as well: Ahmadinejad's son is married to the daughter of his advisor, close confidant and former vice-president, Rahim Mashaei. See Ehteshami, *After Khomeini*, p. 48, and Theler et al., *Mullahs, Guards and Bonyads*, pp. 37–74.

16. Ehteshami, *After Khomeini*, pp. 38–9.

17. Behrooz, 'The Islamic State and the Crisis of Marja'iyat in Iran'.

18. Keddie and Richard, *Modern Iran*, p. 263; Tezcür, *Muslim Reformers in Iran and Turkey*, p. 94.

19. Buchta, *Who Rules Iran?*, p. 47.

20. Shakibi, *Khatami and Gorbachev*, p. 122.

21. Künkler, 'The Special Court of the Clergy (dādgāh-ye vizheh-ye ruhāniyat) and the Repression of Dissident Clergy in Iran'.

22. Saeidi, 'The Accountability of Para-Governmental Organizations (bonyads)', pp. 479–88.

23. Kamrava and Hassan-Yari. 'Suspended Equilibrium in Iran's Political System'.

24. Mavani, 'Khomeini's Concept of Governance of the Jurisconsult', p. 207.

25. Shakibi, *Khatami and Gorbachev*, p. 123.

26. Arjomand, *After Khomeini*, p. 63.

27. Quoted in Omid, *Islam and the Post-Revolutionary State in Iran*, pp. 106–10.
28. Farhi, 'The Antinomies of Iran's War Generation', pp. 101–21.
29. Theler et al., *Mullahs, Guards and Bonyads,* pp. 59–64.
30. Golkar, 'Paramilitarization of the Economy'.
31. Voiced most prominently by Vali Nasr in the mid-2000s, this view gained traction in the West after the 2009 presidential election. Most notably, then US Secretary of State Hillary Clinton argued the Guards were 'supplanting the government of Iran'. 'Clinton: Iran moving toward military dictatorship', *Reuters*, 15 February 2010.
32. Safshekan and Sabet, 'The Ayatollah's Praetorians'; Hen-Tov and Gonzalez, 'The Militarization of Post-Khomeini Iran'.
33. Harris, 'The Rise of the Subcontractor State'.
34. Quoted in Shakibi, *Khatami and Gorbachev*, p. 127.
35. Frings-Hessami, 'The Islamic Debate over Land Reform in the Iranian Parliament (1981–1986)', p. 145.
36. Farhi, 'The Antinomies of Iran's War Generation', p. 3.
37. *Ettela'at*, 28 March 1992.
38. Abrahamian, *A History of Modern Iran*, p. 183.
39. I briefly discuss the fifth presidency, that of Ebrahim Raisi which started in 2021, at the end of Chapter 7. Suffice it to say for now that it represents a new era in which the traditionalist guardians have marginalised all other factions, completely emasculated the republican institutions and dominated both pillars of the regime for the first time in history of the Islamic Republic.
40. Arjomand, *After Khomeini*, p. 37.
41. The eight-year war with Iraq claimed nearly a million lives in total and left millions more disabled and traumatised. Its direct and indirect cost on the Iranian economy was calculated at USD 627 billion. By 1989, per capita income had fallen by nearly 45% from 1977/78. See Rajaee, *Iranian Perspectives on the Iran-Iraq War*.
42. By 1991, the total trade volume had become 3.5 times the pre-revolutionary level. St. Marie and Naghshpour. *Revolutionary Iran and the United States*, p. 134.
43. Ehteshami, *After Khomeini*, p. 56.
44. Ansari, *Iran, Islam and Democracy*, pp. 52–79.
45. Keshavarzian, 'Regime Loyalty and *Bazari* Representation under the Islamic Republic of Iran'.
46. *Kayhan*, 27 June 1991.
47. In a 1992 address, for example, Khamenei publicly criticised the direction of reconstruction: 'The enemy claims that during the period of reconstruction,

revolutionary spirit and morality must be put aside', he said. 'Is this the meaning of reconstruction? Surely it is not. [. . .] If we spend billions on development projects and ignore moral issues in the country, all the achievements will amount to nothing'. *Ettela'at*, 20 October 1992.

48. Khamanei, *Farhang va Tahajom-e Farhangi.*
49. Moslem, *Factional Politics in Post-Khomeini Iran*, pp. 221–4
50. *Iran*, 31 March 1996. Quoted in Takeyh, *Guardians of the Revolution*, p. 125.
51. Breckenridge, 'Sanction first, ask questions later'.
52. In a 2012 interview, Rafsanjani recalled the constraints and frustrations he faced both at home and abroad in the foreign policy arena during his presidency: 'I wanted to re-establish relations with Egypt, but I could not. I wanted to begin negotiations with America, based on the terms I had set, but I could not. Could not is not the same as did not want to'. Editorial, 'Editorial Board Roundtable with Ayatollah Hashemi Rafsanjani.
53. Arjomand, *After Khomeini*, p. 37.
54. Patrick E. Tyler, 'Pragmatism Emerging in Iran', *Washington Post*, 11 July 1989.
55. The GC had disqualified 124 of 128 candidates, and those who were approved all belonged to the conservative faction.
56. Put forth by Rafsanjani's Deputy President Ata'ollah Mohajerani and Chief of Staff Hossein Marashi, the proposal was vehemently opposed by the traditionalists, 'politely rejected' by the reformists and ultimately dismissed by Khamenei. See Moslem, *Factional Politics in Post-Khomeini Iran*, pp. 240–1.

4

DEMOCRACY UNDER TUTELAGE
IN TURKEY

My biggest defeat is my greatest victory.
   – İsmet İnönü, after the election loss on 14 May 1950
that ended the CHP's single-party rule

The Armed Forces had no choice but to seize power [. . .] to restore the unity of the homeland and the nation, to bolster the principles of Atatürk, to put democracy which has been unable to control itself on firm grounds, and to reestablish the state's lost authority.
   – Kenan Evren, 12 September 1980

Guardianship in Turkey was institutionalised more gradually and less overtly than in the Islamic Republic of Iran. The Kemalist regime originally stood on three pillars: the leader, the party and the military. With his unmatched charisma, the founder and the first president of the republic, Mustafa Kemal Atatürk, stood above the fray of everyday politics and governed virtually undisputed during his lifetime. Organised out of the popular mobilisation networks of the Anatolian resistance movement, the Republican People's Party (CHP) served as the main institutional bridge between the state and society and as the organisational vehicle of mass socialisation into the regime. In the absence of a formal opposition party between 1925 and 1946, the CHP was the only platform on which factional differences amongst the republican elite could emerge. Following Atatürk's death in 1938, the ruling party, which had already become synonymous with the state, emerged as the regime's foremost pillar. Finally, tasked by Atatürk with 'guiding' the nation, the Turkish Armed Forces (*Türk Silahlı Kuvvetleri*, TSK) were the regime's coercive arm, enforcer of its reforms and authority and the provider of many of the young republic's senior statesmen and bureaucrats.

Turkey's transition to multiparty politics after World War II and the subsequent end of the CHP's single-party rule meant that by the 1950s only one of the regime's original three pillars remained standing: the military. In an uncertain environment of nascent democracy at home and ideological polarisation abroad, this new situation led members of the TSK to reinterpret their duty of 'guiding the nation' and 'guarding the regime' as licence for a more robust tutelary role than was explicitly outlined by Atatürk himself. Following the first military coup in 1960, proponents of Kemalist guardianship invoked various sociological, historical and geopolitical arguments to justify the growing tutelary powers of the military and senior bureaucracy. These found consistent support not only among a significant minority of the population but also, crucially, among Turkey's new Western partners in NATO, which came to view the Turkish military as a strategic bulwark against Soviet expansionism. Still, in the absence of an institutional blueprint drawn up by the charismatic leader himself, akin to Khomeini's *velayat-e faqih* system, guardianship was built on more tenuous grounds in Turkey than in Iran.

Tracing the long-term institutional trajectory of guardianship in Turkey reveals two intertwined stories: the first is a story of continual expansion of the guardians' 'reserved domains' vis-à-vis electoral politics, marked by periodic military coups and subsequent legal-constitutional amendments. The second is a story of repetitive 'course corrections' by the guardians, wherein each military intervention since 1960 is an attempt to fix the unintended socio-political consequences of the previous intervention. The outcome of these two stories is a paradox: although military tutelage grew consistently in the twentieth century, it also contributed to creating the conditions that ultimately brought about the fall of Kemalist guardianship in Turkey in the twenty-first century.

Electoral Politics and Transition to Multiparty Democracy

The death of the charismatic leader in 1938 did not immediately alter the basic institutional character of the Turkish Republic. By then, Turkey had already become a party-state, with the CHP chairman simultaneously serving as the president of the republic, deputy party chairman as prime minister, party general secretary as interior minister, and local party leaders as provincial governors. From 1925, when the TCF was shut down, until 1946, the CHP ruled without a formal opposition.[1] Under President İnönü, the statist military-bureaucratic wing of the leadership elite came to dominate the ruling CHP, while the CHP dominated political life in the young republic. The İnönü government pursued state-driven industrialisation schemes and pressed on with Atatürk's secularisation and Turkification projects, while pragmatically maintaining Turkey's neutrality during World War II.

It was the Allied victory in that war and the subsequent resurgence of the historically rooted Turkish fear of Russian expansionism that convinced İnönü to start navigating Turkey's strategic alignment with the emerging Western axis. While the president and the proponents of alignment with the West justified this move as compliant with Atatürk's ideal of participating in 'contemporary civilisation', others saw it as a compromise on the country's hard-won sovereignty. Indeed, the strategic rapprochement also entailed ideological re-alignment and political commitments. In exchange for economic assistance, military aid and security guarantees from the US, as part of the Truman Doctrine, the İnönü government put in place a series of economic liberalisation reforms. At the same time, İnönü initiated the transition to a multiparty system, although there is no evidence that he was pressured to do so by the Americans, or that a non-democratic Turkey would be left out of the Western alliance, which included Franco's Spain and Salazar's Portugal. Whether İnönü really believed it was time for democracy or that he could still maintain the CHP's hegemonic position in a tightly controlled multiparty system remains disputed.[2] Either way, the first competitive multiparty election in 1950 spelled the end of the CHP-era as it brought to power the coalition of landowners and entrepreneurs, which had been marginalised by the military-bureaucratic alliance following Atatürk's death.

Founded in 1946 by prominent former CHP members Celal Bayar, Adnan Menderes, Fuat Köprülü and Refik Koraltan, the Democrat Party (*Demokrat Parti*, DP) promised to relax the state's social policies and to pursue a liberal economic agenda. The promise of change appealed to large portions of the electorate, who had grown weary of the CHP after a decade of economic stagnation and felt alienated by its enforced modernisation agenda. Securing 53% the vote in the 1950 election, the DP became the first popularly elected party in the history of the Turkish Republic and the first opposition party to take over the government from an incumbent through elections.[3] It was also to become the first in a series of socially conservative, economically liberal mass parties that would achieve overwhelming electoral success in Turkish politics in the decades to come. Following on the political tradition of the DP, the Justice Party (*Adalet Partisi*, AP) of Süleyman Demirel in the late 1960s, the Motherland Party (*Anavatan Partisi*, ANAP) of Turgut Özal in the 1980s and the AKP of Recep Tayyip Erdoğan in the 2000s all succeeded in forming popular single-party governments.

During its one decade in power following two more general election victories in 1954 and 1957, the DP government led by Prime Minister Adnan Menderes and President Celal Bayar anchored Turkey firmly in the Western geopolitical camp, where it would remain during and after the Cold War. Turkey committed troops to the Korean War on the US side in 1950 and became full member of NATO in 1952. At home, the DP carried out a robust capitalist development programme – benefiting both from the industrial foundations laid previously by the CHP and the financial and military assistance provided by the US Marshall Fund – and also relaxed restrictions on the expression of religious identity in the public sphere.

Equally important as the Democrat Party's victory in 1950 was İnönü's recognition of the outcome of the poll and his peaceful handover of power to his rivals, a remarkable event that set three important precedents for Turkish politics. First, in accepting defeat and voluntarily stepping down from the presidency after twelve years in power, İnönü publicly acknowledged that neither he – the most powerful political figure in the country, whom the GNA had given the honorific title of 'National Chief' (*Milli Şef*) – nor the office of the president had inherited the full charismatic authority of Atatürk. Thereafter, no single individual, whether the party head, president or military chief of staff, could enjoy Atatürk's supra-political position.[4] On the one hand, de-personalising Atatürk's charisma arguably spared Turkey the fate of post-revolutionary polities driven towards personal dictatorship under ambitious successors, such as the Soviet Union under Stalin or the Islamic Republic under Khamenei. On the other hand, İnönü's move set the stage not for the disappearance, but for the institutionalisation of the leader's charismatic legacy by the only standing regime pillar, the Turkish Armed Forces.

Secondly, with the introduction of a multiparty system within a parliamentary framework, centralised and hierarchically structured political parties became the main vehicle of Turkish politics. Unlike political factions in the IRI, these parties were 'bureaucratic mass organisations' characterised by patron–client networks.[5] In this arrangement, party mechanisms, which are formally linked to their socio-political constituencies, produce their own leaders from among these constituencies. Although powerful patriarchal figures loom large in Turkish politics and dominate party affairs, these figures tend to be bound to the party mechanism, more than the party mechanism to them.[6]

Last but not least, the smooth transition of power between two political parties created democratic path dependence. Following this first competitive vote, Turkish citizens regularly expressed their will at the ballot box, rewarding or punishing political parties in reasonably free and fair elections. At least until the mid-2010s, when concerns about unfair competition and electoral manipulation became paramount, the vote count and the election results were widely trusted by the public and respected by victors and losers alike.

Turkey still remains a rare example of a voluntary transition from a single-party rule to multiparty democracy initiated from above; in the mid-twentieth century, it was an extremely unusual case. 'The example of Turkey' wrote Maurice Duverger in 1954, 'seems to demonstrate that the technique of the single party, applied with discernment, makes it possible gradually to build up a new ruling class and independent political elite which alone make it possible to establish at some date an authentic democracy'.[7] Despite successful transition and the institutionalisation of multiparty politics, however, democracy never became 'the only game in town' in Turkey.[8] During the second half of the twentieth century, political power frequently oscillated between populist-majoritarian elected governments and tutelary actors intervening in the electoral process, starting with the coup d'état of 1960.

The DP's domination of Turkish politics in the 1950s was facilitated by a winner-takes-all election system that awarded the first party with a disproportionally high number of seats in the parliament, and the 1924 Constitution, which was originally tailored for Mustafa Kemal and vested far-reaching powers in the executive branch over the legislature and the judiciary.[9] The 1924 Constitution enabled a type of 'executive duumvirate' where the president and the prime minister could hail from the same party: the president, elected by the parliament following each general election, could remain a member of his party and seek re-election indefinitely.[10] In the absence of an effective system of checks and balances, the DP displayed an increasingly majoritarian understanding of democracy, using its success at the ballot box as a licence to silence the opposition, especially as the economic boom of the early DP years gave way to stagnation and crisis in the late 1950s. Intolerant of dissent and fearful of being overthrown, the government attempted to seize the assets of the CHP, publicised lists of loyalists on the radio, and, under the guise of fighting communism, carried out McCarthyesque witch hunt of intellectuals, journalists, officers and civil servants.

To be sure, the DP leaders were as careful to promote their policies in Kemalist terms as their predecessors, emphasising President Bayar's close personal relationship with Atatürk. It was the DP government that had criminalised 'insulting the memory and legacy of Atatürk and damaging his statues' in 1951.[11] Regardless of this, for many statist officers and bureaucrats, who viewed the transition to multiparty politics as a premature move that jeopardised the Kemalist project of modernisation, the DP was a counter-revolutionary government backed by regressive elements in society. From this point of view, the coup d'état carried out by left-leaning junior officers on 27 May 1960 that toppled the DP government and executed three of its leaders, including PM Menderes, was a revolutionary act to save democracy and the Kemalist revolution. For nearly two decades after the 1960 coup, 27 May was celebrated as a public holiday as the 'Freedom and Constitution Day'.

Consolidation and Justifications of Military Guardianship

Like the 1950 election, the coup d'état of 1960 also set important precedents. First, it confirmed the TSK's position as the main tutelary pillar of the Kemalist regime, and opened the way for future interventions in civilian politics. Henceforth it was up to the military-as-institution to watch over elected politicians and protect the legacy of the charismatic leader, however that legacy was interpreted. The TSK could force the president to step down, as in 1960, or shut down political parties, including the CHP, as happened after the 1980 coup. Military officers acting in the name of protecting the order could even defy their own superiors, including chiefs of the general staff. The junta that carried out the 1960 coup arrested General Rüştü Erdelhun, the TSK chief appointed by Bayar, and sentenced him to death alongside the DP leaders for collaborating with the counter-revolutionaries.[12]

Secondly, the 1960 coup laid the institutional groundwork for a system of indirect tutelage, rather than direct military rule. Unlike its counterparts in Southern Europe, Latin America, Africa or Southeast Asia at the time, the Turkish military on the whole refrained from governing the country directly. After the 1960 coup, the TSK overthrew elected governments three more times, in 1971, 1980 and 1997. Yet after every successful coup, it eventually returned power to civilian politicians and allowed competitive elections to be organised.[13] This transfer of power led some scholars of political transitions to assume, rather incorrectly, that Turkey was on the path to re-democratisation following a spell of authoritarian rule.[14] In reality, the impact of coups was not limited to those brief periods of direct military government. All of the four major coups that the TSK carried out between 1960 and 1997 resulted in profound changes in Turkey's political and constitutional landscape that tilted the civil–military balance in favour of the generals. A new constitution was drafted by the generals following two direct interventions in 1960 and 1980, while the 1971 and 1997 interventions led to critical amendments to the exiting constitutions.

Every coup and subsequent constitutional change expanded the legal/institutional remit and influence of the military guardians at the expense of elected officials. Consequently, even when the soldiers returned to the barracks, the generals were able to influence events through the veto institutions they put in place as well as through their associates within the state bureaucracy, the judiciary and civil society as well as civilian politics. The resultant hybrid structure demarcated the affairs of the state (*devlet*) from the affairs of government (*hükümet*). Government came to indicate the realm of everyday politics – issues that could be entrusted to elected politicians and discussed publicly within 'permissible' boundaries drawn by the guardians. Beyond these boundaries started the realm of state affairs, understood as the exclusive domain of the guardians, who were deemed to possess the necessary personal, ideological and institutional credentials to make decisions on matters of national security, foreign policy orientation or the general socio-economic direction of the country.

At the root of the TSK's reluctance to govern directly was an issue of legitimacy. As noted earlier, even though Atatürk had bestowed upon the military the duty of guiding the nation and guarding the revolution, he did not articulate or design an explicit political role for it the way Khomeini did for the clergy in Iran. In fact, as early as in 1924, the GNA passed a law barring active officers from becoming members of the parliament.[15] Moreover, the military lacked an explicit constitutional basis for its tutelary role. In contrast to the constitutions of the IRI, none of Turkey's constitutions, even the junta-made 1961 and 1982 versions, included a reference to the TSK as the guardian of the regime, the republic or the constitution. The legality of military interventions was based on the ambiguously worded Article 35 of the TSK's Internal Service Act. Added after the 1960 coup, it defined the duty of the TSK as 'to protect and watch over the Turkish homeland and the Turkish Republic as delineated by the Constitution'.[16] Turkish generals boasted their role as the 'unwavering custodians of Atatürk's material and moral legacy'. But quite unlike the IRI system, where *velayat* and *vali-ye faqih* are formally held in the highest esteem, the Turkish guardians never embraced the term *vesayet* (tutelage), which gained a negative political connotation and, together with *statüko* (status quo), has been used by critics to denounce an autocratic and intransigent state elite.

This had two contradictory implications for the Turkish guardians: on one side, by avoiding direct engagement in politics, the TSK managed to present itself as uninvolved and uninterested in government affairs, conveniently placing responsibility for the country's socio-economic problems on the shoulders of civilian politicians. This may even help explain the relative longevity of Turkey's military guardianship compared with the shorter life span of military dictatorships elsewhere. On the flipside, however, it meant that whenever the military did intervene in politics, it could be accused of committing an act that was not explicitly sanctioned by the founding father or the constitution (i.e., an illegitimate act). Consequently, the institutional arrangement that was established as a result of military coups in Turkey was also built upon shaky legal and ideological grounds and needed constant justification.

These justifications were based on historical, cultural and geopolitical grounds. The Turkish military's carefully cultivated nationalist image was that of an institution with a glorious past dating from the Hunnic invasions of China to the heroic defence at the Battle of Gallipoli in WWI; the institution that produced Mustafa Kemal, brought victory in the War of Liberation, and built a sovereign nation from the ruins of a defunct empire.[17] Furthermore, despite the strictly secular training of its officer corps, the TSK continued to command respect and loyalty through deep-rooted symbols of patriarchal authority in a society that refers to the military as 'the prophet's hearth' (*peyg-amber ocağı*) and considers soldiering not only a sacred duty towards the state, religion and the nation, but also a necessary sacrifice for attaining manhood.[18]

In part thanks to this aura of sanctity, which kept the TSK's internal affairs off limits to public scrutiny for decades, the military was able to count on a popular reputation as the country's most professional, meritocratic and trust-worthy institution. This reputation, in turn, was used to justify periodic coups as unfortunate but necessary acts that patriotic officers had to carry out reluctantly in order to save the republic, democracy and the gullible electorate from self-serving, inept or manipulative politicians. In other words, while the guardians on the one hand exhibited a classic distrust of the masses, on the other hand, they relied on a narrative of popularity to legitimise their socio-political position. The need to sustain this narrative ultimately rendered the Turkish guardians more exposed and vulnerable to shifts in public opinion than their Iranian counterparts.

Finally, guardianship was justified on the basis of the existence of various external threats emanating from Turkey's sensitive geopolitical location. The TSK's threat perception evolved over time. During the Cold War, communism was the usual suspect. Both the 1971 and 1980 coups primarily targeted the wide spectrum of left-wing and socialist movements across the country. Following the end of the Cold War, political Islam and Kurdish separatism replaced communism at the top of the list of existential threats that were used to justify imposing limitations on democracy and civil liberties.[19] Crucially, these justifications were aimed not only at a domestic audience to keep up nationalistic fervour and popular support for the tutelary establishment, but also at the country's Western allies in NATO.

During the Cold War, Turkey's 'geostrategic indispensability' at the frontline of the East-West axis prompted the Western security establishment to actively support the Kemalist guardians' efforts to keep politics and society under control. As maintaining Turkey's pro-Western orientation was of a higher priority than supporting democracy, Turkey's NATO allies, the US in particular, either tacitly approved or directly backed the military's interventions and turned a blind eye to violations of civil liberties and human rights. The heavy-handed right-wing coup of 12 September 1980, for instance, was welcomed in Washington, DC, for anchoring Turkey in the Western orbit shortly after the Iranian revolution and the Soviet occupation of Afghanistan.[20] Whether carried out by left-leaning junior officers as in 1960, or senior generals as in 1971 and 1980, coup makers immediately declared their commitment to the NATO structure after each intervention – a kind of institutional dependence, it should be noted, the guardians of the Islamic Republic did not have towards any major international security alliance.

The end of the Cold War did not immediately alter the core dynamics of this strategic relationship. During the 1990s, Turkey continued to provide military and logistical assistance to US and NATO-led operations, including the Gulf War, Somalia, Yugoslavia and, in the aftermath of the 11 September 2001 attacks in the US, against the Taliban in Afghanistan. For its part, Washington increased security coordination with Turkey, which included subsidised arms sales to the Turkish military in support of its campaign against the Kurdish insurgents.[21] Likewise, both the US and the European Union quietly approved the guardians' last successful intervention against a civilian government in 1997.

Institutions of Kemalist Guardianship

Regular competitive elections took place in relatively free and fair conditions in Turkey. The Kemalist guardians maintained no formal link with any political party, including the CHP. In rare cases when senior generals indicated a party preference – such as Kenan Evren's support for the uninspiring and short-lived Nationalist Democracy Party, which was led by a retired general, ahead of the 1983 elections – they did not campaign or attempt to fabricate a victory on their behalf. In fact, partisan support by the military routinely backfired as voters tended to defy the generals' wishes and choose leaders and parties that were least favoured by the guardians. When faced with undesirable election outcomes, the guardians did not contest, annul or attempt to overturn the results. Elections thus served as an effective popular response to tutelary power.

The guardians had little interest in manipulating votes or pre-determining outcomes also because they did not compete in them and did not risk being voted out of office.[22] Moreover, as I noted above, the maintenance of a functioning procedural democracy was necessary to legitimise the existence of tutelary institutions as well. Instead of determining who should govern, they focused on how (and how much) elected governments would be permitted to govern. Consequently, the basic logic of guardianship as it was institutionalised after the 1960 coup was to draw and enforce the boundaries of the playing field in which elected officials were permitted to operate and to demarcate the *devlet* from *hükümet* through restraining executive power by dividing it among rival actors and establishing and expanding veto institutions. This section provides a brief overview of these institutions.

National Security Council

The establishment of the National Security Council (*Milli Güvenlik Kurulu*, NSC) after the 1960 coup had the most profound impact on Turkey's institutional landscape. 'The embodiment of the bureaucracy's primacy over the popularly elected parliament', the NSC was founded as a governmental advisory body that brought together cabinet ministers and the prime minister, the president and the military high command on regular intervals to exchange views on developments.[23] With every intervention, the Council's influence over the elected government and the parliament increased, as did the clout and the number of its military members over their civilian counterparts. The 1982 Constitution expanded the authority of the NSC general secretary, who was always a military officer until 2004, and ensured that the NSC's recommendations to the elected government were given 'special consideration', making them in effect equivalent to official edicts (Articles 118–20). Although NSC meetings were confidential, critical messages were routinely leaked to trusted media outlets as a way for the generals to make their position public.

Through the NSC, the military guardians also came to control the drafting of the National Security Policy Document (*Milli Güvenlik Siyaseti Belgesi*, NSPD). Dubbed Turkey's 'secret constitution', the NSPD is a classified document that outlines Turkey's national security policy, identifies internal and external threats and thus determines the permissible boundaries of public politics. The NSPD is prepared by the NSC general secretariat and submitted to the NSC for approval without any parliamentary oversight of the drafting process.[24] Illustrating the importance of the document, former TSK Chief of

Staff Doğan Güreş once described it as 'the god of all policies, the mother of all constitutions: it is unthinkable to act against it'.[25]

The security bureaucracy's influence over the NSC allowed the generals to pressurise the government to declare emergency laws in parts or the whole of the country in the name of national security. The definition of national security, meanwhile, was revised in a 1983 law in such broad and ambiguous terms that it could be interpreted to cover any policy field. Most of the country was under martial law from 1978 until 1983. In the Kurdish-majority provinces of southeast Turkey, emergency laws remained in place until 2002, suspending the democratic process and giving senior generals and centrally appointed bureaucrats a free hand in governing the region with little parliamentary scrutiny, under the pretext of combating terrorism.

Finally, the military's influence over the NSC and the NSPD limited the civilian bodies' ability to monitor the TSK's economic activities. Institutions that were nominally charged with overseeing military procurements and the defence budget (i.e., the National Defence Commission, the Parliamentary Planning and Budget Commission, and the Court of Accounts) were legally constrained by constitutional amendments and also lacked the political clout to fulfil their oversight duties.

The Presidency

An extension of the ruling party under the 1924 Constitution, the presidency was transformed into a tutelary institution after the 1960 coup. The 1961 Constitution split up the 'executive duumvirate' that had allowed the president and the prime minister to be from the same party, turning the presidency into a non-partisan office, whose occupant would be elected by the GNA for a single seven-year term. The parliament was expected to seek a nod of approval from the NSC before electing a presidential candidate. Until the election of Abdullah Gül in 2007 against the expressed will of the TSK, Turkey's presidents were either former generals, bureaucrats with proven Kemalist credentials or civilian politicians who had received the guardians' nod of approval.

The presidency remained a largely ceremonial office until the junta that carried out the 12 September 1980 coup expanded its powers. The 1982 Constitution equipped the presidency with enhanced monitoring and veto capabilities over the government, as well as the authority to appoint senior judges, prosecutors, senior bureaucrats and university rectors. The constitution also bestowed upon the president a number of legislative and executive powers, including declaring states of emergency and issuing decrees during these periods.[26] This power would prove critical years later under the presidency of Recep Tayyip Erdoğan, when he started to rule by executive decree following the failed coup attempt and the subsequent declaration of a state of emergency in July 2016.

The Judiciary

In his comparative study of new constitutionalism, Hirschl noted 'the global trend towards juristocracy', driven by 'a strategic pact led by hegemonic yet increasingly threatened political elites, who seek to insulate their policy preferences from the changing fortunes of democratic politics'.[27] Before it was systematically transformed and brought under the political control of the executive branch in the 2010s, the judiciary in Turkey had been a symbol and mechanism of tutelary control of democratic politics. After carrying out the 1960 coup, the statist wing of the Kemalist elite went on to tighten its grip over the judiciary through a system of close-circuit recruitment and appointment of judges and prosecutors.[28] Established with the 1961 Constitution, the authority of the military courts was expanded with the 1973 constitutional amendments and the 1982 Constitution. While they acquired the power to try civilians, civilian courts' jurisdiction over military personnel was restricted.[29]

Military coups further shaped the structure of the civilian justice system. Also established after the 1960 coup, the Constitutional Court (*Anayasa Mahkemesi*) was tasked with reviewing the constitutionality of legislature enacted by the parliament and was equipped with the power to dissolve political parties and ban or imprison politicians on the grounds of acting against the constitution. According to the 1961 Constitution, military and civilian high judiciary, the President, the GNA and the Senate (which was established in 1961 and abolished in 1980) each appointed a fixed number of members to the Constitutional Court. The 1982 Constitution transferred the power of appointment exclusively to the president, who would choose from candidates presented to him by various state institutions. Between 1963 and 2008, the Constitutional Court outlawed 25 political parties, 19 of which were banned after 1980. These were almost exclusively socialist, Kurdish nationalist or Islamist parties.[30]

The 1982 Constitution re-established the State Security Courts (*Devlet Güvenlik Mahkemeleri*, SSC), which were first created in 1973 but abolished two years later. These were tasked with overseeing cases that included 'crimes against state security', an expansive jurisdiction based on a highly ambiguous offence. A law that was in effect from 1991 to 1999 required one member in every three-judge panel to be a military officer. The SSCs were the main judicial instrument with which the state attempted to suppress left-wing movements in the 1980s and the Kurdish uprising in the 1990s. Characterised by weak defendant rights, extremely long detention periods, systematic torture and heavy prison sentences, these courts became the embodiment of the military's dominance over the state, and the state's authoritarian grip over politics and society in the post-1980 era.[31]

The 'Deep State'

The geopolitical dimension of military tutelage in Turkey went beyond the expression of support for its periodic coups by the country's Western allies. The Western security alliance was particularly instrumental in laying the foundations of a shadowy extra-legal network within the security bureaucracy, often referred to in Turkey as the 'deep state'. Within the framework of a US-led initiative to set up anti-communist 'stay behind' paramilitary groups and sleeper cells across NATO member states in Europe, a secret Special Warfare Department (*Özel Harp Dairesi*) was founded inside the Turkish military in cooperation with US intelligence services.[32] The department was set up in September 1952, but for the next two decades neither the Turkish public nor its elected representatives had any knowledge of its existence or activities, let alone being able to hold it to account.

Discovering it almost by accident in 1974, Prime Minister Bülent Ecevit was the first elected official to publicly question the presence of a secretive paramilitary network within the state. Trained in unconventional warfare methods and drawing their recruits mainly from members of far-right nationalist groups – in particular, the so-called 'Grey Wolves' – the counter-guerrilla units attached to this department were invisible to law or to the parliament. During the Cold War, they functioned as assassination squads, targeting communist 'subversives' and have been widely suspected of instigating some of the most critical (and unresolved) episodes of political violence in Turkey, such as the Taksim Square massacre on May Day 1977 or the sectarian killings in the city of Maraş in 1978, which were in turn used to justify the 1980 coup.

While the demise of the left in Turkey following the 1980 coup, and the collapse of the Soviet Union a decade later, stripped the Turkish counter-guerrilla network of its original raison d'être, institutions of the deep state did not abrogate themselves. Nor were they exposed and disassembled by public prosecutors or the government of the day. There was, in other words, no public trial in Turkey similar to Italy's Operation *Gladio* in the 1990s. Instead, the conflict with the Kurdish separatists provided the deep state with a new focus, as well as a new terrain on which to operate with considerable freedom. In the atmosphere of legal and political impunity created by the state of emergency laws and the SSCs that governed public life in the Kurdish-majority provinces during the 1990s, the underground counter-guerrilla network, along with quasi-official intelligence units and members of the special police forces, routinely carried out extra-legal detainment, torture and assassination of civilians in the region. It was also at this intersection that the politico-economic interests of these security sector actors became increasingly embroiled with those of civilian politicians, big business and organised crime groups, united under an ultra-nationalist banner.[33]

Here lies another difference between the Turkish and Iranian systems of tutelage that is a factor of their sources of legitimation. The self-justification for an ultra-nationalist paramilitary structure in Turkey doing the guardians' dirty work has been based on the enduring idea of the state's sanctity and ensuring its survival (*devletin bekası*) – but it had no solid legal or constitutional foundation. In a country that at least paid lip service to democracy and the rule of law, such an entity could not function overtly; hence the *deep* state. Its secretive nature – operating behind the scenes and underground – created fertile ground for popular myths and conspiracy theories to flourish around the concept, which in turn made it easier to deny its existence altogether. In contrast, as one observer put it, 'Iran's deep state can be summed up in one name: the Islamic Revolutionary Guards Corps'.[34] Although also highly non-transparent and unaccountable to the public, the existence of a constitutionally sanctioned parallel security apparatus loyal to the Leader and tasked with 'guarding the revolution' gave the Iranian guardians' greater power and freedom than that of their Turkish counterparts.

The Vicious Cycle of Self-correcting Coups

As I noted at the beginning of this chapter, the evolution of military tutelage in Turkey displayed two interconnected logics: one of expansion, whereby each coup and subsequent constitutional change increased the socio-political and institutional remit of the guardians at the expense of civilian politics, and the other of a series of 'course corrections', with each intervention aimed at fixing the unintended consequences of past attempts at socio-political engineering by a previous generation of guardians. These dual logics did not only create a vicious cycle of periodic interventions, but also inadvertently helped prepare the ground for the emergence of socio-political and institutional challenges that would ultimately bring about the fall of military tutelage in the 2000s.

The 1960 Coup and its Legacies

The aim of the military intervention of 27 May 1960 was to undo the perceived damage to the Kemalist revolution that was a consequence of the 'premature' decision to transition to multiparty politics. The junior officers who carried out the coup were convinced that the degeneration of democracy, the erosion of secularist principles and the deterioration of their own socio-economic standing were a result of the concentration of excessive executive power in the wrong hands.[35] Correspondingly, the post-1960 changes were focused on limiting the authority of elected governments by breaking apart the 'executive duumvirate' and de-politicising the presidency, establishing new veto institutions and replacing the winner-takes-all voting system with the D'Hont method of proportional allocation of seats, which diffused parliamentary representation and made single-party governments more difficult to form.[36] Indeed, for the next two decades, coalition governments became the norm and not the exception. Finally, reflecting the left-leaning ideological orientation of the coup makers, the 1961 Constitution expanded civil rights and workers' rights, which the 1924 Constitution provided scant protection to and which successive DP governments had liberally abused.

The senior officers that carried out the 1971 and 1980 coups believed that the rights and liberties enshrined in the 1961 Constitution were excessive and open to abuse by socialist movements and parties. The right-wing coup of 12 March 1971, which came three days after a failed attempt by leftist junior officers, sought to stem the rising left-wing tide by purging the left-leaning officers from the TSK, arresting and executing leaders of the revolutionary student movement, outlawing socialist parties and amending the constitution to criminalise political activism.[37] Yet it fell short of a complete overhaul of an unstable system that tolerated too many 'fringe elements'.

The 1980 coup-makers were determined to finish this job. The constitution they put in place brought in further restrictions on civil rights and liberties under the pretext of safeguarding 'national sovereignty, the republic, national security, public order, general peace, the public interest, public morals and public health'.[38] For instance, it became illegal for labour unions to 'pursue a political cause, engage in political activity, receive support from political parties or give support to them' (Article 52). In an effort to confine parliamentary representation to the tolerated mainstream, a 10% national election threshold was introduced. Finally, two new regulatory institutions staffed with representatives from the military and senior bureaucracy – the Council of Higher Education (*Yüksek Öğretim Kurulu*, YÖK) and the Higher Council of Radio and Television (*Radyo Televizyon Üst Kurulu*, RTÜK) – were set up to bring the universities and the media under stringent state control.

The 1980 Coup and its Legacies

The new order that the junta which carried out the coup of 12 September 1980 sought to establish produced its own institutional, economic and political legacies, all of which eventually came back to haunt the guardians in unforeseen ways. Institutionally, the 1982 Constitution created a weakened parliamentary system with semi-presidential characteristics.[39] In strengthening the presidency, Kenan Evren wanted to transform this office, which he assumed in 1982, into a leading institution of guardianship. But similar to Rafsanjani's attempt to create an executive presidency for himself in Iran after 1989, Evren's institutional re-engineering unwittingly turned a previously ceremonial post into a strategic target for populist politicians after him. Meanwhile, confining the parliamentary space to the mainstream created new opportunities for future populist-majoritarian contenders. In the post-1980 order, if a leader or party could gain the majority in the GNA, which had become more feasible with the 10% threshold and the abolition of the Senate, and also capture the presidency, they could recreate a type of executive duumvirate similar to that of the DP in the 1950s.

Indeed, this was soon achieved under Turgut Özal, who owed his political fortunes to the 1980 coup, having served as the chief economic adviser to the military junta, overseeing Turkey's transition to free market economy. After six years as prime minister at the head of centre-right ANAP, he succeeded Kenan Evren as president in 1989. Despite assuming the presidency with the consent of the NSC, Özal soon made it clear he had no intention to heed the constitutional boundaries of his office or the guardians' unwritten rules. Acting as de facto head of his former party, he often clashed with the parliamentary opposition. Nor did he shy away from defying the generals.[40] An admirer of the US political system, he started advocating for a transition to presidentialism, which he praised as efficient and entrepreneurial. He also flirted with the idea of federalism in place of Turkey's rigidly centralised administrative structure as a possible solution to the country's increasingly violent Kurdish conflict.[41] These ideas did not endear him to the generals. At an NSC meeting shortly before his death, the military representatives reportedly expressed their dissatisfaction and cautioned the president against encouraging public discussions about the regime's basic principles.

Özal's unexpected death in April 1993, which has long been a source of conspiracy theories as it came in the midst of sensitive peace negotiations with the Kurdish militants, meant that he could not fulfil his political ambitions.[42] The guardians made sure that Özal's successors – his long-time rival Süleyman Demirel (1993–2000) and former Constitutional Court chief Ahmet Necdet Sezer (2000–07) – would serve as active veto players defending the interests of the tutelary establishment. Yet the idea of re-creating an executive duumvirate and pushing for presidentialism continued to inspire popular challengers and was picked up in earnest by the AKP government in the 2000s.

The economic legacy of the 1980 coup was Turkey's overnight transition from an import-substitution model to a free market economy, which happened in the context of the global advent of neoliberalism. Sharp spikes in oil prices in the 1970s meant that resource-poor Turkey could no longer afford its energy-intensive industrial development agenda. By 1979, facing economic bankruptcy, the import-substitution model was largely defunct. One of the key objectives of the 1980 coup was to create a favourable socio-political environ-ment for the implementation of vastly unpopular shock therapy programmes prescribed by the IMF and the World Bank. This meant not only suppressing labour union resistance and left-wing activism but also suspending parliamen-tary politics, characterised in this period by weak coalition governments and frequent legislative deadlocks. With lightning speed under the military's iron fist, social services and enterprises were deregulated, a series of privatisation schemes were launched, trade tariffs were brought down and Turkey's doors were swung open to foreign capital and investors.

The TSK itself made significant forays into the business world in this new period via the Armed Forces Pension Fund (*Ordu Yardımlaşma Kurumu*, OYAK). Another product of the 1960 coup, OYAK enjoyed tax exempt status, while its properties, revenues and debts benefited from all the rights and privi-leges of state properties.[43] As a major beneficiary of the post-1980 privatisation schemes, it became a giant conglomerate with more than 60 affiliated compa-nies involved in strategic sectors of the economy, from banking to energy, car manufacturing to construction. By the 2000s, it was one of Turkey's top three holding companies.[44]

But unrestrained integration into the international markets also imposed further sovereignty-reducing constraints on Turkey's guardians. The transi-tion to a free market economy did stimulate growth at first, but this did not last long. Frequent boom-and-bust cycles, balance of payments crises, run-away inflation, currency devaluations and widening income inequality increasingly characterised the period from the late 1980s onwards, during which the IMF came to play a tutelary role over Turkish politics. Between 1983 and 2002, Turkey's governments signed six standby agreements with the IMF, agree-ing to implement strict austerity measures. Growing dependence on volatile foreign capital, in turn, rendered direct military interventions unaffordable in both macroeconomic and political terms and therefore less desirable for an institution that valued its popular reputation.

Furthermore, it wasn't just the TSK or the secular bourgeoisie that ben-efited from the new economic system. Deregulations and privatisation schemes allowed successive centre-right governments starting with ANAP to redistribute public resources and rent to their own conservative base. As part of the export-driven growth strategy, incentives were given to small-and-medium sized enterprises, helping them turn from family-owned manufacturing operations into export giants. The result was the rise of a new class of pious Muslim entrepreneurs based not in the traditional centres of industry and finance, but in sleepy Anatolian towns, which experienced an economic boom.[45] Known as the 'Anatolian Tigers', this fledgling bourgeoisie established business lobbies – MÜSIAD (Independent Industrialists and Businessmen Association) in 1990 and TUSKON (Turkish Confederation of Businessmen and Industrialists) in 2005 – which served as a conservative counterbalance to TÜSİAD (Turkish Industry and Business Association), the main business lobby of the secular bourgeoisie, which was founded in 1971 and had enthusiastically supported the 1980 coup.

Meanwhile, the state's abdication of its social welfare provision duties as a result of the neoliberal turn created a vacuum that was filled in the Anatolian countryside and the peripheries of major metropolises by various Islamic networks and fraternities. One of these networks, the *Hizmet* (Service) Movement founded by Sufi cleric Fethullah Gülen emerged in this period as a faith-based social movement providing free dormitories and preparatory schools to low-income students preparing for university entrance exams. Many of these students eventually reached prominent positions in the private and public sector, providing the movement with a growing base of highly qualified loyalists. By the mid-1990s, Fethullah Gülen's disciples were running an international network of schools and businesses, rising within the state bureaucracy, enjoying close relations with the political establishment and harbouring a growing appetite to shape Turkey's future.

While the power of the Gülenists grew quietly, the same era saw the Welfare Party (*Refah Partisi*, RP) of seasoned Islamist politician Necmettin Erbakan explode onto the political scene. The RP was the latest in a series of Islamist parties in Turkey's *Milli Görüş* (National View) tradition, which shared ideological roots with Egypt's Muslim Brotherhood. In contrast to Gülen's emphasis on pragmatism over ideology, avoidance of confrontation with the guardians, and reluctance to engage in party politics, Erbakan's parties openly railed against Turkey's pro-Western orientation and state-enforced secularism. They were repeatedly outlawed by the Constitutional Court, but reopened under a new name. In the 1990s, the RP's sharp moralistic discourse against injustice and inequality and effective grassroots organisation in urban working-class neighbourhoods helped the party to capture the metropolitan municipalities of Istanbul and Ankara in the local elections of March 1994.[46] The party stunned the Kemalist establishment once again in the general election of December 1995, securing 22% of the vote and forming Turkey's first Islamist-led coalition government.

The rise of political Islam was a conscious legacy of the 1980 coup, and not merely its accidental by-product. To discourage political activism and counter leftist movements, the junta promoted – alongside consumerism and a depoliticised version of Kemalism, known as *Atatürkçülük*, which was little more than state and leader veneration – a mix of Turkish nationalism and Sunni Islam. This so-called 'Turkish–Islamic synthesis' emphasised the sanctity of state authority and loyalty to its traditional symbols.[47] As the head of the supposedly secular Turkish military and state, Kenan Evren led the way by quoting passages from the Quran in his speeches. The result was a sudden opening for religion in the public sphere, including a rapid rise in the number of state-run mosques,[48] the introduction of mandatory religion classes into school curricula, the expansion of clerical schools, known as *İmam Hatip* and new recruitment opportunities in the state bureaucracy for members of Islamic networks.[49]

Finally, we should mention the rise of the Kurdistan Workers' Party (*Partiya Karkerên Kurdistan*, PKK) and the beginning of the most violent phase yet in Turkey's Kurdish conflict as a brutal legacy of the 1980 coup. It was the junta's repression of non-violent Kurdish political alternatives, wholesale rejection of Kurdish cultural rights, and systematic abuse and torture of Kurdish civilians, most notoriously in the military prison of Diyarbakır, which after 1984 prepared the ground for an armed insurrection led by the Marxist–Leninist militant organisation. As the PKK turned into the defender of Kurdish rights and national aspirations in the eyes of many Kurds, it became the enemy number one in the eyes of the Turkish state and public. By the 1990s, in other words, the political legacies of the 1980 coup had already become the official justifications for preserving military tutelage. However, in the age of liberal triumphalism, with direct coups no longer as easily justifiable as in the Cold War, the public image of guardianship also needed a make-over. Post-modern times called for 'post-modern guardianship'.

The 1997 Coup and 'Post-modern Guardianship'

Post-modern guardianship, as envisioned by the influential generals and bureaucrats of the era, embodied two basic characteristics. First, it was based on a significantly broadened threat perception, formulated upon the ambiguous and sweeping description of national security, set out by the abovementioned 1983 law. Second, it focused on indirect ways of keeping politics and society in check, namely through the guardians' civilian associates. The broad-based reformulation of security threats allowed the guardians to maintain an open-ended list of internal and external enemies to pick from, while reducing Turkey's complex socio-economic problems to a narrow security paradigm. Referred to as the 'national security system' in a booklet published by the NSC General Secretariat in 1990, this approach further divorced the state from society, conceptualising the former as an innately sacred entity that required protection from an inherently menacing (or at best, immature) population.[50]

The two national security threats that received the most attention in the NSC meetings, the NSPDs and the mainstream media throughout the 1990s were ethnic separatism (*bölücülük*) and religious reaction (*irtica*). The former term was used to refer to Turkey's multi-faceted Kurdish conflict. Downplaying its socio-economic, political and humanitarian roots and implications, the conflict was presented in an official narrative of an international conspiracy by Turkey's enemies who were aiding and abetting terrorists to divide the Turkish homeland. In turn, this narrative was used to justify the state's heavy-handed policies and continued imposition of emergency laws in the Kurdish provinces. *İrtica*, on the other hand, had long been a byword for Islamic fundamentalism in the Kemalist lexicon, and could be used to refer to any socio-political movement that took Islam as its guiding reference.

Convinced that their predecessors' social engineering project had backfired and the rise of the Islamists constituted a direct threat to the regime, the senior cadre of the TSK decided that the RP government had to go. However, as Vice Admiral Güven Erkaya, a member of the NSC, put it, 'this time the job has to be done by the unarmed forces'.[51] These would be the generals' civilian associates in politics, academia, the judiciary, labour unions and other civil society organisations. Often under instruction from senior generals, these groups and individuals issued statements of alarm and organised public events, conferences and mass rallies to provoke the public sentiment against the threat of *irtica*.[52] Even though opinion polls consistently showed that only a very small minority of the population expressed desire to be governed by Sharia law, mainstream newspapers ran hysterical headlines and doomsday stories, some serviced directly by the military high command, heralding the collapse of the secular order.[53] In the words of Ismet Berkan, the Ankara correspondent of the daily *Radikal* at the time:

> Without the media, [the coup] would not have succeeded. The media almost voluntarily became part of the psychological operation [against the Welfare Party]. We were used and allowed ourselves to be used. We are all responsible for the 28 February process.[54]

Tensions boiled over in January 1997 when an RP-run district municipality in Ankara organised an event in support of Palestine, called 'Jerusalem night'. Posters of Hamas and Hezbollah adorned the walls of the venue, where amidst religious slogans the Iranian ambassador gave a speech that called on the Turkish people to obey 'the precepts of Islam'.[55] In response, the army moved tanks across the district. This was followed by an ultimatum to government issued by the senior generals during the NSC meeting on 28 February 1997. Speaking to journalists after the meeting, Vice Admiral Erkaya said, 'extremist religious currents present a vital threat to the future of Turkey. *İrtica* has become a more urgent matter than the PKK. I voiced this opinion at the NSC, and will do so again. Turkey is not without its owners'.[56]

After three months of resistance and attempted negotiation, Erbakan finally dissolved the government in June and stepped down as prime minister. In January 1998, the Constitutional Court outlawed the RP for anti-secular activities and banned its leaders from politics.[57] In the months that followed the NSC meeting, in what came to be known as the '28 February process', the generals pressured the parliament to roll back the influence of *İmam Hatip* schools. A dormant ban on wearing the Islamic headscarf in public universities was reinforced, while a semi-official department formed under the TSK chief of staff, known as the 'Western Working Group' (*Batı Çalışma Grubu*), was tasked with monitoring Islamist activities within the bureaucracy, civil society, universities and the media. The organisers of the 'Jerusalem night', including the Welfare district mayor, were tried in a State Security Court and sentenced to between four and seventeen years in prison. In 1999, Istanbul mayor Erdoğan received a ten-month prison sentence for 'inciting religious hatred' at a political rally. The same year, Fethullah Gülen, facing mounting legal and political pressures despite having originally supported the generals' 'soft coup', left Turkey for the United States on self-imposed exile.

Asked whether the military's ultimatum had meant a coup, General Erol Özkasnak, then secretary of the NSC, responded that coups were a thing of the past: 'The military of the 21st century acts in accordance to the 21st century'. But the ultimatum went down in history as the 'post-modern coup', labelled thus by General Çevik Bir, the deputy head of the TSK. One of the architects of the intervention, General Bir reportedly suggested that the military had merely carried out a 'wheel balancing on democracy'. In an NSC meeting in January 1999, the TSK Chief of Staff General Hüseyin Kıvrıkoğlu reminded Prime Minister Bülent Ecevit that 'the 28 February is not over. [. . .] If necessary, it will last a thousand years'.[58] At the turn of the millennium, post-modern guardianship appeared firmly entrenched in Turkey.

Notes

1. Mustafa Kemal briefly experimented with multiparty politics in 1930, ordering the creation of *Serbest Cumhuriyet Fırkası* (Free Republican Party, SCF) as a 'loyal opposition' only to have it disbanded after three months.
2. Danforth, 'Why a Turkish Dictator Let Himself Lose an Election'. Also see Chapter 3. The Transition to Competitive Politics in Turan, *Turkey's Difficult Journey to Democracy*.
3. Karpat, *Turkey's Politics*.
4. For two Turkish eye-witness accounts of this era, see Aydemir, *İkinci Adam*, and Arcayürek, *Açıklıyor*.
5. Tuğal, *Passive Revolution*, p. 257; Tezcür, *Muslim Reformers in Iran and Turkey*, p. 108.
6. Even though charismatic populists like Turgut Özal and Recep Tayyip Erdoğan can be considered exceptions to this rule, their political success also depended in large part to their parties' organisational capacities.
7. Duverger, *Political Parties*, p. 280.
8. Democracy is consolidated when it becomes 'the only game in town; when no one can imagine acting outside the democratic institutions, when all losers want

to do is to try again within the same institutions under which they have just lost'. (Przeworksi, *Democracy and the Market*, p. 23.)

9. In 1950, for instance, the DP won 55% of the overall vote but took 416 of the 487 seats (85%) in the parliament.

10. On paper, the presidency was a ceremonial office; however, presidents serving under this constitution (Atatürk, İsmet İnönü and Celal Bayar) played oversized roles due to their charismatic authority.

11. Göktepe, '1960 "Revolution" in Turkey and the British Policy Towards Turkey'.

12. Erdelhun's sentence was subsequently commuted to life imprisonment. He was granted presidential amnesty in 1964 and forced into retirement.

13. After the 1960 coup, the military allowed an elected government to reassume authority in 1961. After the 1971 intervention, the junta returned power to civilian authorities in 1973. The longest period of direct rule by a military junta was between the coup of 12 September 1980 and the general elections that took place on 6 November 1983.

14. See for example Brownlee, *Authoritarianism in an Age of Democratization*, pp. 515–32.

15. The political context of this law was the challenge Mustafa Kemal and the CHP were facing from senior commanders and leaders of the Anatolian resistance movement, such as General Kazım Karabekir and Rauf Orbay, who had just established the Progressive Republican Party. Forcing them to resign from the military was expected to limit their power. Otherwise, the law had limited practical impact, given that the top cadres of the CHP and the state bureaucracy were already dominated by former military officers at the time. As usual, Mustafa Kemal was above the norms: he continued to wear his uniform and maintained his military titles until 1927.

16. The reference in this law is to the first three articles of the 1961 and 1982 constitutions, defining Turkey's regime type as republic (Article 1), outlining its fundamental characteristics (Article 2) and emphasising its unitary structure on the basis of official language, flag and capital (Article 3). In the 1961 Constitution, Article 2 defined the Turkish Republic as 'a nationalistic, democratic, secular and social State governed by the rule of law, based on human rights and fundamental tenets set forth in the preamble'. Reflecting the restrictive socio-political environment of the post-1980 coup era, Article 2 of the 1982 Constitution included the phrases 'within the notions of public peace, national solidarity and justice' and 'loyal to the nationalism of Atatürk', while a new Article 4 declared that the first three articles 'shall not be amended, nor shall their amendment be proposed'.

17. See 'History' in the official website of the Turkish General Staff, http://www.tsk.tr.

18. Akkoyunlu, *Military Reform and Democratisation*, pp. 21–5.

19. İnsel, Ahmet and Ali Bayramoğlu, *Bir Zümre, Bir Parti*.

20. TBMM, *Darbeleri ve Muhtıraları Araştırma Komisyonu Raporu*; Birand, *The Generals' Coup in Turkey*.

21. Turkey's arms purchases from the US exceeded USD 6 billion in worth between 1992 and 1999. In 1997 alone, the US delivered more weapons to the Turkish military than in the entire period between 1950 and 1983 (Gabelnick et al., *Arming Repression*).

22. Akkoyunlu, 'Electoral Integrity in Turkey'.

23. Cizre, 'The Anatomy of the Turkish Military's Political Autonomy', pp. 157–8.

24. Cizre, *Almanac Turkey 2005*, p. 56

25. İnsel and Bayramoğlu, *Bir Zümre, Bir Parti*, p. 92.

26. The 1961 Constitution authorised the Council of Ministers to declare a state of emergency under the approval of the GNA. The 1982 Constitution required the Council of Ministers to meet under the chairmanship of the President and seek the opinion of the National Security Council before declaring emergencies and issuing decrees (Articles 119–21). See Göztepe, 'The Permanency of The State of Emergency in Turkey'.

27. Hirschl, *Towards Juristocracy*, p. 49.

28. Özbudun, *The Constitutional System of Turkey*, p. 32.

29. Akay, *Security Sector in Turkey*, pp. 15–17

30. 'Anayasa Mahkemesi 44 Yılda 24 Parti Kapattı', *Bianet*, 21 November 2007, http://www.bianet.org/bianet/siyaset/103054-anayasa-mahkemesi-44-yilda-24-parti-kapatti.

31. Article 143 of the 1982 Constitution established the SSCs 'to deal with security offenses against the indivisible integrity of the State with its territory and nation, the free democratic order, or against the Republic whose characteristics are defined in the Constitution, and offenses directly involving the internal and external security of the State'.

32. TBMM, *Darbeleri ve Muhtıraları Araştırma Komisyonu Raporu*, pp. 115–32.

33. For further discussion, see 'The transformation of the deep state into *the* state (1990–2000)' in Söyler, *The Turkish Deep State*, p. 143.

34. Vatanka, 'How Deep is Iran's State?'.

35. Belge, *Militarist Modernleşme*, pp. 617–18.

36. Law 306 dated May 25, 1961 on the Election of Parliamentary Deputies.

37. For more on factional power struggles within the military in the 1960s and 70s, see Esen, 'Praetorian Army in Action'.
38. Amendment to Article 11 of 1961 Constitution, http://www.tbmm.gov.tr/anayasa/anayasa61.htm. For a comparison of the 1961 and 1982 constitutions (in Turkish), see Parla, *Türkiye'de Anayasalar*.
39. Heper and Çınar, 'Parliamentary Government with a Strong President'.
40. The most memorable clash was over Turkey's participation in the Gulf War against Saddam Hussein in 1990, which Özal supported despite opposition from the military top brass. Faced with the president's intransigence, Chief of Staff Necip Torumtay resigned in protest and was replaced by the more acquiescent Doğan Güreş. This was the first instance a civilian politician openly insisted on his prerogatives and prevailed over the military since the 1980 coup.
41. Bilici, 'Sistem Tıkandı İstikamet Başkanlık Sistemi'; Çandar, 'Özal federasyonu istemedi ama tartıştı eyaleti istedi ama sustu'.
42. In June 2012, a report by the State Audit Board ruled the circumstances of Özal's death suspicious and that his death may have been caused by poisoning. In September, a state prosecutor ordered his remains to be exhumed for investigation. The results of the investigation were not made public.
43. 1961 OYAK Law, No. 205.
44. Akça, *Military-Economic Structure in Turkey*.
45. World Bank, *Rise of the Anatolian Tigers*.
46. Recep Tayyip Erdoğan rose to national prominence in this election, when he became the municipal mayor of Istanbul from the Welfare Party.
47. The geopolitical background for the promotion of the Turkish–Islamic synthesis was the US strategy to promote Sunni Islamist movements against communists in the 1980s. Other cases included the US-Saudi-Pakistani support for the mujahedeen against the Soviet occupation of Afghanistan, and the Israeli facilitation of the rise of Hamas against the secular-nationalist Fatah in Palestine.
48. As many as 1500 mosques were built every year in the 1980s. By 1988 there was a mosque for every 857 people. Kasaba, *The Cambridge History of Turkey*, p. 390.
49. First established by the Democrat Party as vocational schools to train religious personnel, the curricula of *İmam Hatips* were eventually expanded and restrictions on their students to take the university entrance exams were lifted. As a result, for pious Muslims, *İmam Hatips* became competitive alternatives to regular public high schools. The number enrolments in these institutions rose from 34,570 in 1974 to 511,502 in 1997. Erdoğan himself is an *İmam Hatip* alum. See Çakır et al., *İmam Hatip Liseleri*.

50. MGK, *Devletin Kavram ve Kapsamı*.

51. The statement was reported by then editor-in-chief of *Hürriyet* newspaper, Ertuğrul Özkök in his column on 20 December 1996.

52. For an account of the involvement of five prominent civil society organisations (two labour unions, two merchant organisations and one employers' union, known as the 'Gang of Five') in this process, see Baydur, *Bizim Çete*.

53. Between August 1996 and April 1997, the daily *Milliyet* ran 16 headlines, which reported a stern 'warning' to the government – six in the month of April alone. See section on the role of the media in the 1997 coup in TBMM, *Darbeleri ve Muhtıraları Araştırma Komisyonu Raporu*, pp. 969–79.

54. 'Medya olmasaydı 28 Şubat olmazdı', *Yeni Şafak*, 16 April 2012.

55. Eligür, *The Mobilisation of Political Islam in Turkey*, p. 219.

56. 'Erbakan'ın MGK'daki zor anları', *Milliyet*, 12 August 1997.

57. The ruling was eventually upheld by the European Court of Human Rights. Case of 'Refah Partisi (Welfare Party) and Others vs. Turkey', Grand Chamber ruling, 13 February 2003.

58. 'Kıvrıkoğlu'dan Ecevit'e: "28 Şubat daha bitmedi!"', *Habertürk*, 28 February 2012.

Part III

CONTESTATION

5

THE STRANGLING OF THE REPUBLICAN
PILLAR IN IRAN

Neither the laws nor the officials of the state have any legitimacy unless and until they meet with the vali-ye faqih's approval.

– Ayatollah Mesbah Yazdi

If I retreated, I retreated against the system I believed in.

– Mohammad Khatami

The institutional tension and imbalance between the Islamic and the republican pillars of the IRI was the central issue of the Khatami presidency. The aim of the reformists was to strengthen the presidency and the Majles vis-à-vis the Leader and the Guardian Council. Khatami argued that this was Khomeini's true legacy. Led by intellectuals who were part of the 1979 revolution and the IRI's first decade, the reformists had little appetite for another revolution. They wanted change to come from within the system. But hopes for gradual transformation, briefly raised following sweeping electoral victories for reformist candidates, were soon dashed as the traditionalist guardians demonstrated none of Khatami's restraints and went on to suppress the popular challenge to the status quo. Khatami's reluctance to avoid instability ultimately sealed the fate of the movement, alongside the guardians' intransigence, the reformists' inability to appeal to the working class and unfavourable economic and geopolitical conditions.

A more unexpected and destabilising challenge to the tutelary establishment came from Khatami's populist neo-conservative successor, Mahmoud

Ahmadinejad. Eager to avoid the type of institutional clashes that characterised the Khatami presidency, the traditionalists mistook Ahmadinejad as a little-known layman who would remain loyal to the Leader and the *velayat-e faqih* system and supported him in two presidential elections. Yet driven by a dogged determination and sense of divine destiny, and displaying none of his predecessor's concerns for regime stability, Ahmadinejad turned, especially after 2009, into a fierce critic of clerical tutelage and a champion of the powers of the presidency.

The traditionalists' attempt to subdue the reformist and the neo-conservative challenges led them to systematically undermine the regime's republican pillar. As evidence of organised electoral manipulation mounted, the popular expectation of a just and predictable, if heavily constrained, voting process gradually eroded. Widespread belief in massive fraud committed under the supervision of the regime's top guardians in the 2009 presidential election dealt a major blow to the IRI's democratic legitimacy. In an environment of institutional paranoia and geopolitical crisis, with elections no longer serving as a mechanism of managing factional rivalries and popular pressures, the Islamic Republic veered deeper into insecurity and autocracy.

Change from Within: The Khatami Presidency

The Intellectual Discourse of Reform

A critical reappraisal of the *velayat-e faqih* system had started in earnest during the early 1990s as part of the Islamic left's intellectual evolution. These criticisms formed the core of the reform movement's intellectual discourse, and were important because they came from within the system – from theologians, philosophers and political activists, who had supported the revolution and were influential during the IRI's first decade and thus implicitly claimed the authority to comment on its trajectory in the absence of the system's founder. For this reason, they presented an acute ideological challenge to the traditionalist interpretation of the institutional architecture of the IRI and promises of the revolution.

The origins of the reform movement can be traced to the emergence in 1991 of *Kiyan*, the leading religious intellectual journal of the decade, which provided a platform for debate among influential philosophers like Abdolkarim Soroush, Mohammad Mojtahed Shabestari and Mohsen Kadivar. *Kiyan* itself was a continuation of *Kayhan-e Farhangi*, the first major monthly journal on culture, literature and philosophy in the Islamic Republic, which was banned in 1990 for publishing a series provocative articles written by Abdolkarim Soroush, titled 'The Theoretical Contraction and Expansion of Religious Knowledge'. Educated in Tehran and London, Soroush was a supporter of Khomeini in the 1970s, and upon his return to Iran after the revolution, served in the seven-member committee overseeing the implementation of the leader's Cultural Revolution.

In his 'Theory of Contraction and Expansion', which forms the basis of his philosophy as well as that of religious revivalism in post-Khomeini Iran, Soroush tackled the dilemma of change and perfection in religion. Stressing the impossibility of grasping the totality of religion, Soroush argued that 'religious knowledge' (*marifat-e dini*) is a form of human knowledge; sincere but fallible and therefore subject to change.[1] He was therefore critical of the presentation of religious knowledge as sacred and absolute.[2] Building on this premise, Soroush claimed that Islamic jurisprudence (*fiqh*) constitutes only one aspect of religious knowledge and cannot singularly provide the basis of 'just government'.[3] Identifying justice as a 'meta-religious concept',[4] he suggested that for a modern administration to be just, it had to derive its sources both from within religion, including *kalam* (discursive theology) and *akhlaq* (ethics) alongside *fiqh*, and from outside of it (i.e., modern sciences and secular knowledge), ultimately making the case for 'religious democracy' that is based on pluralism, human rights and the rejection of dogma.[5]

While Soroush argued that religious knowledge was variable, Shabestari emphasised its limitations and the need to seek secular sources to complement it.[6] As a *mojtahed* who, by his own claim, worked strictly within the boundaries of Islamic tradition, Shabestari presented a religious case for separating the divine from the worldly and challenged the legitimate authority of absolute guardianship.[7] Whereas Shabestari was indirect and non-confrontational in his critiques, Mohsen Kadivar, who was also a *mojtahed*, took on Khomeini's formulation of the absolute guardianship of the jurisprudent directly and refuted it openly from the perspective of *fiqh*. In *Government by Mandate*, the second volume of his trilogy on political theology, Kadivar launched 'a frontal and unabashed attack' on Khomeini's theory, concluding that it is 'neither intuitively obvious, nor rationally necessary':

It is neither a requirement of religion, nor a necessity for denomination (*mazhab*). It is neither a part of the general principles of Shiism (*osoul*), nor a component of detailed observances (*forou'*). It is, by near consensus of Shiite *ulama*, nothing more than a jurisprudential minor hypothesis and its proof is contingent upon reasons adduced from the four categories of Quran, Traditions, Consensus and Reason.[8]

Besides such philosophical challenges, overtly political criticisms of the system and the Leader by dissident clerics, lay intellectuals and political activists became more vocal and commonplace following Khatami's election. In November 1997, Grand Ayatollah Ahmad Azari-Qomi published an open letter blaming Khamenei for sanctioning extra-judicial killings and torture and the pervasive culture of corruption and moral decadence within the regime. He went on to propose dividing the leadership into two departments, with Khamenei being responsible for political affairs and Grand Ayatollah Montazeri for religious affairs.[9] For his part, Montazeri openly questioned the constitutionality of Khamenei's extensive authority, arguing that it should be limited to a supervisory role, and criticised the GC's interference in elections.[10] Former IRGC officer-turned-dissident journalist Akbar Ganji was more blunt and provocative. In a public lecture shortly after Khatami's election, Ganji labelled the traditionalist supporters of the regime 'totalitarian Islamofascists'.[11]

It is important to stress that Khatami typically disapproved of the tone and the openness of the criticisms and attacks levied against the regime and the Leader. He preferred a less confrontational approach that emphasised the loyalty of the reform movement to *velayet-e faqih* and the legacy of Khomeini.[12] Frequently stressing Khomeini's support for republicanism and mass participation in politics, Khatami attempted to present the goals of the reform movement – emphasised as establishing rule of law, strengthening civil society (*jame'e-ye madani*) and defining the limits of the 'guardianship society' (*jame'e-ye velai*) – as necessary for the fulfilment of the charismatic leader's vision and the promises of the revolution. He summarised these goals in his inaugural speech in the following words:

Establishment of the rule of law is an Islamic, revolutionary and national obligation, and an absolute imperative, which requires a conducive and enabling environment, as well as a legal means and instruments coupled with public involvement and assistance.[13]

Shakibi notes that Khatami's position regarding the power and the responsibilities of the Leader remained ambiguous throughout his presidency:

> His public stance indicated support for the broad supervisory role that permits intervention on decisive and politically paralysing issues in the hope that the Leader would support those positions on which Khatami and the proponents of politics of change were attached given their electoral success. Yet, the practical consequences of his rhetoric and programme would result in a Leadership position similar to that propagated by Montazeri.[14]

This ambiguity may have been a result of Khatami's expressed faith in the hybrid system as formulated by Khomeini – that ultimately the Islamic and republican pillars could co-exist and work in a harmonious fashion. For this, he believed, the constitution had to be fully implemented, and the guardians had to accept institutional checks on their existing prerogatives. He would be disappointed.

Khatami wanted to reform the IRI from within, without breaking the system.[15] In other words, while he dared to initiate the Iranian *perestroika*, he did not wish to go down in history as Iran's Gorbachev; the man responsible for the collapse of the system that he tried to improve. At critical junctures when he suspected that the forces unleashed by the reform movement would challenge the core institution of the IRI's hybrid regime, he consistently refrained from confronting the guardians, which ultimately sealed the fate of his presidency and the reform movement itself.

The Reformist Surge and the Traditionalist Backlash

By the mid-1990s, as the Rafsanjani administration was grappling with the complexities of economic development, a growing number of observers inside and outside Iran noticed the simmering popular discontent caused by the lack of political reform.[16] It was this overwhelming demand for political change, expressed primarily by the country's urban lower-middle and middle classes, youth population and women, that carried Khatami into office in 1997 with an unprecedented popular mandate. The outcome took the traditional-ist guardians by surprise: Khatami's resounding defeat of Nateq-Nuri (70% against 25%) despite the Leader's presumed support for the latter was coupled with the high turnout of 80% (up 30% from the previous election). The impact of the reformist victory and the extent of the desire for change soon became apparent as Khatami's call for popular participation in politics found spirited response in increased civil society activism. NGOs began to emerge in large numbers and student movements were mobilised into vocal advocacy and political pressure groups.[17] Under Culture Minister Ata'ollah Mohajerani (for-mer Rafsanjani vice president and a founder of *Kargozaran*), reformist news-papers and journals proliferated, criticising and challenging official viewpoints represented in the traditionalist-controlled TV and radio.[18]

Riding on the back of this popular wave, the reformists swept the local council elections held in February 1999 and the Majles elections in February and May 2000. The 1999 elections for city, district and village councils were particularly significant as they were the first to be organised in the IRI despite being stipulated in the 1979 Constitution. Also notable was the fact that a parliamentary commission had handled the vetting of candidates, instead of the GC. With this election, the authority of appointing town mayors was transferred from the interior ministry to elected councils. As such, the local elections symbolised a key step towards realising Khatami's vision of grassroots participation in decision-making.[19] 'With the implementation of the provision on municipal councils', the president said, 'the people will be given the oppor-tunity to restore their rights. [This] will help remove the chronic mentality of law breaking'.[20]

Following on the success of the local elections, the victory in the sixth Majles elections gave the reformist Participation Front (*Moshakerat*) 189 of the 290 seats (as opposed to 54 for the traditionalist Society of the Militant Clergy and 42 for *Kargozaran*). This appeared at the time as a turning point for the balance of power among rival factions, and more importantly, between the two pillars of the IRI hybrid regime. It was not to be. The reformists were denied the veto-busting two-thirds majority they looked to have secured after the Guardian Council strategically annulled a number of reformist victories in provinces where the potential for unrest was low or easily containable. This signalled the beginning of a backlash by the traditionalist guardians, who regarded the reformist surge as an internal coup d'état and realised the existing filters of the electoral system had failed to block it.

By this point, with the traditionalists having already shaken off their initial surprise at the outcome of the 1997 presidential election, the reformists were facing growing resistance, obstruction and intimidation from their opponents in the guardianship institutions. Like Khatami, the Leader and his traditionalist supporters had also learned from the experience of Gorbachev and the Soviet *perestroika* the dangers of opening up the political system to accommodate wider criticism and opposition, which they were determined to resist. Consequently, while Khatami was focusing on mobilising the masses for increased political participation, the Leader put his weight behind strengthening his personal control over key state institutions through strategic appointments and representatives. The judiciary, in particular, emerged as the vanguard of tutelary resistance. Politicised courts, populated by former Ministry of Intelligence and Security interrogators recruited by the head of the judiciary, Ayatollah Mohammad Yazdi, took upon themselves the task of silencing the reformist press and harassing the leading reformists.

Within a couple of years of Khatami taking office, many of the newspapers that had opened after 1997 were banned. Montazeri was placed under house arrest shortly after challenging Khamenei. In February 1998, the Special Court of the Clergy sentenced former Tehran mayor and *Kargozaran* founder Gholamhossein Karbaschi to two years in prison on corruption charges. In April 1999, in a trial that attracted considerable international attention, the same court sentenced Mohsen Kadivar to eighteen months in prison for spreading propaganda against the regime.[21] In November, Abdollah Nuri was found guilty of insulting Ayatollah Khomeini. The attempt to suppress and intimidate the movement took a violent turn with the physical attacks and harassment of pro-reform students, activists and clerics by state-backed vigilante groups, as well as the murders of outspoken artists and intellectuals.[22] The investigation and the ensuing trial of the intelligence agents, whose involvement in a spate of high-profile killings in late 1998 was admitted to by regime officials after sustained public pressure, were watered down and failed to disclose the full extent of senior officials' involvement.[23] The assassination attempt that permanently disabled Saeed Hajjarian, who had worked to uncover the murders, shortly after the Majles election in 2000, was a clear message that those behind the campaign of intimidation were not daunted by the judicial process.

The perpetrators of these acts took courage from hardliner traditionalist clerics who openly sanctioned the use of violence against the opposition. Ayatollah Mesbah Yazdi, for instance, argued that the enemies of Islam 'present principles such as tolerance and compromise as absolute values while violence is regarded as a non-value. [. . .] The taboo that every act of violence is bad and every act of tolerance is good must be broken'.[24] They would also be encouraged by the fact that Khamenei himself did not explicitly denounce violence. For his part, aside from expressing his sympathy and support for the victims of violence and condemning its perpetrators, Khatami was neither able to prevent these attacks from occurring, nor ensure that the trials were conducted in a just and transparent manner. In the absence of an organised party structure and meaningful support from inside the guardianship pillar, Khatami's faith in the ability of loosely coordinated civil society activism to instigate change appeared increasingly naïve.

Against Hajjarian's consistent advice to push for permanent institutional reform while the traditionalists had yet to figure out an effective strategy to thwart the reformist challenge, Khatami was reluctant to confront the traditionalist guardians openly. In August 2000, he missed an important opportunity to start a debate to define the limits of the Leader's authority, when Khamenei took advantage of the legal ambiguity surrounding his powers to issue a governmental decree (*hokm-e hokumati*) ordering the newly formed Majles to stop deliberating a new press law. A failed initiative in early 1999 to make the *bonyads* answerable to the Ministry of Finance was the only (rather timid) attempt at structural reform during Khatami's first term. By the time he finally came to accept in his second term that some confrontation was unavoidable and perhaps necessary, he was already facing a united guardianship front determined to contain the threat posed by the reformist-dominated republican pillar.

As the threat from the reformist camp increased, the GC, with the Leader's blessing, came to fulfil its role as the first line of defence against the bills proposed by the reformist Majles. But it was the Expediency Council, tasked with mediating disputes between the GC and the Majles, which served as the institution that ultimately tipped the scale against the reformists by siding with the

GC at every critical juncture. At the head of the EC was Rafsanjani, who in the early 2000s had once again switched sides to cooperate with the traditionalists, after facing scathing personal attacks and criticisms from the reformist camp. Khatami did not approve of these attacks but nor did he attempt to contain them until Rafsanjani had moved closer to the traditionalist camp. With the EC's support, the GC successfully struck down two major bills aimed at shifting the institutional balance of power in the republican pillar's favour. Introduced in September 2002, the first of the 'twin bills' was an attempt to roll back the supervisory powers that the GC had assumed after 1991. The second bill was intended to enhance the president's authority as the protector of the constitution on the basis of Article 113.

Following the bills' rejection, some reformists suggested that the president should resign in protest and as a tactical push for national referendum. In response, Rahim Safavi, commander of the IRGC, issued a thinly veiled threat of violent reprisal.[25] Withdrawing the bills from the parliament in April 2004, Khatami wrote a letter expressing dashed hopes of reform and frustration at the recalcitrance of the GC.[26] The letter was remarkable not so much as an admission of defeat, which had become fairly clear by that point, but rather as an example of Khatami's unrealistic expectation, maintained until very late, that the guardians would give up power willingly.

The loss of hope among the reformists translated into political apathy and dwindling participation, depriving Khatami of the movement's most valued asset. The first electoral defeat came in the local elections of 2003, in which many reformist councillors were replaced by traditionalists, as well as members of the emerging neo-conservative faction, including Mahmoud Ahmadinejad, who became the mayor of Tehran. In January 2004, in the run up to the elections for the seventh Majles, the GC disqualified 3,600 out of nearly 8,200 candidates, including eighty sitting reformist MPs. With an expanded budget approved by the EC, the GC was able to employ thousands of 'investigators' to produce incriminatory evidence against potential candidates, a capability it had lacked in 2000.[27] Khatami once again refrained from challenging the guardians when he failed to support the 123 reformist MPs, who had threatened to resign in protest and demanded rescheduling of the elections. Acquiescing to the Leader's wishes, Khatami 'had unwillingly become complicit in the emasculation of the republican part of the IRI'.[28] The subsequent defeat in the Majles election was followed by the presidential election in June 2005, which large portions of the demoralised reformist base boycotted instead of voting for Rafsanjani or his populist neo-conservative rival.

Behind the Defeat: Structure and Agency

In explaining the defeat of the reform movement, the institutional obstructions put up by the traditionalist guardians outlined above loom large. But also important was the wider socio-economic and geopolitical context in which the reformists had to operate, as well as the agency of Khatami-as-leader. The international environment in the late 1990s and the early 2000s did not facilitate Khatami's reform attempts. Given oil's predominance in the Iranian economy, the historical lows in petroleum prices experienced during Khatami's presidency forced the reformists to work with a contracted budget. As fallout from the global economic slowdown spearheaded by the Asian financial crisis, Iran's oil export revenues fell by nearly 20% and non-oil exports by 7% during 1997–98.[29]

Despite some success in taming runaway inflation, managing an average annual growth of 5.6% between 2001 and 2005 and starting a programme of diversification from oil, the government's economic performance did not translate into electoral support. Unemployment remained high. The working class saw little tangible improvement in their lot. Khatami's economic programme remained ambiguous, especially during his first term, in part due to the necessity of balancing between his liberal and statist supporters. The emphasis on economic liberalism during his second term did not make the government particularly popular among the working class. Ultimately, economic policies were overshadowed by the overriding rhetoric of political change. Although promoting social justice was articulated as one of the Participation Front's goals, it did not constitute a major policy area or a prominent rhetorical point.[30] Preoccupied with the philosophy of political change, the reformist leadership appeared distant to the day-to-day economic struggles of the urban working class and rural population. As a result, the movement's popular base became limited to the urban middle class. Putting social justice at the forefront of his platform, Ahmadinejad was able to garner support from those classes that were ignored under both Rafsanjani and Khatami.

In foreign affairs, Khatami's policy of gradual rapprochement with the West, especially the US, met with resistance from the traditionalists and was left largely unreciprocated by Washington. Holding foreign policy firmly in his reserved domain, the Leader provided Khatami with a degree of autonomy at the beginning of his first term, taking credit for his fleeting achievements, while capitalising on his failures. Despite the budding strategic cooperation and intelligence sharing between the US and Iran after the 11 September 2001 attacks and during the US invasion of Afghanistan, Iran's classification as part of an 'Axis of Evil' by the US President George W. Bush in February 2002 undermined Khatami's position at home and abroad. The 2003 US occupation of Iraq freed Iran of a historical rival in Saddam Hussein and inadvertently exposed Iraq to greater Iranian influence, which benefited mostly Khatami's successor as well as the IRGC. But the heavy presence of US troops surrounding Iran became a cause for alarm for the regime. The heightened militaristic rhetoric against the Islamic Republic coming from the US and Israel during this period rendered Khatami's policy of reconciliation redundant, culminating in Ahmadinejad's policy of confrontation.

Khatami preached a 'dialogue among civilisations' at a time when the dominant foreign policy thinking in the United States was shaped by the 'clash of civilisations' thesis and the dichotomous worldview of the American neo-conservatives that assigned to the US an enlightening mission in the Middle East.[31] The George W. Bush administration's attempts to justify military occupations in the region through the rhetoric of liberty and democracy were detrimental to the legitimacy of local struggles for democracy and civil rights across the region, including in Iran. Moreover, the spread of pro-Western colour revolutions in the former Soviet republics gave Iran's traditionalist guardians an extra cause for caution and resistance to Khatami's reform agenda. The Leader, the IRGC commanders and the traditionalist clergy frequently stressed the need to remain vigilant against foreign-backed plots, which Khamenei referred to as 'soft overthrow' (*barandazi-ye narm*).[32] It was also in this light that the traditionalists viewed and responded to the popular support expressed for the Green Movement and the mass demonstrations that followed the presidential election in June 2009.

Despite all the economic, geopolitical and institutional woes that the reformists had to contend with, it appears in hindsight that events could have taken a different turn had Khatami chosen not to retreat against his rivals at each of the several critical junctures that he faced as president. As early as in

1999, at the height of the student protests that were triggered by the closure of the reformist *Salam* newspaper and that quickly spread across all the major Iranian cities, one of the popular slogans alongside 'Freedom of thought, always, always' and 'Khamenei must go!' was 'Khatami, where are you?' Unable to calm down or respond to the protestors, and in fear of being responsible for throwing the country into anarchy, the reformist leadership had chosen not to stand behind the students, even as they were being attacked by the *Hezbollahi* vigilantes and the *Basij* militia. During a heated exchange in a ceremony marking the student day at the University of Tehran in December 2004, students angry with Khatami's failure to stand up for the thousands of reformist candidates banned from the seventh Majles elections chanted 'Khatami, Khatami, shame on you!' and 'Incompetent Khatami'. In response, the beleaguered president admitted:

> If I retreated, I retreated against the system I believed in. I considered it necessary saving the established order. [. . .] Either we had to hold the elections or face riots. [. . .] I didn't consider it in the country's interests that riots erupt.[33]

In the end, Khatami's fear of civil strife and institutional collapse of the IRI tutelary democracy led him to grudgingly accept the systematic suppression of democracy by the tutelary establishment. Some observers suggested that this fear was exaggerated and successfully manipulated by the traditionalists. Writing during the standoff over the disqualification of reformist candidates by the GC in January 2004, Ali Ansari argued that the proponents of change should resist the temptation to compromise and make good on their threat to resign en masse:

> Only this way can they potentially re-energise a public hungry for genuine, decisive leadership. In short, they will have to call the hardliners' bluff, by ignoring the much over-used threat that confrontation could lead to the disintegration of the Iranian state through civil strife.[34]

By this time, however, many supporters of the president had given up not only on Khatami but also on the possibility of reform from within the system. Boycotting the Majles election, the main student organisation, *Daftar-e Tahkim-e Vahdat*, argued:

Unless elections lead to systematic and fundamental change they will only legitimise autocracy. [. . .] The constitution of the Islamic Republic in its present form, with institutions such as the Guardian Council, the Expediency Council and [the office of] the Leader leaves no further room for democratisation.[35]

In an open letter titled 'The Tragedy of Khatami', jailed dissident Hashem Aghajari warned about the possible collapse of the hybrid regime:

In a very short period of time, the democratic face of the Iranian constitution is going to be turned into an autocratic face. [. . .] Alongside this comical repetition of history we are also witnessing a tragedy: the tragedy of Khatami. [. . .] During the six years that have elapsed for the reformist government and the four years of the reformist parliament, because of a lack of will and courage great opportunities were missed.[36]

An Unexpected Challenge: The Ahmadinejad Presidency

Mesbah Yazdi and the Neo-conservative Project

Despite being outdone by the Leader and the traditionalists, during the eight years of Khatami presidency, the reformists demonstrated that a popular movement could pose a significant threat to the guardians and the *velayet-e faqih* system by gaining control of the republican institutions. The reformists were defeated, but not without inflicting considerable damage on the guardians, whose increasingly blatant meddling in the electoral and legislative processes brought the democratic legitimacy and the feasibility of the hybrid system under greater popular scrutiny. On balance, the instability caused by sustained conflict between the two pillars did not seem to benefit the guardians. Thus, towards the end of Khatami's second term the traditionalist guardians set out to look for a successor to Khatami, who could both compete in popular politics and also remain loyal to the Leader.

The most resourceful of these guardians was Ayatollah Mesbah Yazdi. A founder of the influential Haqqani seminary in Qom (along with his ally Ahmad Jannati, the head of the GC), Mesbah Yazdi was one of the fiercest critics of the drive for political reform and pluralism under Khatami.[37] A firm believer in the absolute guardianship of the jurisprudent, he claimed that the Leader derived his legitimacy directly from the Twelfth Imam and delegated authority out of his own volition.[38] People, according to Mesbah Yazdi, played no role in legitimising the political system:

> In our view, the validity of the laws enacted in the Islamic Republic of Iran stems from the orders and the signature of the *vali-ye fiqh*. Without his approval, a matter has no validity. [. . .] Had he not signed it, [the constitution] would have been null. Even if everyone had voted for it, it would have no legal or religious validity. [. . .] [Imam] orders you to vote and elect a president; presidential elections derive their validity from his will. He saw it expedient in the current conditions for people to vote.[39]

Mesbah Yazdi openly declared his opposition to the institutional division of powers in the IRI, arguing that Islamic jurisprudence entitled the Leader to control all three branches of government: the executive, legislative and the judiciary.[40] In his view, the conflict between the two pillars of the hybrid system had to be resolved in favour of the divinely appointed guardians.[41] At the same time, however, Mesbah Yazdi was also aware of the practical importance of popular politics and the necessity to devise more subtle and effective methods of controlling public opinion. His formula entailed promoting a populist counter-narrative to the reformist discourse based on a sense of public nostalgia for the moral purity and the religious fervour of the martyrs of the revolution, a spirit embodied in the veterans of the war with Iraq and especially the *Basij* militia.

This narrative was embodied by the neo-conservative faction that had emerged in the mid-1990s and grew in prominence towards the end of Khatami's presidency. This faction consisted mainly of non-clerical second-generation revolutionaries and particularly veterans of the war with Iraq, who became active inside the security and intelligence sectors in the 1990s. Their worldview combined the Islamic left's social justice-based economic agenda and anti-imperialist stance in foreign policy with the traditionalists' strict views on religious morality and defence of traditional jurisprudence.[42] A representative of this faction, a former member of the *Basij* and the mayor of Tehran since 2003, Mahmoud Ahmadinejad seemed to fit the bill of a true loyalist and a sincere populist. Ahmadinejad had become Yazdi's follower in the early 2000s as the two shared a millenarian belief in the imminent return of the Hidden Imam. Mesbah Yazdi was the only high-profile cleric to endorse Ahmadinejad openly at a time when few people gave the little-known mayor much chance in the 2005 election. Encouraging his followers to support the young and eccentric candidate, he declared that participating in the elections was a religious duty. Speaking of the Rafsanjani and Khatami administrations, he said, 'we have not had an Islamic government yet, but we would like to have that government now and that means we cannot afford not voting'.[43]

Ahmadinejad's second place showing in the first round, behind Rafsanjani and just ahead of reformist former Majles speaker Mehdi Karroubi, and his convincing victory over Rafsanjani by securing 61% of the vote in the second round, thus came as a surprise to many Iranians and foreign observers alike, but not so much to Mesbah Yazdi.[44] Many reformists had chosen to boycott the election. Turnout was 63% and 59% in the two rounds respectively, compared with 80% in 1997. The reformist vote that did come was divided between Karroubi, Mostafa Moin and Mohsen Mehralizadeh. It was also rumoured that the Leader, who initially favoured Mohammad Baqer Qalibaf, had switched his support shortly before the first round and put his resources behind Ahmadinejad.[45]

As the Khamenei–Rafsanjani rivalry resurfaced ahead of the second round, the traditionalist guardians mobilised the mosque networks, the IRGC and *Basij* volunteers in support of Ahmadinejad.[46] Shunned by the reformists, the traditionalists and the neo-conservatives alike, Rafsanjani spent most of his campaign lobbying for alliances in Tehran and Qom. In contrast, an energetic Ahmadinejad visited the urban poor and toured the neglected countryside to deliver his message of social justice. Significantly, his campaign featured conspicuously few references praising the clerical leadership of the IRI, including Khomeini. Ironically, although backed by the traditionalist guardians, the victory of this unassuming man against the Iran's wealthiest cleric and ultimate regime insider was also an expression of popular discontent with the clerical elite.

Ahmadinejad's first term did not provide the type of dramatic institutional and ideological conflicts that had characterised the Khatami presidency. Behind the carefully maintained image of unity and harmony, however, tensions between the traditionalists and the neo-conservatives – and the two pillars of the regime – were brewing. A key point of discord in this period, which would become a major cause of the breakdown of relations between the president and the Leader during Ahmadinejad's second term, was over the appointment of cabinet ministers. Constitutionally within the president's authority, it had become commonplace for the Leader to interfere in the appointment process. In a surprisingly defiant attempt to enforce his presidential prerogatives, shortly after being elected, Ahmadinejad fired the chiefs of four major public banks and went on to form his cabinet and senior administration without consulting Khamenei. Most of his appointees were second generation revolutionaries: former IRGC members, *Basijis*, intelligence officials and prison administrators outside the core circle of the revolutionary elite and with little or no experience in government. He also picked loyal disciples of Mesbah Yazdi from the Haqqani seminary for key positions.[47] Faced with this unexpected affront, the traditionalists in the Majles joined forces with Rafsanjani and the EC to block four of the president's nominees, including three nominations for the oil ministry.[48]

In the process, it became apparent that populism – at least the type Ahmadinejad represented – and loyalty to the tutelary establishment did not sit well together. The president's sharp attacks against Iran's 'oil mafia' and 'economic aristocrats' (targeting in particular Rafsanjani), together with his redistributive policies that included heavy injection of oil funds into the economy, increased subsidies and cash hand-outs for low income families, drew the ire of the traditionalists and the modernists as well as some of his own followers.[49] Nor were these factions particularly pleased with Ahmadinejad's confrontational anti-Western rhetoric, finding his conduct of foreign policy imprudent and too independently driven. The Leader's distrust in the president's policies and his instinct to protect and control the clerical establishment became visible in October 2005 when he issued a decree to expand the supervisory powers of the Expediency Council over the judiciary, the executive and the legislative branches.[50] He also instructed the EC to prepare an economic programme parallel to that of the president's. Furthermore, the establishment of the Strategic Council for Foreign Relations (*Shora-ye Rahbordi-ye Ravabet-e Khareji*, SCFR) in 2006 with another decree from the Leader was meant as a check on the president's ambitious forays into foreign policy.[51]

Another controversial aspect of Ahmadinejad's presidency for the clerical establishment, leading to his eventual confrontation with the Leader, was the millenarian propaganda disseminated by the president's circle about the purported link between Ahmadinejad and the Twelfth Imam. In contrast to Khatami, who had shunned religious dogma and emphasised reason (*aql*), Ahmadinejad and his mentor Mesbah Yazdi passionately embraced it.[52] Mesbah Yazdi declared Ahmadinejad's 2005 victory a miraculous event and part of a divine plan.[53] Another cleric close to Mesbah Yazdi, Ayatollah Meshkini claimed that all members of the seventh Majles were approved by the Twelfth Imam.[54] Ahmadinejad often commented that his presidency had ushered in a new 'wave of spirituality' (*mowj-e manaviyat*) across the region.[55] He stirred controversy after his address to the UN General Assembly in September 2005 when he claimed that he was surrounded by a halo of light – a reference to divine grace – and that an invisible force had fixated the delegates' attention on him. He paid frequent visits to an obscure shrine in Jamkaran, south Tehran, where, according to popular legend, the Hidden Imam would reappear.[56] He spoke with conviction of the Mehdi's imminent return and said that the main duty of his government was to prepare for his arrival.[57]

For all its bizarre and superstitious characteristics, the neo-conservatives' emphasis on miraculous occurrences and prophetic expectations had distinct populist and pragmatic elements. By suggesting a link between himself and the Twelfth Imam, Ahmadinejad was effectively circumventing the clerical guardians to lay direct claim on divinely ordained guardianship. The elevation of Jamkaran as an alternative pilgrimage site to the traditional Shi'a shrines in Qom and Mashhad was one way in which the neo-conservatives attempted to popularise a messianic version of Shiism that was deeply mystical and occultist. Naturally, the 'Jamkaranisation of Shiism', as reformist cleric Majid Ansari called it, by the followers of Ahmadinejad and the small cohort of clerics around Mesbah Yazdi, drew the ire of senior clergy and triggered accusations of 'deviation'.[58] Mesbah Yazdi, too, increasingly became a target of clerical criticism, as his position came to represent an affront against the hybrid regime in favour of absolute guardianship.

These tensions were carefully managed between 2005 and 2009. Indeed, the overall record of the neo-conservative and traditionalist dominated seventh Majles displayed a marked loyalty to the authority of the Leader. Most vividly, in 'an astounding feat of self-limitation', the Majles in December 2008 undermined its own authority by relinquishing its theoretical right to oversee the financial and political activities of the Leader, the GC and the EC.[59] Ahmadinejad, too, frequently stressed his loyalty to the Leader, while the Leader strove to maintain a public image as above the fray of day-to-day politics. That image was to come undone after the presidential election in 2009, when the traditionalists and the neo-conservatives temporarily bridged their differences to counter what appeared to both factions to be a more imminent threat: the unexpected resurgence of the reformists.

The 2009 Presidential Election and the Loss of Democratic Legitimacy

The presidential election of 12 June 2009 and its turbulent aftermath provided Iran with its most critical socio-political juncture since the 1979 revolution. The path taken at that juncture culminated in an unprecedented loss of legitimacy for the Islamic Republic and the temporary collapse of the electoral process as the IRI's flawed but relatively effective method of managing popular demands and factional rivalries. The election, in which former reformists were mobilised at a speed and efficiency that took most regime insiders by surprise, resulted in a proclaimed victory for Mahmoud Ahmadinejad by a suspiciously wide margin in the first round. This led to allegations of extensive fraud, the largest mass demonstrations since the revolution, direct confrontation between the tutelary establishment and the people, and the eventual suppression of the reformist 'Green Movement' (*Jonbesh-e Sabz*) by the traditionalist/ neo-conservative alliance.

Several interrelated factors explain the widespread enthusiasm behind the Green Movement. Domestically, increasing economic hardship for the lower middle and working classes as a result of high inflation, spurred by Ahmadinejad's poorly managed redistributive policies, coupled with growing social restrictions and the loss of the few civil liberties secured during the Khatami presidency, drove a new generation of young urban voters, especially women, into political activism.[60] In their attempts to appeal to these voters, the two presidential candidates of the movement – former Prime Minister Mir Hossain Mousavi and former Majles speaker Mehdi Karroubi – demonstrated that they had learned from the reformists' past failures.

Mousavi and Karroubi built their political campaigns on a platform of 'freedom, social justice and national sovereignty'.[61] Moving away from the relatively abstract and discredited notion of reform towards a more tangible and universal rights discourse, both campaigns issued their human rights charter and pledged to push for the ratification of the UN Convention on the Elimination of Discrimination Against Women.[62] The more popular of the two candidates, Mousavi was able to unite the reformist base with the modernist right faction thanks to his personal relations with both Khatami and Rafsanjani. But the emphasis of his campaign on economic justice and the elimination of corruption revealed a conscious effort not to be identified strictly with the upper and middle classes – roughly associated with Rafsanjani and Khatami, respectively – and to reach out to working class Iranians as well. Mousavi's own reputation as a long-time champion of socio-economic justice and competent manager of the economy during the war with Iraq lent credibility to his message.

Geopolitically, the election of Barack Obama as the new US president in November 2008, and his expressed desire to reverse his predecessor's belligerent policies in the region and especially towards Iran, created a sense that a more reconciliatory Iranian foreign policy rhetoric could help defuse military tensions over Iran's nuclear programme and help restore its economic ties with the Gulf monarchies and the West.[63] This appetite for reduced tensions, following a period of exceptional geopolitical strain under Ahmadinejad, contributed to the popular enthusiasm behind the Green Movement. It is important to remember, however, that both Mousavi and Karroubi consistently emphasised their firm support for Iran's right to develop nuclear power. Alongside freedom and social justice, the two leaders highlighted the defence of national sovereignty as a key component of their platform, presenting the Green Movement as a continuation of the Constitutional Revolution, the movement for the nationalisation of the oil industry (1951–3) and the Islamic Revolution.[64]

The lively and remarkably candid televised debates between the candidates before the election, a first in the country's history, allowed the voters to see the major differences between the candidates – not only between the reformists and the neo-conservatives, but also within the security establishment, thanks to the heated exchange between Ahmadinejad and former IRGC commander Mohsen Rezai. The debates generated a sense of genuine choice that would not transpire through political rallies and slogans alone. Finally, the extensive and highly effective use of new social media platforms by a younger generation of Iranians played a role in the emergence of an organic grassroots political movement and popular mobilisation both before and after the election.[65]

The Green Movement's strategy was to drive people out to vote and achieve a similarly high turnout as in the 1997 presidential election, which they presumed would secure victory with a margin wide enough to be too risky for manipulation. Yet although the turnout of 85% on 12 June was indeed the highest in any Iranian election to that date, the following morning the Interior Ministry announced a landslide victory for Ahmadinejad. Claiming that the same ministry had informed him overnight that he had won and that Majles speaker Ali Larijani had even congratulated him on his victory, Mousavi disputed the outcome and called it illegitimate.[66] Karroubi and Rezai also challenged the declared outcome. Three days before the election, several reformist websites had published a letter, allegedly written by Mesbah Yazdi to the Interior Ministry staff, encouraging them to ensure his protégé's victory, saying 'for you, everything is permitted'.[67] Shortly afterwards, Rafsanjani issued an open letter to Khamenei, calling on him to guarantee a fair election. Building on these earlier suspicions, the seemingly implausible announced outcome convinced many Iranians that their vote had been stolen and drove them en masse to the streets.[68]

The swift and heavy-handed response to the mass demonstrations by the IRGC and the *Basij*, organised raids against Mousavi and Karroubi campaign offices and the arrest of prominent Green activists within twenty-four hours of the election, followed by televised confessions by activists and unknown protestors of their complicity in a Western plot to overthrow the regime, suggested that the guardians had been gearing up for open confrontation. Even so, they could not have predicted the intensity of the demonstrations or control the flow of events during the highly volatile first week after the election. The same argument goes for Mousavi and Karroubi, who at times appeared to be following the masses rather than leading them, as the protests spread and the slogans transformed in a matter of days from challenging the election to challenging the IRI. Notably, however, neither man backed down from their call for a fresh election, even when the clashes turned deadly and Khamenei intervened publicly on behalf of Ahmadinejad. Ultimately, open confrontation with the Leader led to a heavy-handed crackdown against the Green Movement, which was labelled by its opponents the 'green path of sedition', the imprisonment of thousands of its supporters, including the eventual home arrest of Mousavi and Karroubi, and the intense securitisation of the IRI regime, which was facing its most acute domestic legitimacy crisis since institutional consolidation.

A critical turning point for the Green Movement, as well as the fate of the IRI hybrid regime, was the Friday prayer sermon that the Leader delivered at the University of Tehran on 19 June. During this widely anticipated sermon, Khamenei uncharacteristically stepped out of his public image as the arbiter of disputes, and unequivocally endorsed Ahmadinejad, thus becoming a direct party to the conflict. Calling the election a 'historic moment' that 'put religious democracy on display for the whole world to see', he declared that Ahmadinejad's ideas were closer to his, accused foreign powers of being behind the unrest ('They thought that Iran is Georgia') and warned opposition leaders of retribution for the 'bloodshed and chaos' to come if they did not end the protests.[69]

The extent of the rupture among the regime's top guardians became fully visible when Rafsanjani publicly defied Khamenei in another Friday sermon on 17 July. Having become the primary target of Ahmadinejad's attacks over the years, Rafsanjani had put his support behind Mousavi before the election. After 12 June, he met with senior clerics in Qom and reportedly called for a meeting of the Assembly of Experts, the only body with the power to remove the Leader. Two days after Khamenei's Friday sermon, Rafsanjani's daughter was arrested and sentenced to prison for spreading propaganda against the regime. Delivering his sermon against this backdrop, Rafsanjani spoke about 'doubts' regarding the credibility of the election and the loss of trust in the country's institutions, and he emphasised the centrality of the concepts of just rule and popular legitimacy to Iran and Shiism. 'Legitimacy of the country comes from its people's consent', he stated and added that Khomeini had given the utmost importance to popular will. He made the case for the necessity to have both the Islamic revolutionary and the republican pillars functioning side by side and pleaded for the release of political prisoners.[70] In response, the Leader stripped Rafsanjani of his role as Friday prayer leader, and in March 2011 he was not re-elected as the head of the Assembly of Experts. This period also marked the end of the private meetings that Khamenei and Rafsanjani had held every Tuesday for years, even at the height of their personal rivalry.[71]

The 2009 presidential election and its aftermath marked the failure of the IRI's electoral system to carry out its fundamental functions: managing popular participation in politics, socialising new generations into the IRI system and negotiating factional competition. Indeed, electoral politics not only failed to diffuse, but actually provoked, existing tensions. The Leader's direct involvement on one side of the divide made the most powerful guardian complicit in this failure. In the eyes of many Iranians, rebellion against an illegitimate government had become not only justifiable, but an obligation.

Leader–President Rivalry after 2009

Rafsanjani's marginalisation and the suppression of the Green Movement left the traditionalist and neo-conservative factions to compete for political influence. Political contestation during Ahmadinejad's second term took place in an atmosphere of heightened social and institutional distrust, compounded by growing regional tensions following the outbreak of the 'Arab Spring' uprisings and the Syrian civil war, as well as an acute economic crisis caused by both governmental mismanagement and a new round of international sanctions.[72] In this environment, the underlying rivalry between the Leader and the president surfaced and morphed into a new power struggle played out mainly in the shape of byzantine palace intrigues.

Emboldened by his re-election and convinced of his popularity and divinely guided destiny, Ahmadinejad set out to enhance the institutional powers of his office, challenging in the process the authority of the guardians as well as the Majles. As regards the latter, Ahmadinejad even contradicted Khomeini's dictum to claim that the presidency – and not the Majles – was 'the most important branch of government'. His remarks drew criticism from traditionalist MPs. One of the president's fiercest opponents, Ali Motahari, the brother-in-law of Ali Larijani, warned that 'the parliament is still on top of affairs and has the authority to impeach the president and remove him from power'.[73] In January 2011, following a dispute over the appointment of a new governor for the Central Bank, Ahmadinejad published an open letter accusing the Majles, the judiciary and the EC of meddling in his administration's affairs.[74] The EC responded by instructing the president to perform his duties and stop imposing his personal interpretations of the law.[75]

The tension over the right to appoint and dismiss ministers, which had started in 2005 and grew in early 2008 when Ahmadinejad abruptly fired Mostafa Pourmohammadi, the interior minister imposed on him by the Leader, took a more open and destabilising turn after the presidential election. In July 2009, Ahmadinejad fired two key cabinet members close to Khamenei: Minister of Culture and Islamic Guidance Hossein Saffar

Harandi and Minister of Intelligence Gholam Hossein Mohseni Ejei. The president was particularly intent on enhancing his authority over the conduct of foreign and national security policies, both of which traditionally fell within the Leader's reserved domains. His appointment of personal confidants as special envoys for foreign affairs to work independently from the foreign ministry led Khamenei to declare that 'parallel diplomacy is not acceptable'. Foreign Minister Manouchehr Mottaki described the practice as 'naïve' and 'unwise'.[76]

In December 2010, without consulting the Leader, Ahmadinejad fired Mottaki while the latter was on a foreign visit. This act of defiance was condemned by the *Kayhan* newspaper as exceptionally insulting but celebrated by the pro-Ahmadinejad *Rajanews* website as 'long overdue'.[77] In April 2011, the president forced the Minister of Intelligence Heydar Moslehi to resign. When the Leader promptly reinstated Moslehi, Ahmadinejad protested in a dramatic manner by not appearing in public or attending cabinet meetings for eleven days. This was the clearest sign yet of the deepening crisis between the 'representative of God' and the 'representative of the People'.

At the centre of the traditionalists' attacks were Ahmadinejad's aides and confidants, especially Esfandiar Rahim Mashaei, his most trusted advisor and the father of his daughter-in-law. Mashaei's friendship with Ahmadinejad dated back to their years in the IRGC. By 2009, Mashaei had already made enemies among the traditionalist guardians for his anti-clerical views, occasional praise for Iran's pre-Islamic history and messages of friendship to Israel. Immediately after the 2009 election, Ahmadinejad's appointment of Mashaei as his first vice president triggered a clerical backlash and a standoff that led the Leader to instruct the president to remove Mashaei from the post.[78] Ahmadinejad obliged, and subsequently made Mashaei his chief of staff. In September 2010, when the president was in New York to address the UN General Assembly, Mashaei stirred controversy by suggesting that the clergy should be removed from power in order to 're-establish a great civilisation without Arab-style clerics who have tainted and destroyed the country for the past 31 years'.[79] At the same time, Hamid Baqai, one of the president's closest allies and senior advisors, likened Ahmadinejad to Cyrus the Great, a provocative comparison given the taboo surrounding the glorification of the country's pre-Islamic past.[80]

Such declarations may be viewed both as expressions of genuine conviction among Ahmadinejad's entourage in the president's divinely ordained authority, as well as their recognition of the clergy's diminishing popularity and the need to dissociate themselves from it by using an alternative discourse. Indeed, from the outset, both Ahmadinejad and Mashaei's image as modest, self-made men and regime outsiders stood in stark contrast with the exclusive personal networks of the IRI's ruling clerical elite. But to portray the president's circle as the secular nationalist antithesis of the clerical establishment would be misleading. As much as their ideological differences, the feud between the neo-conservatives and the traditionalists was an outcome of the purges that left the two groups without a common foe and fuelled an internecine rivalry in an increasingly insecure political atmosphere.[81]

By 2011 the traditionalist guardians were channelling their full energy into eliminating what they now called the 'deviant current' (*jarayan-e enherafi*). A *Kayhan* editorial in May argued that the president's team was 'contaminated' and had to be 'quarantined'.[82] Conservative clerics labelled the 'deviant current' a foreign conspiracy and its members 'infiltrators'.[83] Showing that the security establishment was not immune to factional fighting, but also leaving no doubt as to where the loyalties of the top brass lay, senior IRGC commanders swore oaths of allegiance to the Leader. The *Basij* carried out manoeuvres to defend the revolution against the 'foreign-backed deviant current'.[84] Onetime supporter of the president, Ayatollah Jannati announced during a Friday prayer sermon that the 'perverted team is gradually being eliminated'.[85] Even Mesbah Yazdi had to distance himself from the group. Labelling Mashaei a freemason and comparing him to Ali Mohammad Shirazi – the founder of Bab'ism, which is viewed as heretical by the Shi'a clergy – Mesbah Yazdi accused Ahmadinejad's advisors of 'bewitching' the president.[86]

Between 2010 and 2013, in coordination with the judiciary, the Majles impeached nine of Ahmadinejad's ministers. The president himself was also threatened with impeachment. In May 2011, dozens of people with close ties to Mashaei were arrested on charges of sorcery. In late 2011, the president had to fight allegations that his chief of staff was involved in the country's biggest banking scandal, which involved USD 2.6 billion in illegally obtained credit from state banks, channelled to private companies to purchase state entities.[87] As the president responded to accusations by threatening to reveal incriminating evidence against major regime figures, one MP to commented, 'We do not need an enemy when we have Ahmadinejad'.[88]

The power struggle also had a destabilising effect on Iran's foreign relations, particularly on the nuclear issue. Faced with rising inflation and a budget deficit that forced him to slash his populist government's two signature policies, fuel and food subsidies and cash hand-outs for the poor, Ahmadinejad appeared more eager in his second term to negotiate a nuclear agreement with the P5+1 (the five permanent UN Security Council members and Germany) that could ease the tightening economic sanctions.[89] Not trusting the president with the issue and unwilling to allow him a popular victory, his traditionalist rivals put up obstacles. When the government signed a nuclear swap deal with Turkey and Brazil in May 2010 (which was ultimately ignored by the West), Ali Larijani and his cousin, traditionalist MP Ahmad Tavakkoli, dismissed the agreement as misguided and foolish.[90] In December 2011, in the midst of a behind-the-scenes diplomatic exchange between the representatives of the Obama and Ahmadinejad governments, came the storming of the British embassy in Tehran, reportedly carried out by plainclothes *Basij* members acting on the orders of Ali Larijani, a former Guardsman himself.[91]

Thus, as the Majles elections in March and May 2012 approached, not only were the battle lines clearly drawn, but also the neo-conservatives had already suffered significant setbacks. In this first election since 2009, which Khamenei declared 'more sensitive than all others', the traditionalists had two objectives: to marginalise the neo-conservatives in the Majles, while creating an impression of popular support for the IRI system to restore its legitimacy.[92] The traditionalists accused the 'deviationists' (neo-conservatives) of secretly forming alliance with the 'seditionists' (reformists) to derail the elections, which the Intelligence Minister Moslehi called 'the most complex problem facing the established order' (*nezam*).[93] In fact, facing an ongoing crackdown and with their leaders banned from politics or in prison, the vast majority of the reformist groups did not participate in the election and called for a boycott.[94] In contrast, the guardians made a concerted effort to increase participation, arguing that a low turnout would give the US and Israel an excuse for military aggression.

Whether the election restored the regime some of its lost legitimacy remained questionable, in part due to the inability to rely on the veracity of the declared results, including the official turnout figure of 64%, which the state media declared a victory of the people (*piroozi-ye mellat*) and an expression of outpouring of support for the regime. The figure may have been exaggerated, given the reformist boycott, but it is unlikely to have been dramatically inflated. It is important to note that, unlike presidential elections, legislative elections in the IRI historically have been less about national issues and more about local, even personal issues – given the amount of competition among the large number of candidates running for office in 207 districts and 31 provinces.

The declared outcome was a clear victory for the Leader's supporters. The traditionalists claimed a majority of the 290 seats in the Majles. An important indicator of change was the large number of candidates from Mesbah Yazdi's United Front (*Jebhe Paydari*), a key source of support for Ahmadinejad in 2005 and 2009, which had publicly distanced itself from the president in 2012. Ahmadinejad's support base reduced to a small minority in the Majles. Stories such as the failure of the president's sister to get elected in her hometown made the defeat seem even worse.[95] With the Majles now firmly in the Leader's hand, Ahmadinejad was reduced to a lame duck president during his last year in office, although the open confrontation between the Leader and the president continued to escalate. Unable to run for a third term, Ahmadinejad presented Mashaei as his preferred candidate for the June 2013 presidential election. Unsurprisingly, the GC rejected Mashaei's candidacy. Much more unexpected was the rejection of Hashemi Rafsanjani's application, which came as a vivid demonstration of the level of distrust among the top guardians and the extent to which Khamenei had succeeded in personalising his control over the institutions of the IRI.

The clerical guardians' effort to suppress the populist neo-conservative challenge via the judiciary did not come to an end after Ahmadinejad's presidency. Shortly after Hassan Rouhani took office, members of the former's president's inner circle and businesspeople close to his administration were put on trial as part of an anti-corruption drive. In December 2013, one of Iran's richest men, Babak Zenjani, was arrested and charged with embezzling billions of dollars while assisting the government to circumvent economic sanctions; he was given a death sentence in March 2016. The execution of Mahafarid Amir-Khosravi, the businessman at the centre of the banking scandal of 2011, was carried out in December 2014. In January 2015, Ahmadinejad's former vice president Mohammad Reza Rahimi was sentenced to five years in prison for embezzlement. Baqai was arrested in June 2015 and subsequently sentenced to fifteen years. Finally, Mashaei was arrested in March 2018 and received a six-and-a-half-year sentence for threatening national security and engaging in propaganda against the regime.

In response, Ahmadinejad stepped up his attacks against the clerical establishment and continued to threaten senior regime figures with releasing incriminating evidence against them, although he never carried out these threats.[96] In April 2017, he openly defied Khamenei by registering himself as a candidate for the presidential elections and was subsequently barred from running by the GC. In February and March 2018, he published two open letters addressing Khamenei, in which he warned of extreme popular dissatisfaction with the system, called for free elections without tutelary intervention and demanded 'fundamental reforms' limiting the powers of the guardians, including that of the Leader.[97]

Notes

1. Soroush, *Qabd va Bast-e Teorik-e Shari'at*. Also see Sadri, 'Sacral Defense of Secularism'.
2. Soroush, *Qabd va Bast-e Teorik-e Shari'at*, pp. 206–8.
3. Soroush, 'Saqf-e Maishat bar Sotoon-e Shariat', p. 28.
4. See 'Bavar-e dini, Davar-e dini' in Soroush, *Farbihtar az Idioloji*, and 'Tolerance and Governance: A Discourse on Religion and Democracy' in Soroush, *Reason, Freedom and Democracy in Islam*, p. 132.
5. Soroush, *Farbihtar az Idioloji*, p. 52; Soroush, *Reason, Freedom and Democracy in Islam*, pp. 131–55.
6. Shabestari, *Hermenutik, Ketab va Sonnat*.
7. For his views on secularism, see Shabestari, *Iman va Azadi*.
8. Kadivar, *Hokumat-e Velai*; quoted in Sadri, 'Sacral Defense of Secularism', p. 265.
9. 'Name-ye Azari-Qomi be jame-ye modaresin', *Rahesabz*, 3 August 2013.
10. 'Montazeri: Khamenei Should Have Supervisory Role', *Reuters*, 19 November 1997.
11. Ganji was subsequently prosecuted and jailed for three months on the basis of his speech.
12. This view apparently predated Khatami's election. In the words of Abdolkarim Soroush, 'I remember that Mr Khatami was culture minister at the time or he was the head of the Kayhan Institute. He criticized some of *Kayhan Farhangi*'s

methods; quite fierce criticism. I know that Mr. Rokhsefat [one of the founders of *Kayhan Farhangi*] and Mr. Khatami had some heated arguments'. Official website of Abdolkarim Soroush, http://www.drsoroush.com/English/Interviews/E-INT-Kian.html.

13. Khatami, *Hope and Challenge*, p. 81. Note the inclusion of 'the national' alongside 'Islamic' and 'revolutionary' in this formulation, which can be seen as another subtle indication of a return from Islamic revolutionary universalism to nation-state rationale.

14. Shakibi, *Khatami and Gorbachev*, p. 308.

15. Arjomand, *After Khomeini*, p. 92.

16. One of these observers, Ehteshami noted: 'The Rafsanjani government [. . .] has been reluctant to legalise channels of political opposition, content with the belief that if economic channels of self-expression exist the need for political reform diminishes. The emergence of new class factions at the ruler level, or a return of the old ones, will, however, increase pressures for political reform. Indeed, if economic reform does not bear fruit, then pressure for change at the political level may become overwhelming'. (Ehteshami, *After Khomeini*, p. 124).

17. Mashayekhi, 'The Revival of the Student Movement in Post-Revolutionary Iran'.

18. 'Print Media Triumphs in Iranian Elections', *BBC World Monitoring*, 21 February 2000.

19. *Ettela'at*, 19 April 1999; Akbari and Aganji, 'Why Iran's City Council Elections Matter'.

20. 'Iran Prepares for First-Ever Local Elections', *BBC World Monitoring*, 10 February 1999.

21. Kadivar was arrested not for his theological works but for a sermon in which he criticised the guardians for involvement in political assassination of dissidents. For the text of Kadivar's defence see Kadivar, *Baha-ye Azadi*.

22. State-sanctioned assassinations targeting non-conformist individuals took place throughout the 1990s, resulting in 'a massive emigration of the Iranian intelligentsia and the death of nearly 100 people connected with art, letters, and literature'. (Rajaee, *Islamism and Modernism*, pp. 170–1). The assassinations reached a climax in late 1998. In November, political dissidents Dariush and Pervaneh Forouhar were murdered in their home, while journalist Majid Sharif and editor Pirouz Davani 'disappeared' after being abducted by plainclothes intelligence agents. The following month saw the assassinations of authors Mohammad Jafar Pouyandeh and Mohammad Mokhtari.

23. 'Iranian Journalist Names Names', *BBC News*, 30 November 2000; '"Cover-up" in Iran Murder Trial', *BBC News*, 7 January 2001; 'Iranian Killers Spared Death Penalty', *BBC News*, 29 January 2003.

24. *Kayhan*, 5 August 1999.

25. 'Iran's Long Power Struggle Nears Climax', *Financial Times*, 2 November 2002.

26. 'Name baraye farda', *Mehrnews*, 3 May 2004.

27. Ehsani, 'Round 12 for Iran's Reformists'.

28. Shakibi, *Khatami and Gorbachev*, p. 318.

29. Amuzegar, 'Khatami's Economic Record'.

30. Behdad, 'Khatami and His Reformist Economic (Non-)Agenda'; Askari, 'Iran's Economic Policy Dilemma'.

31. Huntington, *The Clash of Civilizations and the Remaking of World Order*; Lewis, 'Time for Toppling'.

32. Arjomand, *After Khomeini*, p. 178.

33. 'Students Heckle Iranian President', *BBC News*, 6 December 2004.

34. Ansari, *Iran, Islam and Democracy*.

35. Ehsani, 'Round 12 for Iran's Reformists'.

36. 'Iranian Dissident Says Reforms at an End', *Al Jazeera English*, 15 February 2004.

37. Rejecting the Participation Front's slogan 'Iran for all Iranians', Mesbah Yazdi retorted: 'What does this slogan mean? Muslims are Iranians, but so are Baha'is. Does this mean Baha'is have the right to govern as well? [. . .] It is the wish of the United States to have Baha'ism recognised as an official religion. [. . .] The slogan 'Iran for all Iranians' is a ploy to bring minority religions into government'. Speech, 5 June 2001; in San'ati, *Gofteman-e Mesbah*, p. 734.

38. 'Fasl-e Panjom: Mafhoom-e Velayat-e Motlagheh-e Faqih', Official website of Ayatollah Mesbah Yazdi, https://mesbahyazdi.ir/node/2345/فصــل-پنجــم .مفهــوم-ولایــت-مطلقــه-ی-فقیه.

39. 'Mesbah Yazdi: E'tebar-e Velayat-e Faqih be Ghanoon-e Asasi nist', *Radio Farda*, 15 October 2009.

40. Speech titled 'Velayat-e faqih va Khobregan', 15 March 2006, Official website of Ayatollah Mesbah Yazdi, http://www.mesbahyazdi.org/farsi/speeches/lectures/lectures21.htm.

41. Mesbah Yazdi, *Pasokh Ostad be Javanan Porseshgar*, pp. 160–1; Rahnema, *Superstition as Ideology in Iranian Politics*, p. 91.

42. Ehteshami and Zweiri, *Iran and the Rise of its Neoconservatives*.

43. San'ati, *Gofteman-e Mesbah*, p. 858.

44. Karroubi contested the first-round results, claiming vote rigging, but was not able to push for a recount.

45. Takeyh, *Guardians of the Revolution*, p. 235.

46. Deputy commander of the Guards, Mohammad Baqir Zulqadr, boasted: "Traditionalist forces won the election thanks to the smart and multi-front plan and through massive participation of the *basij*." *Sharq*, 14 July 2005; quoted in Takeyh, *Guardians of the Revolution*, p. 236.

47. Morteza Agha-Tehrani was appointed as the cabinet's 'ethics advisor'. Gholamhossein Mohseni-Ejei became the minister of intelligence, Manoucher Mohammadi the deputy foreign minister and Mohammad Naser Saghaye Biriya a senior advisor to the president. Gholam-Hossein Elham, also a member of the GC, whose journalist wife Fatameh Rajabi wrote a book titled *Ahmadinejad: Miracle of the Third Millennium*, was first appointed as spokesperson to the president then the minister of justice.

48. 'Ahmadinejad Embarrassed Again', *Economist*, 23 November 2005

49. Mohammad Khoshchehreh, who was an economic adviser to Ahmadinejad but quit within three months of his election, became an outspoken critic of his economic policies. *Ettela'at,* 14 September 2006.

50. 'Iran Moves to Curb Hard-Liners', *Washington Post*, 8 October 2005.

51. Bill Samii, 'Iran: New Foreign Policy Council Could Curtail Ahmadinejad's Power', *RFE/RL*, 29 June 2006.

52. Khatami, *Hope and Challenge*, p. 26–7.

53. 'Ayatollah Mesbah Yazdi: Tashkil-e Dowlat-e Ahmadinejad Ne'mati Elahi Ast', *Aftab News*, 16 November 2005.

54. Rakel, *Power, Islam, and Political Elite in Iran*, p. 58.

55. See for example his comments on the spiritual resistance emerging in Palestine against Israel, 26 October 2005, official website of the presidency of the IRI, http://www.president.ir/fa/2288.

56. Ahmadinejad built a rail connection from the capital to Jamkaran when he was the mayor of Tehran. Mesbah Yazdi and Agha-Tehrani often expounded on the miraculous powers of the shrine and worked to elevate its status in the eyes of the pious folk.

57. Nazila Fathi 'Iranian Clerics Tell the President to Leave the Theology to Them', *New York Times*, 20 May 2008.

58. Rahnema, *Superstition as Ideology in Iranian Politics,* pp. 70–5.

59. Arjomand, *After Khomeini*, p. 174; 'More Power to Iran's Most Powerful Leader', *RFE/RL*, 19 December 2008.

60. In order to emphasise the electoral importance of this young urban demographic, note that in 2009 nearly 70% of Iranians lived in cities, more than half of the university students were women who faced systematic legal and professional discrimination, the median age was twenty-six and the voting age was sixteen.

61. These were enshrined as the key demands of the movement in the charter adopted by Mousavi and Karroubi the following year. 'Musavi Posts Green Movement Charter, Calls for Trial of Vote Saboteurs', *RFE/RL,* 15 June 2010.

62. Nabavi, *Iran: From Theocracy to the Green Movement.*

63. 'Barack Obama Offers Iran "New Beginning" with Video Message,' *Guardian,* 20 March 2009.

64. Holliday, *Defining Iran,* p. 149; Dabashi, *The Green Movement in Iran.*

65. Mottahedeh, 'Green is the New Green'; Cross, 'Why Iran's Green Movement Faltered'; Kamalipour, *Media, Power, and Politics in The Digital Age.*

66. Significantly, the allegation about Larijani's access to classified information and his phone conversation with Mousavi first appeared on a pro-Ahmadinejad website *Rajanews* and was later removed.

67. 'Mesbah Yazdi's Decree to Rig Votes', *Rooz Online,* 9 June 2009.

68. For example, Ahmadinejad had supposedly defeated Mousavi in every major city, including in the latter's hometown of Tabriz. Karroubi, who commands a proven support base, had received less than 1% of the overall vote.

69. '[English voiceover] Imam Khamenei (HA) – Friday Sermons – June 19, 2009', *YouTube,* posted by 'altigerr', 19 June 2009, http://www.youtube.com/watch?v=hLiBp8qxuMA.

70. For an English translation of the sermon, 'IRAN: Full text of Rafsanjani's lengthy speech', *LA Times,* 17 July 2009.

71. Eshraghi and Baji, 'Debunking the Rafsanjani Myth'.

72. On the impact of sanctions on Iran's economy see Cheraghali, 'Impacts of International Sanctions on Iranian Pharmaceutical Market'; Farzanegan, 'Effects of International Financial and Energy Sanctions on Iran's Informal Economy'; Peterson, 'EU Sanctions on Iran'.

73. 'MPs Respond to President's Remarks on the Role of Majlis', *Tehran Times,* 20 September 2010.

74. 'President Ahmadinejad Accuses Majlis, Judiciary, EC of Interference in Administrative Affairs', *Tehran Times,* 26 January 2011.

75. 'Hashdar-e Majma'-e Tashkhis be Dowlat', *Rooz Online,* 6 February 2011.

76. 'Enteqad-e tond-e vezir-e omor-e khareje az movaziye kari dar dowlat', *Jahannews,* 6 September 2010.

77. *Kayhan*, 14 December 2010; 'Taghir-e dorengam dar reis-e vazaret-e khareje', *Rajanews*, 13 December 2010.

78. 'Nameh-ye Rahbar-e Moazzam-e Enqelab-e Islam be Reis-e Jomhoor dar morad-e Agha-ye Mashaei', official website of the supreme leader of IRI, 18 July 2009, http://farsi.khamenei.ir/message-content?id=7495.

79. For Mashaei's views on *velayat-e faqih*, see 'Daramadi bar qeranet motefaved mohandes Rahim Mashaei az velayat-e faqih', official website of Rahim Mashaei, http://www.rahimmashaei.ir/mashaei/6.

80. 'Ahmadinejad's Nationalist Attack on the Islamic Republic', *World Politics Review*, 27 September 2010.

81. Alavi, 'Iran: An Elite at War'.

82. *Kayhan*, 11 May 2011.

83. 'A'zai-ye jarian-e enherafi shenasaye'i va shenasnamedar mishavand', *Jahannews*, 5 May 2011.

84. 'Basij beraye moqabeleh ba 'jarian-e enherafi' amade mishavad', *BBC Persian*, 20 May 2011.

85. 'Jannati: Per o bal-e jarian-e enherafi dar hal ghichi shodan ast, kheyli devam nemiavarand', *Aftab News*, 13 May 2011.

86. 'Hashdar-e Mesbah Yazdi nesbet be nofooz-e feramasonri dar Iran', *BBC Persian*, 13 April 2011; 'Mesbah Yazdi: Ba'zi mikhahand ba in harf ke Imam Zaman jam'e ra edareh mikonad, lozoom-e vali-ye faqih ra zir soal beberand', *Entekhab*, 13 May 2011.

87. 'Iranian President Ahmadinejad Denies Aide Is Linked to Bank Scam', *Guardian*, 15 September 2011; 'Iran Sentences 4 To Death in Biggest Bank Fraud Case', *Press TV*, 13 February 2013.

88. 'Ba vojood-e Ahmadinjead Iran niyaz be doshman nadarad', *Rooz Online*, 14 November 2011.

89. 'Iran Redistributes Wealth in Bid to Fight Sanctions', *Wall Street Journal*, 27 July 2011

90. 'Hashdar-e Larijani be keshvarha-ye gharbi', *Rooz Online*, 23 May 2010; 'Enteqad-e shadid-e Ahmad Tavakkoli az biyani-ye Tehran', *Tabnak*, 18 May 2010.

91. Parsi, 'Why the UK Embassy in Iran Was Attacked'.

92. 'Ayatollah Khamenei: Hesasiyat-e in entekhabat az defa'at-e pish bishtar ast', *BBC Persian*, 29 February 2012.

93. Vazir-e Ettela'at-e Iran: Nemigozarim Entekhabat-e Majles be Enheraf Keshide Shavad', *BBC Persian*, 6 September 2011.

94. Opposition websites reacted angrily when former president Khatami, who had personally supported the boycott, did show up to vote on the day.

95. While the official media carried the story as proof of the president's dwindling popularity, the reformist media and the Western press questioned whether this amounted to a 'sign of fraud'. 'Ahmadinejad's Sister Loses in Iran Vote', *CNN International*, 3 March 2012, http://edition.cnn.com/2012/03/03/world/ meast/iran-parliamentary-elections/.

96. 'Ahmadinejad Fails to Produce Evidence, Calls for Top Judge's Resignation', *Radio Farda*, 20 December 2017.

97. 'Ahmadinejad Discloses Harshly Critical Letters to Khamenei', *Radio Farda*, 19 March 2018.

6

THE DISMANTLING OF KEMALIST
GUARDIANSHIP IN TURKEY

They toppled a great army, it turns out it was just a paper tiger; we thought
it was a real army, but apparently, the USA had hollowed it out. They just
knocked down that huge tree in one go.
                    – Süheyl Batum, Deputy Chairman of the CHP, 5 February 2011

In [Batum's] eyes, the army only becomes respectable when it is capable of
staging a coup.
                    – Ömer Çelik, Deputy Chairman of the AKP, 7 February 2011

The post-modern guardianship that the military put in place in the 1990s
proved to be short lived. Coming to power in 2002 and enlisting the
support of a coalition of liberals, conservatives and Kurds at home, and both
the US and the EU abroad, the AKP government succeeded in disassembling
Kemalist tutelage following a bitter power struggle that took place both within
and outside of the realm of democratic politics. The defeat of the guardians
came about gradually, through the course of three general elections, the EU-
backed institutional reforms, one presidential election, two constitutional referenda, and two highly politicised court cases ostensibly against coup plotters,
but implicating a wide range of Kemalist opponents of the government. Of
crucial importance to the outcome of this power struggle were the divisions
among the guardians regarding the course of action to be taken in response to
the changing status quo. These internal disagreements, which reflected a wider

division within society between reform and resistance, split open the institutions of guardianship, ultimately benefitting the liberal–Islamist alliance supporting the AKP government.

Beginning of the End: The 'Lost' 1990s

Contrary to General Kıvrıkoğlu's prediction of a 'thousand-year 28 February', the political and institutional arrangement that followed the 1997 intervention unravelled in little more than a decade. The process of unravelling, however, had already begun in the 1990s, which was a decade of failures, frustrations and crises for many people in Turkey. Between 1991 and 2001, the country suffered four major economic crises. The gloomy economic atmosphere was compounded by a political picture featuring weak coalition governments, parties embroiled in corruption scandals and state collusion in organised crime. The Kurdish conflict, which claimed over 40,000 lives and displaced millions, took a particularly violent turn after 1993, following the back-to-back deaths of key public figures advocating a negotiated resolution.[1]

The extent of the collusion between politics, the security establishment and organised crime fully came into public view literally by accident, on 3 November 1996. From the wreckage of a Mercedes that collided with a truck near the town of Susurluk in northwest Turkey came out the bodies of a former deputy police chief and an ultra-nationalist mafia boss sought by Interpol for drug trafficking and assassination of Kurdish dissidents and businessmen. A minister of parliament representing an influential Kurdish clan, which collaborated with the state against the PKK, emerged wounded. The trio was said to have left a meeting with Mehmet Ağar, then interior minister and founder of the counter-terrorism unit within the police. The public inquiry and the court case that followed the 'Susurluk scandal' fell short of exposing the shadowy connections within the 'deep state'. However, the scandal did trigger one of Turkey's first concerted civil society campaigns for justice and transparency in the post-1980 period.[2]

A major earthquake hit the country's industrialised northwest region in August 1999, killing more than 17,000 people, devastating infrastructure and triggering a new economic crisis. While civil society took the lead in conducting relief efforts, the state's lack of preparation and disorganised response to a long-anticipated disaster put its intent and competence to provide for the wellbeing of its citizens under further public doubt.³ In 2001, the lira collapsed, public debt reached three quarters of GDP and the IMF was once again called for rescue.⁴ While banks embroiled in corruption scandals were bailed out, ordinary citizens lost life-long savings. For many people, this was the straw that broke the camel's back.

The EU Accession Process and the Rise of the AKP

Two dynamics emerged out of the turbulent 1990s and defined Turkey's politics in the 2000s: the European Union accession process and the rise of the AKP as a popular and highly effective political movement. Turkey had been seeking European integration officially since the 1960s and applied for full membership of the European Community (the predecessor of the EU) in 1987. But it was the signing of a customs union in 1995 followed by Turkey's formal admission by the European Commission as a candidate for full membership in 1999 that transformed a slow-moving bureaucratic process into a tangible prospect that captured the public's imagination and became the primary issue in the country's political agenda. At the turn of the millennium, popular support in Turkey for full membership in the EU rose significantly, with an increasing number of Turkish citizens looking to European integration as a solution to chronic crises and instabilities.⁵

As Brussels' influence on Turkey's domestic affairs grew, Europe increasingly became the focal point of Turkey's engagement with the West. This relationship was based on a liberal reform agenda, unlike the security-focused agenda of the US–Turkish relationship. The EU accession process entailed the implementation of a wide range of social, economic and political liberalisation measures by the candidate country within the framework of 'harmonisation packages', monitored closely by the European Commission. In the run up to the general election held in April 1999, all mainstream national parties, including the far-right Nationalist Action Party (*Milliyetçi Hareket Partisi*, MHP) and the Islamist Virtue Party (*Fazilet Partisi*, FP; the successor to the outlawed RP), were campaigning in favour of the EU accession. Until its dissolution in 2002, the unlikely coalition government that emerged from the 1999 election, made up of the centre-left Democratic Left Party (*Demokratik Sol Parti*, DSP), the centre-right ANAP and the nationalist MHP, put in place a number of key political reforms. These included 34 amendments to the 1982 Constitution, the drafting of a new civil code, revised anti-terrorism legislation, the abolition of the death penalty, the easing of cultural restrictions on minorities and the permission to broadcast in languages other than Turkish.[6]

By mid-2002 the coalition government had collapsed, with an early election called for November. In that election, the voters punished all the major parties involved in the 'lost' 1990s, leaving them below the 10% threshold and out of the parliament. The only two parties to pass the threshold were the CHP, with 19% of the vote, and the newly established AKP, which secured 34%. Controlling 363 seats in the 550-seat parliament, the AKP went on to form Turkey's first single-party government since Özal's ANAP in the 1980s. However, representing only 53% of the overall votes cast due to the high election threshold, the 2002 Assembly also exposed the underlying democratic deficit of the post-1980 institutional arrangement.

The founders of the AKP, led by Recep Tayyip Erdoğan and Abdullah Gül, consisted of a younger generation of Islamist politicians, who rose from among the Welfare Party ranks but split from the senior leadership after the 1997 intervention. This 'reformist wing' had concluded that open ideological confrontation with the Kemalist guardians had, on the one hand, limited their movement's popular appeal and, on the other hand, triggered a heavy-handed response from the tutelary establishment. Abandoning their predecessors' anti-secularist discourse, they went on to emphasise a pragmatic service-based politics at home, focusing on economic development, political stability, good governance and better provision of social services. They signalled continuity in the country's market-friendly macro-economic direction by appointing technocrats to oversee the implementation of the IMF's austerity programme, and sought to placate suspicions of an anti-Western foreign policy by underlining the party's commitment to NATO and the EU.[7] In other words, by appearing to conform to the guardians' basic redlines, the AKP founders moved from the contested boundaries of the tolerated space in Turkish politics, where their Islamist predecessors had lingered, to the fertile ground of centre-right politics, occupied in the past by the DP and ANAP. At a moment when the mainstream parties of the post-1980 coup era were discredited and pushed out of the parliament, this timely shift provided the young Islamists with a virtually uncontested political space and an electoral support much wider than that enjoyed by the RP.[8]

Still, even though the 'reformed Islamists' were elected to govern, they were not truly in power. With their cadres purged and marginalised after 1997, they lacked support within state institutions. This institutional fragility is crucial to explaining the party's choice of alliances in its first years in government. Facing a distrustful military and senior bureaucracy, the AKP forged a coalition of convenience with two groups at home: first, a small but vocal group of liberal intellectuals, many members of which had been part of leftist parties or movements before 1980, and second, the rising class of conservative entrepreneurs (the 'Anatolian tigers') united and mobilised through Islamic trust networks, the most important of which was Gülen's Hizmet movement.

Despite their historical and ideological differences, these groups came together in the early 2000s on the basis of their shared opposition to Kemalist tutelage and support for the EU accession process. The alliance with Hizmet was crucial for the AKP in terms of the movement's financial and media support, established networks abroad, as well as its cadres within the state bureaucracy. Even after the 1997 intervention, when the guardians sought to keep the movement in check through the Western Working Group, and launched a court case against Gülen in absentia, the Gülenists had succeeded in maintaining a quiet presence within key institutions, especially the judiciary and the police force.[9]

Meanwhile, since the late 1980s, members of the liberal intelligentsia had come to see the top-down imposition of Kemalist secular nationalism not only as an anachronistic straightjacket in a post-modern age of globalisation, cultural pluralism and liberal democracy but also as the source of many of Turkey's most persistent socio-political problems. In turn, they viewed the AKP as the representative of a conservative grassroots movement from the 'periphery' that could take on the secular Kemalist 'centre' and act as the agent of a potentially historic reconciliation between Islam, Europe and democracy.[10] At home, the liberals strove to contain the socially conservative urges of the party's core constituency by insisting on a reform agenda in line with the EU accession process.[11] Abroad, they helped improve the party's image by presenting it as a movement of business-minded reformists rather than dangerous Islamists.

It was not only with the EU that the AKP built positive relations during its first term in government. The changing geopolitical conjuncture of the Middle East in the post-September 11 context also brought the party in close strategic cooperation with the US. Neo-conservative strategists in the George W. Bush administration as well as influential foreign policy pundits in the US started to view and promote Turkey's governing party as a moderate antidote to radical Islamist movements in the US's self-styled 'war against terror'. Popularly elected, pro-Western and pro-market, Turkey's 'moderate Islamists' came to represent the ideal response to both violent jihadi movements like al-Qaeda and the revisionist anti-Westernism of Iran.[12] For instance, describing Turkey as a 'free society [. . .] which has always embraced religious pluralism' and its 'moderate branch of [. . .] Islam' as the 'real Islam', *New York Times* columnist Thomas Friedman wrote:

> If we want to help moderates win the war of ideas within the Muslim world, we must help strengthen Turkey as a model of democracy, modernism, moderation and Islam all working together.

The US government endorsed this viewpoint explicitly within the framework of its 'Broader Middle East and North Africa Initiative', a democracy promotion project adopted by the G8 at the Sea Island summit in June 2004.[13] Speaking at a NATO summit in Istanbul a few weeks later, President Bush praised Turkey as a 'Muslim country, which embraces democracy, rule of law and freedom'.[14]

Mindful of the Kemalist guardians' suspicions of its Islamist roots and intentions, the AKP insisted on being described as a 'conservative democratic' party similar to Europe's Christian democrats, rather than 'moderate Islamist'. The party leaders carefully avoided any public criticism of Atatürk or his legacy and, in the centre-right tradition, presented their developmentalist policies as in line with the charismatic leader's civilisational mission. Nonetheless, the party's representation by the US foreign policy circles as a model to the wider region did resonate with its leading ideologues, especially with then foreign policy advisor, and future foreign and prime minister, Ahmet Davutoğlu. As laid out in his book *Strategic Depth*, Davutoğlu envisioned a Turkey no longer at the cultural and political periphery of a Western-led order, desperately seeking acceptance by the West, but rather as an 'order setting agent' at the centre of a wide geography spanning from the Balkans to the Middle East, drawn together by trade and diplomatic ties and a shared Ottoman heritage.[15]

Addressing the neo-conservative think tank American Enterprise Institute in January 2004, Prime Minister Erdoğan echoed this vision in these words:

> Turkey in its region and especially in the Middle East will be a guide in overcoming instability, a driving force for economic development, and a reliable partner in ensuring security [. . .] I do not claim, of course, that Turkey's experience is a model that can be implemented identically in all other Muslim societies. However, the Turkish experience does have a substance which can serve as a source of inspiration for other Muslim societies, other Muslim peoples.[16]

In short, backed by the liberals, religious conservatives and a surging popular demand for the pursuit of the EU membership at home, and by Turkey's two strategic Western allies abroad, the AKP pressed on with the political and economic reform process, which had started in the aftermath of the 2001 financial crisis. The momentum for the EU-backed reforms was at its highest during the party's first three years in government. Within weeks of assuming office in December 2002, the AKP-controlled GNA passed two legal packages that operationalised reforms passed into law by the previous government, revised the penal code to eradicate systematic torture and called for the retrial of all past cases decided in the SSCs. These courts were abolished altogether in May 2004. In 2002, the government lifted the emergency laws that had been in place in the Kurdish provinces since 1987. In 2003, the parliament ratified two UN conventions, which Turkey had previously expressed reservations about, strengthening the protection of civil liberties and cultural rights.[17]

The most critical reform initiative that aimed directly at weakening the military's tutelary dominance was the restructuring of the powerful National Security Council. Between August and December 2003, the Turkish GNA passed laws that increased the number of civilian members of the Council, tipping the balance for the first time in the civilians' favour. The AKP also successfully curtailed the NSC secretary general's influence over the cabinet and the parliament. The first civilian secretary general of the NSC was appointed in August 2004. On the eve of the first NSC reforms journalist Berkan wrote:

If we were to search for a 'deep state' in Turkey, until the day before yesterday this would be the NSC General Secretariat. [. . .] Today this monopoly of information no longer exists. No longer can the NSC general secretary write to ministries and demand classified files, or send them instructions to do this or that. On its own, this is not a sufficient step to democratise Turkey, but it is a beginning.[18]

Other reforms aimed at rolling back the guardians' institutional preroga-tives included the removal of the NSC representatives from the Turkish Radio Television Corporation, as well as the two monitoring agencies, the Higher Council of Radio and Television and the Council of Higher Education. How-ever, the government stopped short of shutting down these agencies, which, albeit under civilian control, continued to represent the state's patriarchal authority over society. A judicial reform bill passed in 2003 ended the military courts' ability to try civilians during peacetime.[19] From 2005 onwards, civilians also gained greater influence over the drafting of the NSPDs, whose contents nevertheless remained confidential. Finally, although there were initiatives to expand the parliament's oversight capabilities over the economic activities of the TSK, their implementation remained problematic due to the persistence of a culture of secrecy within the military, as well as a reluctance by politicians to scrutinise publicly what had been for decades a taboo subject.[20]

These political changes took place at the same time as Turkey's economy recovered consistent growth rates. Buoyed by the global surge in liquidity in the 2000s, the country attracted record amounts of foreign direct investment. Together with the most extensive privatisation scheme in the country's history, which generated nearly as much capital for the government during 2005 and 2006 as in the previous two decades, this windfall cash allowed the govern-ment to stimulate growth, tame inflation, improve the country's ailing hous-ing, transportation and health infrastructure, while distributing rent to its clients in exchange for political support.[21] Coming on the heels of a decade of turbulence, this newfound stability and the positive outlook contributed to the popular image of the AKP as competent managers of the economy. As a consequence, the ruling party's share of the vote increased – first to 42% in the local elections held in 2004, and then to 46% in the early general election in June 2007.

Under the AKP, Turkey also came closer to realising its European integration goals. In November 2004, the European Union responded to the government's reform initiatives by launching full membership negotiations with Ankara. A BBC commentary from May 2004 praised the Turkish government's 'obsession' with EU membership:

> The list [of the government's constitutional and legal reforms] is long and impressive. Little if any of this would have come about were it not for Turkey's obsession with EU entry. [. . .] No one in the Turkish government is taking success for granted, but Turkey seems closer than ever to achieving its European ambitions.[22]

Alongside the political and institutional reforms, another important aspect of this period was the extent to which nationalist taboos about the state and society came to be discussed and challenged in remarkably candid and heated discussions that took place in the media, academia and other public fora. The subjects ranged from deconstructing the official historiography of the republic and engaging in a critical introspection about the demise of Anatolia's Christian communities and heritage in the course of the nation-building process, to examining the causes and consequences of military coups and the plight of various social and cultural minority groups. This was an exceptional period of political openness that was encouraged by the EU accession process, driven by the liberal intelligentsia and a new generation of scholars and political activists, and carefully managed by a governing party that strove to strike a balance between the interests of its diverse supporters without overplaying its hand against the guardians. Thus, although Kemalist guardianship was still very much alive and standing, it was increasingly on the defensive and divided over how to respond to the growing domestic and international challenges to its authority.

The Guardians' Dilemma: Reform or Resistance?

Shifting Attitudes within the Tutelary Establishment: The Rise of Eurasianism

In the late 1990s, Turkey's military-bureaucratic guardians appeared confident of their socio-political and institutional hegemony in the unfolding 'post-modern' age. By the mid-2000s, this confidence had largely disappeared as the guardians faced unprecedented political and ideational challenges to their hegemonic position both at home and abroad. As a consequence, in the course of the decade, 'post-modernism' started featuring prominently among the guardians' list of threats to the order. In his inaugural address as the new head of the TSK, General Işık Koşaner summarised what seemed to be the prevalent worldview within the Kemalist establishment:

> The network of propaganda and influence made up of a post-modern class orchestrated by global powers and nested within the domestic media, certain academic and business circles and civil society organisations, is hard at work to weaken and dissolve our national unity, national values and national security parameters.[23]

Koşaner's attack on the 'post-modern class' was a reference to the liberal intelligentsia, and its alliance with the Islamists and global powers to reshape Turkey by eliminating the guardians of the secular nation-state, while empowering separatists and reactionaries. This reading pointed to a remarkable shift in the dominant worldview of the guardians within the span of only a few years. Not only was it the previous generation of senior officers who had encouraged, in close cooperation with the now-maligned global powers, the rise of political Islam while forcing open the country's economy to global markets in the early 1980s, but it was also Koşaner's own generation, whose ultimatum to the Welfare-led government in February 1997 had included directives to maintain Turkey's Western geopolitical orientation, pursuit of the EU membership and the implementation of free market reforms.[24]

Instead of being an essentially ideological transformation, then, this sudden shift in attitudes towards the West, neo-liberalisation and globalisation in the early 2000s primarily reflected a realisation on the part of the guardians that they were losing the strategic backing of the West to the liberal–Islamist alliance. In the 1990s, Erbakan's RP, with its open hostility towards the West and free-market capitalism, had presented a relatively straightforward challenge to the Kemalist guardians, who could justify intervening against the Islamists as a necessity for anchoring Turkey in the West and safeguarding Atatürk's legacy. In contrast, at a time when 'entering contemporary civilisation' had become, in the eyes of a majority of Turkey's voters, synonymous to entering the EU, the idea of a popular Islamist-led project of European integration presented the guardians with a difficult dilemma, pitting their geopolitical priorities against their ideological commitment to Westernisation as well as sensitivity to their own public image.

The outcome of this dilemma was the re-emergence of one of the key divisions within the Kemalist establishment that dated to İnönü's decision to embed Turkey inside the Western security alliance in the early years of the Cold War: the division between those who saw Westernisation as the essence of Atatürk's legacy versus those who interpreted this legacy primarily as an anti-imperialist mission that placed national sovereignty above all else. While in the course of the Cold War and during the 1990s, the former interpretation was institutionalised and the latter marginalised, at the turn of the millennium, with shifting geopolitical dynamics and alliances, the emphasis on sovereignty once again became resurgent among the guardians and their civilian associates. The geopolitical worldview and discourse that grew out of this process was Eurasianism (*Avrasyacılık*).

Kemalist Eurasianism brought together two political groups, secular nationalists and (some) socialists, who had clashed frequently during the Cold War, but now formed an emerging national front against liberalism, Islamism and globalisation. As a general stance, the Eurasianists regarded revisionist efforts to cast light on the darker founding chapters of the Turkish nation-building project as an imperialist ploy to weaken and divide the nation-state. They opposed the prospect of the EU membership and the reform agenda promoted by the EU-backed liberal–Islamist alliance as an existential threat to the country's sovereignty and the regime's unitary and secular character.[25] Increasingly convinced that Turkey's geopolitical interests no longer lay with the United States and Europe, and inspired in part by Russian geostrategist Alexander Dugin's ideas on establishing a new Eurasian geopolitical space to counter the politico-economic hegemony of the West, the Turkish Eurasianists advocated strategic rapprochement with Russia, China and Iran.[26] This, they argued, was in line with the true principles of Kemalism:

> We suggest that Kemalism, as it is understood by its adherents today, has never been synonymous with Westernisation, but rather with anti-Imperialism. Indeed, this has always been the main motivation behind the convergence of

Kemalists with a segment of the Socialists and sections of the military elite in Turkey. The most recent and important outcome of this convergence is the current support of these groups for Eurasianism, an intellectual movement originally developed by Russian émigrés which rejected a Western-centric understanding and explaining of world history, geography and politics.[27]

Two regional developments in 2003 and 2004 strengthened the appeal of Eurasianism among the Kemalist guardians: the occupation of Iraq by the US military in 2003 and the Annan Plan for the reunification of Cyprus in 2004. The Iraqi occupation confirmed fears that, following the Turkish parliament's refusal in March 2003 to grant the American troops the use of Turkish territory for the land invasion, the US would forsake its strategic partnership with Turkey and support Iraqi Kurds' aspirations for independence.[28] The proposal for the Cypriot unification as advocated in the Annan Plan, on the other hand, was opposed by a number of senior figures within the Turkish military as well as by the nationalist leadership of the Turkish Cypriot community, led by Rauf Denktaş, as undermining Turkey's strategic interests and insistence for a two-state solution on the island.[29] With these developments in the backdrop, Dugin paid his first visit to Turkey in December 2003, delivering a lecture on Eurasianism at Istanbul University.

Two further events organised in 2004 brought together the leading Eurasianists within the military, politics and the civil society. In September, a conference titled 'Turkish, Russian, Chinese and Iranian relationships on the Eurasian axis' held at Istanbul University was chaired by Professor Nur Serter, who went on to become an MP from the CHP in 2007, and featured as keynote speakers Onur Öymen, the Deputy Chairman of the CHP, General Tuncer Kılınç, former NSC General Secretary, the Worker's Party Chairman Doğu Perinçek, alongside the Iranian and Russian ambassadors to Turkey. In his address to the conference, General Kılınç, an outspoken proponent of Turkey's shift away from the West, proposed a 'Eurasian Union', modelled after the EU and led by Turkey, Russia, China and Iran, to counter the hegemonic ambitions of the US and to combat terrorism, ethnic separatism and other disputes in the region.[30]

A second conference held in Ankara in December was jointly sponsored by Dugin's International Eurasianist Movement, the Confederation of

Turkish Trade Unions (*Türkiye Işçi Sendikalari Konfederasyonu*, Türk-İş), the Atatürkist Thought Association (*Atatürkçü Düşünce Derneği*, ADD) and *Ulusal Kanal* (National Channel; a TV-channel linked to Perinçek's Worker's Party). Dugin himself was in attendance, alongside former president Süleyman Demirel, retired former head of the gendarmerie General Şener Eruygur, as well as Kılınç and Perinçek, among others.[31] These events provided the opposition to the AKP within the tutelary establishment with a new geopolitical framework and a more coherent political agenda.

Guardians Divided: Reform versus Resistance

During the first five years of the AKP government, the growing split among the Kemalist guardians between those who saw the ongoing process of change in Turkey as an inevitable outcome of the post-Cold War order and thought it wiser to adapt to it and those who rejected the change and resisted the loss of power became increasingly visible. As senior military officers, acting and retired, started publicly contradicting each other and exchanging thinly veiled criticisms, the carefully maintained reputation of the military as a highly disciplined, secretive and hierarchical institution was undermined. The senior command structure of the TSK reflected this split: at the highest echelon of power was a group of officers who first became known as activist supporters of the 1960 coup while still students at the War Academy and had gone on to play prominent roles in the military's subsequent interventions. Many of the senior officers of the 1990s, such as Generals Bir and Kılınç, former Gendarmerie Commander and Intelligence Chief Teoman Koman, and the former TSK Chief Hakkı Karadayı (1994–8) belonged to this group.

With the notable exception of the then head of the TSK, these activist officers dominated the military top brass in the early 2000s. This included three commanders of the First Army, Generals Çetin Doğan (2001–3, also the director of the West Working Group after the 1997 coup), Yaşar Büyükanıt (2003–4) and Hurşit Tolon (2004–5). Generals Eruygur and Tolon were known as the leaders of the anti-AKP camp. Following their retirement in 2004, Tolon and Eruygur, who assumed the leadership of the ADD, continued their active opposition to the AKP government. Although not part of this group, General İbrahim Fırtına and Admiral Özden Örnek, the air force and navy chiefs between 2003 and 2005, were also closer to the

Eurasianists due to their discomfort with the ruling party. These officers did not hide their displeasure with General Hilmi Özkök, the TSK chief of general staff between 2002 and 2006, who did not belong to the activist group, opposed Eurasianism as a geopolitical blueprint for Turkey and opted for reform rather than resistance, and was seen as an American lackey and 'closet Islamist' by his detractors.[32]

In many ways, Özkök was a typical Turkish officer, sharing the same threat perception as his fellow soldiers. His speeches often included declarations of vigilance against ethnic separatism and religious reactionism.[33] Yet he also appeared to believe that the Cold War-era guardianship role of the TSK could no longer be sustained in the post-Cold War environment, and that the military could no longer afford to appear anti-democratic. In a notable departure from common practice, under Özkök's leadership the TSK refrained from declaring an official stance on some of the most pressing issues of the day – including the parliamentary bill on the use of Turkish territory by the US forces ahead of the Iraqi invasion, the Annan Plan referendum on Cyprus and the European Union reforms – thereby allowing the parliament to lead the debate on these matters. To a question about why the military had remained silent on the failed bill on Iraq, which most of the senior staff – including himself – had privately supported, Özkök replied in a way that defied the traditional notion of guardianship: 'We, the soldiers, do not consider ourselves the most knowledgeable in every issue. Had we made a statement with only the security dimension in mind, we could have misled the public'.[34] When criticised for his leniency on the governing party, he responded: 'I am a democrat, is that a crime?'[35]

Following Özkök's retirement in 2006, the restraint he imposed on the military disappeared. His successor, General Büyükanıt, brought tutelary activism back to the fore and took a tough stance against the AKP and the liberal–Islamist alliance. In March 2007, the weekly political newspaper *Nokta* published a classified military document listing scores of Turkish journalists according to their 'levels of loyalty' to the regime.[36] The same journal then went on to publish a leaked diary that allegedly belonged to Admiral Örnek, detailing two advanced coup plans against the AKP government in 2004, which were reportedly aborted when discovered by Özkök.[37] Shortly afterwards, the offices of *Nokta* were raided by the police upon the directives of the military prosecutor. The newspaper was shut down, while its editor-in-chief and lead reporter were sued for 'insulting and denigrating Turkishness, the republic and the institutions of the state'. The charges were based on the ambiguously worded Article 301 of the Penal Code, which allowed nationalist lawyers and prosecutors to open a barrage of court cases against prominent liberal intellectuals.[38] On the eve of a crucial presidential election, the government appeared reluctant to challenge the guardians directly.

The year 2007 proved to be a critical juncture for Turkish politics. The central issue was the parliamentary election of President Ahmet Necdet Sezer's successor. As the former chief of the Constitutional Court and a staunch Kemalist, Sezer had come to symbolise the bulwark of the tutelary resistance against the AKP government. He used his veto rights more than any other president, sending seventy-two bills back to the parliament and appealing to the Constitutional Court twenty-six times to review the constitutionality of legislation.[39] The government's nomination of then Foreign Minister Abdullah Gül to replace Sezer ignored the tradition of nominating presidential candidates with the generals' nod of approval and constituted a direct affront to the guardians. The Kemalists attempted to prevent the Islamist capture of this important tutelary post by blocking the presidential election process, organising mass demonstrations and issuing a military ultimatum.

On 27 April, MPs from the opposition CHP boycotted the first round of voting and appealed to the Constitutional Court to annul the outcome on the grounds that the parliament had failed to reach the necessary two-thirds quorum. Following the vote, a statement appeared on the official website of the TSK at midnight, expressing 'grave concern' over 'recent debates about secularism surrounding the presidential election process'. The statement emphasised the military's role as 'the absolute defender of secularism' and emphasised its 'legal duty' to take the necessary action to protect the 'fundamental values' of the republic.[40] Senior CHP figures and leading Eurasianists hailed the ultimatum, which came to be known as the 'e-memorandum'.[41] Meanwhile, mass demonstrations against Gül's candidacy were held in major urban centres throughout April and May. These were co-organised by the ADD and the secularist 'Association in Support of Contemporary Living' (*Çağdaş Yaşamı Destekleme Vakfı*, ÇYD). Some of the popular slogans from these rallies included: 'Neither the US, nor the EU, fully sovereign Turkey', 'We do not want an Imam for president' and 'We are Mustafa Kemal's soldiers'. The paradoxical appearance of signs calling the army to duty alongside chants of 'Neither sharia, nor coup d'état; we demand a fully democratic Turkey' revealed a lack of consensus among the participants regarding military intervention.

The government's immediate response to the e-memorandum was one of caution, but also – unlike the Welfare Party in 1997 – a refusal to back down. This refusal grew more resolute as it became apparent that, for the first time in its long history of interventions, the military had managed to secure neither enough public support nor the backing of Turkey's strategic Western partners. On 28 April, the EU Commissioner for Enlargement, Olli Rehn, cautioned the military to respect democratic values and processes.[42] The official US response was mixed and muted, yet on balance unsupportive of the generals.[43] In May, shortly after the Constitutional Court announced the annulment of the first round of the vote in line with the opposition's appeal, the government withdrew Gül's candidacy and called for an early general election.

The AKP won the general election held in July 2007 by a wider than predicted margin, increasing its share of the vote by 12% from 2002 (but losing 22 seats based on proportional distribution, as the new parliament also featured 71 new MPs from the MHP and 26 mostly Kurdish independents). While the CHP's vote remained static, the party lost 66 seats in total. The rise in the AKP's support did not only come as a verdict on its five-year record, but also as an expression of public disapproval of tutelary intervention. Buoyed by the victory, the government re-nominated Gül as its candidate for the presidency, and with the participation and partial backing of the MHP delegates, succeeded in getting him elected as Turkey's first president with an Islamist background in August 2007. Marking the historical significance of Gül's election, Ertuğrul Özkök, then editor of the daily *Hürriyet,* declared him 'the first president of the second republic'. Buoyed by its success, in October, the AKP organised and won a constitutional referendum to elect future presidents by general vote instead of by parliament, thereby popularising the presidency and opening the way for Prime Minister Erdoğan to become Turkey's first directly elected president in August 2014.

A final act of resistance from the guardians came the following year, when Abdurrahman Yalçınkaya, the chief state prosecutor, brought charges against the ruling party on the grounds of engaging in anti-secular activities, demanding its closure and a ban on politics for its senior members. As in the case of the e-memorandum, the CHP expressed support for the chief prosecutor's request, with its leader Deniz Baykal stating 'the judiciary is all we have left'. On 31 July 2008, the Constitutional Court ruled, with five votes to six, against the chief prosecutor's demands. The ruling laid bare a similar division within the high judiciary as in the military. The court did find the AKP guilty of damaging secularism, but decided to impose a monetary fine instead of closure; a much lighter punishment, apparently produced in part as a result of some of the judges' reluctance to upset Turkey's delicate political stability and macroeconomic balance. Having previously expressed concern over the case, the European Union and the financial markets, both of which acted as independent pressure mechanisms that decision makers in Turkey have found difficult to ignore, reacted positively to the ruling.[44]

Here, the role that Chief Justice Haşim Kılıç played in the outcome must be emphasised. Not only did he cast the deciding vote, but he was also the only judge to vote against both closure and monetary fine. The presence of a sympathetic judge at the head of the Constitutional Court at such a critical moment was highly opportune for the AKP, yet it was hardly a coincidence. Kılıç was a conservative judge appointed to the Constitutional Court by President Özal in 1990. President Gül made him Chief Justice in October 2007. Between 1990 and 2009 Kılıç took part in eighteen closure cases, and in fourteen of these he voted for closure. All of these fourteen parties were of leftist and/or Kurdish political orientation. Three of the four times he voted against closure were in the Welfare, the Virtue and, in 2008, the AKP cases.[45] His presence, in other words, was a direct outcome of the institutional and political legacies of the 1980 coup and its move towards semi-presidentialism and promotion of the Turkish–Islamic synthesis.

In short, in contrast to the 1990s, the guardians encountered a much more challenging domestic and international environment in the 2000s. As the primary agent of these challenges, the ruling AKP was not only more popular at home than its Islamist predecessors, but it had also managed to secure key alliances and win over Turkey's Western partners. Faced with a difficult dilemma, the tutelary establishment appeared increasingly and visibly divided. The presence of two individuals that erred on the side of reform rather than resistance (namely, General Özkök and Chief Justice Kılıç) at the helm of the two key tutelary institutions at these critical junctures played a decisive role in favour of the elected government and contributed to the unravelling of Kemalist guardianship.

Resistance Suppressed: The Fall of Kemalist Guardianship

Having survived two alleged coup plans in the early 2000s, a military ultimatum in 2007 and a closure case in 2008, the ruling Islamists went on the counter-offensive during the AKP's second term in office. Between 2008 and 2011, as the AKP wrested control of the military and the judiciary, the tutelary structure of the Turkish Republic collapsed. The mechanisms through which resistance within the Kemalist establishment was suppressed included two high profile court cases driven by Gülenist judges and prosecutors against the Eurasian-ists, and a constitutional referendum for a major restructuring of the judiciary. Equally significant was the role that the media played in this period in challenging the military's sacrosanct popular image and untarnished reputation.

The Coup Trials and the Emasculation of the TSK

Following the Constitutional Court's ruling, the governing party put its weight behind a criminal investigation that had started the previous year into an alleged clandestine ultra-nationalist network embedded within the security establishment, civil society and the criminal underworld. Prosecutors claimed that this shadowy organisation, called Ergenekon, had been planning political assassinations, bomb attacks in public places, organised riots and mass demonstrations (i.e., psychological warfare tactics from the playbook of the TSK's Special Warfare Department) to create an atmosphere of socio-political instability that would justify a military takeover.

Launched following the discovery of a hidden cache of arms and explosives linked to two retired officers in June 2007, the Ergenekon investigation was eventually merged with other ongoing criminal cases, including bombing of the secularist daily *Cumhuriyet* and the fatal attack targeting the Council of State (*Danıştay*) following a ruling upholding the headscarf ban in public offices in 2006.[46] Prosecutors suggested links between this network and a series of recent murders of non-Muslims, namely that of a Greek Orthodox priest and three Protestant missionaries in 2006, as well as prominent Turkish–Armenian journalist Hrant Dink in January 2007. The assassination of Dink, an outspoken advocate of an honest reconciliation between Turks and Armenians, in broad daylight in central Istanbul triggered mass demonstrations against the culture of impunity surrounding crimes committed in the name of 'the state's perpetuity' (*devletin bekası*). The first indictment in July 2008 implicated eighty-six people with conspiring against the government, including several retired officers and well-known Kemalist and Eurasianist figures such as Doğu Perinçek, ultra-nationalist lawyer Kemal Kerinçsiz, former Istanbul University rector Kemal Alemdaroğlu and veteran journalist İlhan Selçuk.

Coinciding with the highly anticipated final days of the closure case, the timing of the indictment revealed the intensity of the power struggle within the state bureaucracy between the AKP and the Gülenists on one side and the Kemalists on the other: nearly all of the leading police investigators and prosecutors involved in the Ergenekon case were, as it turned out, associated with Gülen's Hizmet movement. But it was the second and the third indictments, accepted in March and August 2009, that expanded the scope of the case significantly and covered, among other allegations, the aborted coup plans of 2003 and 2004. These indictments followed the detainment and arrest of retired generals, including Eruygur, Kılınç and Tolon, along with prominent Kemalist scholars, journalists and civil society activists, increasing the total number of suspects in the case to nearly 200.

From its inception, the Ergenekon trial exposed and intensified the polarisation of Turkey's politics and society into two seemingly irreconcilable camps. Kemalist opponents of the AKP immediately declared the investigation a conspiracy against the secular regime, while members of the ruling party and its staunch supporters in the media and civil society categorically ignored the presumed innocence of the defendants until proven guilty. In the ensuing race to win over public opinion, Prime Minister Erdoğan declared himself the unofficial 'prosecutor' of the case, while the CHP leader Deniz Baykal said he was the 'defendants' lawyer'. If in its early days the investigation raised hopes among ordinary Turks and Kurds for being a belated Operation Gladio (i.e., a historic opportunity to push back the uncontrolled powers of the tutelary establishment and expose and cleanse the state of its extra-legal criminal elements), such hopes were soon dashed under mounting concerns over the disregard of the law, evidence fabrication and political revanchism.

Such concerns peaked following the launch of a separate investigation in 2010 into another alleged scheme to topple the government, referred to as

'Operation Sledgehammer' (*Balyoz*). The scheme's details, involving the bombing of historical mosques in Istanbul and provoking a conflict with Greece on
the Aegean Sea, were discussed at a First Army staff seminar in March 2003.
The military acknowledged that such discussions took place in the seminar, but
insisted that they were part of a routine war scenario, and did not constitute
a coup plan. Both the Ergenekon and Sledgehammer cases were handled by a
Heavy Penal Court (also known as Specially Authorised Court, *Özel Yetkili
Mahkeme*) as terrorism trials. Established in June 2005, these courts dealt exclusively with organised crime and terrorism cases. The extensive authority of the
prosecutors and judges in these courts, and the lengthy detention periods were
reminiscent of the practices of the notorious State Security Courts.

Between early 2010 and late 2011, a total of 365 suspects were charged
with conspiring against the government in the Sledgehammer investigation.
All except one of the suspects were retired or serving officers who had taken
part in the seminar or were believed to have been informed of its contents
(despite, for instance, serving in NATO missions outside Turkey at the
time). Among the detainees were General Çetin Doğan, the chief of the
First Army at the time of the seminar and the prime suspect in the case, as
well as retired General Fırtına and Admiral Örnek, the author of the so-
called 'coup diaries'. Arguing that the reports forming the backbone of the
trial were forgeries created on backdated computers, Doğan's daughter,
academic Pınar Doğan, and her husband, Harvard economist Dani Rodrik
brought concerns over the coup trials' integrity into the international spotlight.[47] Their meticulous documentation of forensic inconsistencies, however, was drowned out in the country's increasingly toxic atmosphere of
socio-political polarisation.

One newspaper, in particular, played a leading role in publishing the
incriminating evidence and shaping public opinion around the trials. Founded
after the closure of *Nokta* in 2007, and featuring prominent liberal journalists
and intellectuals led by editor-in-chief Ahmet Altan, the daily *Taraf* quickly
became the source of some of the most unreserved criticisms of the military
and Kemalist tutelage.[48] It was to this newspaper that unnamed sources inside
the police, the state bureaucracy and the military leaked classified information
about the secretive internal world of the TSK. The revelations included not
only anti-government activism, but also gross misconduct, inefficiency and

oversight, leading in some instances to preventable deaths of military personnel.[49] Almost single-handedly, *Taraf's* reporting challenged the TSK's long-standing reputation as Turkey's most successful, patriotic and professional institution.[50] Its critics accused *Taraf* of being funded by the Gülenists and the Open Society Foundation of George Soros and launched a series of court cases against its reporters and editors.

In July 2011, the entire military senior command, led by the Chief of the General Staff Işık Koşaner, resigned in protest over the sheer number of TSK members incarcerated and subjected to lengthy detention periods. In a written statement, Koşaner lamented the general staff's inability to protect the military personnel in the face of what he described as an unlawful and politically motivated process.[51] This was indeed no less than a remarkable admission of defeat by the once powerful guardians. A senior member of the CHP expressed his disappointment with the generals' failure to defend the regime: 'We thought they were soldiers', Deputy Chairman Süheyl Batum said in a speech delivered at an ADD meeting, 'but turns out [the military] was a paper tiger. The United States had simply carved a hole in it. They were able to fell that gigantic tree within seconds'.[52]

Another previously unthinkable development as part of the Ergenekon investigation took place in January 2012, when former Chief of General Staff, General İlker Başbuğ (2008–10), was arrested on charges of 'forming and leading a terrorist organisation'. The primary accusation against Başbuğ was his knowledge of another confidential plan, the so-called 'Action Plan to Combat Reaction', drawn up by a colonel in April 2009 with the aim of manipulating public opinion against the AKP government and the Hizmet Movement.[53] In September 2012, amidst clashes between the police and anti-government protestors outside the high security courthouse, the judges in the Sledgehammer trial found 322 of the suspects guilty as charged and delivered prison sentences between five to twenty years.[54] Similar dramatic scenes unfolded in August 2013, when the same court reached a verdict in the Ergenekon trial, sentencing 275 suspects to prison. Başbuğ, Eruygur and Tolon were given life sentences.

The outcome of the trials was a historic victory for the Islamists, who had managed to turn the tables against the Kemalists and bring the once mighty military guardians to their knees. It would prove, however, no triumph for democracy or rule of law in Turkey. Despite the widening scope of the indictments and the sheer number of suspects, the investigations never confronted the role of the security sector and the 'counter-guerrilla' in the political violence and human rights abuses, especially in the Kurdish conflict of the 1990s. Instead of clearing the smokescreen around the deep state and exposing crimes committed under the guise of a particular ideology – whether Kemalism, Eurasianism or ultra-nationalism – the prosecutors built their own myth of an omnipresent deep state, which they then used to criminalise the ruling Islamists' political opponents. Mixing incredulous claims and fabricated evidence with serious fact-based allegations of criminality, targeting secular academics alongside notorious paramilitary leaders, they damaged the credibility of those allegations and indeed the entire notion of deep state, which increasingly appeared like a front used by the AKP and the Gülenists for state capture.

In total, twelve defendants and witnesses died in the course of the trials, nine of them committing suicide and two passing away in custody during months-long detention periods.[55] The arrests of two prominent journalists, Ahmet Şık and Nedim Şener, in March 2011 as part of the Ergenekon investigation, cast further doubt on the true nature of the trials.[56] Şık was a member of the *Nokta* team that had published the 'coup diaries' attributed to Admiral Örnek in 2007 and was working on a book manuscript on the growing Gülenist presence inside the police force, titled 'The Imam's Army' (*İmam'ın Ordusu*). Şener's reporting implicated senior police officers with ties to the Hizmet Movement in the murder of Hrant Dink.[57] After five years of bureaucratic foot dragging, covered up evidence and disappearing suspects, the Dink trial ended in January 2012 with a verdict that left senior officials and police officers implicated in the assassination untouched and, eventually, promoted.[58]

The Constitutional Reforms, Judicial Restructuring and State Capture

While the coup trials were ongoing, the AKP government presented to the GNA a constitutional reform package, which was put to referendum on 12 September 2010. The package contained amendments to the 1982 Constitution for a far-reaching judicial restructuring, alongside provisions for the protection of individual privacy, freedom of speech and various socio-economic rights in line with EU requirements. By scheduling the referendum to coincide with the 30th anniversary of the 1980 coup, the government framed it as a choice between the authoritarian old Turkey and the democratic new Turkey. Indeed, one of the proposed amendments was to scrap the provisional Article 15 of the 1982 Constitution, which granted legal immunity to the perpetrators of past coups. The day after the reform package was approved by 58% of the voters in the referendum, prosecutors launched an investigation against the aging leaders of the 1980 coup, Kenan Evren and Tahsin Şahinkaya, with a formal indictment brought against them in January 2012. This was followed by the arrest of thirty-one people as part of an investigation into the 'post-modern coup' of 1997. Among the detainees was General Bir, the mastermind of the intervention.[59]

The constitutional reforms enabled a further shift in the civil–military balance in civilians' favour. In a move with direct impact on the Ergenekon and Sledgehammer trials, Article 145 of the Constitution was revised to restrict the military courts' ability to try civilians, while expanding the civilian courts' remit in trying military personnel in cases involving crimes against the state, including coup plotting. Another amendment granted former officers dismissed from the TSK by the Supreme Military Council (*Yüksek Askeri Şura*, YAŞ) the right to appeal, opening the way for those who were expelled from the military due to 'anti-secular tendencies' to return to service. By December 2012, 690 of over 2,000 officers expelled by the Supreme Military Court after 1997 had been reinstated.[60]

The most crucial and controversial aspect of the reform package concerned the restructuring of the civilian judiciary. The proposed amendments included increasing the number of members in the Constitutional Court (from eleven to seventeen) and the Supreme Board of Prosecutors and Judges, which made judicial appointments (from seven to twenty-two). Alongside the president, the parliament was given the right to appoint members to the Constitutional Court. The election process to the Supreme Board of Prosecutors and Judges was also restructured. Whereas previously the Supreme Court of Appeals (*Yargıtay*) and the Council of State (*Danıştay*) controlled the make-up of the board, the new arrangement allowed judges and prosecutors to elect half the members and the president another four. The government claimed the amendments were aimed at democratising the judiciary by breaking the Kemalist 'juristocracy'.[61] In reality, the Kemalists' control over the judiciary had already been weakened as a result of the post-1980 rise of conservative judges and prosecutors, facilitated by the Özal and Gül presidencies. The coup trials and the outcome of the closure case had put to lie the spectre an almighty Kemalist juristocracy. However, the ruling Islamists still had a tenuous grip over the higher echelons of the judiciary, which the reform package would allow them to enhance.

Critical observers warned that by empowering the legislative and executive branches over the judiciary, the changes would go beyond disassembling tutelage and undermine the democratic separation of powers, allowing for popular single-party governments to pack the courts with their own supporters.[62] The preparation and packaging of the amendments also raised concern. The government had put together the reform package without a public debate and prior consultation with the parliamentary opposition or civil society. Some argued, justifiably in hindsight, that the democratic amendments were mere 'window dressing', strategically bundled with the critical changes to the judiciary to make the package more palatable to the liberals at home and in the West.[63]

With the judicial restructuring and the coup cases, the ruling Islamists put the final nail in the coffin of Kemalist guardianship. Whereas the TSK's traditionally sacrosanct image as selfless servants of the nation had been tarnished in the course of this process, the AKP's growing popularity was reconfirmed when it won a third consecutive general election victory in June 2011, securing one out of every two votes cast. The triumph of the elected government over the unelected guardians meant that politics in the AKP's 'New Turkey' would no longer be under the tutelage of a secular nationalist military and bureaucracy. Yet it would also not be a consolidated democracy, as the ruling Islamists had prioritised 'state conquest over state democratisation'.[64] The extra-legal means they employed in achieving this outcome and the vicious power struggle that would erupt between the victorious coalition partners would plunge the country into a new kind of authoritarianism under Erdoğan's populist leadership.

Notes

1. In January 1993, prominent Kemalist journalist Uğur Mumcu was assassinated. At the time, he was investigating suspected links between the PKK and the Turkish intelligence services. The blame was officially put on Iran. Adnan Kahveci, a liberal politician close to President Özal, was killed in a car crash in February. Two weeks later, General Eşref Bitlis, the reform-minded commander of the gendarmerie and NSC member who had publicly criticised the security forces' conduct

in the Kurdish provinces, died in a mysterious plane crash. Finally, President Özal passed away in April 1993.

2. 'Söyler, *The Turkish Deep State*, pp. 143–57.
3. Jalali, Rita, 'Civil Society and the State: Turkey After the Earthquake', *Disasters*, 26 (2), 2002, June, pp. 120–39.
4. Macovei, *Growth and Economic Crises in Turkey*.
5. Public support for EU membership in Turkey consistently came out above 50% in opinion polls during the early-to-mid 2000s, reaching a high of 67% in 2004. See European Council, 'Turkey 2005 Progress Report', *Eurobarometer 63*.
6. Müftüler Bac, 'Turkey's Political Reforms and the Impact of the European Union'.
7. See the party's 2002 election manifesto, AKP, *Herşey Türkiye İçin*.
8. Somer, 'Moderation of Religious and Secular Politics'.
9. Berlinski, 'Who is Fethullah Gülen?'; Daloğlu, 'Leak Deepens AKP-Gulen Rift'.
10. As noted in Chapter 1, the centre–periphery argument, originally developed by Şerif Mardin, offered a straightforward and powerful yet arguably reductionist lens through which many intellectuals, journalists and politicians came to read Turkey's socio-political cleavages at the turn of the millennium. Some well-known scholarly examples include: Göle, 'Secularism and Islamism in Turkey; Heper and Toktaş, 'Islam, Modernity, and Democracy in Contemporary Turkey'; Yavuz, 'Political Islam and the Welfare (Refah) Party in Turkey.
11. One example is the debate over the criminalisation of adultery in 2005. The government floated the idea but backtracked when faced with resistance from the EU, the liberals and the Kemalists. In these early years, the AKP would often point to the constraints imposed by the EU and the guardians to justify to their conservative base why they could not push a more religious social agenda.
12. Friedman, 'War of Ideas, Part 2'.
13. 'Broader Middle East and North Africa Initiative', US Department of State Archive 2005–9, http://bmena.state.gov.
14. Quoted in Altunışık,'The Turkish Model and Democratization in the Middle East', p. 46. Also see Bağcı and Kardaş, 'Post- September 11 Impact', pp. 429–32.
15. Davutoğlu, *Stratejik Derinlik*.
16. Yavuz, *The Emergence of a New Turkey*, Appendix 1, p. 337.
17. Müftüler Bac, 'Turkey's Political Reforms and the Impact of the European Union', pp. 25–7. There is the International Covenant of Civil and Political Rights and the International Covenant on Economic, Social and Cultural Rights.

However, Turkey maintained some reservations to the latter convention, mainly regarding women's and minorities' socio-economic rights.

18. Berkan, 'MGK'sız hayat: Siviller hazır mı?'.
19. Amendments to Law No. 353, adopted on 7 August 2003. This commentary was also another example of how the concept of the deep state was frequently conflated with tutelage, as there was nothing 'deep' about the NSC and its secretariat, whose undemocratic powers were formally recognised by law.
20. The 'Public Financial Management and Control Law' (Law No. 5018, adopted on 10 December 2003), was passed into law with the aim of expanding financial transparency of state institutions, but its efficacy was curtailed by subsequent amendments. Similarly, a 2005 bill that would do away with the legal hurdles before the Court of Accounts in carrying out its oversight role into the budget and expenditures of the military passed into law after much delay in December 2010 (Law No. 6085) and only after being watered down to keep the military's financial autonomy largely intact.
21. OECD, *Economic Surveys Turkey*; Karataş and Ercan, 'The Privatisation Experience in Turkey and Argentina.
22. Jonny Dymond, 'Turkey Edges Toward EU Goal', *BBC News*, 18 May 2004.
23. 'Topluma müdahale', *Sabah*, 31 August 2008.
24. According to the leaked text of the ultimatum, the generals had insisted that 'Turkey's goal to become a full member of the EU must be maintained' and that 'economic efforts to unite Turkey with the outside world, including privatisation schemes, must be intensified'. 'İşte tarihi değişiklikler', *Hürriyet*, 4 November 1997.
25. For a detailed content analysis of the leading Eurasianist publications, see Eren-Webb, 'To Which Eurasia Does Turkey Belong?
26. Translated to Turkish, Dugin's works became popular among socialists and secular nationalists and were reportedly included in the curricula in the War Academy. Dugin established the 'International Eurasianist Movement' in November 2003, of which the Turkish Worker's Party (İşçi Partisi, IP) of Doğu Perinçek became an active member.
27. Akçalı and Perinçek, 'Kemalist Eurasianism', p. 559.
28. See 'A Partnership at Risk?', *Economist*, 10 July 2003; 'Rumsfeld Faults Turkey for Barring Use of Its Land in '03 to Open Northern Front in Iraq', *New York Times*, 21 March 2005. For a detailed account of the internal politics of the Iraqi invasion in Turkey as observed by a veteran Ankara journalist, see Bila, *Sivil Darbe Girişimi ve Ankara'da Irak Savaşları*.

29. The plan, backed by the AKP government, the European Union and a majority of Turkish Cypriots, failed when put to referendum in April 2004, as the majority of Greek Cypriots, led by the nationalist government of Tassos Papadopoulos, voted against it. In 2005, Cyprus was admitted to the EU as a divided island.

30. Speech titled 'The Greater Middle East and the Future and Security of Eurasia', Istanbul, 3 September 2004. In an earlier speech to the War Academy in Istanbul on 7 March 2002, General Kılınç had argued, 'Turkey has not seen the tiniest assistance from the European Union in matters concerning its national interests. On the contrary, the EU regards issues that concern Turkey's interests in complete negativity, this is obvious. Russia is in isolation. I believe it would be in Turkey's benefit to engage in a search that includes [Russia] and if possible Iran, without disregarding the US'. In 2007, Kılınç called for Turkey to pull out of NATO altogether. 'Turkey and Its Army: Military Manoeuvres', *Economist*, 7 July 2007.

31. Shortly after the conference, Russian President Vladimir Putin paid a state visit to Turkey, while Dugin travelled to the Turkish-controlled Northern Cyprus to express support for Denktaş and the nationalists opposed to the UN and EU policies on the island (Akçalı and Perinçek, 'Kemalist Eurasianism', p. 562.)

32. Internal complaints about Özkök were typically aired through deliberately leaked reports and anonymous criticisms, usually published by Mustafa Balbay, a columnist for the daily *Cumhuriyet*. These leaks would then be officially denied by the TSK. 'TSK'daki iki eğilim ve Kıbrıs', *Radikal*, 9 January 2004.

33. See speeches commemorating the 'Victory Day' celebrations, 30 August 2002 and the death of Atatürk, 10 November 2002.

34. Statement made on 5 March 2003. 'İz bıraktı', *Milliyet*, 28 August 2006. In 2012, Özkök revealed that alongside his own junior staff, he also had to resist demands from the Bush administration to put pressure on the Turkish parliament for the passage of the bill. 'ABD 1 Mart tezkeresinde baskı yapmamı istedi!', *Milliyet*, 4 August 2012.

35. 'İz bıraktı', *Milliyet*, 28 August 2006.

36. 'Askerin medya notları', *Radikal*, 8 March 2007.

37. 'İçinden iki darbe girişimi geçen günlük', *Radikal*, 29 March 2007. Örnek has consistently asserted that the diaries were forgeries.

38. They were eventually acquitted of the charges. Other high-profile figures taken to court under article 301 during the mid-2000s included novelist and Nobel laureate Orhan Pamuk, academic Murat Belge and journalist Hrant Dink.

39. Gönenç, 'Presidential Elements in Government'.

40. 'Excerpts of Turkish Army Statement', *BBC News*, 28 April 2007.

41. CHP deputy chairman Onur Öymen praised the statement, adding that his party shared the TSK's concerns on secularism. Addressing a rally the following day, the ADD vice president Nur Serter said: 'Long live the Turkish army! On 27 April, the Turkish army heard our voice, supported our voice and supported democracy. [. . .] It supported the true will of the Turkish Republic'. See 'CHP Genel Başkan Yardımcısı: Dayatmayla cumhurbaşkanı seçmek istiyorlar', *Hürriyet*, 28 April 2007; 'Prof. Nur Serter: Ordumuz 27 Nisan'da demokrasiye sahip çıktı', *Hürriyet*, 30 April 2007.

42. 'Turkish Army Statement Sparks EU Concern', *EUobserver*, 30 April 2007.

43. 'For the First Time, US Warns Against Army Intervention', *Hürriyet Daily News*, 4 May 2007.

44. 'Rehn Warns Turkey on Closure Case Against Ruling Party', *Hürriyet Daily News*, 29 March 2008; 'AKP Case Depresses Istanbul Stock Market', *Financial Times*, 1 April 2008; 'Financial markets welcome Turkish court's decision not to close AKP', *Hürriyet Daily News*, 1 August 2008.

45. Çelik, 'Haşim Kılıç'a hatırlatmalar ve sorular'.

46. 'Ergenekon ile Danıştay davaları birleştirildi', *Sabah*, 4 August 2009.

47. Rodrik, 'The Plot Against the Generals'.

48. Some of the prominent names were editor-in-chief Ahmet Altan, Murat Belge, journalist Yasemin Çongar and former chief editor of *Nokta*, Alper Görmüş.

49. On at least three occasions the paper claimed that serious oversight of intelligence and failures in the chain of command had led to the avoidable casualties in clashes with the PKK. See *Taraf* reports by Mehmet Baransu, 'Dağlıca baskını biliniyordu' 24 June 2008; 'Aktütün'ü itiraf edin demiştik . . . Biz açıklıyoruz'; 14 October 2008, and 'Hantepe ile Gediktepe ihmalleri', 17 August 2010.

50. For many years, the TSK led public opinion polls as Turkey's most trusted institution. At the height of *Taraf*'s reporting in the late 2000s, this confidence appeared to be shaken. In at least one poll (by Metropoll) the military was ranked for the first time after the presidency as the most trusted institution, while in another (by Genar), it came after the presidency, the parliament and somewhat surprisingly, the police force. See Genar, 'Türkiye Sosyal, Ekonomik ve Politik Analiz – 3' and Sencar, 'Liderlerin İtibarı ve Kurumlara Güven'.

51. 'Koşaner'den veda mesajı', *Sabah*, 29 July 2011.

52. 'Batum: Asker meğer kağıttan kaplanmış', *NTV*, 6 February 2011.

53. 'AKP ve Gülen'i bitirme planı', *Taraf*, 12 June 2009. 'Ergenekon'da delil uçurumu', *Milliyet*, 17 October 2012.

54. The three most senior officers, Doğan, Fırtına and Örnek were handed life sentences, which were subsequently reduced to 20 years in prison.
55. 'Ergenekon ve Balyoz'da sır dolu 12 ölüm', *Milliyet*, 23 October 2013.
56. See chapter on Turkey in HRW, *World Report 2013*, pp. 487–93.
57. 'Arrest of Turkish Reporters Raises Doubts Over Ergenekon Case', *Index on Censorship*, 11 March 2011.
58. 'Turkey Fails to Deliver Justice for Murdered Armenian Journalist as Trial Ends', *Amnesty International*, 16 January 2012.
59. By late 2013, all the top suspects had been released from custody. 'Five More Released in Feb 28 Trial, No Arrested Suspect Left', *Hürriyet Daily News*, 19 December 2013.
60. 'Kaç YAŞ mağduru memuriyete döndü?', *Zaman*, 8 December 2012.
61. Shambayati and Kirdiş, 'In Pursuit of "Contemporary Civilization"'; Ergil, Doğu, 'Constitutional Referendum'.
62. Yeğinsu, Can, 'Turkey Packs the Court'; Kalaycıoğlu, 'Kulturkampf in Turkey'.
63. 'The Battle for Turkey's Constitution', *Guardian*, 4 September 2010.
64. Somer, 'Conquering Versus Democratizing the State'.

Part IV

THE OUTCOME

7

THE ROUHANI PRESIDENCY AND
THE LIMITS OF MODERATION

The people have nothing to do and are not considered part of the republic. [. . .]
And the republic, in front of everyone in the world, is being slaughtered and
finally being completely eliminated.
        – Zahra Rahnavard, in response to the engineered election of 2021

Although by 2012 Khamenei and the traditionalists had greatly tightened
their grip over both pillars of the Islamic Republic, the expansion of the
Leader's patriarchal authority and the suppression of the three major factions,
as well as the republican pillar, put the stability of the regime and the security
of the guardians into jeopardy. Unfolding as Iran faced a deepening economic
crisis due to new international sanctions, a geopolitical crisis as a result of the
Syrian civil war and a societal crisis emanating from the post-2009 clampdown, the power struggle between Ahmadinejad and the clerical establishment brought the Islamic Republic of Iran closer to the brink of unravelling
than at any time since its establishment. Against this backdrop, the election
of Hassan Rouhani – a cleric, regime insider and self-declared moderate (i.e.,
the antithesis of Ahmadinejad) – in a vote widely seen to be free from massive fraud briefly brought the IRI hybrid regime back from the brink, helped
restore its electoral legitimacy and established a new modus vivendi among its
main political factions. The centrepiece of this modus vivendi was the support
Khamenei lent to Rouhani in pursuing a negotiated settlement over Iran's

nuclear programme. The signing of the Joint Comprehensive Plan of Action (JCPOA) with P5+1 countries in July 2015 and the subsequent lifting of sanctions brought Rouhani and his allies victories in the 2016 Majles and the 2017 presidential elections.

Success and stability, however, proved to be fleeting, with geopolitics once again shaping the dynamics of domestic politics in Iran. The sudden withdrawal of the US from the JCPOA under President Trump, who issued new sanctions on Tehran and allied with Saudi Arabia and Israel in reviving a hostile front against Iran, tested the limits of the factional modus vivendi and re-securitised the political discourse in the Islamic Republic. In the process, the death of Rafsanjani, economic crisis and new waves of popular unrest fatally weakened the Rouhani administration, setting the stage for Khamenei and the traditionalists to finalise their direct takeover of the republican pillar. With power fully concentrated in the hands of a single, unaccountable actor and his tightknit entourage, and with large segments of the population disenchanted and disenfranchised, the clashes and confrontations that took place after 2017 increasingly assumed a familiar 'patriarchal state versus society' appearance.

The Leader and the Perils of Presidentialism

In the Islamic Republic of Iran, the expansion of the guardians' autonomy and authority over the republican pillar took place gradually as a result of two intertwined processes, one formal and the other informal. The formal process consisted of the constitutional amendments of 1989 canonising and expanding the ambiguously defined role and unwritten powers of the *faqih*, which had hitherto relied on Khomeini's charismatic authority, the 1991 expansion of the Guardian Council's authority to supervise elections and to vet and qualify candidates, as well as the Majles decision in 2008 exempting the *faqih* from parliamentary oversight. The informal process accompanying this formal accumulation of power included the expansion of the Leader's personal grip over key state institutions through his representatives, his control over the *bonyads*, the growing economic prominence of the IRGC, and the guardians' extensive manipulation of the electoral process by methods that went beyond their formal prerogatives. The weakening of the republican pillar was also an outcome of factional struggles, which took place along the guardianship versus democracy cleavage during the Khatami and Ahmadinejad presidencies.

With the defeat of Ahmadinejad's anti-establishment challenge in the 2012 Majles elections, Khamenei had greatly expanded his personal grip over the regime's institutional architecture, save for the one office that consistently challenged his political and ideological authority: the presidency. Consequently, in late 2011 Khamenei publicly suggested eliminating the presidency altogether and to have the Majles select a prime minister instead. Echoing the Leader's words, Majles speaker Ali Larijani said that a 'parliamentary system could be more efficient for Iran'.[1] The proposal reflected the guardians' discomfort with the existence of an executive presidency locked in institutional rivalry with the Islamic pillar and able to cater to the popular demand for charismatic leadership that could counterbalance the Leader's authority. It also demonstrated the traditionalists' discomfort with holding presidential elections, especially after the experience of 2009. Finally, given that it was Khamenei, together with Rafsanjani, who had abolished the office of the prime minister to marginalise their Islamic leftist rivals back in 1989, the proposal exposed the unintended long-term consequences of institutional engineering by the guardians.

In theory, a transition to parliamentarism could mitigate the threat posed by a popular charismatic president to the guardians by de-popularising the executive branch and opening the way for coalition governments that would be easier to manipulate than a single-faction presidency. In other words, it could protect the guardians from 'the perils of presidentialism' and allow the Leader to maintain a grip over the political system without having so much to engage in open confrontation with elected officials.[2] In July 2012, a Majles group was tasked by the Leader to assess the feasibility of switching from a presidential to a parliamentary system. The group's conclusions were not made public. However, the fact that the traditionalists did not pursue the matter beyond this point suggests that they found the socio-political conditions at the time unfavourable for such a transition.

The fact that this idea was flaunted but not pursued attested to two important points: first, while the Leader's institutional authority had grown consistently and become extensive, in practice it had not become absolute even after 2009. Secondly, while some guardians (such as Mesbah Yazdi) openly supported the absolute control of *vali-ye faqih* over the entire political system, having taken part in the 1979 revolution, many were also aware of the inherent risks and insecurity of such domination and saw some degree of democratic legitimacy as necessary for the regime's survival. As one observer noted at the time, 'if such a change materializes, the Islamic Republic's political system will come to more closely resemble the regime it toppled in 1979'.[3]

Even without a transition to a parliamentary system, Khamenei's position was already drawing comparisons with that of the Pahlavi shahs. Kadivar described the IRI as a monarchy (*saltanat*) in the mid-2000s. After the 2009 election, Ata'ollah Mohajerani suggested that the Leader had replaced the Islamic Republic with an Islamic government, thereby bringing to an end the era of republicanism in Iran.[4] In July 2009, Grand Ayatollah Montazeri issued a series of *fatwas* declaring *velayat-e faqih* illegitimate and unjust in the absence of 'proper and free popular elections'.[5] In a joint statement issued on the anniversary of the IRI's founding in February 2011, Mousavi and Karroubi described the political system as 'monarchism without hereditary rule'.[6] Arjomand described the post-2009 arrangement in Iran as clerical monarchism with a neo-patrimonial feature:

> The IRI is now critically dependent on decisions made by one man, the Leader, and is for that reason of a comparable degree of fragility to the neo-patrimonial regime of the Shah in the latter part of the 1970s, obvious differences between the two notwithstanding.[7]

As discussed in Chapter 1, both Iranian revolutions of the twentieth century targeted rulers who were in control of a patrimonial state apparatus, yet whose popular base had diminished due to widening social perceptions of unjust and inept rule. Historically, popular support has proven at least as important as institutional power for the security and stability of a regime or ruler in Iran. By the end of Ahmadinejad's second term, the formal political space had shrunk so much that it accommodated little more than the Leader's loyal followers within the two pillars, alongside those within the state bureaucracy, *bonyads*, the clerical establishment and the IRGC, who either benefited from his extensive patronage or were not openly engaged in factional rivalries. Perhaps the clearest expression of this new status quo was the disqualification of Rafsanjani, one of the regime's founding fathers and key players, from the presidential race in 2013. The controversial decision prompted outspoken conservative Majles deputy Ali Motahari to complain publicly to the Leader that were Khomeini still alive, he would also be disqualified by the GC.[8] Ayatollah Khomeini's daughter, Zahra Mostafavi, wrote an open letter to Khamenei, protesting the decision.[9] Years later, Heydar Moslehi, the minister for intelligence at the time, would reveal that Rafsanjani was disqualified because his victory seemed 'imminent' and this was deemed to be 'not in the interest of the system', which by this point had come to mean the interest of the Leader and his supporters.[10] By personalising power in the IRI to such an extent, Khamenei had tied his fate to that of the regime – and the regime's fate to his.

Furthermore, despite his increasingly bitter feud with Ahmadinejad, having supported him in the 2005 and 2009 elections, it was difficult for the Leader to simply disassociate himself from the state of affairs in the country under the neo-conservative government. Iran faced socio-economic crisis during Ahmadinejad's second term, caused both by governmental mismanagement and the new set of international sanctions imposed after 2010. In 2012, oil production fell to a 25-year-low and oil exports dropped by nearly 40% on the previous year – the lowest level since 1986.[11] Banking sanctions blocked international money transfers to and from Iran and forced the government and private traders to engage in barter through third parties. The impact of the crisis was felt throughout the country, as the purchasing power of the Iranian currency dropped 75% between 2005 and 2013. By October 2012, the rial had depreciated 80% on the previous year. By the end of the Iranian year in March 2013 inflation had climbed to 40% and the GDP contracted by 6%. There were reports of food and medicine shortages.[12] Finally, Ahmadinejad's poorly managed redistributionist policies came with a cost as he left the government in USD 67 billion in debt, despite receiving USD 600 billion in oil revenues, the highest in the IRI history, during his eight-year tenure.[13]

Complementing Iran's economic hardships was the increasingly volatile geopolitical atmosphere in the Middle East following the outbreak of the 'Arab Spring' uprisings. Iran's early attempts to present the uprisings across the Arab world as an 'Islamic Awakening', inspired by its own 1979 revolution, were quietly abandoned as it became clear that Sunni Islamist movements that replaced Tunisia and Egypt's secular dictators preferred to emulate the geopolitical pragmatism of Turkey's AKP rather than the anti-Westernism of the IRI. Tensions between Iran and the Gulf Arab monarchies, particularly Saudi Arabia, which were already high before 2011, turned into proxy conflict in Bahrain and Yemen.[14] Sponsored by the Gulf monarchies and Turkey and backed by the West, a disparate range of Sunni Islamist movements defied Iran's main strategic ally in the region, the regime of Bashar al-Assad in Syria. The uprising that started in Syria in March 2011 gradually evolved into a violent civil war fought along sectarian fault lines and became the centre stage of a geopolitical power struggle drawing in regional and global players. It was in this volatile geopolitical environment and amidst heightened Israeli threats of a military strike on Iran's nuclear facilities that the new sanctions regime came into effect.

In short, as the 2013 presidential election approached, the Leader found himself in an institutionally powerful but strategically weakened position. The fact that in the third presidential debate held on 5 June, all of the candidates who were approved by the GC condemned Ahmadinejad's economic and foreign policies, criticised the state of affairs in the IRI and in varying degrees supported a move away from international confrontation came as evidence of a system-wide recognition of the crisis that had engulfed the regime. This crisis and the Leader's predicament are crucial to explaining Hassan Rouhani's unexpected victory on 15 June 2013.

The Election of Hassan Rouhani and the New Modus Vivendi

A mere week before the presidential election, a first-round victory by Hassan Rouhani would come as a surprise to most Iranians, outside observers as well as many regime insiders, including arguably the Leader himself. Yet Rouhani managed to secure just over 50% of the vote and win the race in the first round, avoiding a run off. The official participation rate of 73% was not the highest but also did not suggest voter apathy, such as in the 1993 or 2005 presidential elections. Unlike in 2009, there were no protests or widespread claims of vote rigging – on the contrary, there were street celebrations by Rouhani's supporters in major cities across the country. The outcome was quickly endorsed by the GC and the Leader, as well as sidelined opposition figures, such as Rafsanjani and Khatami.

The election of Hassan Rouhani helped restore crucially needed electoral legitimacy to the IRI and signalled a new modus vivendi between the regime's three main factions: the traditionalists, the modernists and the reformists. An academic, diplomat and cleric, Hassan Rouhani was the ultimate establishment insider, having held numerous bureaucratic and technocratic posts since the Islamic Republic's inception. He was a commander in the war with Iraq, serving as the head of *Khatam al-Anbiya*, the engineering arm of the IRGC, as well as the air force. A five-time Majles deputy, a member of the Expediency Council from 1991 and the Assembly of Experts from 1998, he was also the secretary of the Supreme National Security Council from 1989 until 2005, national security advisor to presidents Rafsanjani and Khatami, and Khatami's chief nuclear negotiator between 2003 and 2005. Often described as a centrist, Rouhani was not formally associated with any of the IRI's main political factions. However, partly due to his close personal relationship with Rafsanjani, he was viewed with distrust among some reformists and traditionalists, and mostly disliked by the neo-conservatives. Even so, the fact that he never played an overtly political role meant that he had not become the target of sustained political attention – either positive or negative – until a week before the election. Ehteshami described him as an 'establishment rebel who has a mind of his own in socio-political and foreign policies, and does not blindly tow regime lines'.[15] His public criticism in 2006 of Mesbah Yazdi's argument that legitimate authority can only be divinely obtained represented a philosophical defence of the tutelary hybrid regime:

> Everyday some people pit national sovereignty (*hakimiyat-e melli*) against religious sovereignty (*hakimiyat-e dini*). National sovereignty is inseparable from religious sovereignty. [. . .] Can we say that the government of the Islamic Republic of Iran is not democratic? Ours is a religious democracy (*mardom-salari dini*). Can we say that the people's votes are purely ceremonial? It was the will of the Imam [Khomeini] that votes should matter.[16]

Rouhani was not the Leader's preferred candidate; that person was Saeed Jalili, whose campaign stirred little public enthusiasm. But like the seven other candidates who were ultimately approved by the GC, Rouhani was not perceived as a potential threat to the Leader or the regime either. This was an election designed to be safe for the Leader.[17] Rouhani was also not a front-runner until a few days before the election, when both Rafsanjani and Khatami publicly endorsed him. With the withdrawal of Mohammad Reza Aref, the only reformist candidate on the list, Rouhani suddenly turned into the preferred candidate of the modernists, the reformists and other critics of the Leader and the status quo, against five conservative establishment figures. Khatami campaigned on behalf of Rouhani in an attempt to energise the reformist base, where there was an ongoing debate about boycotting the election. For example, Mostafa Tajzadeh, a prominent reformist politician jailed after 2009, called for a boycott following Rafsanjani's disqualification, by which, he claimed, the regime had displayed its incompetence and admitted Rafsanjani's popularity among the people.[18] Tajzadeh withdrew his call once Rafsanjani expressed his open support for Rouhani.

Rafsanjani's predicament after 2009 was the opposite of Khamenei's. At the same time as he was being marginalised institutionally, the former president's popularity surged based on the perception that he was sacrificing his position to defend a just cause. Increasingly before the election, Rafsanjani became portrayed as the only person capable of standing up to the Leader and managing economic and political normalisation, as he did after the Iraq war.[19] His disqualification was meant to prevent his return to power. In fact, it added to his popularity, casting him as the victim of a personal vendetta, while painting the Leader and the traditionalist guardians as weak, insecure and vengeful. Khamenei could have presumably stemmed this trend by reversing the GC's decision and allowing Rafsanjani to run, therefore appearing magnanimous and sensitive to public opinion. But the Leader was apparently more willing to contend with public disapproval than to face the prospect of another Rafsanjani presidency. In the end, more than anyone else, it was Rafsanjani's support that boosted Rouhani's campaign in the final hour.[20]

The fact that the two sidelined former presidents, Rafsanjani and Khatami, were able to generate considerable public excitement in a matter of days and influence the outcome of the vote attested to the two men's continued importance as providers of popular legitimacy to the IRI system. At the same time, however, it also showed their continued loyalty and dependence to that system: Rafsanjani and Khatami did not merely put their weight behind Rouhani to defy the Leader; as regime insiders their fate was also tied to the future of the IRI. Khamenei and the traditionalists could only marginalise the two leaders at the expense of crucial popular legitimacy for the regime, in which Rafsanjani and Khatami also remained deeply invested. Last but not the least, the unexpected level of support Rouhani received from small towns and the urban working class suggested that the traditionalists were losing grip over their core support base as a result of the constant economic instability and crises in the country.

This complex web of elite inter-dependencies, which formed the basis of the modus vivendi that emerged from the 2013 election, helps explain why the Leader and the traditionalists favoured a return to hybridity instead of manipulating the outcome of the poll. Given the precarious state of the IRI's domestic legitimacy and geopolitical position, the guardians were not willing to risk another wave of mass demonstrations four years after the 2009 protests. In any case, a Rouhani presidency did not mean a defeat for the Leader, even if it was a victory for Rafsanjani. Rouhani was not a reformist and, unlike Khatami and the ideologues of the reform movement, he did not make promises that would challenge the Leader's institutional authority or the hybrid status quo.[21] The return of the presidency to a cleric would bring an end to the anti-clerical tide that peaked under Ahmadinejad. Furthermore, as a centrist and establishment insider, Rouhani would be aware of the delicate power dynamics amongst the IRI elite and could be expected to thread a careful balance.

Finally, Rouhani's emphasis on 'moderation' (*etedal*) and experience as chief nuclear negotiator could relieve the regime of some of the economic and geopolitical pressures, and help regain some of its lost popular legitimacy. His platform of 'prudence and hope' (*tadbir va omid*) symbolised a rejection of Ahmadinejad's confrontational socio-economic and foreign policies.[22] Overall, a degree of socio-political, economic and international normalisation appeared necessary for the IRI – and the Leader – to overcome the numerous crises surrounding it. And if a Rouhani presidency meant the return of the modernists and reformists to the formal political space, the Leader could still rely on his extensive patronage over the regime's key institutions to contend with rising factional challenges in due course, as he did during the previous three presidencies.

The first years of the Rouhani presidency demonstrated that the regime elite was indeed engaged in such strategic calculations and adjustments to the changing status quo. The new president put together a cabinet of moderates that featured traditionalists, modernists and reformists, many of whom were known for their experience in government and technical expertise, rather than overt factional affiliations. While the traditionalist-dominated Majles rejected three of Rouhani's ministerial nominations for being too close to the Green

Movement, it did approve Khatami-era officials Bijan Namdar Zanganeh as oil minister, Massoumeh Ebtekar as vice president and Mohammad Javad Zarif as foreign minister. The key ministries of intelligence, interior and justice were given to the traditionalists. In particular, the appointment as justice minister of Mostafa Pourmohammadi, whom Ahmadinejad had sacked in 2009, demonstrated that the new president was not interested in confronting the Leader over presidential appointees as his successor had done.[23]

One of Rouhani's earliest initiatives was to re-engage with the P5+1 group of countries to work towards a negotiated settlement of the nuclear issue. This happened with the explicit blessing of the Leader, who declared that solving the nuclear issue would be 'simple and easy' if Western countries put aside 'their stubbornness'[24] and described the government as a champion wrestler that needed to show 'heroic flexibility' without forgetting 'who the opponent is'.[25] This way Khamenei was positioning himself strategically: ready to take credit for success, but also prepared to put the blame on the government and say 'I warned you' in case of failure. Reflecting both the pragmatism of Khamenei's decision as well as the regime's difficult geopolitical predicament, Mohammad Ali Jafari, the head of the IRGC, likened the Leader's position to Khomeini's expression of 'drinking from the poisoned chalice' as the latter agreed to the ceasefire that ended the war with Iraq in 1988.[26] As they abandoned their traditional hardliner stance on the nuclear issue and lent tacit support to the government in negotiations, the Guards also seemed to have strategic calculations in mind, namely, the potential economic benefits of sanctions relief on their own vast business interests.[27]

On 28 September 2013, shortly after they addressed the UN General Assembly in New York, Presidents Obama and Rouhani held a phone conversation, the highest-level contact between the two countries since the 1979 revolution. On 24 November, Iran and the P5+1 countries reached a preliminary deal over the nuclear issue, whereby Iran agreed to stop uranium enrichment above 5% and accepted stricter inspections in exchange for limited sanctions relief. The deal, which the US and Iranian governments described as a historic breakthrough as well as the first step towards a permanent solution, marked a notable change in the nature of bilateral relations and a turn away from the Ahmadinejad–Bush era ideological confrontations. The public reaction to the deal in Iran's urban centres was one of widespread jubilation and cautious optimism regarding the country's economic future, reflected in the street celebrations and the sudden rise in the Tehran Stock Exchange.[28] The subsequent negotiation phase led to the signing of the Joint Comprehensive Plan of Action (JCPOA) in July 2015 and the Obama administration's January 2016 decision to lift sanctions, returning the Islamic Republic to international markets, allowing it to sell its oil abroad and promising access to its assets, worth over USD 100 billion, that were frozen overseas.

Coming against persistent opposition from Israel, Saudi Arabia as well as Republicans in the US Congress and Senate, the nuclear agreement was facilitated by the changing dynamics on the ground in Syria. The Assad regime held on to power with military assistance from Russia and Iran, while jihadi groups like the al-Qaeda affiliated al-Nusra Front and the Islamic State (IS) had become increasingly dominant within Syria's fractured opposition. As Europe faced a wave of incoming refugees and a series of terrorist attacks perpetrated by radicalised local Muslims, the focus in the West shifted from pushing for regime change in Syria towards containing the growing jihadi challenge. The perception of a common foe, in turn, opened space for increased dialogue and mutual toleration between the West and Iran.

Domestically, the government sought to justify the Islamic Republic's extensive military involvement in Syria as a 'war on terror'.[29] Gaining traction after the dramatic expansion of the Islamic State after 2014, this official narrative was aimed at uniting a divided society against the threat of a terrifying foreign enemy. In the process, Qassem Soleimani, the charismatic commander of the IRGC's elite *Quds Force*, emerged as a popular public figure, receiving praise from across the factional divide as a stalwart defender of the nation, the religion and the revolution.[30] Opinion polls featuring Soleimani as the most popular person in Iran, often alongside Foreign Minister Zarif, suggested considerable public approval for the IRI's handling of a region-wide conflagration.[31]

This was a time when even neighbouring Turkey, whose rise as a success story was followed with some envy across the border in Iran, was descending into conflict and authoritarianism. Suddenly, to many Iranians the predicament of their country, which appeared at the cusp of a diplomatic, economic and geopolitical breakthrough, looked less bleak. The Rouhani administration was the principal beneficiary of the turnaround in perceptions and rising expectations, reflected in the gains the reformists and the modernists scored in the 2016 Majles elections and in Rouhani's re-election with more than 57% in May 2017. Crucially, the outcome of these elections did not pose a significant threat to Khamenei and the traditionalists.[32] In contrast to the Khatami and Ahmadinejad periods, the battle lines were not drawn to pit the two pillars against each other. Facing a host of threats and opportunities, the IRI political elite had managed to sideline the populist neo-conservatives and contain factional in-fighting to restore a semblance of stability around the regime. Starting from late 2016, however, developments in and around Iran once again exposed how tentative and fragile this stability was.

Back to State versus Society? Challenges From Below and Beyond

The containment of factional rivalries did not mean there were no underlying tensions. In fact, some of these surfaced soon after Rouhani's ascent to the presidency. In October 2013, the reformist *Bahar* newspaper was shut down by the press-monitoring agency for publishing an article considered an insult to Islam, signalling early on that the guardians were not going to tolerate political reform. The same month, the traditionalist Majles threatened Oil Minister Bijan Zangeneh and Economy Minister Ali Teyebnia with impeachment. Foreign Minister Zarif was summoned to the Majles in December to account for his statement that the United States could 'wipe out Iran's defence systems with just one bomb', with several traditionalist MPs calling for his resignation. In late December, Mesbah Yazdi labelled moderation a threat to Islam similar to reformism and said the guardians would intervene 'if we feel that [. . .] the beliefs and values of Islam are exposed to danger'.[33]

Following the signing of the JCPOA, signs of discord between the government and the IRGC became more visible, with Rouhani accusing the IRGC of trying to thwart the nuclear deal, pushing to slash the Guards' budget and criticising its oversized economic involvement, while increasing the budget of the *Artesh* and praising it for resisting politicisation.[34] In turn, the Guards defended their economic role, criticised the flurry of business deals the government signed with Western companies, and attacked the president for his inability to deliver on his economic promises.[35] Rouhani also faced criticism for pursuing Rafsanjani-era neoliberal policies that served the country's rich but left the poor behind.

Ahead of the 2017 elections, the president's traditionalist rivals Mohammad Baqer Qalibaf and Ebrahim Raisi adopted a populist discourse, with Qalibaf even imitating the slogan of the Occupy Movement to claim that Rouhani represented 'the privileged 4 percent of society against the 96 percent'.[36]

While progress in nuclear negotiations had kept Rouhani's hand strong, the domestic and international turn of events after the signing of the JCPOA dramatically weakened the government's position both at home and abroad. Yet even then, analyses of a major rupture between Rouhani and Khamenei, or between the regime's rival institutions, were for the most part exaggerated and unrealistic. At various key moments, senior regime figures, including the Leader himself, publicly sought to defuse tensions by emphasising unity and patience, and expressing support for the government. Despite the IRI's past record of destabilising power struggles, the guardians seemed to act on the awareness that, amidst renewed societal and geopolitical tensions, keeping the regime afloat was of greater urgency than engaging in factional rivalries.

The first major setback for Rouhani was the election of Donald Trump as President of the United States in November 2016. As candidate, Trump had repeatedly said he would pull out of the JCPOA if he became president, calling it 'the stupidest deal of all time'. His election immediately put the agreement in uncertainty, keeping foreign investors at bay and dampening the already waning post-JCPOA enthusiasm in Iran.[37] In May 2018, despite opposition from the rest of the P5+1 and large parts of the US foreign policy establishment, Trump carried out his threat and pulled out of the 'decaying and rotten' nuclear agreement.[38] European determination to salvage the deal without the US ultimately succumbed under the threat of US sanctions. In November, the US government re-issued sanctions waived under the JCPOA.

The Trump administration also eagerly joined the hawkish anti-Iran regional front, consisting of Israel under Prime Minister Benjamin Netanyahu and Saudi Arabia, now steered by its young and ambitious Crown Prince Mohammad Bin Salman. The US-equipped Saudi military intensified its devastating campaign of attrition against the Houthi rebels in Yemen, allegedly backed by Iran, while the Saudi-dominated Gulf Cooperation Council imposed an economic blockade on Qatar, in part for its closer ties with the IRI.[39] Both governments called for 'urgent action' against the Islamic Republic. As the Saudi crown prince declared 'the Iranian supreme leader makes

Hitler look good' and Netanyahu, tirelessly lobbying against the JCPOA, accused Tehran of violating the nuclear agreement,[40] senior members of the Trump administration started talking about regime change in Iran.[41]

Shortly before being named Trump's national security advisor, John Bolton addressed a rally organised in Paris by the exiled People's Mojahedin of Iran (MEK). 'The declared policy of the United States should be the overthrow of the mullahs' regime in Tehran', Bolton said. 'The behaviour and the objectives of the regime are not going to change and, therefore, the only solution is to change the regime itself'.[42] Attending the same rally, Trump's lawyer Rudy Giuliani hinted at foreign involvement in Iranian protests, saying that they were not 'happening spontaneously' but rather 'because of many of our people here and throughout the world'.[43] Writing for the *Wall Street Journal*, Washington DC-based political analysts Reuel Marc Gerecht and Ray Takeyh argued that US pressure was fuelling a 'vicious infighting' between Rouhani and Khamenei and added: 'As regime-shaking street protests have repeatedly revealed, the country is a volcano. We want it to erupt. For the U.S. and the Middle East, sooner is better than later'.[44]

Actually, far from fracturing Iran's cross-factional coalition, this new belligerence was pushing Rouhani closer to Khamenei and the IRGC. With his government's autonomy and credibility very much depending on the success of the nuclear negotiations, the president found his domestic position severely undermined. Not wanting to appear weak, he abandoned his usual diplomatic style for an increasingly defiant tone, threatening to restart nuclear activities in case of US withdrawal from the JCPOA, labelling the US re-imposition of sanctions on Iran's oil exports as 'economic terrorism', accusing the US and the Saudi regime of being behind the deadly terrorist attack at a military parade in the city of Ahvaz in September 2018, and even calling Israel a 'cancerous tumour' established by the West. This new rhetoric drew accolades in the Iranian media across the factional spectrum, which found a rare common ground in the face of what was widely regarded as brazen and unjustified foreign hostility.[45] Notably, in an open letter to the president, General Qassem Soleimani praised Rouhani's statements against the US and Israel, writing:

This is the same Dr. Rouhani whom we knew and know, and who must be, [. . .] I will kiss your hand for your timely, prudent and correct statement,

and we are ready for any policies that are in the interest of the Islamic establishment.[46]

Rouhani suffered a second setback when Hashemi Rafsanjani died of a
heart attack in January 2018. The loss of a key supporter and eminent inter-
locutor of Rafsanjani's stature was a blow to the president and, more importantly, to reformist and modernist hopes of controlling the process of selecting
Khamenei's successor, given the former president's position of influence in the
Assembly of Experts. Thus, even though Rafsanjani's death did not unravel
the post-2013 modus vivendi, it entailed major ramifications for the future
power balance and potential destination of the Islamic Republic. By simply
outliving Rafsanjani, Khamenei had emerged victorious from one of the most
consequential rivalries at the top of the Islamic Republican pantheon.

The third and arguably the most daunting challenge not only to Rouhani
but to the entire tutelary establishment of the IRI came in the shape of a new
wave of mass protests, the first of which started in late December 2017. Because
the initial protests took place in the city of Mashhad, which is home to Ebrahim
Raisi, and featured occasional 'Death to Rouhani' chants, initial assessments
focused on the likelihood of a traditionalist plot against the president. However, as demonstrations quickly spread across 80 cities and the slogans targeted
not just the government but the entire regime elite, it became evident that this
was not about factional infighting but rather a popular outburst of long simmering socio-economic frustrations and resentments towards the ruling class.

The main causes of the protests included rising prices, weakening currency,
chronic water and electricity shortages, unemployment and inadequate social
services. In this sense, they were more comparable to the 'bread riots' of the
1990s and during Ahmadinejad's second term than to the Green Movement of
2009.[47] In part, they reflected the unmet expectations of economic recovery following the lifting of sanctions. According to one survey, by January 2018, 58%
of Iranians thought their economic conditions were getting worse, up from
29% in August 2015.[48] Indeed, despite rising expectations following Rouhani's
election and the JCPOA, the reality for the Iranian working class had remained
one of continuing hardship. In an attempt to tame inflation and reduce public
debt incurred under Ahmadinejad, the Rouhani government initiated a programme of budget cuts, privatisations, trade liberalisation and tax reform. At

the same time, it relied on a new wave of foreign investment and the removal of sanctions to stimulate the economy and create jobs. These hopes were dashed by the policies of the Trump administration, while unemployment remained high and austerity brought misery to millions.

Another underlying cause for the protests was the country's long-term environmental crisis. In January 2018, Iran's Meteorological Organisation announced that 96% of the country was suffering from prolonged drought.[49] The crisis had global as well as national culprits: while climate change was responsible for reduced rainfall, problems such as air pollution, lack of water and the resultant waves of migration from the countryside to the cities were consequences of unsustainable agricultural practices, industrial mismanagement and the rampant construction of infrastructural megaprojects, especially large dams that overused water and redirected river beds. A vehicle of rent distribution between the government and key economic stakeholders like the powerful *bonyads* or the IRGC, such megaprojects were typically contracted in a non-transparent fashion and carried out with little regard for environmental concerns or the needs of local communities.[50] Sporadic protests by farmers and cattle herders in the countryside were routinely suppressed and attracted little attention in urban centres.

By the end of January 2018, most demonstrations were crushed, with thousands arrested and at least 25 people killed by the security forces. Smaller protests, however, continued to erupt throughout 2018, often giving voice to separate but overlapping issues. In Kurdistan and Khuzestan, economic and environmental woes mixed with frustration over ethnic discrimination and marginalisation. In Tehran, teachers took to the streets to demand higher wages and women to protest the compulsory hijab. There were also expressions of growing anger at Iran's costly military engagement in Syria, captured in the slogan 'Leave Syria, think about us'.[51] The IRGC blamed the unrest on foreign powers. In contrast, Rouhani expressed sympathy with the protestors, who were overwhelmingly young, saying that 'people had economic, political and social demands' and 'our ears must be completely open to listen and know what the people want'.[52]

An embattled Rouhani had little power to command the socio-economic and geopolitical dynamics at work. Still, his government received the lion's share of the blame. In May 2018, thousands of truck drivers across the country went on a strike for ten days. In June, Tehran's Grand Bazaar shut down in protest of the quickly depreciating *rial*, with shopkeepers calling for Rouhani's resignation. Such calls were repeated by traditionalist legislators as well as some reformists.[53] The IRGC Commander-in-Chief Mohammad Ali Jafari issued a harshly worded letter, advising Rouhani not to rely on 'the unique and extensive backing you benefited from us in the past weeks' and to display 'revolutionary determination and decisiveness in dealing with certain managers' weaknesses'.[54] In August, the Majles summoned the president, grilled him over his performance and rejected his justifications. His labour and economy ministers subsequently resigned, followed by the ministers for roads and industry in October.

Rouhani survived in part because Khamenei was opposed to his resignation. At the same time as the Leader instructed the government to find urgent remedies for the economic deterioration, he called for unity in the face of the 'economic war' waged against the Islamic Republic by the US and Saudi Arabia.[55] Indeed, Khamenei had no reason to wish for the downfall of Rouhani, whose government never posed a threat to the tutelary establishment in the first place, and who had become more willing to bend to the traditionalists' demands as his position weakened following the death of Rafsanjani and the demise of the JCPOA.[56] Removing him would only exacerbate the sense of instability surrounding the regime and put the burden of dealing with the socio-economic and geopolitical crisis directly in the hands of the traditionalists.

The scale of the crisis confronting the IRI was starkly displayed in November 2019 – a year in which Iran's economy was forecasted to shrink by almost 10% – with the outbreak and the suppression of yet another round of mass uprisings that followed a government decision to raise petrol prices. The ensuing protests and riots were apparently the largest and the most widespread yet since the revolution. Shortly after they broke out, the government, terrified of a repeat of 2009, suspicious of foreign interference and desperate to maintain control, imposed an unprecedented five-day nationwide internet blackout. In the end, featuring deadly street combats between protestors and the IRGC, attacks on government offices, state-owned bank buildings and gas stations and a crackdown that resulted in the deaths of as many as 1,500 protestors, those five days proved to be more violent and explosive than the events of 2009.[57]

In light of the simultaneous protests erupting in Iraq and Lebanon, the newly appointed IRGC chief, Hussein Salami, commented that Iran was fighting a 'world war' against its enemies on its own soil.[58] To add fuel to fire, President Trump and various senior US officials expressed support for the protestors.[59] Unlike in previous social upheavals, this time all branches of government and major institutions displayed a unified front. Notably, there was also no factional infighting.[60] The assassination of Qassem Soleimani in a targeted drone attack outside the Baghdad airport by the United States on 3 January 2020 further contributed to this semblance of unity. The outpouring of mass anger and mourning in Iran, leading to the largest public funeral since Khomeini's death, allowed the IRI establishment to draw legitimacy from Soleimani's 'martyrdom', cast itself as the epicentre of the global struggle against tyranny and imperialism, and temporarily channel popular frustrations away from the government towards the enemy abroad.

But this was not the relatively balanced factional unity that the post-2013 modus vivendi had established. With Rouhani fatally weakened, Rafsanjani dead, Khatami all but withdrawn from public life, Mousavi and Karroubi still under house arrest and slowly forgotten,[61] and Ahmadinejad and the neo-conservatives long marginalised, the IRI's factional diversity at the leadership level had given way to a single-faction domination under Khamenei. The traditionalists did not miss the opportunity to cement their political hegemony. The GC resorted to mass disqualification of reformists and modernists for the Majles elections in February 2020, including 75% of the sitting deputies. The result of that election put Khamenei's supporters firmly in control of the Majles, with the traditionalists securing 221 of the 290 seats (up from 83 in 2016) and the reformist/moderates dropping to 20 seats (from 121). This proved to be a successful rehearsal for the following year's presidential election, when the GC once again barred all popular contenders, making the victory of Ebrahim Raisi, the arch-conservative head of the judiciary, a foregone conclusion.[62] Deeply loyal to the Leader and tipped as his potential successor, Raisi's election as president in June 2021 brought the presidency under the traditionalists' direct control for the first time. And for the first time since the establishment of the Islamic Republic, a single faction controlled the judiciary, the legislative and the executive branches at the same time.

'The people have nothing to do and are not considered part of the republic', said Zahra Rahnavard about the GC's election engineering. 'And the republic, in front of everyone in the world is being slaughtered and finally being completely eliminated'.[63] But the reaction from the modernist and reformist camps was on the whole muted, muddled and ineffective. More worryingly for the IRI leadership, the Iranian people, for the most part, seemed to have stopped caring. In 2009, they had poured to the streets in hundreds of thousands against vote rigging. This time, there were no protests, as public trust in the IRI's electoral institutions had already plummeted. The turnout in both the Majles and presidential elections – officially at 42% and 48%, respectively – was by far the lowest in the history of the Islamic Republic.[64] The runner-up of the presidential election in 2021 was not one of Raisi's formal rivals, but the spoiled and blank votes, which had increased to 13% from 3% in 2013 and 1% in 2009.[65]

Institutional duality and factional competition had been, paradoxically, both destabilising for the IRI tutelary hybrid regime and yet also essential for its survival as mechanisms of managing and absorbing socio-political tensions, albeit in imperfect and limited fashion. The subjugation of the republican pillar by the Islamic guardianship pillar, and the domination of both pillars by Khamenei and his tight-knit coterie of loyalists rendered these mechanisms useless. Even though the IRI's institutional architecture has remained hybrid, politically it has become a personalistic dictatorship that has alienated the vast majority of Iranians from across the social spectrum, save for its own shrinking base.[66] As a result, Iranian politics post-2017 has once again taken on the ominously familiar 'patriarchal state versus society' appearance. Having failed to deliver the revolution's promises of social justice, economic prosperity and political liberty, the IRI regime resorted to ever more violence and repression to contain increasingly frequent, widespread and radical bouts of popular unrest, led by younger generations who seemed less interested than the protestors in 1999 or 2009 in reforming the system. The monthslong country-wide protests that followed the killing of the young Kurdish woman Mahsa (Jina) Amini in police custody after being detained for 'improper hijab' in September 2022 remarkably featured, among diverse socio-economic groups, schoolgirls defiantly calling for the fall of the theocratic establishment.[67]

Notes

1. 'Parliamentary System Could Be More Efficient: Iran's Parliament Speaker', *Payvand*, 22 October 2011.
2. Linz, Juan J., 'The Perils of Presidentialism'.

3. Alem, 'Is the Islamic Republic of Iran on Its Last Elected President?'.

4. Arjomand, *After Khomeini*, p. 21

5. 'Fatwa-ye_Ayatollah_Al'azami_Montazeri,' *Rahesabz*, 31 August 2009.

6. 'Iran Protests See Reinvigorated Activists Take to The Streets In Thousands', *Guardian*, 14 February 2011.

7. Arjomand, *After Khomeini*, p. 191.

8. 'Name-ye Ali Motahari be Rahbar-e Enqelab derbare redselahiyat-e Hashemi', official website of Ali Motahari, 13 May 2013, http://alimotahari.ir/latest-news/1194.

9. 'Name-ye mohem-e doktor Zehra Mostafavi ferzand-e hazrat-e Imam Khomeini (s) be maqam-e moazzam-e rahbar', *Jamaran*, 22 May 2013.

10. 'Ex-Spy Chief Claims Elimination Of Rafsanjani from Iran's 2013 elections', *Amwaj Media*, 15 June 2021, https://amwaj.media/media-monitor/the-controversial-revelation-about-the-disqialificaiton-of-rafsanjani-in-2013-rac.

11. 'Sanctions Cut Iran's Oil Exports to 26-Year Low', *Wall Street Journal*, 29 April 2013; 'Iran Oil Output Heads to 25-Year Low', *Financial Times*, 4 June 2013.

12. 'Iran Unable to Get Life-Saving Drugs Due to International Sanctions', *Guardian*, 3 January 2013.

13. 'Eraeh-ye gozarash-e a'malkard-e 100 rooz-e aval-e dowlat-e yazdahom be mardom', official website of President Hassan Rouhani, 26 November 2013, http://www.rouhani.ir/event.php?event_id=198.

14. '"Cut off head of snake" Saudis told US on Iran', *Reuters*, 29 November 2010.

15. Ehteshami, 'Iranian Foreign Policy after the Election of Hassan Rouhani'.

16. Rouhani speaking to students at Semnan University, March 2006; quoted in San'ati, Gofteman-e Mesbah, p. 551.

17. The other candidates besides Rouhani and Jalili were Mohammad Bagher Qalibaf, Gholam-Ali Haddad-Adel, Ali Akbar Velayati, Mohsen Rezaei, Mohammad Gharazi and Mohammad Reza Aref.

18. 'Tajzadeh: Agher Rahbari khodsarihaye Jannati ra mehar nakonad mesool-e mostaqim-e entekhabat rasool khahad bood', *Norooz News*, 7 May 2013.

19. Not all those who contributed to this portrayal were modernists or reformists. In March, Foad Sadeghi, founder of the news website *Baztab* (known for being close to Mohsen Rezaei and highly critical of the Ahmadinejad government) wrote an article likening Iran's socio-economic and geopolitical situation to the end of the Iraq war and calling on Rafsanjani and Khatami to assist the Leader in 'saving the country' by participating in the upcoming election. *Baztab Emrooz*, 25 March 2013.

20. Karami, 'Has Rafsanjani Returned to Power?'.
21. To mitigate the distrust among the reformists towards Rouhani, Khatami attempted to reconcile reform with Rouhani's discourse of moderation. Following the election he said, 'We preferred for the reformist discourse to win even if reformists themselves were not the victors . . . Real reformism is compatible with rational moderation. The slogan of moderation is not outside the sphere of reformism'. Gareth Smyth, 'Iran's Khatami Strikes Back', *Guardian*, 19 September 2013.
22. Consequently, his administration was dubbed 'the government of moderation and hope'.
23. The appointment was also condemned by human rights organisations. Having served as a prosecutor in revolutionary courts and as deputy intelligence minister, Pourmohammadi has been implicated in the execution of thousands of political dissidents in the late 1980s.
24. Iran's Khamenei says Nuclear Talks Easy If Enemy Not Stubborn', *Reuters*, 26 June 2013.
25. Thomas Erdbrink, 'Enigmatic Leader of Iran Backs Overture, for Now', *New York Times*, 23 September 2013.
26. 'Dowlat-e_dovom_Khordad_hadaql_hemkari_ra_ba_Sepah_dasht', *Mehr News*, 27 September 2013.
27. 'Though the deal keeps in place US sanctions against the Revolutionary Guards, it removes sectoral bans against areas of Iran's economy that the Revolutionary Guards dominate. The organization, as Iran's economic "gatekeeper", will have the ultimate say on how the country's post-deal windfall will be spent'. Rezaei and Moshirabad, 'The Revolutionary Guards'.
28. Ladane Nasseri, 'Iranians Pile into Stocks as Nuclear Deal Spurs 133% Gain', *Bloomberg*, 26 December 2013.
29. Fathollah-Nejad, 'Iran: Fighting "Terror" Publicly, Mourning the Dead Secretly'.
30. Alipour, 'Soleimani Emerges as Unifying Figure for Iranians'.
31. '"Gen. Qassem Soleimani" is the Most Popular Character in Iran', *ISNA*, 29 July 2017.
32. 'While conservative forces (the theocrats) faced a humbling defeat in the [Majles] elections, the disparity of seats won in parliament by the moderates and reformists (the republicans) do not represent an electoral sweep either. Only in Tehran were the moderates and reformists able to achieve a crushing victory—in the rest of the country the picture is much more balanced and nuanced, reflecting a more even division of power between other major groups. [. . .] The 2016 parliamentary

elections thus did not result in a clear electoral victory for republicans but rather a symbolic one—signalling that the republicans are not only back to stay, but now enjoy the mainstream support of the political establishment'. Mohseni, 'The 2016 Iranian Parliamentary Elections and the Future of Domestic Politics under the JCPOA'.

33. Interview, *9 Day*, 21 December 2013.
34. Qaidaari, 'Rouhani Moves to Slash IRGC Budget, Empower Army'; 'Revolutionary Guards Tried to Sabotage Iran's Nuclear Deal, Says President', *Guardian*, 5 May 2017.
35. Shine et al., 'Iran: Mounting Tension between President Rouhani and the Revolutionary Guards'; 'Iran's Revolutionary Guards Call on Rouhani to Halt Rial's Drop', *Bloomberg*, 31 July 2018.
36. Rivetti, 'Labor and Class in Iran'.
37. 'Trump Rhetoric Rattles Iranian Business', *Financial Times*, 10 February 2017.
38. Sherman, 'How We Got the Iran Deal'.
39. The blockade eventually pushed Qatar closer towards Iran. Six months into the blockade, Qatar resumed full diplomatic relations with the Islamic Republic, broken off 20 months earlier following attacks on Saudi diplomatic targets in Iran. Declan Walsh, 'Qatar Restores Full Relations with Iran, Deepening Gulf Feud', *New York Times*, 25 August 2017.
40. 'Saudi Crown Prince: Iran's Supreme Leader "Makes Hitler Look Good", *The Atlantic*, 2 April 2018; 'Nuclear Deal: Netanyahu Accuses Iran of Cheating on Agreement', *Guardian,* 30 April 2018.
41. 'The Trump Administration Calls on Iranians to "Make a Choice About Their Leadership"', *New Yorker*, 21 May 2018;
42. 'M.E.K.: The Group John Bolton Wants to Rule Iran', *New York Times*, 7 May 2018. 'Iran Says Saudis Back Terrorism After Senior Prince Attends Rebel Rally', *Reuters*, 10 July 2016.
43. 'Rudy Giuliani calls for Iran regime change at rally linked to extreme group', *Guardian*, 30 June 2018.
44. Gerecht and Takeyh, 'Let Rouhani and Khamenei Fight'.
45. 'Iranian Media Hails Rouhani for Scoring in UN Battle Against Trump', *Al Monitor*, 26 September 2018.
46. 'Payam-e Sarashkar Soleimani be Reis-e Jomhoori', *ISNA*, 5 July 2018.
47. Batmanghelidj, 'Iranian Protests and the Working Class'.
48. Amir Farmanesh, 'Iranian Attitudes on JCPOA pre-Trump Announcement'.
49. '96% of Iran Experiencing Prolonged Drought: Official, *Tehran Times*, 8 January 2018.

50. Rivetti, 'Labor and Class in Iran'.
51. Fathollah-Nejad, 'Iranians Respond to the Regime: "Leave Syria Alone!"'.
52. 'Iranian Government Must Listen to Demands of The People: Rouhani', *Reuters*, 6 February 2018.
53. 'Motelefe amadeh janeshini dowlat?', *ISNA,* 27 June 2018.
54. 'Iran's Revolutionary Guards Call on Rouhani to Halt Rial's Drop', *Bloomberg*, 31 July 2018.
55. 'Iran's Khamenei Orders Officials to Resolve Economic Crisis', *Reuters*, 11 October 2018.
56. At a meeting with senior government officials, Rouhani said that he was 'ready to bow to the opposition and all critics and kiss their hands for unity and cooperation'. 27 June 2018, http://www.president.ir/en/104985.
57. 'Special Report: Iran's leader ordered crackdown on unrest – "Do whatever it takes to end it"', *Reuters,* 23 December 2019.
58. 'Iran Guards Commander Issues Harsh Threat Again US, UK, Saudi Arabia', *Radio Farda*, 25 November 2019.
59. 'U.S. Meddles in Iran's Affairs, Again, After Protests Subside', *Tehran Times*, 22 November 2019.
60. 'What's Driving Iran's Crackdown on Protesters? Increased Unity Among the Political Establishment' *Los Angeles Times*, 23 November 2019.
61. Rouhani had failed to deliver on his campaign promise of ending the two reformist leaders' captivity.
62. Even former Majles speaker and establishment insider Ali Larijani was disqualified by the GC.
63. 'Iran Hardliners Fight to Ensure Ebrahim Raisi Wins Presidential Election', *Guardian*, 16 June 2021.
64. The Turnout in Tehran in The Majles Election Was Lower Than 25%.
65. 'Voters Send a Message to Iran's Leaders After Dismal Turnout For Presidential Election', *Radio Free Europe/Radio Liberty*, 22 June 2021.
66. Though it is extremely difficult to get reliable polling data in Iran, as an indicator of widespread disenfranchisement, a survey by state-run ISPA found in 2021 that only 20% of Iranians self-identified as traditionalist or reformist, down from 43% in 2016. *Farsnews*, 2 June 2021.
67. Ghaderi and Goner, 'Why "Jîna"'; 'Woman, Life, Freedom: A Panel on the Protests in Iran (Video)', *Jadaliyya* 10 October 2022, https://www.jadaliyya.com/Details/44500; Bayat, 'Is Iran on the Verge of Another Revolution?'.

8

CHANGE AND CONTINUITY IN THE MAKING OF ERDOĞAN'S 'NEW TURKEY'

Ultimately, this act of betrayal is a great gift to us from God. Because it will lead to the cleansing of our armed forces. [. . .] This is no longer the old Turkey. New Turkey acts differently.

– Recep Tayyip Erdoğan, 16 July 2016

Erdoğan has converged with our line. He has become an Islamic Kemalist.

– Doğu Perinçek, 20 September 2017

The victory of elected challengers over the unelected guardians in the 2000s brought an end to military tutelage, but it did not lead to democratic consolidation in Turkey. Instead, in the 2010s Turkey entered a new phase of conflict and autocratisation under the increasingly personalistic rule of Prime Minister-turned-President Recep Tayyip Erdoğan, who set out to establish a 'New Turkey' in his own patriarchal image and based on a religious–nationalist reimagination of a glorious Ottoman past. The period saw the unravelling of the liberal–Islamist-alliance, followed by the split within the Islamist camp between supporters of Erdoğan and Fethullah Gülen. Erdoğan survived the Gülenist challenge in part by forging a ruthlessly pragmatic pact with his ultra-nationalist and Eurasianist former enemies at home, and by moving closer to Vladimir Putin's Russia abroad. Meanwhile, the concurrent process of power consolidation took place in the context of Turkey's first popular presidential election in 2014, the twin parliamentary elections of 2015, in which Erdoğan effectively cancelled an unfavourable outcome and engineered a 'repeat election' to retain the AKP's parliamentary majority, and the 2017 constitutional referendum held under a state of emergency declared following the failed coup attempt of July 2016 and sounded the death knell of parliamentary democracy in Turkey.

The tactics and the discourse employed to undermine institutional democracy in the 2010s mirrored those that the AKP had used to disassemble the undemocratic tutelage of Kemalist guardians during the previous decade. These included key election and referendum victories that opened the way for far-reaching institutional reforms, continuing politicisation of the judiciary, vindictive court cases and widespread purges to consolidate political and economic power in the hands of the Leader and his increasingly exclusive group of clients and loyalists. In justifying state capture, Turkey's new rulers presented a populist worldview that divided society into a national and authentic 'us' versus a foreign-backed, inauthentic and disloyal 'them', as part of which they used and abused the anti-tutelage and deep state arguments that were part of the discourse of liberal democratisation during the previous decade.

Post-Kemalist Power Struggles, State Capture and Regime Consolidation

Unravelling of the Liberal–Islamist Alliance

The coalition that brought together the AKP with the liberal intelligentsia and the Hizmet movement started to fall apart as its two constituent elements – support for the EU accession and opposition to Kemalist tutelage – disappeared. The fizzling of Turkey's EU membership ambitions was a consequence of the popular backlash within Europe against the twin processes of enlargement and 'Brusselsisation', which were driven by the EU's own liberal politicians and technocratic guardians. When crisis hit Europe in 2008, bringing to surface a host of unresolved socio-economic tensions and resentments, the allure of the EU as an economic and democratic model started to fade away. Meanwhile, the defeat of the Kemalist guardians removed the common foe that had united the liberals and the Islamists, exposing their clashing visions over such issues as the nature and limits of state authority, the boundaries of free speech, the role of religion or the place of women in society. With the waning of the EU as a pressure mechanism for domestic reform, the liberals found it increasingly difficult to influence the direction of change in the country. Unbound by the external anchor of the EU and the internal pressures of the tutelary establishment, and in control of the institutions once dominated by the Kemalist guardians, the AKP officials' rhetoric and policies started to resemble, especially after their third election victory in 2011, a socially conservative version of their patriarchal predecessors.

The post-2011 period also saw a rapid personalisation of power by Prime Minister Erdoğan, who started transforming the AKP from an outward-looking and relatively diverse organisation into a vehicle of his personal ambitions, increasingly characterised by leader veneration and institutional distrust. Personally vetting the party's list of candidates for the 2011 election, he left out liberal-leaning and independent-minded figures, as well as those with close ties to President Gül, seen as a potential rival in a future presidential race. Surrounded by loyalists who owed their political status to the leader, a personality cult started forming around Erdoğan that gradually alienated him from his disillusioned former allies and long-time comrades. Party members started referring to Erdoğan as 'The Great Master' (*Büyük Usta*) or 'The Chief' (*Reis*). To the horror of many pious Muslims, some of his sycophantic associates even attributed divine qualities to their 'prophet-like' leader.[1]

The third AKP government (2011–15) saw the ruling party's domestic and foreign politics become increasingly intertwined, with Turkey's active engagement in the conflicts beyond its borders exacerbating socio-political tensions at home, and domestic tensions fuelling a more confrontational foreign policy abroad. Erdoğan and his ambitious Foreign Minister Ahmet Davutoğlu envisioned a post-Kemalist Turkey that would lead the new Middle East, where popular Islamist movements, like Tunisia's an-Nahda and Egypt's Muslim Brotherhood, which shared ideological references with the Turkish Islamists and looked up to the AKP as an ally and inspiration, were replacing secular dictatorships one after another. The expectation that Syria would soon follow these countries led the Turkish government to burn bridges with Damascus and become an active supporter of an increasingly radicalised opposition in what morphed into a bloody civil war.[2]

In the early days of the 'Arab Spring' uprisings, this vision found strategic support within Western foreign policy circles, where the idea of a Muslim-majority democracy led by a popular pro-Western, pro-Israel and pro-market 'moderate Islamist' government serving as a model for regional transformation appeared more desirable than seeing the rise of anti-Western and anti-Israeli brands of Islam sponsored by Saudi Arabia or Iran.[3] Some observers declared Turkey as the 'biggest winner of the Arab Spring'.[4] The simultaneous unfolding of so many propitious events at home and abroad convinced Turkey's decision-makers that their 'moment in the sun' had arrived and infused an element of imperial hubris to their policies, leading to overreach.[5]

The speech that Prime Minister Erdoğan delivered on the night of the AKP's election victory in June 2011 vividly captured this immense confidence, alongside the interwoven nature of domestic and foreign affairs, and the emerging pyramid-like power structure placing Erdoğan at the centre of the party, the party at the centre of the country, and the country at the centre of a vast Islamic realm corresponding to the former Ottoman territories. 'Believe me', he said, addressing thousands of passionate supporters from the imposing balcony of the AKP's new headquarters in Ankara: 'Sarajevo won today as much as Istanbul, Beirut won as much as Izmir, Damascus won as much as Ankara, Ramallah, Nablus, Jenin, the West Bank, Jerusalem won as much as Diyarbakir'.[6]

At home, the AKP gradually unveiled a state-driven refoundational project that was in many ways a religious–nationalist reproduction of the Kemalist nation-building efforts of the early republic. This vision for 'New Turkey' included a re-imagination of Turkey's Ottoman past as a golden era for Islam and Turkish nationalism; an ambitious economic growth agenda driven by the construction sector that would radically alter the physical landscape of Turkey's cities and countryside; a social engineering project based on Erdoğan's openly articulated desire to 'raise a religious youth'; and a political agenda to replace Turkey's parliamentary system with a strong presidentialism. These goals often overlapped. For example, spectacular construction projects, such as the world's largest mosque built on Istanbul's highest hilltop, the third Bosphorus bridge named after the Ottoman Sultan Selim II, or plans to demolish a public park and the Atatürk Cultural Centre in the historic Taksim Square to build a shopping mall designed after an Ottoman-era barracks and another massive mosque, were at once vainglorious monuments to neo-Ottomanism, symbolic acts of revenge on Kemalist modernism, as well as lucrative enterprises that boosted growth, promoted domestic consumption and distributed rent to government-backed construction tycoons.

As part of its social-engineering project, the AKP passed through the GNA an education bill that increased the number of *İmam Hatip* schools and added new religion courses to public school curricula, while gradually doing away with 'controversial' subjects like evolution in biology textbooks.[7] This was accompanied by the imposition of a conservative public morality, from curbs on alcohol sales and consumption and attempts to restrict abortions, to an intensive campaign of censorship by the state media regulatory agency, RTÜK, to eradicate perceived immorality on television.[8] Meanwhile, courts that previously dished out punishment for insulting Turkishness or Atatürk became increasingly preoccupied with the cases of those charged with insulting Islam, the Prophet, and after 2014, President Erdoğan himself.

Finally, in 2012 Erdoğan announced his long-anticipated plan to replace Turkey's parliamentary system with presidentialism. Declaring the institutional separation of powers as the 'main obstacle' to political expediency, Erdoğan and his advisors called for a system of executive presidentialism, equipped with the power to dissolve the parliament, govern through executive decrees and appoint senior judges and bureaucrats without parliamentary approval.[9] The push for 'Turkish-style presidentialism' was also an attempt at historical score-settling, given that it was the Kemalists' Young Turk predecessors who spearheaded the Constitutional Movement of 1908 that had convened the Ottoman parliament and forced the abdication of Sultan Abdulhamid II, the last absolutist monarch and the first major proponent of Islamism. In Erdoğan's increasingly fiery populist rhetoric, presidentialism came to represent the Muslim Turkish nation's emancipation from the shackles of an 'inauthentic' system and its Western-influenced secular guardians.[10]

Aided by strong economic growth until the mid-2010s, this state-driven refoundational project helped the AKP consolidate a large conservative base, while alienating secular Turks and Kurds, Alevis, feminists, the LGBTQ+ community and other marginalised minorities. In an environment where the government passed legislation without meaningful dialogue with the opposition parties, and major infrastructure projects – from hydroelectric dams threatening sensitive ecosystems to urban regeneration programmes displacing local communities – were awarded to a small number of contractors with personal links to Erdoğan, anti-government protests (and heavy-handed police response) became increasingly commonplace. In late May 2013, when police responded violently to a small protest against the destruction of Gezi Park in Taksim Square, these tensions boiled over to trigger the largest anti-government mass demonstrations in Turkey's modern history.

Framing dissent and protest as an affront to 'the nation's will' (*milli irade*) that emerged from the ballot box, Erdoğan labelled the demonstrators as 'terrorist hooligans' and 'looters and marauders'. This was not only a rhetorical tirade, but also legal labelling. Based on a 2006 amendment to the anti-terrorism legislation that greatly expanded the scope of the term 'terrorism', thousands of journalists, editors, academics, small publishers, student activists and local politicians were arrested on contentious charges. A testament to Turkey's superficial democratisation – and, indeed, selective autocratisation – in the 2000s, the illiberal spirit of this legislation was captured by then Interior Minister İdris Naim Şahin, who in a 2011 speech argued that terrorism was not an act limited to armed militants: 'A poem, a painting, a song, a caricature or an academic article can also support terrorism'.[11] The year 2011 was the first year when Turkey topped the list of countries with most journalists in jail, an unenviable accolade the government only buttressed in the following decade.[12]

The anti-terrorism legislation also provided police officers with extensive legal impunity and armed special police units with military-grade weapons, thereby rolling back the EU-backed police reforms of 2004. Unlike the military, which the ruling Islamists could never fully trust even after a decade of purges, religious–nationalist cadres had grown increasingly influential within the police force since the 1980s. Under the AKP, the police force became the coercive arm of the ruling party and a counterbalance against the armed forces. In 2009, Erdoğan even called the police 'the guarantors of the regime'.[13] As such, the militarisation of the police force took place parallel to the 'demilitarisation' of the state, with the former's budget rising consistently during the first decade of the AKP government.[14] The only other institution whose expenditures increased at similarly steep rates was the Presidency of Religious Affairs (*Diyanet*), which played a prominent role in promoting the ruling party's worldview and interests at home and abroad.[15]

The liberal–Islamist alliance unravelled in these circumstances, with the 'liberal moment' of the early 2000s appearing in retrospect as an interregnum rather than a genuine process of democratisation. Confident in their positions of power, the ruling Islamists no longer felt the need to speak diplomatically of their erstwhile allies or the direction of post-Kemalist Turkey under the AKP. One candid assessment came from Aziz Babuşcu, the AKP chairman, in March 2013:[16]

> Those who were our stakeholders during the past decade will not be our stakeholders in the coming decade. [. . .] The liberals, for instance, were our stakeholders during this process. But the future is the era of construction. And this construction era will not be as [the liberals] wish. Hence, they will no longer be with us. [. . .] The Turkey that we will construct, the future that we will bring about, is not going to be a future that they will be able to accept.

Betrayed and dismayed, not just by their allies at home but also by the global failures of liberal democratisation and, specifically, of the Europeanisation project to which they had tied their political fate, many liberal defenders of the AKP turned into the government's ardent critics and were subsequently hounded by Erdoğan's new regime.[17] They were also stigmatised by Erdoğan's socialist and Kemalist opponents as 'useful idiots' and mockingly compared with Iranian leftists and liberals, who supported Khomeini against the Pahlavi regime, only to be discarded once the Islamic Republic was established. To be sure, there was no inevitability to Turkey's post-Kemalist trajectory to justify the determinism with which the AKP's secular nationalist opponents had denied a chance to the country's democratisation from the outset. Indeed, many self-declared Kemalists and Eurasianists contributed to that trajectory in complex ways, whether by conducting politics on a zero-sum basis during the early years of the AKP government, or by forming a coalition of convenience with President Erdoğan following the intra-Islamist split.

But there were also signs of caution early on, from the anti-terrorism legislation to the conduct of the Ergenekon and Sledgehammer cases, that the AKP's most vocal liberal supporters, in their determination to dismantle Kemalist tutelage, either missed or chose to overlook. The liberals had hoped that exposing the darker chapters of Turkey's nation-building process would usher in a catharsis that would not only break down nationalist taboos but also the barriers to democracy in Turkey. While challenge taboos they did, the singular focus on the 1908–45 period may have blindsided some of these intellectuals to the prevalence of a patriarchal state tradition both pre- and post-dating the Young Turk and Kemalist experiences that cannot simply be explained as a factor of them.[18] As post-Kemalist Turkey under Erdoğan made abundantly clear, the reservoir and repertoire of patriarchal state reflexes ran deeper and wider than many had assumed and hoped for.

Intra-Islamist Split, Failed Coup and State Capture

After mid-2013, the AKP's neo-imperial ambitions suffered multiple setbacks at home and abroad. Abroad, Turkey's active engagement in the Syrian civil war led to the rapid re-securitisation of the country's southern and eastern borders, deteriorating its ties with Iraq, Iran and Russia, and triggering an influx of refugees and foreign fighters onto Turkish soil. Meanwhile, the military coup in Egypt against President Mohammad Morsi in July 2013 did not only deprive Turkey's ruling Islamists of a key regional and ideological ally but also plunged them into a state of existential insecurity, bringing to surface historically rooted fears of violent overthrow and distrust of the West. For Erdoğan, the muted Western response to the Egyptian coup and the swift recognition of the Sisi government came as a confirmation of the West's double-standards against Muslims, especially in light of the extensive media coverage and international condemnation of police brutality in the Gezi protests.

Compounding this resentment was a sense of betrayal resulting from the shift in strategic focus in the West from toppling the Assad regime in Syria to defeating the rising jihadist challenge. This shift followed the capture of the Iraqi city of Mosul by the Islamic State (IS) in June 2014 and a spate of terror attacks linked to IS in Europe in 2015 and 2016. In turn, it opened space for new alliances against IS, most notably between the US and the Syrian Kurdish People's Protection Units (*Yekîneyên Parastina Gel*, YPG), which was established as an offshoot of the PKK. Just as the Syrian Kurds were becoming the object of admiration in the West for their fierce resistance to IS and for championing gender equality and democracy in northeast Syria, Western perceptions of Erdoğan's Turkey were turning from viewing it as a regional model to an authoritarian police state and enabler of violent jihadism.

Temporarily keeping the fighting in Syria from spilling into Turkey were the peace negotiations that started between the Turkish state and the PKK in early 2013. This was a fragile process, fraught with tensions and suspicions on both sides. In October 2014, Ankara's reluctance to assist Kurdish fighters defending the border town of Kobanê in Syria from an IS assault – and Erdoğan's seemingly gleeful anticipation of the town's fall to the jihadists – triggered deadly Kurdish riots in eastern Turkey. By the time the Turkish government bowed to Western pressure and reversed its policy, the damage to Erdoğan's reputation amongst the Kurds had been done. Simmering tensions between an embittered AKP and an emboldened PKK boiled over following the June 2015 general election. This was the first election the AKP contested without Erdoğan officially at the helm of the party. Having won Turkey's first popular vote for the presidency in August 2014, he was constitutionally obliged to step down as party chairman and prime minister.

It was also the first election since 2002 that the AKP failed to secure a parliamentary majority. This failure was in part due to the visible lack of coordination between Erdoğan, who continued to act as de facto head of the AKP, and Davutoğlu, his hand-picked successor as prime minister and AKP chairman, who did not want to remain in the president's shadow. At the same time, its Kurdish policy had cost the AKP its support base among both Turkish nationalists – who despised the talks with the PKK – and conservative Kurds. The former migrated towards the ultra-nationalist MHP, and the latter towards the Peoples' Democratic Party (*Halkların Demokratik Partisi*, HDP), making it the first party of the Kurdish nationalist movement to overcome the election threshold, with 13% of the vote.

Showing no intention to share or relinquish power, Erdoğan immediately set out to engineer a 'repeat election' to reclaim his lost majority. He also abandoned the 'peace process' for a return to the politics of war and nationalism. He found a bellicose counterpart in the PKK, whose fighters, in their newfound zeal and confidence, dug trenches and declared autonomy in densely populated areas in preparation for Kobanê-style urban guerrilla battles. The resulting fighting saw weeks-long twenty-four hour curfews in Kurdish cities and wide-scale destruction of historic neighbourhoods.[19] Emergency laws, which the AKP had prided itself for lifting in 2002, were brought back to the region. Civilian deaths and human rights abuses mounted.[20] Major metropolises suffered some of the deadliest terror attacks in the country's history, attributed both to the PKK and to IS.[21] In the repeat election of November 2015, a terrorised electorate gave Erdoğan the parliamentary majority he had wanted.

In this process, anti-Westernism became a central feature of Erdoğan's increasingly nativist discourse. 'Foreigners don't like us', he argued at a trade summit for Islamic countries in Istanbul in November 2014. 'They love oil, gold, diamonds, and the cheap labour force of the Islamic world [. . .] They look like friends, but they want us dead, they like seeing our children die'.[22] The sycophants surrounding the Turkish leader took this discourse to creative new heights. One prominent example was Erdoğan's special economic advisor Yiğit Bulut, a government-critic-turned-cheerleader, whose outlandish conspiracy theories during the Gezi protests included claiming that the German airliner Lufthansa was behind the protests, and that foreign intelligence agencies were trying to kill the Turkish leader through telekinesis. This combative and conspiratorial discourse reflected both a real sense of existential insecurity among AKP decision-makers, as well as its instrumentalisation to mobilise popular support.

A major cause of this insecurity was the split between the AKP and the Gülenists. With their common enemy, the Kemalists, out of the way, the historical differences and rival political ambitions of the two Islamist camps resurfaced with a vengeance. The result was a much more profoundly destabilising and paranoia-inducing fallout than the liberal–Islamist split. The first signs of a rupture had come as early as in 2010, when Fethullah Gülen, a long-time advocate of close ties with the US and Israel, gave a rare interview to the *Wall Street Journal*, criticising and distancing himself from Erdoğan's sharp public denunciations of Israel.[23] In 2012, Erdoğan intervened personally to block a Gülenist prosecutor from detaining and questioning Hakan Fidan, then chief of Turkey's National Intelligence Agency and a confidant of Erdoğan, for taking part in secret talks with the PKK representatives in Oslo. The details of these talks were leaked to the press by Gülenist police officers.[24] During the Gezi protests, Hizmet newspapers *Zaman* and *Today's Zaman* published unusually harsh criticisms of the AKP government.

The simmering rivalry turned into open hostility in December 2013, following a move by the government to shut down private preparatory schools that had for decades served as a major cash source and recruitment base for Hizmet. In immediate retaliation, Gülenist prosecutors launched a major corruption investigation against the government, implicating senior ministers and businesspeople close to Erdoğan with bribery, money laundering, illegal provision of building permits and public contracts, as well as a breach of US-enforced sanctions against Iran for private gain. The investigation was led by Zekeriya Öz, the chief prosecutor in the Ergenekon case. Calling the operation a 'bureaucratic coup attempt', Erdoğan accused Gülen of building a 'parallel state'. In an attempt to block a second indictment implicating other senior AKP figures as well as Erdoğan's own family, the government abruptly purged hundreds of suspected followers of Gülen in the police force and the judiciary. In response, secretly obtained recordings of incriminating phone conversations between the prime minister and his close entourage were leaked online.[25] In February 2014, the government forced two bills through the GNA aimed at suppressing the indictments and the leaks by tightening the executive's control over the judiciary and expanding internet censorship.

The shattering of the intra-Islamist alliance did not only expose both the extra-legal tactics and the corrupt internal mechanisms of the coalition that governed Turkey since 2002, it also had far-reaching socio-political and international ramifications. In contrast to the fight against the Kemalists, which featured two sides clearly separated by political ideology, socio-economic status and cultural habitus, the split within the Islamist 'tribe' proved to be particularly traumatising and paranoia-inducing.[26] The Islamist fratricide quickly spilled over into international politics. The business and political networks of Hizmet, from which the AKP had benefited generously for over a decade, started functioning as an anti-Erdoğan lobby in the West.[27] In return, the AKP government stepped up diplomatic, lobbying and intelligence efforts to crack down on Gülenist activities abroad. It also launched an intensive propaganda campaign at home, through the national media landscape that it had come to dominate, labelling critics and opponents – whether secular, leftist, liberal, Kurdish or Islamist – as agents of foreign powers, traitors and terrorist supporters.

Byzantine power struggles over key institutions created further conditions for autocratisation and securitisation of the state and society. In late 2015, Hizmet was officially designated a terrorist group. Now referred to as the 'Fethullahist Terror Organisation' (FETÖ) its members and sympathisers were retrospectively criminalised. Ultimately, the zero-sum nature of this power struggle created a downward spiral, culminating in the failed coup attempt of 15 July 2016. This attempt was allegedly spearheaded by Gülenist officers, many of whom had risen through the ranks following the purge of Kemalist officers between 2008 and 2011, but were expected to be discharged in the upcoming meeting of the Supreme Military Council, scheduled for August 2016. It remains a mystery to what extent the government was caught unaware by the intervention, in which over 300 people were killed, many of them civilians confronting soldiers on the streets. What is known is that by declaring the failed coup a 'gift from God', Erdoğan used it as an opportunity to crush his rivals and finally establish the 'Turkish-style presidentialism' that he had long aspired to.[28]

Within days of the coup attempt, amidst government-sponsored public rallies and 'democracy vigils', the Turkish government derogated from its obligations to the European Convention of Human Rights and declared a nationwide state of emergency, giving the president extraordinary powers over the judiciary and the legislature. Henceforth, Erdoğan started to rule by decree, overseeing a new wave of purges and repression, which surpassed even the post-1980 clampdown in its scope and intensity. Within two weeks of the attempted coup, more than 60,000 public officials, including soldiers, police officers, judges, teachers and bureaucrats, were dismissed by emergency decree. Nearly half of all the generals and admirals in the TSK were dishonourably discharged. By March 2019, the number of dismissals from public service had surpassed 150,000, while more than 100,000 people, including more than 300 journalists, had been arrested. Three-thousand schools, universities and dormitories, and 189 media outlets were shut down. More than 6,000 academics lost their jobs.[29] Turkey's top religious official, Diyanet President Mehmet Görmez, declared Fethullah Gülen a heretic.[30] The Gülenist business association TUSKON was shuttered, while the assets of Hizmet-associated banks, media organisations and business conglomerates were expropriated and eventually transferred to the allies of President Erdoğan.

The target of the purges and incarcerations was not limited to suspected members of 'FETÖ'. They included left-wing activists, liberal intellectuals, human rights lawyers, trade unionists, Kurdish politicians and outspoken government critics. Imprisoned at the height of the coup trials for probing Gülenist links in the police force, journalist Ahmet Şık was jailed again for his no-holds-barred critical reporting of the purges. Ahmet Altan was sentenced to life in prison for sending 'subliminal messages' via his newspaper columns to overthrow the government. Scholars who signed an online petition condemning the rights abuses by the security forces in the Kurdish provinces were labelled by the president as 'treacherous pseudo-intellectuals'. Hundreds were stripped of their academic titles, taken to court on terrorism charges and scores were handed prison sentences.[31] After spending nearly five years in pre-trial detention, philanthropist businessman and rights defender Osman Kavala, dubbed and vilified by Erdoğan as the 'Turkish Soros', was handed aggravated life sentence for 'plotting the Gezi upheaval' to overthrow the government, alongside seven other civil society activists, who received eighteen years each. Amnesty International condemned the verdict in the 'Gezi trial' as 'a travesty of justice of spectacular proportions'.[32]

Between November 2016 and March 2017, thirteen HDP deputies, including the party's popular and charismatic co-chair Selahattin Demirtaş, were stripped of their parliamentary immunity and imprisoned, along with eighty-four elected Kurdish mayors, while fifty-four HDP-run municipalities were taken over by the central government. The GNA had approved lifting the deputies' immunities before the coup attempt, in May 2016. The legislation was prepared by the AKP, supported by the MHP and even received partial backing from the CHP, whose leader, Kemal Kılıçdaroğlu, astonishingly said that they would vote for the bill 'even though it violated the constitution'.[33] It seemed Erdoğan had discovered the parliamentary opposition's Achilles heel. Framing his agenda in the language of 'the nation and the state's survival' (*milletin ve devletin bekası*), he managed to drive a wedge between Turkish nationalists and the Kurds, thereby keeping the opposition fragmented.

It was not just the parliamentary opposition that helped clear the way for Erdoğan's pursuit of political domination. In a remarkable act of self-sabotage, the Constitutional Court declared itself unauthorised to review the constitutionality of the presidential decrees, whose scope expanded beyond the legal confines of the state of emergency into all matters of government, from the regulation of commercial transactions to restructuring universities.[34] Without judicial oversight, partisan control of the judiciary also reached unprecedented levels. Over 4,000 judges and prosecutors were dismissed within a year of the failed coup. In January 2017, a presidential decree removed the requirement to obtain a minimum score of 70% in the written examination to become a judge, effectively allowing anyone who participated in the examination to proceed to the interview stage, which was mired with lack of transparency and partisan selection practices. Another presidential decree in July 2018 removed the requirement to have a law degree in order to become a judge, opening the way for anyone with a university diploma to enter the judiciary.

According to the opposition CHP, more than 10,000 new judges and prosecutors were appointed between early 2017 and mid-2019, with party loyalists, personal lawyers and relatives of AKP members being placed in key positions.[35] Some of these appointees played critical roles in politicised court cases, including 'the Gezi trial' and the controversial decision to dismiss – a week before the visit of Saudi Crown Prince Mohammad Bin Salman to Turkey in April 2022 – the murder trial of Saudi journalist Jamal Khashoggi, who was killed inside the Saudi consulate in Istanbul in 2018.[36] In both cases, senior judges who expressed dissenting opinions were summarily exiled to provincial courts.[37] In contrast, judges that defied higher courts – including legally binding decisions by the Constitutional Court and the European Court of Human Rights (ECHR) – in pursuing partisan missions were protected and promoted by the government.[38]

The state of emergency was extended every three months until 17 July 2018. By the time it was lifted, most of its temporary restrictions and emergency decrees had already been made permanent in the constitutional referendum of 16 April 2017. In this referendum, put to vote under conditions of suspended democracy and following a campaign that 'failed to meet international standards' of free and fair competition, the 'Turkish-style' presidentialism was approved by 51% of the voters, formalising Erdoğan's de facto rule.[39] The new system granted the president the powers to bypass the GNA and rule by executive decree, determine the country's budget, appoint ministers, senior bureaucrats, half of the members on the Board of Judges and Prosecutors, and twelve of the fifteen-member Constitutional Court, declare a state of emergency and to dissolve the parliament. It also restricted the legislature and the judiciary's abilities to oversee the executive branch and hold it to account, effectively turning the president into the head of all three branches of power.[40] Publishing its opinion ahead of the referendum, the Venice Commission, the EU's top constitutional law body, warned that the proposed system represented 'a dangerous step backwards in the constitutional democratic tradition of Turkey' and would steer it 'towards an authoritarian and personal regime'.[41]

Finally, the intra-Islamist split allowed Erdoğan to tighten his grip on the ruling party itself, marginalising Gülen sympathisers in the old guard, such as party co-founder Bülent Arınç and his own high school classmate İdris Naim Şahin, the former interior minister. A younger generation of loyalists filled up the vacant spots. Erdoğan's drive to achieve absolute control of the party was completed in May 2016 with the ouster of Ahmet Davutoğlu through an internal party coup that had him replaced by the president's trusted devotee Binali Yıldırım as prime minister and party leader. Erdoğan appeared to hold Davutoğlu responsible for the party's poor performance in the June 2015 election. By early 2016, the president's supporters were publicly questioning Davutoğlu's loyalty to the leader, and blaming him for Turkey's foreign policy debacles, especially in Syria. At a time when anti-Westernism dominated the ruling party's discourse, Davutoğlu drew suspicion for maintaining close working relations with his Western counterparts, particularly with the US State Department.[42] As such, his departure accelerated the AKP's pivot towards a more nationalistic direction at home and a Eurasianist platform in foreign policy.

'Parallel State' Makes Way for the 'Deep State'

With its provisional abolition of the separation of powers, the state of emergency gave President Erdoğan the opportunity – 'the gift from God' – to consolidate his personal authority. But this domination came at the expense of the institutional monopoly of the Islamists. The purge of the Gülenists left a major vacuum within the state bureaucracy and the security establishment, depriving the president of well-trained and competent personnel. The purges did open space for the president's own loyalists, who were mostly educated in *İmam Hatip* schools and hailed from the AKP's youth branches, to rise within the bureaucracy alongside members of lesser-known Islamic fraternities. But these groups lacked both the numbers and the competence to fill the vacuum entirely.[43] As a result, Erdoğan turned to former opponents – the nationalist MHP and the Eurasianists – for an ultra-pragmatic new alliance.

Already during the Gezi protests rumours had emerged of an ongoing operation to replace Gülenist police officers with religious–nationalist cadres close to the MHP.[44] This budding convergence no longer remained a secret after the intra-Islamist split. Following the June 2015 election, the MHP – the party whose rank-and-file members had provided the bulk of the anti-communist militias (the 'Grey Wolves') during the Cold War and for the anti-Kurdish assassination squads in the 1990s – first became an informal and then a formal coalition partner of the AKP. Virtually overnight, the MHP leader Devlet Bahçeli turned from a fierce critic of the government into a key ally. In return for gaining preferential access to state bureaucracy and successfully promoting his party's anti-Kurdish agenda, he lent vociferous support for the post-coup attempt clampdown and the state of emergency measures, as well as for Erdoğan's successful bids for presidency in 2018 and 2023.[45]

At the height of the Gülenist-led corruption probe in early 2014, the government also performed a dramatic volte-face by declaring the Ergenekon and Sledgehammer trials 'a sinister plot against our nation's military' by the Gülenists.[46] Within months, prominent military and civilian suspects were released, pending retrial, while the prosecutors and the reporters driving the investigations themselves turned into suspects. The judiciary subsequently threw out both cases, declaring the evidence fabricated and unacceptable. Among the released suspects was Sedat Peker, an ultra-nationalist mafia boss, who refashioned himself as a loyal servant of 'the Chief', threatening perceived enemies of the state with 'rivers of blood'.[47] Another newly liberated figure that turned into an AKP enthusiast was Mehmet Ağar, the former interior minister and police chief, whose name is inextricably linked with the deep state of the 1990s. In the June 2018 election, Ağar's son was elected MP from the ruling party.

The Eurasianists also walked free, some of whom subsequently joined the anti-liberal, anti-Kurdish, anti-Western, anti-Gülenist patchwork alliance around the president, vying for influence within the military and intelligence agencies.[48] Upon his release from prison in March 2014, Doğu Perinçek publicly swore to seek vengeance from Fethullah Gülen, whom he called the agent of 'crusader reactionism' (*haçlı irtica*), signalling a partnership of convenience with his former enemy, President Erdoğan.[49] In June 2016, immediately after Davutoglu's departure, retired generals and diplomats from Perinçek's circle reportedly acted as intermediaries in the efforts to mend Turkey's broken ties with Russia.[50]

The rapprochement with Russia gained pace following the abortive coup. While the Turkish government blamed the United States for supporting the coup attempt, Russia was seen in a favourable light. Alexander Dugin, the ideologue-in-chief of Eurasianism and briefly an advisor to Russian President Putin, claimed that Moscow had tipped off Ankara about a potential intervention the day before the events. In November 2016, twelve years after his last visit, Dugin was in Turkey once again, but this time as a friend of the AKP. Upon Prime Minister Yıldırım's invitation, he briefed a parliamentary inquiry commission about Russian intelligence into the failed coup and spoke at length about the 'US support for FETÖ'.[51] That same month, Erdoğan supporters welcomed the election of Donald Trump as the US president, despite the latter's brazenly Islamophobic statements and proposals. In Trump, the Turkish government saw an unconventional leader, unbound by institutional constraints and sympathetic to Russia, whom they believed could be swayed on a range of issues.[52] When Turkey's behind-the-scenes lobbying efforts failed to produce intended results, pro-AKP commentators concluded that Trump had 'surrendered to the US deep state'.[53]

In the end, Erdoğan's pragmatic manoeuvres enabled him to break through the isolation his government suffered between 2013 and 2016 and survive the mounting threats to his rule, cementing his legacy as Turkey's most powerful and impactful politician since Atatürk. Erdoğan managed to consolidate his personal authority by securing further (albeit relatively narrow) victories in the 2018 and 2023 presidential elections, which took place under increasingly unfree and unfair conditions. At the same time, however, the return of the ultra-nationalists to the governing fold following the Islamist fratricide threw into sharp relief the unfinished nature of Turkey's hegemonic struggles. The president's continued dependence on the cadres of independent interest groups, whether the Gülenist 'parallel state' or the ultra-nationalist 'deep state', alongside his micromanaging style and inability to groom a successor due to his intensely suspicious nature, as well as the surprising resilience of a democratic opposition in the country, put to question the long-term stability of his regime and portended fresh power struggles after Erdoğan.

The Use and Abuse of 'Tutelage' in the Making of a Party-state

The dramatic power struggles and shifts of alliances that occurred against a backdrop of geopolitical fluidity and insecurity altered Turkey's socio-political and institutional landscape in unmistakable ways. But built upon the institutional, ideological and economic foundations laid by the 1980 military coup (i.e., the creation of a semi-presidential system, the promotion of the Turkish–Islamic synthesis as semi-official state ideology and the reconfiguration of rent distribution and patronage networks through neoliberal reform), the post-Kemalist Turkey that emerged in the 2010s also exhibited important continuities from the past.[54]

At its core, Erdoğan's 'refoundational project', and the monopolisation of state power to forge a new national identity in the charismatic leader's image, is an attempt to reproduce the nation-building projects of the nineteenth and early twentieth centuries, including the Kemalist one, which the Islamists have long resented and sought to undo. Likewise, the emergence of a party-state under supreme executive authority harks back more to the pre-1960 era of Turkish politics under the 1924 Constitution (i.e., the single-party under the CHP and the DP's dominant-party rule) than any arrangement under the Ottoman Empire. In its methods, if not in its idiosyncratic ideology and convictions, Erdoğan's pragmatic making and breaking of coalitions resembles the process of Kemalist regime consolidation in the early republic, as well as the military guardians' logic of expansion through self-correcting coups.

The overarching continuity between Turkey before and under Erdoğan is the enduring attachment of power holders to the idea of a patriarchal state, which has manifested itself under different ideological guises throughout Turkey's modern history. State veneration has been at once a core pillar of Turkish nationalism, both secular and religious, and the excuse that political actors have used to justify using public means and resources for their private, including illicit, interests. This remains unchanged in Erdoğan's 'New Turkey'. What is notable is the degree to which the image and the authority of the state have become enmeshed with the personal image and authority of Erdoğan, both in abstract and institutional terms. In the course of the AKP's two-decade control of the national government, the line separating the ruling party from the state apparatus has become increasingly blurred, rendering Turkey a party-state. With its formidable grassroots organisation, municipal administrations, control of state institutions and access to public resources, the ruling party serves as the bridge between the government, the civil service, coalition partners, allied businesses and voters.[55]

At the centre of the party-state is President Erdoğan, who, with his charisma and presidential powers, holds together a multi-layered network of allies, clients and supporters by negotiating and overseeing the distribution of public posts, contracts and resources. His indispensability to the party, which he dominates, and the party's infusion into the state apparatus, have meant that Turkey's national agenda and interests, the political agenda of the ruling party and the interests of the president and his inner circle have become virtually indistinguishable. It is no surprise, then, with so much depending on the 'Reis', that the AKP government and its supporters see Erdoğan's political survival as necessary not just for the survival of the Turkish nation and the state (*milletin ve devletin bekası*) but also of the entire Islamic realm.[56] Viewing the world through such an existential prism infuses a zero-sum approach to politics, where the end justifies any means.[57]

The legitimising discourse of this dominate-or-perish worldview depicts Erdoğan as fighting a new battle of independence at home and abroad in pursuit of an alternative hegemonic project in the name of 'us, the good and authentic (Muslim/Turkish) people' against 'them, the corrupt, greedy and oppressive (Western/secular) elites'. This simplifying Manicheanism draws both from the deep wells of nationalist and Islamist resentments and conspiracy theories of 'old Turkey'[58] and the rising transnational anti-globalist discourse that brings together right-wing populists and autocrats like Putin, Orbán, Trump and Bolsonaro, against the liberal international order in the twenty-first century.[59]

References to *vesayet* feature prominently in this grand narrative. But while in the 1990s and the 2000s, tutelage had a clear and specific definition, referring to the unelected military and bureaucratic bodies that wielded undue influence over the democratic process, during the 2010s it turned into an empty signifier covering a broad and fuzzy set of often interchangeable and largely unrelated enemies at home and abroad, real and sometimes imagined. In part, this had to do with the changing ownership of the term over time. In their first years in power, the AKP officials largely refrained from referring to *vesayet* in their public statements, invoking instead the less polemical 'respect for democracy and rule of law' argument when faced with military-bureaucratic intransigence. It was the combative liberal intelligentsia that openly called out the guardians and the system of tutelage and labelled their sympathisers *statükocu* and *vesayetçi*.[60] Erdoğan only started using *vesayet* consistently during the 2010 constitutional referendum, which he declared a historic victory against 'the tutelary regime'.[61]

From then on, instead of fizzling out as military tutelage was disassembled, *vesayet* became ubiquitous in the government's discourse. Parliamentarism had to be abandoned to do away with 'the outdated tutelage system that has set us back for years'.[62] The education system had to be reformed 'to liberate science from all sorts of tutelage'.[63] 'Shackles of tutelage' in arts and literature had to be broken to establish 'our social and cultural hegemony'.[64] The two long-standing dreams of Turkey's Islamists that Erdoğan fulfilled – building a mosque in Taksim Square and converting Hagia Sophia into a mosque – were symbolic blows to the tutelage of Western/Kemalist secularists.[65] The president's unorthodox economic policies and personal control of the ostensibly autonomous Central Bank, widely considered to be responsible for Turkey's currency meltdown and skyrocketing inflation after 2018, were part of the resistance to 'global economic tutelage institutions'.[66] ECHR judgements on Kavala and Demirtaş were attempts at exercising tutelage on Turkey's judicial independence.[67] In March 2021, İbrahim Karagül, then chief editor of the pro-government *Yeni Şafak* daily, defended the president's decision to withdraw from the Istanbul Convention, the Council of Europe treaty on preventing and combating violence against women, which the AKP government itself had signed in 2010, in the following words:

> Turkey is removing all tutelary devices in order to become a great power. Political tutelage, military tutelage, economic tutelage, social tutelage, mental tutelage. [. . .] The Istanbul Convention has been transformed into an LGBT convention. It has nothing to do with women's rights. It has been used to organise a new kind of 'social tutelage'. It was the conflict zone chosen to dynamite Turkey. We have taken another weapon off their hands.[68]

In October 2021, the CHP Chairman Kılıçdaroğlu published an online video message calling on public officials not to follow orders that did not comply with the law even if these came from their superiors. 'You cannot serve the mafia order in the name of duty', he said. 'You cannot consider illegal works as orders. You are honourable officers of this state, not servants of the Erdoğan family'. Erdoğan responded in characteristic fashion: 'This statement is a clear admission that the CHP mentality is a tutelage mentality', he said. 'Inviting the bureaucracy to oppose the elected government is nothing but a call for tutelage'.[69] It is not difficult to imagine a similar exchange taking place a decade earlier, when Erdoğan would be praised as a champion of democratisation and his opponent an obstacle to it. This was perhaps the most telling example of the how the authoritarian–democratic cleavage that defined Turkey's politics in the 2000s had turned on its head as the discourse of resisting tutelage was gradually appropriated by the hegemonic project of a populist strongman, who had no patience or respect for the democratic separation of powers, public integrity and the rule of law.

Notes

1. Some memorable statements by Erdoğan's followers include: 'To us, our prime minister is a second prophet', İsmail Hakkı Eser, AKP chair for Aydın province, 3 February 2010; 'Even touching our prime minister is an act of worship', AKP MP Hüseyin Şahin, 21 July 2011; 'I swear to God that Erdoğan is the indefinite and eternal leader of Turkey', AKP Deputy Chairman Süleyman Soylu, 3 February 2013; 'I recognise Erdoğan as a righteous caliph and pay him homage', Twitter message by journalist Atılgan Bayar, 23 August 2013; '[Erdoğan] is a world leader that possesses all the attributes of Allah', AKP MP Fevai Arslan, 16 January 2014.
2. Akkoyunlu et al., 'The Western Condition'.
3. See Ülgen, 'From Inspiration to Aspiration'; Bechev, 'Turkey's Rise as a Regional Power'.
4. 'Turkey is the biggest winner of the Arab Spring. In the five countries polled, Turkey is seen to have played the 'most constructive' role in the Arab events. Its prime minister, Recep Erdoğan, is the most admired among world leaders, and those who envision a new president for Egypt want the new president to look most like Erdoğan. Egyptians want their country to look more like Turkey than any of the other Muslim, Arab and other choices provided'. Telhami, 'The 2011 Arab Public Opinion Poll'.
5. Akkoyunlu, 'The "Turkish model" Isn't Good for Turkey'.
6. Susanne Güsten, 'Mandate for a New Turkish era', *New York Times*, 15 June 2011.
7. Simon Cameron-Moore, 'Turkey Passes School Reform Law Critics View as Islamic', *Reuters*, 30 March 2012.
8. Constance Letsch, 'Istanbul Hospitals Refuse Abortions as Government's Attitude Hardens', *Guardian*, 4 February 2015.
9. 'Separation of Powers an Obstacle, Says Erdoğan', *Hürriyet Daily News*, 18 December 2012.
10. Akkoyunlu, and Öktem, 'Existential Insecurity'.

11. 'İçişleri Bakanı'ndan yeni terör tarifleri', *Radikal*, 26 December 2011.
12. Nina Ognianova, 'Turkey--World's Top Press Jailer Once More', *Committee to Protect Journalists Worldwide*, 18 December 2013.
13. '"Rejimin güvencesi polis" sözleri tartışma çıkardı', *Hürriyet*, 29 June 2009.
14. Gönen et al., *Polis yasalarının ruhu*.
15. Öztürk, 'Turkey's Diyanet Under AKP Rule'.
16. 'AK Partili Babuşcu'dan ilginç değerlendirme', *CNN Turk*, 31 March 2013.
17. A symbolic sign of this divorce was the sentencing of Ahmet Altan, editor-in-chief of *Taraf*, to eleven months in prison in 2013 for insulting Erdoğan.
18. For a critical evaluation of the liberal 'post-Kemalist' theses, see Aytürk and Esen, *Post-Post-Kemalizm*.
19. Demirbaş, 'Undoing Years of Progress in Turkey'.
20. 'Turkey: Mounting Security Operation Deaths', *Human Rights Watch*, 22 December 2015.
21. Major attacks linked to Islamic State included the suicide bombing in Suruç, on the Syrian border, in July 2015, which killed thirty-three youth members of a socialist party; twin explosions in Ankara, which killed 109 civilians at a left-wing peace rally; the Istanbul Atatürk Airport attack in June 2016, which killed forty-eight people; and the attack at an Istanbul night club on New Year's Eve 2017, which killed thirty-nine people. Two explosions in Ankara in February and March 2016, killing sixty-seven people in total, and a suicide attack next to a football stadium in Istanbul in December 2016, killing forty-four people, were claimed by an offshoot of the PKK.
22. 'Foreigners Don't Like Muslims, Only Their Money: Turkish President Erdoğan', *Hurriyet Daily News*, 27 November 2014.
23. Joe Lauria, 'Reclusive Turkish Imam Criticizes Gaza Flotilla', *Wall Street Journal*, 4 June 2010.
24. Daren Butler, 'Turkish Spy Row Hits Kurdish Peace, Democratization Move', *Reuters*, 17 February 2012.
25. Samia Nakhoul and Nick Tattersall, 'Turkish PM Says Tapes of Talk With Son a Fabrication', *Reuters*, 25 February 2014.
26. Akkoyunlu and Öktem, 'Existential Insecurity', p. 515.
27. Lewontin, 'Turkey Coup Attempt Exposes Gülen-Erdoğan Lobbying Battle in the US'.
28. Champion, 'Coup Was "Gift from God" for Erdogan Planning a New Turkey'.
29. Chris Morris, 'Reality Check: The Numbers Behind the Crackdown in Turkey', *BBC News*, 18 June 2018.

30. Öztürk, 'Does Turkey Use "Spying Imams" To Assert Its Powers Abroad?'.

31. 'Turkey: Academics on Trial for Signing Petition', *Human Rights Watch*, 5 December 2017.

32. 'Turkey: Conviction of Osman Kavala A 'Devastating Blow' For Human Rights', *Amnesty International*, 25 April 2022.

33. 'Kılıçdaroğlu: AKP'nin dokunulmazlık teklifi Anayasa'ya aykırı ama "Evet" diyeceğiz', *Diken*, 13 April 2016.

34. See for instance Benjamin Harvey and Ercan Ersoy, 'New Erdogan Law Forces Contracts in Turkey to Be Made in Liras', *Bloomberg*, 13 September 2018.

35. Alican Uludağ, 'Tartışmalı davalarda kıdemsiz hakim imzası', *DW*, 27 April 2022.

36. Birkan Bulut, 'Gezi kararı yargıdaki kadrolaşmayı daha görünür kıldı: Yargıda adım adım kuşatma', *Evrensel*, 28 April 2022.

37. 'Kaşıkçı davasının sürgün edilen hakimi: Mesleği bırakacağım', *Gazete Duvar*, 20 June 2022.

38. One example is Akın Gürlek, who presided over the high profile sentencing of opposition figures, including former HDP co-chair Selahattin Demirtaş, CHP Istanbul chair Canan Kaftancıoğlu and CHP deputy Enis Berberoğlu. The sentencing of Demirtaş took place despite the ECHR ruling for his immediate release on rights violations grounds. Gürlek made headlines in January 2021 for ignoring the Constitutional Court's decision to release Berberoğlu and keeping the opposition MP behind bars. He was promoted to become a first-tier judge in September 2021, before being appointed by President Erdoğan as deputy minister of justice in 2022.

39. OSCE/ODIHR, 'Republic of Turkey Constitutional Referendum 16 April 2017'.

40. Öztürk, Erdi and İştar Gözaydın (2017), 'Turkey's constitutional amendments: A critical perspective', *Research and Policy on Turkey*, 2, pp. 210–24.

41. Venice Commission, 'Turkey: Opinion on the Amendments to the Constitution Adopted by the Grand National Assembly on 21 January 2017 and to be Submitted to a National Referendum on 16 April 2017'. Opinion No. 875/2017, Strasbourg, 13 March 2017.

42. Senior US officials lamented Davutoğlu's fall from grace as the loss of Washington's 'behind-the-scenes ally'. Hudson, 'America Loses its Man in Ankara'.

43. Two fraternities that started to populate several ministries and the police force were the Süleymancılar and Menzil branches of the Naqshbandi Sufi order. 'Boşalan kadrolara Menzil tarikatı mı yerleştiriliyor?', *Evrensel*, 17 August 2016.

44. Çakır, 'Ülkücüler Cemaat-hükümet savaşının neresinde?'. Başaran, 'Cemaatçi polisler gitti, 'dombra'cılar mı geldi'.
45. This sudden shift fractured the MHP. After repeated attempts to challenge Bahçeli's leadership in an extraordinary party congress was blocked by the judiciary, presumably under Erdoğan's directives, dissident MPs led by former interior minister Meral Akşener split to establish the 'Good Party' (*Iyi Parti*), which has allied with the CHP, successfully in the 2019 municipal elections and unsuccessfully in the 2023 presidential and parliamentary elections.
46. 'Yalçın Akdoğan: Cemaat orduya kumpas kurdu', *Cumhuriyet*, 24 December 2013.
47. 'Notorious criminal threatens academics calling for peace in Turkey's southeast', *Hurriyet Daily News*, 13 January 2016.
48. Gürcan, 'Power Struggle Erupts in Turkey's Security Structure'. Tol and Taşpınar, 'Erdogan's Turn to the Kemalists'.
49. Akyol, 'Ak Parti – Doğu Perinçek ittifakı da nereden çıktı?'.
50. The Turkish–Russian relations had entered a crisis in November 2015, when the Turkish Air Force shot down a Russian fighter jet on its border with Syria. This led Moscow to suspend intelligence sharing with Ankara, accuse the AKP of supporting IS, issue trade sanctions and threaten to cut energy supplies. In June 2016, Erdoğan's public apology for the jet incident, which was blamed on rogue Gülenist officers, was followed by the lifting of Russian sanctions. Renewed dialogue with Russia and Iran on Syria, and Turkey's decision to buy an anti-missile system from Moscow marked the beginning of a new era of strategic convergence between Putin and Erdoğan.
51. 'FETÖ'nün arkasında ABD var', *Hürriyet*, 8 November 2016.
52. Key issues included the extradition demand for Fethullah Gülen, US support for Syrian Kurds, and influencing the outcome of a federal court case in New York, in which senior Turkish government officials were implicated for directing a scheme to evade US sanctions against Iran.
53. 'Ex-Trump Aide Mike Flynn "Offered $15m by Turkey for Gulen"', *BBC News*, 11 November 2017; Küçük, 'Trump, Amerikan derin devletine teslim oldu'.
54. Christofis, 'Kemalism vs Erdoğanism'.
55. As of January 2023, the AKP had 11.2 million registered members, eight times more than the CHP, its next closest rival. In Erdoğan's neoliberal party-state, membership in the ruling party has increasingly become a guarantor of social status and security, especially in the provinces, where it can grant privileged access to services, cadres and promotions. The Supreme Court of Appeals Prosecutors' Office, https://www.yargitaycb.gov.tr/kategori/109/siyasi-parti-genel-bilgileri.

56. Karakaş, 'Milli İrade ve Beka Kavramlarını 24 Haziran 2018 Türkiye Başkanlık Seçimi Üzerinden Okumak'.
57. Akkoyunlu, and Öktem, 'Existential Insecurity'.
58. Gürpınar, *Conspiracy Theories in Turkey*, pp. 74–97.
59. Guimarães and Oliveira e Silva, 'Far-Right Populism and Foreign Policy Identity'; Rogenhofer, 'Antidemocratic Populism in Turkey after the July 2016 Coup Attempt'.
60. Compare, for instance, the AKP spokesperson Cemil Çiçek's otherwise stern response to the military's e-memorandum in April 2007, which does not reference tutelage, to the open letter by 500 intellectuals condemning military tutelage and calling for an end to tutelary democracy. 'Cemil Çiçek'ten "muhtıra" ile ilgili açıklama', *sendika.org*, 28 Nisan 2007, https://sendika.org/2007/04/cemil-cicek-ten-muhtira-ile-ilgili-aciklama-13063/; 'Muhtıraya karşı aydınlardan 500 imzalı bildiri', *dunyabulteni.net*, 14 May 2007, https://www.dunyabulteni.net/arsiv/muhtiraya-karsi-aydinlardan-500-imzali-bildiri-h14013.html.
61. 'Erdoğan: Vesayetçi anlayış kaybetti', *BBC Türkçe*, 12 September 2010.
62. 'President Erdoğan: "There is no Point in Reviving the Outdated Tutelage System That Has Set Us Back For Years"', Presidency of the Republic of Türkiye, Directorate of Communications, 30 Sept 2021, https://www.iletisim.gov.tr/english/haberler/detay/president-erdogan-there-is-no-point-in-reviving-the-outdated-tutelage-system-that-has-set-us-back-for-years.
63. 'Erdoğan: Science Should Be Liberated From Political Tutelage', *Daily Sabah*, 24 December 2014.
64. 'Cumhurbaşkanı Erdoğan: "Sosyal ve kültürel iktidarımız konusunda sıkıntılarımız var"', *Hürriyet*, 28 May 2017.
65. Tweet by Soylu, 25 December 2021, https://twitter.com/suleymansoylu/status/1474844128923906051.
66. 'Cumhurbaşkanı Erdoğan: Türkiye istikbalini asla küresel ekonomik vesayet kurumlarının reçetelerine teslim etmeyecek', *Anadolu Agency*, 1 December 2021, https://www.aa.com.tr/tr/politika/cumhurbaskani-erdogan-turkiye-istikbalini-asla-kuresel-ekonomik-vesayet-kurumlarinin-recetelerine-teslim-etmeyecek/2435519.
67. 'Şimdi de AİHM vesayeti mi?', *Akşam*, 25 December 2020.
68. Tweets by Karagül, 20 March 2021, https://twitter.com/ibrahimkaragul/status/1373374154506911746?; https://twitter.com/ibrahimkaragul/status/1373179604039573505 (author's translation).
69. 'Inviting Bureaucracy to Oppose Govt Is Call For Tutelage: Erdoğan', *Daily Sabah*, 17 Oct 2021.

CONCLUSION

Erdoğan is your Ahmadinejad. But now he wants to be Khamenei.
— Tabriz taxi driver, September 2015

At the turn of the millennium, Iran and Turkey saw the rise of popular movements that challenged the institutional hegemony of their powerful guardians. A decade later, the ensuing power struggles had yielded results that were, on the one hand, markedly different, and on the other, depressingly similar. In Iran, the traditionalist guardians were able to obstruct and ultimately suppress both the reform movement led by Khatami and the more unexpected populist challenge by the Ahmadinejad presidency, although this happened at the expense of the IRI's democratic legitimacy and stability. Meanwhile, in Turkey the AKP governments and their allies had succeeded in overcoming tutelary resistance to dismantle the system of military-bureaucratic guardianship, despite subsequently descending into an even more vicious power struggle, existential insecurity, social polarisation and authoritarian decline.

How did the guardians survive in Iran while they were defeated in Turkey? And what to make of the fact that these divergent paths ultimately led to the transformation of both tutelary hybrid regimes into more autocratic entities?

259

Divergent Paths

The guardians' victory in Iran and defeat in Turkey can be explained based on three interconnected dimensions: the legal/constitutional sanction of guardianship in both tutelary hybrid regimes, the nature of the two countries' relationship with the West, and the role of human agency in grappling with these institutional and geopolitical constraints. Simply put, guardianship survived in the IRI because, in comparison to Turkey, it was built on firmer legal/constitutional and charismatic grounds, more divested from the West geopolitically and economically, and more tightly controlled by a single faction under the personal leadership of a supreme authority.

Legal and Constitutional Sanction

As discussed in Chapter 3, the system of Islamic guardianship of the Iranian state and society was laid out and enshrined explicitly in the IRI's constitutions on the basis of Ayatollah Khomeini's *velayat-e faqih* theory. The powers and responsibilities of every major institution of the Islamic pillar were outlined in the IRI's first constitution, which was drafted under Khomeini's supervision and presented to popular vote in 1979. Although critical changes to the guardians' legal powers were made soon after Khomeini's death, the foundational legitimacy of these institutions as direct products of the revolution and its leader remained intact. This explicit constitutional and charismatic sanction, in turn, allowed the Iranian guardians to exert their authority openly and forcefully when challenged both by the reformists and the neo-conservatives – by impeaching ministers or influencing their appointment, disqualifying candidates, blocking legislation and using force to intimidate or suppress popular dissent.

In Turkey, on the other hand, the guardianship role of the TSK was based on tenuous legal and historical grounds from the outset. Although the institutions established as a result of military coups, such as the NSC, the RTÜK or the YÖK, were constitutionally enshrined, there was no direct reference to the military's guardianship role in any of the country's constitutions. The legal justification used for military interventions, Article 35 of the TSK's Internal Service Law, was itself a product of the 1960 coup. Furthermore, despite Atatürk's designation of the Turkish military as the guide and guardian of the

Turkish nation, the hybrid institutional architecture that emerged after 1960 was not designed by the charismatic leader nor had his explicit blessing. As I noted in Chapter 6, Atatürk even outlawed active duty officers from engaging in politics, whereas Khomeini strongly encouraged the clergy to participate in politics.

Lacking a clear mandate from the charismatic leader and a firm constitutional backing, the hybrid system that emerged in Turkey as a result of successive military coups needed constant justification. This forced the guardians to assume a less visible role than their Iranian counterparts: compare the attempts to create a 'post-modern' guardianship or to conceal the existence of an extra-judicial mechanism of socio-political control and coercion (the 'deep state') against the publicly visible and institutionalised nature of this mechanism in Iran in the shape of the IRGC, the *basij* or the Hezbollahi vigilante groups. While Turkey's position as a frontier country along the East/West axis during the Cold War provided the tutelary establishment with a strategic raison d'être, the end of the Cold War made Kemalist guardianship more vulnerable to changes in the public opinion. In the early 2000s, defending the military's undemocratic prerogatives had become harder than calling for their dismantling. The AKP politicians even framed their reform agenda as fulfilling Atatürk's goal of 'reaching contemporary civilisation' on the path to EU membership, instead of undoing his secular nationalist legacy, even though this was where some of the deepest grievances of the ruling Islamists lay. In contrast, the battle over political reform in the IRI has been directly and inseparably linked to Khomeini's ideological and institutional legacy. It has never become permissible to publicly advocate undoing *velayat-e faqih* in Iran.

This difference is rooted in the original mission of guardianship as set out by the two charismatic leaders. Even though Khomeini sought revolutionary change in society and the global order, he envisioned *velayat-e faqih* as a permanent political fixture until the return of the Mahdi. In contrast, Atatürk's vision of guardianship was meant to be temporary. Like Lenin's vanguard party, Kemalist single-party tutelage over society would in theory give way to democracy once Turkey's modernisation had been achieved. Many in the statist faction of the CHP saw President İnönü's decision to switch to a multiparty system in the late 1940s as a premature move and a fatal blow to the Kemalist revolution. During 1950s, these critics became convinced that henceforth the revolution had to be protected through the indirect tutelage of the military and the senior bureaucracy. As Kemalist guardianship assumed an increasingly permanent and conservative character, so did the guardians' claim that the people were too immature to be trusted. Over the following decades, this claim generated opposition from those who argued, increasingly convincingly, that it was precisely the guardians' paternalism that had stunted Turkey's democratic and economic development. The liberal democratic critiques of Kemalist guardianship were built on this counter-argument.

There might be a silver lining here for the Kemalists. The ability to dissociate Atatürk from military tutelage may have facilitated the undoing of the latter, but it has arguably allowed for Atatürk's popular legacy to persist beyond the system of guardianship built in his name. Indeed, at the centenary of the Turkish Republic, eighty-five years after his passing, and following two decades of Islamist rule, Atatürk remains as popular and publicly sanctified as ever in Turkey.[1] Even President Erdoğan, who has spent a career undoing the Kemalist legacy and sees himself as the founding father of 'New Turkey', appears to have figured it does not serve him to openly attack Atatürk, and he has assumed a more respectful tone. The fact that the Islamist project has steered Turkey towards conflict, crisis and autocracy gives a new generation of activists and scholars a chance to rehabilitate Kemalism as a social democratic and civic idea.[2] In contrast, having been so inseparably associated with *velayat-e faqih* and its failures in Iran, it is difficult to imagine Khomeini and Khomeinism to retain such popularity beyond the institutional lifetime of the Islamic Republic.

The Role of Geopolitics

It is difficult to overestimate the impact of geopolitics on Turkish and Iranian domestic politics, although these have been to different effects as far as the configuration and fate of guardianship in the two countries are concerned. Since its 1979 revolution, Iran has been locked into a path of confrontation with the United States. Successive US administrations have made no secret of their desire to see regime change in Iran. Instead of weakening it, however, this confrontation has arguably strengthened and sustained the Islamic guardianship pillar of the IRI vis-à-vis the republican pillar. This has happened in two interconnected ways: first, the diversion from strategic reliance on the US and the concomitant diversification of Iran's political, economic and military partnerships to non-Western counterparts has rendered the Iranian regime more resilient in the face of sustained Western pressure. The guardians of the Islamic Republic, in other words, have learned to survive and even thrive under institutionalised hostility and pressure emanating from the world's only superpower. Here, Iran's natural resource wealth needs to be emphasised. While its oil wealth has been on the whole more of a curse than a blessing for Iran as a source of foreign imperial attraction, its role in sustaining the IRI's economy and providing alternative trade partners in spite of Western-backed sanctions cannot be ignored. The prominence of the energy sector allowed for the state to remain the dominant actor in the national economy, providing a lifeline to key guardianship institutions such as the IRGC. The distribution of oil rent has also helped sustain a dependent social base that could be mobilised in support of the regime whenever it faced popular challenges. Without this rent, one could argue that the guardians of the IRI would be both more beholden to public opinion and more exposed to the entrapments of the global economy, as was the case in Turkey.

Secondly, the existence of sustained hostility with the United States and its allies has bolstered the regime's anti-imperialist and anti-Western image, allowing for the institutionalisation of a permanent state of emergency at home at the expense of democracy, civil liberties and rule of law. US, Saudi and Israeli belligerence have helped reinforce this image and, far from delegitimising the regime, strengthened its raison d'être. As such, leaders like Rafsanjani, Khatami or Rouhani, who advocated politics of rapprochement with the US and its regional allies, had to tread a highly precarious line, exposing themselves to attacks from their domestic rivals for jeopardising the IRI's hard-earned sovereignty or, worse, collaborating with the enemy. Similarly, the reformist discourse of strengthening civil society and the rule of law was readily portrayed by the traditionalists as a manifestation of Western cultural invasion, which needed to be resisted and eradicated. The reformists had to fight an uphill battle to frame their agenda not as Western-inspired or liberal, but rather, authentic to the revolution and the true interpretation of the charismatic leader's legacy.

Successive US administrations repeatedly ignored, turned down or sabotaged delicate attempts by Iranian presidents to improve bilateral ties, severely undermining their position vis-à-vis the advocates of continued confrontation within Iran. The Clinton administration responded to Rafsanjani's overtures with the Iran and Libya Sanctions Act. The George W. Bush administration squandered the goodwill coming from the Khatami government and the Iranian people after the September 11 attacks by labelling Iran as part of an 'axis of evil'. The unilateral scrapping of the JCPOA, and the hostile front formed by the US, Saudi Arabia and Israel during the Trump administration, united a bitterly divided regime elite under Khamenei's tight control, while dealing a fatal blow to the Rouhani administration. Thus, whether a degree of sustained normalisation of US-IRI ties would ultimately weaken the guardians' grip over the Iranian state and society still remains a matter of speculation. While the devastating war of economic attrition waged by the United States has contributed to ordinary Iranians deepening misery and desperation, there is little evidence that it has made the traditionalist elite less resilient, especially in light of the growing strategic support Iran has been receiving from the emerging anti-Western axis led by China and Russia.[3]

In contrast to the IRI, the two fundamental principles of Kemalism – national sovereignty and cultural Westernisation – pulled Turkey in opposite directions and created an internal tension among the guardians as to which principle had to be prioritised. Turkey's membership in NATO in 1952 was not driven primarily by cultural concerns, but rather by geostrategic pragmatism and the historically rooted fear of Russian expansionism. Nonetheless, it did cost the Turkish Republic its sovereignty as Turkey's ideological and geopolitical trajectory had to henceforth conform to the priorities of the US-led Western security establishment. As the TSK became firmly embedded within the NATO structure, it also came to rely on the technical and strategic support provided by the United States to maintain its supra-political position. Every successful military intervention had to be backed or approved by NATO. The transfer of this support from the guardians to their elected challengers in the 2000s, in the framework of the European Union's liberal democratisation agenda and the US promotion of the AKP as a 'moderate Islamist model' played a crucial role in dismantling the system of Kemalist guardianship.

Unlike the Iranian reformists, Turkey's reformists in the 2000s had the advantage of both geopolitics and discourse. Resource-poor Turkey's deep integration into international markets and reliance on foreign investment as a result of the post-1980 neoliberal turn meant that the Kemalist guardians in the twenty-first century were unable to intervene in the political process as openly and decisively as their predecessors, or indeed, their Iranian counterparts. The liberal–Islamist coalition was able to promote the AKP government's reform agenda on grounds of macro-economic stability and growth, Europeanisation and democratisation; goals which the military guardians themselves had claimed to uphold as recently as in the late 1990s. These goals attracted greater domestic and international support than the discourse of national sovereignty and anti-Westernism that the Eurasianist opposition championed in the 2000s.

Nonetheless, the popularity of Eurasianism among Turkish officers and senior bureaucrats in the 2000s cannot be simply be explained as a matter of ideological doggedness or nationalist reactionism, as their liberal detractors tend to suggest. This was a pragmatic – if rather desperate – survival attempt on the part of the Kemalist guardians, who realised they were abandoned by the West. Similarly, Erdoğan's anti-Western turn and alliance with his old enemies, ultra-nationalists and the Eurasianists, has also been primarily driven by pragmatic survival instincts. Having been on the winning side of the West's strategic support, Erdoğan knew what losing that support implied. As his distrust of the US grew after the Gezi protests and the Egyptian coup of 2013, and especially following the failed coup attempt in July 2016, the Turkish president started seeking alternative alliances to secure his position. Crucially, unlike that of the Kemalists in the 2000s, Erdoğan's diversification attempt came at a time when the EU's political and normative influence on Turkey had reached an all-time low, the US had turned increasingly unpredictable and inward-looking, and Russia and China were resurgent. Rather than just a stroke of good fortune, this was testament to Erdoğan's ability to manoeuvre strategically and maintain a difficult balancing act in an increasingly fluid multipolar order.

Human Agency: Intra-elite Divisions and Leadership

To paraphrase Marx, human beings make their own history, but they do so within given structural constraints. While in hindsight it appears clear that institutional and geopolitical conditions favoured traditionalist guardians over the elected reformists in Iran, and vice versa in Turkey, in neither case were the outcomes pre-determined. In fact, an observer in 1997 could be excused for thinking that Iran, where a reformist administration had just been elected on the back of overwhelming popular support, held greater democratic promise than Turkey, where the military had just ousted another democratically elected government. Human agency played a decisive role in the critical political junctures that determined the fate of the ensuing power struggles. A key contrast appears to be the strategic shrewdness combined with political perseverance displayed by the AKP leadership during the 2000s and their absence in the reformist and neo-conservative contenders in Iran.

Power was not handed over to Erdoğan and the AKP on a golden platter. When the Islamists came to power in 2002, they not only had to overcome suspicions at home and abroad, they also had to face a powerful military-bureaucratic establishment that had only removed the AKP's Islamist predecessor five years previously. The elected challengers in Turkey created their own chances by striking alliances of convenience with key actors – the US and the EU abroad, and the Gülenists and the liberal intelligentsia at home – with all of whom the Islamists shared a history of mutual distrust. Supported by this strategic coalition, they were able to stand their ground during moments of conflict with the guardians. The AKP government's persistence to nominate Abdullah Gül as its presidential candidate in 2007, despite the Constitutional Court's attempt to block the vote, the secularist mass rallies and the military's 'e-memorandum', stands out as a particularly fateful decision and, in hindsight, a tipping point. Coming at the height of the power struggle when neither side had established their hegemony, the government's risky decision to call for an early general election paid off, as it emerged victorious from the ballot box and went on to have the new parliament elect Gül as president. It was this victory over the guardians that tilted the institutional balance of powers in the government's favour for the first time.

But the elected Islamists may still not have triumphed had it not been for the divisions among senior generals and judges. Here, we should underline General Özkök's role in allegedly blocking at least two advanced coup plans by his senior staff in 2003 and 2004 and Chief Justice Kılıç's stance in opposition to the closure case against the AKP in 2008. Of course, these fissures did not occur by chance. I discussed the existence of internal rivalries in the TSK, which surfaced as early as in the 1960 and 1971 coups and intensified in the 2000s when the guardians were forced to choose between reform and resistance. Meanwhile, the presence of a conservative judge at the top of the Turkish high judiciary was a consequence of the promotion of conservative bureaucrats by the military junta and later by Turgut Özal's ANAP government in the 1980s.

It would be simplistic to explain the defeat of the Iranian reform movement by merely pointing to Khatami's reluctance to defy the guardians out of a fear of civil strife or the institutional collapse of the hybrid regime. The reformists' failure to institutionalise an effective party structure to organise and lead civil society, or to communicate an agenda of socio-economic justice to appeal to the working class, and above all, the traditionalists' readiness to resort to systematic violence were also crucial factors in the reformist defeat. However, considering the dogged determination with which Ahmadinejad defended the prerogatives of his office against the Leader's interventions, leading to confrontations that arguably rattled the feathers of the traditionalists more than any reformist challenge, it does not sound far-fetched to suggest that more determined leadership by Khatami at critical junctures could have delivered strategic victories to the reformists, who after all enjoyed much wider popular support than the neo-conservatives. Khatami's instinct to preserve the hybrid system kept him from picking risky fights with the guardians. Ahmadinejad did not have such inhibitions, but without an active support base and owing his rise and status to the guardians he later turned against, he overplayed his hand. Ultimately, it was the traditionalist guardians, under the personal authority of Khamenei and in control of the state's coercive apparatus, that overcame initial periods of discord and confusion, and presented a united and ruthlessly determined front against both the reformist and the neo-conservative challenges.

The unity of the traditionalists in Iran under the personal authority of Khamenei, in contrast to the divisions among the Kemalist guardians, is also a reflection of the personalised nature of tutelary power in the IRI versus its bureaucratised character in Turkey. The Islamic Republic's institutional architecture – featuring a duality between 'the representative of God' versus 'the representative of the People' – reflects the personality-driven nature of Iranian politics, which has been shaped around the charisma and networks of key individuals, rather than rule-bound bureaucratic bodies or party organisations. In contrast, in Turkey, bureaucratisation dates back to the Ottoman Empire, where sultans' personal authority was gradually checked and transferred to an abstract notion of the state. Even Mustafa Kemal's unmatched personal charisma and authority did not reverse this trend. He was, after all, a product of the same military-bureaucratic tradition, and built his reputation and success on these qualities. İnönü's decision to step down as president and leader of the CHP in 1950 further ensured that authority would be bestowed upon institutions and not to single individuals in the Turkish Republic. In this regard, the dramatic de-bureaucratisation and personalisation of state authority under President Erdoğan, rendering decision-making dependent on the interests and ambitions of a powerful executive president, stands to mark a critical turning point for the nature of state authority in Turkey, especially if it persists beyond Erdoğan's tenure.

Converging Destinations: Enduring Patriarchy

On a visit to northwest Iran in September 2015, upon hearing that I was from Turkey, the driver I was traveling with offered a casual yet also remarkably prescient take on the state of affairs in our two countries. Weeks before the signing of the JCPOA, this was a time of cautious optimism in Iran, while Turkey was descending into conflict and instability, with renewed violence between the PKK and the Turkish security forces making regular trips across the border too dangerous for this driver and many others like him. 'Erdoğan is your Ahmadinejad', the man exclaimed. 'But now he wants to be Khamenei'.

Obvious differences between them notwithstanding, it is possible to think of Erdoğan as the more popular, more pragmatic and ultimately more successful version of Ahmadinejad. Coming from working class backgrounds, both men first emerged on the national spotlight as elected mayors of their country's biggest cities. Driven by a sense of divine destiny – an image propagated and opportunistically used by their loyal supporters – they set out to empower the presidency against the parliament, the judiciary and the institutions of Kemalist and Khomeinist guardianship. Their measured stance towards the powerful guardians in their early years in office gradually gave way to a scathing religious-nationalist populism targeting the tutelary establishment and the socio-economic elite – whether Turkey's 'whisky-sipping' secular bourgeoisie or Iran's clerical 'oil mafia'. Notably, despite drawing their legitimacy singularly from the ballot box – with Erdoğan, unlike Ahmadinejad, mastering the art of winning successive elections – both men showed little respect for the democratic process when they came out on the losing side.

It is also true that as he succeeded in overcoming the guardians, and amassed more wealth and power, Erdoğan became insecure in his position, despised the democratic opposition to his authority and grew impatient with the unpredictable nature of the electoral process. Yet, like the Kemalist and Khomeinist guardians, he could not afford to do away with elections. Thus, in order to reduce their unpredictability, he criminalised dissent, tightened his grip over state institutions and the media, engaged in strategic electoral manipulation, changed the constitution and created the legal basis for a permanent state of emergency that let him rule by decree. The repeat elections of 2015, the post-coup attempt crackdown and the establishment of a 'Turkish-style' presidentialism can all be seen as steps in the 'Khameneisation' of Erdoğan. And like Khamenei, by personalising power to such a great extent, Erdoğan has tied the fate of the regime he has built to his own personal fate, and vice versa.

The Turkish case under Erdoğan demonstrates – and there would be little reason to expect differently had Ahmadinejad got his way – that the victory of popular contenders over the guardians in tutelary hybrid regimes does not guarantee democratic consolidation. On the contrary, the presidentialisation of the executive branch as a populist majoritarian antidote to tutelary power is highly susceptible to give way to personalised illiberal rule through executive aggrandisement.[4] More than a restructuring of institutions or a changeover of political elites, substantial democratisation requires an evolution in dominant socio-political attitudes from a patriarchal view of state and society towards an inclusive and pluralistic view that considers government an open-ended and self-reproducing process of public reasoning, deliberation and participation.

This is also a reminder to avoid depicting politics in tutelary hybrid regimes as a black-and-white struggle between autocratic-minded guardians and democratic-minded civilian politicians. Such a binary approach, which has been influential among democracy promoters in the post-Cold War era, minimises democracy to the ballot box and overlooks the democratic deficits of elected officials that confront overbearing militaries and bureaucracies. As Levitsky and Ziblatt have observed, democracies in the twenty-first century often die 'at the hands not of generals but of elected leaders – presidents or prime ministers who subvert the very process that brought them to power'.[5] Democracy, in other words, needs democrats, not merely election winners. That is a lesson that many liberal supporters of the AKP in Turkey and the EU, who hoped or assumed that undoing the military's tutelage would lead the country to democracy, have bitterly learnt.

Notes

1. Asked whether they felt gratitude towards Atatürk's service to the country, and if they thought recent times had made them better appreciate Atatürk's value, respectively 93% and 73% of the respondents to a nationwide poll conducted in November 2021 answered yes. 'MetroPOLL'den Atatürk anketi', *Diken*, 27 November 2021.
2. Akkoyunlu, 'One Hundred Years of Kemalisms'.
3. Farnaz Fassihi, 'With BRICS Invite, Iran Shrugs Off Outcast Status in the West', *New York Times*, 25 August 2023.
4. Bermeo, 'On Democratic Backsliding'.
5. Levitsky and Ziblatt, *How Democracies Die*.

BIBLIOGRAPHY

Abrahamian, Ervand. *Khomeinism*. New York: I. B. Tauris, 1993.

Abrahamian, Ervand. *Tortured Confessions*. Berkeley, CA: University of California Press, 1999.

Abrahamian, Ervand. *A History of Modern Iran*. Cambridge: Cambridge University Press, 2008.

Afary, Janet. 'Social Democracy and the Iranian Constitutional Revolution of 1906–11'. In Foran, John, ed. *A Century of Revolution: Social Movements in Iran, Social Movements, Protests and Contention*. Volume 2. Minneapolis: University of Minnesota Press, 1994.

Afary, Janet and Kevin B. Anderson. *Foucault and the Iranian Revolution: Gender and the Seductions of Islamism*. Chicago and London: The University of Chicago Press, 2005.

Akalın, Güneri. *Atatürk Dönemi Maliye Politikaları*. Ankara: TC Maliye Bakanlığı, 2008.

Akarlı, Engin D. 'The Tangled Ends of an Empire: Ottoman Encounters with the West and Problems of Westernization – an Overview'. *Comparative Studies of South Asia, Africa and the Middle East*, 26 (3), 2006, pp. 353–66.

Akarlı, Engin D. *The Long Peace: Ottoman Lebanon 1861–1920*. Berkeley: University of California Press, 1993.

Akarlı, Engin. 'Maslaha from "Common Good" to "Raison d'Etat" in the Experience of Istanbul Artisans, 1730–1840'. In Durukan, Kaan, Robert W. Zens and Akile Zorlu-Durukan, eds. *Hoca, 'Allame, Puits de Science: Essays in Honor of Kemal H. Karpat*. Istanbul: Isis Press, 2010.

Akay, Hale. *Security Sector in Turkey: Questions, Problems and Solutions*. Istanbul: TESEV, 2010.

Akbari, Reza H. and Saeed Aganji. 'Why Iran's City Council Elections Matter'. *Al Monitor*, 19 May 2013.

Akça, İsmet. *Military-Economic Structure in Turkey: Present Situation, Problems and Solutions*. Istanbul: TESEV, 2010.

Akçalı, Emel and Mehmet Perinçek. 'Kemalist Eurasianism: An Emerging Geopolitical Discourse in Turkey'. *Geopolitics*, 14 (3), 2009, pp. 550–69.

Akhavi, Shahrough. 'The Thought and Role of Ayatollah Hossein'ali Montazeri in the Politics of Post-1979 Iran'. *Iranian Studies* 41 (5), 2008, pp. 645–66.

Akın, Yiğit. *When the War Came Home: The Ottomans' Great War and the Devastation of an Empire*. Stanford, CA: Stanford University Press, 2018.

Akkoyunlu, Karabekir and Kerem Öktem. 'Existential Insecurity and The Making of a Weak Authoritarian Regime in Turkey'. *Southeast European and Black Sea Studies*, 16 (4), 2016, pp. 505–27.

Akkoyunlu, Karabekir, Kalypso Nicolaidis and Kerem Öktem. 'The Western Condition: Turkey, the US and the EU in the New Middle East'. *SEESOX Paper Series on Turkey*, February 2013.

Akkoyunlu, Karabekir. 'Electoral Integrity in Turkey: From Tutelary Democracy to Competitive Authoritarianism'. In Başer, Bahar and Erdi Öztürk, eds. *Authoritarian Politics in Turkey: Elections, Resistance and the AKP*. London: I. B. Tauris, 2017.

Akkoyunlu, Karabekir. 'One Hundred Years of Kemalisms', in Alpaslan Özerdem and Ahmet Erdi Öztürk, eds. *A Companion to Modern Turkey's Centennial: Political, Socioeconomic and Institutional Transformations since 1923*. Edinburgh: Edinburgh University Press, 2023.

Akkoyunlu, Karabekir. 'The "Turkish model" isn't good for Turkey'. *Hürriyet Daily News*, 8 February 2012.

Akkoyunlu, Karabekir. *Military Reform and Democratisation: Turkish and Indonesian Experiences at the turn of the Millennium*. Adelphi Paper no. 392, London: Routledge, 2007.

AKP. *Herşey Türkiye İçin: AKP Seçim Beyannamesi*. Ankara: AK Parti Yayınları, 2002.

Akyol, Mustafa. 'Ak Parti – Doğu Perinçek ittifakı da nereden çıktı?', *Al Monitor*, 25 January 2016.

Akyol, Taha. *Ama Hangi Atatürk*. Istanbul: Doğan Kitap, 2008.

Alavi, Nasrin. 'Iran: An Elite at War'. *Open Democracy*, 27 May 2011.

Alem, Yasmin. 'Is the Islamic Republic of Iran on Its Last Elected President?'. *Al Monitor*, 7 August 2012.

Alex Vatanka. 'How Deep is Iran's State? The Battle Over Khamenei's Successor'. *Foreign Affairs*, 96 (4), 2017, pp. 155–61.

Alipour, Farahmand. 'Soleimani Emerges as Unifying Figure for Iranians'. *Al Monitor*, 17 April 2015.

Altunışık, Meliha B. 'The Turkish Model and Democratization in the Middle East'. *Arab Studies Quarterly*, 27 (1–2), 2005, Winter-Spring, pp. 45–64.

Amanat, Abbas and Assef Ashraf, eds. *The Persianate World: Rethinking a Shared Sphere*. Leiden: Brill, 2018, pp. 63–83.

Amnesty International. *Iran: Violations of Human Rights: 1987–1990*, 1 December 1990.

Amuzegar, Jahangir. 'Khatami's Economic Record: Small Bandages on Deep Wounds'. *Global Dialogue*, 3 (2–3), 2001, pp. 104–14.

Ansari, Ali M. 'The Myth of the White Revolution: Mohammad Reza Shah, "Modernization" and the Consolidation of Power'. *Middle Eastern Studies*, 37 (3), 2001, pp. 1–24.

Ansari, Ali M. *Iran, Islam and Democracy: The Politics of Managing Change*. London: Chatham House, 2006.

Arcayürek, Cüneyt. *Açıklıyor*. Volume I – IV. Istanbul: Bilgi, 1983.

Arjomand, Said Amir. *After Khomeini: Iran Under His Successors*. Oxford: Oxford University Press, 2009.

Arsan, Nimet, ed. *Atatürk'ün Söylev ve Demeçleri*. Volume I–III, Atatürk Araştırmaları Vakfı, Ankara: Türk Tarih Kurumu Basımevi, 1989.

Arshin Adib-Moghaddam, ed. *A Critical Introduction to Khomeini*. Cambridge: Cambridge University Press, 2014.

Ashraf, Ahmad and Ali Banuazizi. 'Classes in the Qajar Period', *Encyclopedia Iranica*, Costa Mesa: Mazda, 1999, pp. 667–77.

Askari, Hossein. 'Iran's Economic Policy Dilemma'. *International Journal*, 59 (3), 2004, pp. 655–68.

Atabaki, Touraj and Erik Jan Zürcher. *Men of Order: Authoritarian Modernization Under Atatürk and Reza Shah*. London: I. B. Tauris, 2004.

Atabaki, Touraj. *The State and the Subaltern: Modernization, Society and the State in Turkey and Iran*. London: I. B. Tauris, 2007.

Atatürk Araştırma Merkezi. *Atatürk'ün Tamim, Telgraf ve Beyannameleri*. Volume VI. Ankara: Türk Tarih Kurumu Basımevi, 1991.

Atatürk, Mustafa Kemal. *The Great Speech*. Ankara: Ataturk Research Center, 2005.

Atay, Falih Rıfkı. *Çankaya*. Istanbul: Pozitif, 2009.

Axworthy, Michael. *Iran: Empire of the Mind*. London: Hurst, 2007.

Aydemir, Şevket Süreyya. *İkinci Adam*. Volume III (1950–64). Istanbul: Remzi, 1975.

Aytürk İlker and Berk Esen, eds. *Post-Post-Kemalizm: Türkiye Çalışmalarında Yeni Arayışlar*. Istanbul: İletişim, 2022.

Aytürk, İlker. 'Turkish Linguists against the West: The Origins of Linguistic Nationalism in Atatürk's Turkey'. *Middle Eastern Studies*, 40 (6), 2004, pp. 1–25.

Bağcı, Hüseyin and Şaban Kardaş. 'Post- September 11 Impact: The Strategic Importance of Turkey Revisited'. In İdris Bal, ed. *Turkish Foreign Policy in Post-Cold War Era*. Boca Raton, FL: Brown Walker, 2004.

Bairoch, Paul and M. Levy-Leboyer, eds. *Economic Development since the Industrial Revolution*. New York: St. Martin's Press, 1981.

Bakiner, Onur. 'A key to Turkish Politics? The Center–Periphery Framework Revisited'. *Turkish Studies*, 19 (4), 2018, pp. 503–22.

Bani Sadr, Abol Hassan. *The Fundamental Principles and Precepts of Islamic Government*, Costa Mesa, CA: Mazda Publishers, 1981

Barkey, Henri J., ed. *Reluctant Neighbour: Turkey's Role in the Middle East*. Washington, DC: United States Institute of Peace Press, 1996.

Barkey, Karen. *Bandits and Bureaucrats: The Ottoman Route to State Centralization*. Ithaca and London: Cornell University Press, 1994.

Barkey, Karen, 'The Ottoman Empire (1299–1923): The Bureaucratization of Patrimonial Authority'. In Crooks, Peter and Timothy H. Parsons, eds. *Empires and Bureaucracy in World History: From Late Antiquity to the Twentieth Century*. Cambridge: Cambridge University Press, 2016.

Başaran, Ezgi. 'Cemaatçi polisler gitti, 'dombra'cılar mı geldi', *Radikal*, 8 May 2014.

Bashiri, Iraj. *Firdowsi's Shahname: 1000 Years After*. Dushanbe: Academy of Sciences of Tajikistan, 1994.

Batmanghelidj, Esfandyar. 'Iranian Protests and the Working Class'. *LobeLog*, 1 January 2018.

Bayat, Asef. 'Is Iran on the Verge of Another Revolution?'. *Journal of Democracy*, 34 (2), 2022, pp. 19–31.

Baydur, Refik. *Bizim Çete*, Istanbul: Self-published, 2000.

Bayne, E. A. *Persian Kingship in Transition*. New York: American Universities Field Staff, 1969.

Bechev, Dimitar. 'Turkey's Rise as a Regional Power'. *European View*, 10 (2), 2011, pp. 173–9.

Behdad, Sohrab. 'Khatami and His Reformist Economic (Non-)Agenda'. *Middle East Research and Information Project*, 21 May 2001.

Behnam, M. Reza. *Cultural Foundations of Iranian Politics*. Salt Lake City: University of Utah Press, 1986.

Behrooz, Maziar. 'The Islamic State and the Crisis of Marja'iyat in Iran'. *Comparative Studies of South Asia, Africa and the Middle East*, 16 (2), 1996, pp. 93–100.

Belge, Murat. *Militarist Modernleşme: Almanya, Japonya ve Türkiye*. Istanbul: İletişim, 2011.

Benard, Cheryl and Zalmay Khalilzad. *The Government of God – Iran's Islamic Republic*. New York: Columbia University Press, 1984.

Berkan, İsmet. 'MGK'sız hayat: Siviller hazır mı?'. *Radikal*, 8 August 2003.

Berlinski, Claire. 'Who is Fethullah Gülen?'. *City Journal*, 22 (4), Autumn, 2012.

Bermeo, Nancy. 'On Democratic Backsliding'. *Journal of Democracy*, 27 (1), 2016, pp. 5–19.

Bila, Fikret. *Sivil Darbe Girişimi ve Ankara'da Irak Savaşları*. Ankara: Ümit, 2003.

Bilici, Abdülhamit. 'Sistem Tıkandı İstikamet Başkanlık Sistemi'. *Aksiyon*, 7–13 January 1995.

Birand, Mehmet Ali. *The Generals' Coup in Turkey: An Inside Story of 12 September 1980*. New York: Elsevier, 1987.

Bora, Tanıl. *Cereyanlar: Türkiye'de Siyasî İdeolojiler*, Istanbul: Iletisim, 2017.

Bozarslan, Hamit. 'Rejecting Democracy: What Turkey has in common with Russia and Iran'. *The Turkey Analyst*, 9 October 2022.

Breckenridge, Charles. 'Sanction First, Ask Questions Later: The Shortsighted Treatment of Iran under the Iran and Libya Sanctions Act of 1996'. *The Georgetown Law Journal*, 88 (8), 2000, pp. 2439–72.

Brownlee, Jason. *Authoritarianism in an Age of Democratization*. Cambridge: Cambridge University Press, 2007.

Buchta, Wilfried. *Who Rules Iran? The Structure of Power in the Islamic Republic*. Washington, DC: Washington Institute for Near East Policy, 2000.

Cabi, Marouf. 'The Roots and the Consequences of the 1979 Iranian Revolution: A Kurdish Perspective'. *Middle Eastern Studies*, 56 (3), 2020, pp. 339–58.

Çakır, Ruşen, İrfan Bozan and Balkan Talu, eds. *İmam Hatip Liseleri: Efsaneler ve Gerçekler*. Istanbul: TESEV, 2004.

Çakır, Ruşen. 'Ülkücüler Cemaat-hükümet savaşının neresinde?', *Vatan*, 10 February 2014.

Çandar, Cengiz. 'Özal federasyonu istemedi ama tartıştı eyaleti istedi ama sustu'. *Hürriyet*, 4 March 2007.

Canfield, Robert L. *Turko-Persia in Historical Perspective*. Cambridge: Cambridge University Press, 2002.

Canovan, Margaret. 'Trust the People! Populism and the Two Faces of Democracy'. *Political Studies*, 47 (1), 1999, pp. 2–16.

Carlos Closa and Stefano Palestini. 'Tutelage and Regime Survival in Regional Organizations' Democracy Protection: The Case of Mercosur and Unasur'. *World Politics*, 70 (3), 2018, pp. 443–76.

Çelik, Aziz. 'Haşim Kılıç'a hatırlatmalar ve sorular'. *T24*, 20 May 2013.

Champion, Marc. 'Coup Was "Gift from God" for Erdogan Planning a New Turkey', *Bloomberg*, 17 June 2016.

Chehabi, Houchang E. 'The Political Regime of the Islamic Republic of Iran in Comparative Perspective'. *Government and Opposition*, 36 (1), 2001, pp. 48–70.

Cheraghali, Abdol Majid. 'Impacts of International Sanctions on Iranian Pharmaceutical Market'. *Daru (1560–8115)*, 21 (1), 2013, p. 64.

Chomsky, Noam and Edward S. Herman. *Manufacturing Consent: The Political Economy of the Mass Media*. London: The Bodley Head, 2008.

Christofis, Nikos. 'Kemalism vs Erdoğanism: Continuities and Discontinuities in Turkey's Hegemonic State Ideology'. *Middle East Critique*. Published online 25 August 2023.

Cizre, Ümit, ed. *Almanac Turkey 2005: Security Sector and Democratic Oversight*. Istanbul: TESEV, 2006.

Cizre, Ümit. 'The Anatomy of the Turkish Military's Political Autonomy'. *Comparative Politics*, 29 (2), 1997, pp. 151–66.

Clayer, Nathalie, Fabio Giomi, and Emmanuel Szurek, eds. *Kemalism: Transnational Politics in the Post Ottoman World*. London: Bloomsbury Publishing, 2018.

Cleveland, William L. *A History of the Modern Middle East*. Boulder, CO: Westview, 2004.

Coşar, Nevin. 'The Mosul question and the Turkish Republic: Before and after the Frontier Treaty, 1926'. *Middle Eastern Studies*, 42 (1), 2006, pp. 123–32.

Cronin, Stephanie. *The Army and The Creation of the Pahlavi State in Iran, 1910–1926*. London: I. B. Tauris, 1997.

Cross, Kevin. 'Kamalipour Why Iran's Green Movement Faltered: The Limits of Information Technology in a Rentier State'. *SAIS Review of International Affairs*, 30 (2), 2010, pp. 169–87.

Dabashi, Hamid. *The Green Movement in Iran*. New Brunswick, NJ: Transaction, 2011.

Dabashi, Hamid. *Theology of Discontent: The Ideological Foundation of the Islamic Revolution of Iran*. New Brunswick, NJ: Transaction Publishers, 2006.

Dahl, Robert. *Democracy and its Critics*. New Haven, CT: Yale University Press, 1989.

Daloğlu, Tülin. 'Leak deepens AKP-Gulen rift'. *Al Monitor*, 2 December 2013.

Danforth, Nicholas. 'Why a Turkish Dictator Let Himself Lose an Election'. *Al Monitor*, 6 August 2021.

Danforth, Nicholas. *The Remaking of Republican Turkey: Memory and Modernity since the Fall of the Ottoman Empire*. Cambridge: Cambridge University Press, 2021.

Darling, Linda T. *A History of Social Justice and Political Power in the Middle East: The Circle of Justice from Mesopotamia to Globalization*. London: Routledge, 2013

Davutoğlu, Ahmet. *Stratejik Derinlik: Türkiye'nin Uluslararası Konumu*. Istanbul: Küre Yayınları, 2001.

Demirbaş, Abdullah. 'Undoing Years of Progress in Turkey'. *New York Times*, 26 January 2016.

Demirel, Ahmet. *Birinci Meclis'te Muhalefet: İkinci Grup*. Istanbul: İletişim, 1993.

Deringil, Selim. *The Well-Protected Domains: Ideology and the Legitimation of Power in the Ottoman Empire 1876–1909*. London: I. B. Tauris, 1998.

Di Cosmo, Nicola. 'From Alliance to Tutelage: A Historical Analysis of Manchu-Mongol Relations before the Qing Conquest'. *Frontiers of History in China*, 7 (2), 2012, pp. 175–97.

Diamond, Larry. 'Thinking About Hybrid Regimes'. *Journal of Democracy*, 13 (2), 2002, pp. 21–35.

Dmytryshyn, Basil. *The Soviet Union and the Middle East: a documentary record of Afghanistan, Iran and Turkey. 1917–1985*. Princeton, NJ: Kingston Press, 1987.

Duverger, Maurice. *Political Parties*. New York: Wiley, 1954.

Eatwell, Roger. 'The Concept and Theory of Charismatic Leadership'. *Totalitarian Movements and Political Religions*, 7 (2), 2006, pp. 141–56.

Ehsani, Kaveh. 'Round 12 for Iran's Reformists'. *Middle East Research and Information Project*, 29 January 2004.

Ehteshami, Anoushiravan and Mahjoob Zweiri. *Iran and the Rise of its Neoconservatives: The Politics of Tehran's Silent Revolution*. London: I. B. Tauris, 2007.

Ehteshami, Anoushiravan. 'Iranian Foreign Policy after the Election of Hassan Rouhani' Lecture, Middle East Centre, London School of Economics, London, 27 November 2013.

Ehteshami, Anoushiravan. *After Khomeini: The Iranian Second Republic*. London, 1995.

Eligür, Banu. *The Mobilisation of Political Islam in Turkey*. Cambridge: Cambridge University Press, 2010.

Ellidge, Jonn. 'Don't fall for Boris Johnson's 'Deep State' Conspiracy Theory', *New Statesman*, 20 July 2022.

Eren-Webb, Ebru. 'To Which Eurasia Does Turkey Belong? A Comparative Analysis of Turkish Eurasianist Political Discourses'. *Boğaziçi Journal*, 25 (2), 2011, pp. 59–82.

Ergil, Doğu. 'Constitutional Referendum: Farewell to "Old Turkey"'. *Insight Turkey*, 12 (4), pp. 15–22.

Esen, Berk and Sebnem Gumuscu, 'Rising Competitive Authoritarianism in Turkey', *Third World Quarterly*, 37 (9), 2016, pp. 1581–606.

Esen, Berk. 'Nation-Building, Party-Strength, and Regime Consolidation: Kemalism in Comparative Perspective'. *Turkish Studies*, 15 (4), 2014, pp. 600–20.

Esen, Berk. 'Praetorian Army in Action: A Critical Assessment of Civil–Military Relations in Turkey'. *Armed Forces and Society*, 47 (1), 2021, pp. 201–22.

Eshraghi, Ali Reza and Yasaman Baji. 'Debunking the Rafsanjani myth'. *Al Jazeera English*, 21 February 2012.

Eurobarometer. *Eurobarometer 63: Public Opinion in the European Union*. European Commission, Spring 2005, http://ec.europa.eu/public_opinion/archives/eb/eb63/eb63_exec_tr.pdf.

European Council. *Turkey 2005 Progress Report*. Brussels, 9 November 2005.

Farazmand, Ali. *The State, Bureaucracy, and Revolution in Modern Iran: Agrarian Reforms and Regime Politics*. New York: Praeger, 1989.

Farhi, Farideh. 'The Antinomies of Iran's War Generation'. In Lawrence G. Potter and Gary Sick, eds. *Iran, Iraq and the Legacies of War*. New York: Palgrave Macmillan, 2004.

Farmanesh, Amir. 'Iranian Attitudes on JCPOA pre-Trump Announcement'. Iran-Poll for University of Maryland (CISSM), 8 May 2018, https://www.iranpoll.com/publications/pre-trump.

Farzanegan, Mohammad Reza. 'Effects of International Financial and Energy Sanctions on Iran's Informal Economy'. *SAIS Review of International Affairs*, 33 (1), 2013, pp. 13–36.

Faslnameh Motaale'at-e Beynelmelali. 'Editorial Board Roundtable with Ayatollah Hashemi Rafsanjani'. *Faslnameh Motaale'at-e Beynelmelali,* 32 (4), 2012, pp. 1–28.

Fathollah-Nejad, Ali. 'Iran: Fighting "Terror" Publicly, Mourning the Dead Secretly'. *Al Jazeera English*, 1 May 2018.

Fathollah-Nejad, Ali. 'Iranians respond to the regime: "Leave Syria alone!"'. *Al Jazeera English*, 2 May 2018.

Ferrari, G. R. F. *Plato: The Republic*. Cambridge: Cambridge University Press, 2000.

Friedman, Thomas. 'War of Ideas, Part 2'. *New York Times*, 11 January 2004.

Gabelnick, Tamar, William D. Hartung, and Jennifer Washburn. *Arming Repression: U.S. Arms Sales to Turkey During the Clinton Administration*. A Joint Report of the Federation of American Scientists and the World Policy Institute, Washington, DC, 1999.

Gellner, Ernest. *Thought and Change*. London: Weidenfeld and Nicolson, 1964.

Genar, 'Türkiye Sosyal, Ekonomik ve Politik Analiz – 3'. Genar Araştırma Danışmanlık Eğitim, January 2012.

Gerecht, Reuel Marc and Ray Takeyh. 'Let Rouhani and Khamenei Fight'. *Wall Street Journal*, 6 March 2018.

Ghaderi, Farangis and Ozlem Goner. 'Why "Jîna": Erasure of Kurdish Women and Their Politics from the Uprisings in Iran'. *Jadaliyya*, 1 November 2022.

Gibbons, H. A. *The Foundation of the Ottoman Empire: A History of the Osmanlis up to the Death of Bayezid I (1300–1403)*. Oxford: Clarendon Press, 1916.

Gilbert, Leah and Payam Mohseni. 'Beyond Authoritarianism: The Conceptualization of Hybrid Regimes'. *Studies in Comparative International Development*, 46, 2011, pp. 270–97.

Gingeras, Ryan, 'How the Deep State came to America: A History', *War on the Rocks*, 4 February 2019.

Göktepe, Cihat. '1960 "Revolution" in Turkey and the British Policy Towards Turkey'. *The Turkish Yearbook of International Relations*, 30, 2000, pp. 140–89.

Göle, Nilüfer. 'Secularism and Islamism in Turkey: The Making of Elites and Counter-Elites'. *Middle East Journal*, 51 (1), 1997, pp. 46–58.

Golkar, Saeid. 'Paramilitarization of the Economy: The Case of Iran's Basij Militia'. *Armed Forces and Society*, 38 (4), 2012, pp. 625–48.

Gönen, Zeynep, Biriz Berksoy, Zeynep Başer and Mehmet Uçum. *Polis yasalarının ruhu: Mevzuatta söylemler, araçlar ve zihniyet*. Istanbul: TESEV, 2014.

Gönenç, Levent. 'Presidential Elements in Government: Turkey'. *European Constitutional Law Review*, 4 (3), 2008, pp. 488–523.

Göztepe, Ece. 'The Permanency of the State of Emergency in Turkey'. *Zeitschrift für Politikwissenschaft*, 28, 2018, pp. 521–34.

Grigera, Juan. 'Populism in Latin America: Old and New populisms in Argentina and Brazil'. *International Political Science Review*, 38 (4), 2017, pp. 441–55.

Guarneri, Carlo and Patrizia Pederzoli. *From Democracy to Juristocracy? The Power of Judges: A Comparative Study of Courts and Democracy*, Oxford: Oxford University Press, 2002.

Guimarães, Feliciano De Sá and Irma Dutra de Oliveira e Silva. 'Far-Right Populism and Foreign Policy Identity: Jair Bolsonaro's Ultra-Conservatism and the New Politics of Alignment'. *International Affairs*, 97 (2), 2021, pp. 345–63.

Gürcan, Metin. 'Power Struggle Erupts in Turkey's Security Structure'. *Al Monitor*, 12 October 2016.

Gürpınar, Doğan. *Conspiracy Theories in Turkey: Conspiracy Nation*. Abingdon and New York: Routledge, 2020.

Hanioğlu, M. Şükrü. *Atatürk: An Intellectual Biography*. Princeton, NJ: Princeton University Press, 2012.

Harris, Kevan. 'The Rise of the Subcontractor State: Politics of Pseudo-Privatization in the Islamic Republic of Iran'. *International Journal of Middle East Studies*, 45 (1), 2013, pp. 45–70.

Hathaway, Jane. *The Politics of Households in Ottoman Egypt: The Rise of the Qazdağlıs*. Cambridge: Cambridge University Press, 1997.

Hazır, Agah. 'Comparing Turkey and Iran in Political Science and Historical Sociology: A Critical Review'. *Turkish Journal of Middle Eastern Studies*, 2 (1), pp. 1–30, 2015.

Hemmat, Kaveh. 'Completing the Persianate Turn'. *Iranian Studies*, 54 (3–4), 2021, pp. 633–46

Hen-Tov, Elliot and Nathan Gonzalez. 'The Militarization of Post-Khomeini Iran: Praetorianism 2.0'. *The Washington Quarterly*, 34 (1), 2011, pp. 45–59.

Heper, Metin and Menderes Çınar. 'Parliamentary Government with a Strong President: The Post-1989 Turkish Experience'. *Political Science Quarterly*, 111 (3), 1996, pp. 483–503.

Heper, Metin and Şule Toktaş. 'Islam, Modernity, and Democracy in Contemporary Turkey: The Case of Recep Tayyip Erdoğan'. *The Muslim World*, 93 (2), 2003, pp. 157–85.

Heper, Metin. 'Center and Periphery in the Ottoman Empire with Special Reference to the Nineteenth Century. *International Political Science Review*, 1, 1980, pp. 81–105.

Hinnebusch, Raymond and Anoushiravan Ehteshami, eds. *The Foreign Policies of Middle East States*. Boulder, CO: Lynne Rienner Publishers, 2002.

Hirschl, Ran. *Towards Juristocracy: The Origins and Consequences of the New Constitutionalism*. Cambridge, MA: Harvard University Press, 2004.

Hobson, J. M. *The Eastern Origins of Western Civilisation*. Cambridge: Cambridge University Press, 2004.

Holliday, Shabnam J. *Defining Iran: Politics of Resistance*. Farnham: Ashgate, 2011.

HRW. *World Report 2013*. New York: Human Rights Watch, 2013.

Hudson, John. 'America Loses its Man in Ankara'. *Foreign Policy*, 5 May 2016.

Huntington, Samuel P. *Political Order in Changing Societies*. New Haven, CT: Yale University Press, 2006.

Huntington, Samuel P. *The Clash of Civilizations and the Remaking of World Order*. New York: Simon & Schuster, 1996.

Huntington, Samuel P. *The Third Wave: Democratization in the Late Twentieth Century*. Norman: University of Oklahoma Press, 1991.

Ibn Khaldun. *The Muqaddimah: An Introduction to History*. Princeton, NJ: Princeton University Press, 2015.

İnalcık, Halil, ed. *The Middle East and the Balkans under the Ottoman Empire: Essays on Economy and Society*. Bloomington: Indiana University Turkish Studies and Turkish Ministry of Culture Joint Series, 1993.

İnsel, Ahmet and Ali Bayramoğlu, eds. *Bir Zümre, Bir Parti: Türkiye'de Ordu*. Istanbul: Bilgi, 2004.

Issawi, Charles. *Economic History of Iran 1800–1914*. Chicago: The University of Chicago Press, 1971.

Jalali, Rita. 'Civil Society and the State: Turkey after the Earthquake'. *Disasters*, 26 (2), 2002, pp. 120–39.

Kadıoğlu, Ayşe, Mehmet Karlı and Kerem Öktem, eds. *Another Empire? Turkey's Foreign Policy in a New Century*. Istanbul: Bilgi University Press, 2012.

Kadivar, Mohsen. 'God and His Guardians'. *Index on Censorship*, 33 (4), 2004, pp. 64–71.

Kadivar, Mohsen. *Baha-ye Azadi: Defa'iyyat-e Mohsen Kadivar*. Tehran: Nashr-e Ney, 1999.

Kadivar, Mohsen. *Hokumat-e Velai*. Tehran: Nashr-e Ney, 1999.

Kafadar, Cemal. *Between Two Worlds: The Construction of the Ottoman State*. Berkeley: University of California Press, 1995.

Kalaycıoğlu, Ersin. 'Kulturkampf in Turkey: The Constitutional Referendum of 12 September 2010'. *South European Society and Politics*, 17 (1), 2012, pp. 1–22.

Kamali, Masoud. *Multiple Modernities, Civil Society and Islam: The Case of Iran and Turkey*. Liverpool: Liverpool University Press, 2006.

Kamalipour, Yahya R., ed. *Media, Power, and Politics in the Digital Age: The 2009 Presidential Election Uprising in Iran*. Lanham, MD: Rowman & Littlefield, 2010.

Kamrava, Mehran and Houchang Hassan-Yari. 'Suspended Equilibrium in Iran's Political System', *The Muslim World*, 94 (4), 2004, pp. 495–524.

Kara, Ismail. *Şeyhefendinin Rüyasındaki Türkiye*. Istanbul: Dergah, 2011.

282 | GUARDIANSHIP AND DEMOCRACY

Karabekir, Kazım. *İstiklal Harbimiz*. Volume II. Istanbul: Yapı Kredi, 2008.

Karami, Arash. 'Has Rafsanjani Returned to Power?'. *Al Monitor*, 19 June 2013.

Karataş, Cevat and Metin Ercan. 'The privatisation experience in Turkey and Argentina: A Comparative Study, 1986–2007'. *METU Studies in Development*, 35 (2), 2008, pp. 345–84.

Karateke, Hakan T. and Maurus Reinkowski, eds. *Legitimizing the Order: The Ottoman Rhetoric of State Power*. Boston: Brill, 2005.

Karateke, Hakan T. and Maurus Reinkowski, eds. *Legitimizing the Order: The Ottoman Rhetoric of State Power*. Boston: Brill, 2005.

Karpat, Kemal H. *Turkey's Politics: The Transition to a Multiparty System*. Princeton, NJ: Princeton University Press, 1959.

Karpat, Kemal. *Osmanlı'dan Günümüze Elitler ve Din*. Istanbul: Timaş, 2008.

Kasaba, Reşat, ed. *The Cambridge History of Turkey, Volume 4: Turkey in the Modern World*. Cambridge: Cambridge University Press, 2008.

Katouzian, Homa. 'Legitimacy and Succession in Iranian History'. *Comparative Studies of South Asia, Africa and the Middle East*, 23 (1/2), 2003, pp. 234–45.

Katouzian, Homa. *State and Society in Iran: The Eclipse of the Qajars and the Emergence of the Pahlavis*. London: I. B. Tauris, 2000.

Keddie, Nikki R. and Yann Richard. *Modern Iran: Roots and Results of Revolution*. New Haven, CN: Yale University Press, 2006.

Keddie, Nikki R. *Iran: Religion, Politics and Society, Collected Essays*. London: Frank Cass, 1980.

Keddie, Nikki R. *Religion and Politics in Iran: Shi'ism from Quietism to Revolution*. New Haven, CN: Yale University Press, 1984.

Khamanei, Ali. *Farhang va Tahajom-e Farhangi*. Tehran: Sazmen-e Farhangi-ye Enqelab-e Eslami, 1996.

Khatami, Mohammad. *Hope and Challenge: The Iranian President Speaks*. Binghamton, NY: Institute of Global Cultural Studies, 1997.

Khomeini, Ayatollah Ruhollah, *Hokumat-e Islami*. Translated by Hamid Algar, Najaf. Third edition, 1971.

Khomeini, Ayatollah Ruhollah. *Islam and Revolution*. Translated by Hamid Algar. London: Kegan Paul, 2002.

Khomeini, Ayatollah Ruhollah. *Pithy Aphorisms: Wise Sayings and Councils*. Edited by Mansoor Limba. Tehran: The Institute for Compilation and Publication of Imam Khomeini's Works, 2006.

Khosrokhavar, Farhad. 'Toward an Anthropology of Democratization in Iran'. *Critique: Critical Middle East Studies*, 16, 2000, pp. 2–29.

Koçak, Cemil. *Birinci Meclis*. Istanbul: Sabancı Üniversitesi Yayınları, 1998.

Kocatürk, Utkan, ed. *Atatürk'ün Fikir ve Düşünceleri*. Ankara: Atatürk Araştırma Merkezi, 1999.

Köprülü, Fuad. 'Bizans Müesseselerinin Osmanlı Müesseselerine Te'siri Hakkında Bazı Mülahazalar'. *Türk Hukuk ve İktisad Tarihi Mecmuası* (1), 1931, pp. 165–313.

Küçük, Cem. 'Trump, Amerikan derin devletine teslim oldu'. *Türkiye*, 14 March 2018.

Künkler, Mirjam. 'The Special Court of the Clergy (dādgāh-ye vizheh-ye ruhāniyat) and the Repression of Dissident Clergy in Iran'. In Said Arjomand and Nathan Brown, eds. *Constitutionalism, the Rule of Law and the Politics of Administration in Egypt and Iran*. New York: SUNY Press, 2012.

Kunt, Metin and Christine Woodhead, eds. *Suleyman the Magnificent and His Age*. London: Longman, 1995.

Kushner, David. 'Self Perception and Identity in Contemporary Turkey'. *Journal of Contemporary History*, 31, 1997, pp. 219–33.

Lenczowski, George, ed. *Iran Under the Pahlavis*, Stanford, CA: Hoover Institution Press, 1978.

Levitsky, Steven and Daniel Ziblatt. *How Democracies Die*. New York: Broadway Books, 2018.

Lewis, Bernard. 'Iran in History'. Middle Eastern Lectures, Moshe Dayan Center, Tel Aviv, 2001.

Lewis, Bernard. 'Time for Toppling'. *Wall Street Journal*, 27 September 2002.

Lewontin, Max. 'Turkey Coup Attempt Exposes Gülen-Erdoğan Lobbying Battle in the US'. *Christian Science Monitor*, 19 July 2016.

Linz, Juan J. 'The Perils of Presidentialism'. *Journal of Democracy*, 1 (1), 1990, pp. 51–69.

Linz, Juan J. *Totalitarian and Authoritarian Regimes*. London: Lynne Reinner, 2000.

Lord, Ceren. *Religious Politics in Turkey: From the Birth of the Republic to the AKP*. Cambridge: Cambridge University Press, 2018.

Lull, James. *Media, Communication, Culture: A Global Approach*. Cambridge: Polity Press, 2000.

Macovei, Mihai. *Growth and Economic Crises in Turkey: Leaving Behind a Turbulent Past?* European Commission Economic and Financial Affairs, Economic Papers No. 386, Brussels, 2009.

Mainwaring, Scott, Guillermo O'Donnell and J. Samuel Valenzuela, eds. *Issues in Democratic Consolidation: The New South American Democracies in Comparative Perspective*. Notre Dame, IL: University of Notre Dame Press, 1992.

Mango, Andrew. 'Reviewed Work: The First Ottoman Constitutional Period'. *Middle Eastern Studies*, 1 (1), 1964, pp. 91–5.

Mango, Cyril. *Byzantium: The Empire of New Rome*. London: Weidenfeld and Nicolson, 1980.

Mardin, Şerif. 'Center-Periphery Relations: A Key to Turkish Politics?'. *Daedalus*, 102 (1), 1973, pp. 169–90.

Mashayekhi, Mehrdad. 'The Revival of the Student Movement in Post-Revolutionary Iran'. *International Journal of Politics, Culture and Society*, 15 (2), 2001, pp. 283–313.

McDonnell, Duncan. 'Populist Leaders and Charisma'. *Political Studies*, 64 (3), 2015, pp. 719–33.

Mavani, Hamid. 'Khomeini's Concept of Governance of the Jurisconsult "(Wilayat al-Faqih)" Revisited: The Aftermath of Iran's 2009 Presidential Election'. *Middle East Journal*, 67 (2), 2013, pp. 207–28.

Meeker, Michael E. *A Nation of Empire: The Ottoman Legacy of Turkish Modernity*. Berkeley, CA: University of California Press, 2002.

Mesbah Yazdi, Mohammad Taqi. *Pasokh Ostad be Javanan Porseshgar*. Qom: Markaz-e Entesharat-e Moaseseh-ye Amuzeshi va Pajuheshi-ye Emam Khomeyni, 2006.

MGK. *Devletin Kavram ve Kapsamı*. Ankara: Milli Güvenlik Kurulu Genel Sekreterliği Yayınları, 1990.

Migdal, Joel S. *State in Society: Studying How States and Societies Transform and Constitute One Another*. Cambridge, NY: Cambridge University Press, 2001.

Mitchell, Colin P. *The Practice of Politics in Safavid Iran: Power, Religion and Rhetoric*. London: I. B. Tauris, 2009.

Moazami, Behrooz. *State, Religion, and Revolution in Iran, 1796 to the Present*. London: Palgrave, 2013.

Mohseni, Payam. 'The 2016 Iranian Parliamentary Elections and the Future of Domestic Politics under the JCPOA'. Report for the Belfer Center for Science and International Affairs, Harvard Kennedy School, 10 December 2016.

Moin, Baqer. *Khomeini: Life of the Ayatollah*. London: I. B. Tauris, 1999.

Molavi, Afshin. *The Soul of Iran*. London: Norton, 2002.

Momen, Moojan. *An Introduction to Shi'i Islam: The History and Doctrines of Twelver Shi'ism*. New Haven, CN: Yale University Press, 1987.

Moslem, Mehdi. *Factional Politics in Post-Khomeini Iran*. Syracuse, NY: Syracuse University Press, 2002.

Mottahedeh, Negar. 'Green is the New Green: Social Media and the Post-Election Crisis in Iran, 2009'. *New Politics*, 13 (1), 2010, pp. 65–8.

Mudde, Cas. 'The Populist Zeitgeist'. *Government and Opposition*, 39 (4), pp. 541–63.

Müftüler Bac, Meltem. 'Turkey's Political Reforms and the Impact of the European Union'. *South European Society and Politics*, 10 (1), 2005, pp. 16–30.

Nabavi, Negin, ed. *Iran: From Theocracy to the Green Movement*. New York: Palgrave Macmillan, 2012.

Nabi, Yaşar. *Tek Yol: Atatürk Yolu*. İstanbul: Varlık, 1974.

Nowell-Smith, Geoffrey, ed. *Selections from the Prison Notebooks of Antonio Gramsci*, London: Lawrence & Wishart, 2005.

OECD, *Economic Surveys Turkey*, Issue 15, 2006, pp. 28–53.

Öktem, Kerem and Karabekir Akkoyunlu, 'Exit from Democracy: Illiberal governance in Turkey and beyond'. *Southeast European and Black Sea Studies*, 16 (4), 2016, pp. 469–80.

Olson, Robert. *Turkey – Iran Relations 1979 – 2004: Revolution, Ideology, War, Coups and Geopolitics*, Costa Mesa, CA: Mazda Publishers, 2004.

Omid, Homa. *Islam and the Post-Revolutionary State in Iran*. London: Macmillan, 1994.

OSCE/ODIHR. 'Republic of Turkey Constitutional Referendum 16 April 2017: Limited Referendum Observation Mission Final Report', Warsaw, 22 June 2017.

Özbudun, Ergun. 'Khomeinism – A Danger for Turkey?'. In Menashri, David, ed. *The Iranian Revolution and the Muslim World*. Boulder, CO: Westview Press, 1990.

Özbudun, Ergun. *The Constitutional System of Turkey: 1876 to the Present*. New York: Palgrave Macmillan, 2011.

Özel, Oktay. 'Limits of the Almighty: Mehmed II's "Land Reform" Revisited'. *Journal of the Economic and Social History of the Orient*, 42 (2), 1999, pp. 226–46.

Öztürk, Ahmet Erdi. 'Does Turkey use "Spying Imams" to Assert Its Powers Abroad?'. *The Conversation*, 15 April 2017.

Öztürk, Ahmet Erdi. 'Turkey's Diyanet under AKP Rule: From Protector to Imposer of State Ideology?'. *Journal of Southeast European and Black Sea Studies*, 16 (4), 2016, pp. 619–35.

Pahlavi, Mohammad Reza. *Mission for My Country*. London: Hutchison, 1960.

Pahlavi, Mohammad Reza. *The White Revolution of Iran*. Tehran: Imperial Pahlavi Library, 1967.

Pamuk, Şevket. *A Monetary History of the Ottoman Empire*. Cambridge: Cambridge University Press, 2001.

Parla, Taha. *Türkiye'de Anayasalar*. İstanbul: İletişim, 2007.

Parsi, Trita. 'Why the UK Embassy in Iran Was Attacked: The Domestic Angle'. *Huffington Post*, 2 December 2011.

Parsi, Trita. *Treacherous Alliance: The Secret Dealings of Israel, Iran, and the U.S.* New Haven, CN: Yale University Press, 2007.

Perry, John R. 'Language Reform in Turkey and Iran'. *International Journal of Middle East Studies*, 17 (3), pp. 295–311, 1985.

Peterson, Ruairi. 'EU Sanctions on Iran: The European Political Context'. *Middle East Policy*, 20 (1), 2013, pp. 135–46.

Pezeshkzad, Iraj. *My Uncle Napoleon.* New York: Random House, 2006.

Polk, William R., Richard L. Chambers, eds. *Beginnings of Modernization in the Middle East: The Nineteenth Century.* Chicago: The University of Chicago Press, 1968.

Przeworksi, Adam. *Democracy and the Market: Political and Economic Reforms in Eastern Europe and Latin America.* Cambridge: Cambridge University Press, 1991.

Qaidaari, Abbas. 'Rouhani Moves to Slash IRGC Budget, Empower Army'. *Al Monitor*, 5 May 2016

Rad, Assal. *The State of Resistance: Politics, Culture and Identity in Modern Iran.* Cambridge: Cambridge University Press, 2022.

Rahnema, Ali. *Superstition as Ideology in Iranian Politics: From Majlesi to Ahmadinejad.* Cambridge: Cambridge University Press, 2011.

Rajaee, Farhan. *Islamism and Modernism: The Changing Discourse in Iran.* Austin, TX: University of Texas Press, 2007.

Rajaee, Farhang, ed. *Iranian Perspectives on the Iran-Iraq War.* Gainsville, FL: University Press of Florida, 1997.

Rajaee, Farhang, *Islamic Values and Worldview: Khomeini on Man, the State and International Politics.* Volume XIII. New York: University of America Press, 1983.

Rakel, Eva Patricia. *Power, Islam, and Political Elite in Iran: A Study on the Iranian Political Elite from Khomeini to Ahmadinejad.* Boston: Brill, 2009.

Razavi, Reza. 'The Road to Party Politics in Iran (1979 – 2009)'. *Middle Eastern Studies*, 46 (1), 2010, pp. 79–96.

Rezaei, Farhad and Somayeh Khodaei Moshirabad. 'The Revolutionary Guards: From Spoiler to Accepter of the Nuclear Agreement'. *British Journal of Middle Eastern Studies*, 45 (2), 2016, pp. 138–55.

Rivetti, Paola. 'Labor and Class in Iran: An Interview with Mohammad Maljoo'. *Middle East Research and Information Project*, 26 May 2017.

Rodrik, Dani. 'The Plot Against the Generals'. June 2014: https://drodrik.scholar.
harvard.edu/files/dani-rodrik/files/plot-against-the-generals.pdf
Rogenhofer, Julius M. 'Antidemocratic Populism in Turkey after the July 2016 Coup
Attempt'. *Populism*, 1 (2), 2018, pp. 116–45.
Root, Margaret Cool. *The King and Kingship in Achaemenid Art*. Leiden: Brill,
1979.
Rubenstein, Alvin and Oles M. Smolansky, eds. *Regional Power Rivalries in New
Eurasia: Russia, Turkey and Iran*. New York: M. E. Sharpe, 1995.
Sadri, Mahmoud. 'Sacral Defense of Secularism: The Political Theologies of Soroush,
Shabestari and Kadivar'. *International Journal of Politics, Culture and Society*, 15
(2), 2001, pp. 257–70.
Saeidi, Ali. A. 'The Accountability of para-Governmental Organizations (bonyads):
The case of Iranian Foundations'. *Iranian Studies*, 37 (3), 2004, pp. 479–88.
Safa, Peyami. *Reflections on the Turkish Revolution*. Translated by Y. T. Kurat, Ankara:
Atatürk Research Centre, 1999.
Safshekan, Roozbeh and Farzan Sabet. 'The Ayatollah's Praetorians: The Islamic
Revolutionary Guard Corps and the 2009 Election Crisis'. *Middle East Journal*,
Autumn, 64 (10), 2010, pp. 543–58.
St. Marie, Joseph J. and Shahdad Naghshpour. *Revolutionary Iran and the United States:
Low Intensity Conflict in the Persian Gulf*. Farnham: Ashgate, 2011.
Salvatore, A., R. Tottoli, B. Rahimi, M. Fariduddin Attar and N. Patel, eds. *The Wiley
Blackwell History of Islam*. Oxford: John Wiley & Sons, 2018.
San'ati, Reza. *Gofteman-e Mesbah*. Tehran: Markaz-e Asnad-e Enghelab-e Eslami,
2008.
Sarfati, Yusuf. 'How Turkey's Slide to Authoritarianism Defies Modernization
Theory'. *Turkish Studies*, 18 (3), pp. 395–415.
Sencar, Özer. 'Liderlerin İtibarı ve Kurumlara Güven'. Metropoll Stratejik ve Sosyal
Araştırmalar, January 2013, http://www.metropoll.com.tr/report/liderlerin-
itibari-ve-kurumlara-guven-ocak-2013.
Shabestari, Mohammad Mojtahed. *Hermenutik, Ketab va Sonnat*. Tehran: Tarh-e
Now, 1995.
Shabestari, Mohammad Mojtahed. *Iman va Azadi*. Tehran: Tarh-e Now, 1998.
Shakibi, Zhand. *Khatami and Gorbachev: Politics of Change in the Islamic Republic of
Iran and the USSR*. London: I. B. Tauris, 2010.
Shambayati, Hootan and Esen Kirdiş. 'In Pursuit of 'Contemporary Civilization':
Judicial Empowerment in Turkey'. *Political Research Quarterly*, 62 (4), 2009,
pp. 767–80.

Shambayati, Hootan. 'A Tale of Two Mayors: Courts and Politics in Iran and Turkey', *International Journal of Middle East Studies*, 36 (2), 2004, pp. 253–75.

Sheikholislami, Reza. *The Structure of Central Authority in Qajar Iran 1871–96.* Atlanta, GA: Scholars Press, 1997.

Sherman, Wendy. 'How We Got the Iran Deal'. *Foreign Affairs*, September/October, 2018.

Shine, Sima, Raz Zimmt and Anna Catran. 'Iran: Mounting Tension between President Rouhani and the Revolutionary Guards'. *INSS Insight* No. 956, 16 July, 2017.

Shirazi, Asghar. *The Constitution of Iran: Politics and the State in the Islamic Republic.* Translated by John O' Kane. London: I. B. Tauris, 1998.

Skocpol, Theda. 'Rentier State and Shi'a Islam in the Iranian Revolution'. *Theory and Society*, 11 (3), 1982, pp. 265–83.

Smith, Anthony D. *Nations and Nationalism in a Global Era.* London: Polity, 1995.

Sohrabi, Nader. *Revolution and Constitutionalism in the Ottoman Empire and Iran.* Cambridge: Cambridge University Press, 2011.

Somer, Murat. 'Moderation of Religious and Secular Politics, a Country's "Centre" and Democratization'. *Democratization*, 21 (2), 2014, pp. 244–67.

Somer, Murat. 'Conquering Versus Democratizing the State: Political Islamists and Fourth Wave Democratization in Turkey and Tunisia'. *Democratization* 24 (6), 2017, pp. 1025–43.

Soroush, Abdolkarim. 'Saqf-e Maishat bar Sotoon-e Shariat', *Kiyan*, 5 (26), 1995, pp. 24–32.

Soroush, Abdolkarim. *Farbihtar az Idioloji.* Tehran: Serat, 1993.

Soroush, Abdolkarim. *Qabd va Bast-e Teorik-e Shari'at: Nazariat-e Takamul-e Ma'rifat-e Dini,* Tehran: Serat, 1994.

Soroush, Abdolkarim. *Reason, Freedom and Democracy in Islam: Essential Writings of Abdolkarim Soroush.* Translated and edited by Mahmoud Sadri and Ahmad Sadri. Oxford: Oxford University Press, 2000.

Soudavar, Abolala. *The Aura of Kings: Legitimacy and Divine Sanction in Iranian Kingship.* Costa Mesa, CA: Mazda, 2003.

Söyler, Mehtap. *The Turkish Deep State: State Consolidation, Civil-Military Relations and Democracy.* London: Routledge, 2015.

Streeck, Wolfgang and Kathleen Thelen, eds. *Beyond Continuity: Institutional Change in Advanced Political Economies.* Oxford: Oxford University Press, 2005.

Takeyh, Ray. *Guardians of the Revolution: Iran and the World in the Age of the Ayatollahs.* Oxford: Oxford University Press, 2009.

Tamadonfar, Mehran. 'Islam, Law, and Political Control in Contemporary Iran'. *Journal for the Scientific Study of Religion*, 40 (2), 2001, pp. 205–19.

Taş, Hakkı. 'Turkey – from Tutelary to Delegative Democracy', *Third World Quarterly*, 36 (4), 2015, pp. 776–91.

Tavakoli-Targhi, Mohamad. *Refashioning Iran: Orientalism, Occidentalism and Historiography*. New York: Palgrave, 2001.

TBMM. *Darbeleri ve Muhtıraları Araştırma Komisyonu Raporu*. The Grand National Assembly of Turkey, November 2012, http://www.scribd.com/doc/115000348/TBMM-Darbeleri-ve-Muhtıraları-Araştırma-Komisyonu-Raporu.

Telhami, Shibley. 'The 2011 Arab Public Opinion Poll: Report'. *Brookings Institution*, 21 November 2011.

Tezcan, Baki. *The Second Ottoman Empire*. Cambridge: Cambridge University Press, 2010.

Tezcür, Güneş Murat, ed. *The Oxford Handbook of Turkish Politics*. Oxford: Oxford University Press, 2020.

Tezcür, Güneş Murat. *Muslim Reformers in Iran and Turkey: The Paradox of Moderation*. Austin, TX: University of Texas Press, 2012.

Theler, David E., Alireza Nader, Shahram Chubin, Jerrold D. Green, Charlotte Lynch and Frederic Wehrey. *Mullahs, Guards and Bonyads: An Exploration of Iranian Leadership Dynamics*. Santa Monica, CA: RAND Corporation, 2010.

Tol, Gönül and Ömer Taşpınar. 'Erdogan's Turn to the Kemalists'. *Foreign Affairs*, 27 October 2016.

Topuz, Hıfzı. *Türk Basın Tarihi: II. Mahmut'tan Holdinglere*. Istanbul: Remzi, 1996.

Tugal, Cihan. 'Turkey Coup Aftermath: Between Neo-Fascism and Bonapartism'. *Open Democracy*, 18 July 2016.

Tuğal, Cihan. *Passive Revolution: Absorbing the Islamic Challenge to Capitalism*. Stanford, CA: Stanford University Press, 2009.

Tunçay, Mete. *Türkiye Cumhuriyeti'nde Tek Parti Yönetiminin Kurulması (1923–1931)*. Istanbul: Cem Yayınevi, 1989.

Tunçay, Mete. *Türkiye'de Sol Akımlar (1908–1925)*. Volume II. Istanbul: İletişim, 2009.

Turam, Berna. *Secular State and Religious Society: Two Forces in Play in Turkey*. New York: Palgrave Macmillan, 2012.

Turan, Ilter. *Turkey's Difficult Journey to Democracy: Two Steps Forward, One Step Back*. Oxford: Oxford University Press, 2015.

Türkyılmaz, Zeynep. 'Maternal Colonialism and Turkish Woman's Burden in Dersim: Educating the "Mountain Flowers" of Dersim'. *Journal of Women's History*, 28 (3), 2016, pp. 162–89.

Ülgen, Sinan. 'From Inspiration to Aspiration: Turkey in the New Middle East'. *Carnegie Endowment for International Peace*, December 2011.

Vaziri, Mostafa. *Iran as Imagined Nation: The Construction of National Identity*. New York: Paragon House, 1993.

Volkan, Vamık and Norman Itzkowitz. *The Immortal Atatürk: A Psychobiography*. Chicago: The University of Chicago Press, 1984.

Weber, Max. *Economy and Society*. Vol. II, ed. by Guenther Roth and Claus Wittich, New York: Bedminster Press, 1968.

Whittow, Mark. *The Making of Orthodox Byzantium, 600–1025*. London: Macmillan, 1996.

Wigell, Mikael, 'Mapping Hybrid Regimes: regime types and concepts in comparative politics'. *Democratization*, 15 (2), 2008, pp. 230–50.

Willner, Ann Ruth. *The Spellbinders: Charismatic Political Leadership*. New Haven, CT: Yale University Press, 1984.

Wittek, Paul. *The Rise of the Ottoman Empire*. London: B. Franklin, 1938.

World Bank. *Rise of the Anatolian Tigers: Turkey Urbanization Review*. Policy Brief, Washington, DC, 2015, https://openknowledge.worldbank.org/handle/10986/22388.

Yaşar Yücel. 'Atatürk İlkeleri'. *Belleten Dergisi*, 52 (204), 1988, pp. 810–24.

Yavuz, Hakan. 'Political Islam and the Welfare (Refah) Party in Turkey'. *Comparative Politics*, 30 (1), 1997, pp. 63–82.

Yavuz, M. Hakan, ed. *The Emergence of a New Turkey: Democracy and the AK Party*. Salt Lake City: University of Utah Press, 2006.

Yaycıoğlu, Ali. 'Janissaries, Engineers and Preachers: How Did Military Engineering and Islamic Activism Change the Ottoman Order?'. *Revue d'histoire du XIXe siècle*, 53 (2), 2016, pp. 19–37.

Yeğinsu, Can. 'Turkey Packs the Court'. *New York Review of Books Blog*, 22 September 2010.

Yılmaz, Zafer and Bryan S. Turner, 'Turkey's Deepening Authoritarianism and the Fall of Electoral Democracy'. *British Journal of Middle Eastern Studies*, 46 (5), 2019, pp. 691–98.

Zarakol, Ayşe. *Before the West: The Rise and Fall of Eastern World Orders*. Cambridge: Cambridge University Press, 2022.

Zia-Ebrahimi, Reza. *The Emergence of Iranian Nationalism: Race and the Politics of Dislocation*. New York: Columbia University Press, 2016.

Zürcher, Erik Jan. 'The Young Turk Revolution: Comparisons and Connections'. *Journal of Middle Eastern Studies*, 55 (4), 2019, pp. 481–98.

Zürcher, Erik Jan. *Political Opposition in the Early Turkish Republic (1924–1925)*. New York: Brill, 1991.

Zürcher, Erik Jan. *The Unionist Factor: The Role of the Committee of Union and Progress in the Turkish Nationalist Movement 1905–1926*. Leiden: Brill, 1984.

INDEX